South-Western

Foundations Series in Management

THOMSON
™
SOUTH-WESTERN

Australia · Canada · Mexico · Singapore · Spain · United Kingdom · United States

OTHER BOOKS IN THE SERIES

Human Resource Management: Essential Perspectives, 3e

Robert L. Mathis and John H. Jackson

0-324-20217-2   Available January, 2004

The management of human resources is growing in impact in the United States and throughout the world. Frequent headlines in the news media include downsizing, workforce shortages, sexual harassment, union activity, and U.S. business practices abroad. HR issues affect us all, which makes it beneficial to become more knowledgeable about HR management. *Human Resource Management: Essential Perspectives* provides a thorough and well-researched overview of HR management that both HR practitioners and students can use. The condensed and streamlined text content is presented in a way that makes sense to a variety of learners. Its brevity allows instructors to tailor courses by incorporating additional readings and cases of their choosing.

Foundations of Strategic Management, 3e

Jeffrey S. Harrison and Caron H. St. John

0-324-25917-4   Available January 2004

Foundations of Strategic Management provides a concise and balanced introduction to the important theories and views in the field of strategy. The authors present an up-to-take look at the most critical topics in strategy today and use examples from cutting-edge firms to help learners begin to understand and develop decision-making and analysis techniques that are relevant in all types of organizations. Its brevity allows instructors to tailor their courses by incorporating additional readings and cases of their choosing.

A Primer
for Management

Michael P. Dumler

Illinois State University

Steven J. Skinner

University of Kentucky

THOMSON

SOUTH-WESTERN

Australia · Canada · Mexico · Singapore · Spain · United Kingdom · United States

THOMSON
———✳———™
SOUTH-WESTERN

A Primer for Management

Michael P. Dumler   Steven J. Skinner

VP/Editorial Director:
Jack W. Calhoun

VP/Editor-in-Chief:
Mike Roche

Senior Publisher:
Melissa Acuña

Acquisitions Editor:
Joe Sabatino

Senior Developmental Editor:
Judy O'Neill

Marketing Manager:
Jacquelyn Carrillo

Production Editor:
Cliff Kallemeyn

Media Developmental Editor:
Kristen Meere

Media Production Editor:
Karen Schaffer

Senior Designer:
Anne Marie Reckow

Manufacturing Coordinator:
Rhonda Utley

Production House:
Graphic World, Inc.

Cover Image:
© Photodisc

Printer:
Quebecor World, Dubuque IA

For permission to use material from this text or product, contact us by
Tel (800) 730-2214
Fax (800) 730-2215
http://www.thomsonrights.com

For more information
contact South-Western,
5191 Natorp Boulevard,
Mason, Ohio 45040.
Or you can visit our Internet site at:
http://www.swlearning.com

To my family, Kathleen, Irena, and Danny, for their unconditional love and understanding.

—MPD

To my parents, John and Dorothy Skinner, for all their love and support.

—SJS

Brief Contents

Contents

Preface

A Primer for Management is the result of many discussions with and suggestions from our colleagues and students. These discussions and suggestions seemed to center on two broad, related issues: the cost of textbooks and the fact that they often include material not everyone uses. You probably have had some of these discussions yourself and you know the comments made and questions asked. From students: Are you going to test us over the boxes? Why don't you use the cases since we paid for them? Couldn't someone write a paperback without all the color pictures and charge less? And from instructors: I don't like to use the exercises in the book; I prefer to assign my own readings. I don't use all these ancillaries, only the test bank. Why do students ask me if they have to read the boxes? Why doesn't someone write a shorter book that covers all the important material and still gives me the flexibility to use my own material in class? Wouldn't this result in a lower-priced book? You know the discussion, and you know that these issues are complicated with no easy answers.

In more than twenty years of teaching, we both have heard similar questions, and we began to formalize our thoughts on these issues. Maybe a paperback book in the range of 300 pages would be ideal for teaching students the principles of management. Perhaps some instructors would prefer the flexibility of a book that covers the concepts of management without trying to include everything—cases, experiential exercises, research applications, and so on. Some students just might benefit from a book without all these extras, especially if the instructor supplements the book with other material, such as videos, articles, and the like. Of course, we had a few questions of our own. Can a management book be shortened dramatically without compromising its integrity? If that is possible, could it be done at a substantial reduction in price, while providing instructors with the supplemental material they need to teach the course? Answering these questions fostered the conceptual development of the *Primer*. The concept for the *Primer* grew and emerged as a succinct statement of current theory and practice of contemporary management, while at the same time allowing the instructor the flexibility to use supplementary material.

Our objectives in writing *A Primer for Management* were threefold: first, to give the instructor and student a text that presents the basic theories and concepts necessary for gaining an understanding of the process of management; second, to empower the instructor through choice (the *Primer* provides the content, yet allows the instructor the ability to select additional material that adds richness, detail, and flair to the learning environment); and third, to present the material in a format that would offer the market a significantly lower-priced alternative to existing textbooks.

To accomplish these objectives, our book had to be somewhat unique. *A Primer for Management* uses a functional approach to management presented in a streamlined fashion. Fifteen chapters are organized into five parts: I. Managing and the Environment; II. Planning; III. Organizing; IV. Leading; and V. Controlling. While every effort was made to include *all* relevant material necessary to provide readers with a strong foundation in management, our book does not include opening stories, pictures, applications, exercises, or cases. As a result, vital communication flows uninterrupted from the beginning of each chapter to the end. The instructor enjoys the flexibility of a book that covers contemporary management theories and concepts while empowering the instructor to select other material appropriate for the course. And the market benefits from a book that truly answers the call for a lower-priced alternative.

Fundamental Concepts, Not Surplus Features

The important management concepts that instructors try to communicate to their students—how to build, plan, organize, lead, control, and sustain organizations—are covered in the *Primer*. Two concise end-of-book appendixes on the history of management and on production and operations management round out the coverage. A comprehensive ancillary package and resource-rich web site gives instructors a full slate of optional resources for augmenting text essentials without adding unwanted bulk. But all such extras remain in the background until the instructor chooses to direct student attention to them. This is not to say that the *Primer* is either colorless or commonplace, only that we have taken care not to overload it. Its features are few but integral:

- **Chapter introductions** briefly set up topics covered in each chapter.
- **Management Highlights,** used sparingly, emphasize dramatic information, key consolidations, or useful tools or ideas worth special display.
- **Highlighted terms** are defined as chapters unfold, but are not otherwise reiterated in the text. Students can log on to the *Primer*'s companion web site, at **http://dumler.swlearning.com,** to find a flashcard drill of key terms and definitions.
- **Illustrations and examples,** with an eye to student interest, are convincingly rendered.
- **Chapter conclusions** succinctly summarize chapter content.
- **Suggested readings** constitute a basic set of secondary sources.
- **Endnotes,** arranged at the ends of chapters, provide a complete set of citations and links to the research.
- A **unique chapter on managing services** (chapter 14) helps students understand the management challenges associated with this growing sector of the U.S. economy.

Resources, Not Overload

Adopters of *A Primer for Management* have access to a full spectrum of coordinated resources with complete latitude to choose and use only what adds value to their teaching.

InfoTrac® College Edition. Packaged free with every new copy of *A Primer for Management* is a four-month subscription to InfoTrac College Edition, an online research database that amasses over 5 million full-text articles from nearly 5,000 scholarly and popular periodicals. With InfoTrac, your students have anytime, anywhere access to journals like *Business Week, Fast Company, Fortune, Harvard Business Review, Management Review,* and *Newsweek,* to name a few. If you routinely incorporate extra readings or research assignments into your course outline, directing your students to log on to InfoTrac to access particular articles or to conduct their own searches provides a quick and convenient way to gain a comprehensive view of the business environment from the most influential journals from around the world. For more information on InfoTrac, visit **http://www. infotrac-college.com.**

Interactive Self-Assessments (ISBN 0-324-23183-0). If your course includes a self-assessment component designed to get your students to start thinking about the skills they have acquired to date or to evaluate their strengths and developmental needs, a series of online self-assessments is available for free for use in conjunction with the *Primer*. During a quick visit to **http://selfassessments.swlearning.com,** instructors may register and tour the site. Place your order using the designated ISBN (0-324-23183-0), and the *Primer* will ship to your bookstore with pre-assigned passcodes for entering the site. For additional details contact your South-Western/Thomson sales representative (800-423-0563).

Cases. You have three options for selecting companion cases to supplement the *Primer.*

1. You can create a tailor-fitted online case companion with *eCoursepacks,* an easy-to-use custom publishing process that lets instructors combine the *Primer* with cases from NACRA, Darden, and a wide array of South-Western sources. It's also possible to enhance case selections with the currency of the world's most influential journals by selecting articles from *Business Week, Fast Company, Fortune,* or the *Harvard Business Review,* among others, for inclusion. You can even include your own material in an eCoursepack and collect a royalty if you choose. Permissions for eCoursepacks are already secured, saving you the time and worry of clearing rights. To learn more, visit **http://ecoursepacks.swlearning.com** or contact your South-Western/Thomson sales representative (800-423-0563).

2. At your direction, *A Primer for Management* can be packaged with one of several editorially PreBuilt eCoursepacks, providing the ultimate in convenience to instructors who want to enrich their course with cases and additional readings. Established eCoursepacks that you can adopt or further modify to suit particular needs are viewable at **http://ecoursepacks.swlearning.com,** after you receive a passcode from your South-Western/Thomson rep (800-423-0563).

3. Or, if you prefer to build a printed casebook, you can access South-Western's *TextChoice* database of management exercises and cases to create a customized print publication. TextChoice includes a variety of experiential exercises, classroom activities, film-based exercises, and cases. Visit the TextChoice web site at **http://www.thomsoncustom.com** or contact your South-Western/Thomson sales representative for more information (800-423-0563).

Wall Street Journal (ISBN 0-324-23138-5).   A 15-week subscription to this essential business resource, including access to the Online Journal at **http://www.wsj.com,** is available for an additional $15 fee with new copies of the *Primer* at your choosing. Place your order using the designated ISBN (**0-324-23138-5**), and books will ship to your bookstore with an attached student subscription card.

Video.   A range of videos featuring a diverse group of businesses (from Timberland to Ping Golf Clubs to the Buffalo Zoo) are available for viewing at **http://dumler. swlearning.com** via streaming media. These high-interest video assets provide an inside look at how companies address management issues everyday, showing managers—at all levels of an organization—in action. By design, the decision to incorporate video segments into your course outline is yours, but the sample syllabus in the Instructor's Manual provides cues to get you started.

Instructor's Manual with Test Bank (ISBN 0-324-28832-8).   An Instructor's Manual with Test Bank, geared toward making teaching with the *Primer* more effective, is available to faculty who adopt. Learning outcomes; lecture outlines; lecture enhancement material (activities, extra examples, Internet-based exercises); questions for discussion and review (with suggested answers); additional suggested readings linked to student use of InfoTrac's article database; useful web links; and a sample course outline annotated with your options regarding video selections and other available resources are included.

Test questions, written by text authors Mike Dumler and Steve Skinner, fill out the manual, providing instructors with a full complement of questions in true/false, multiple-choice, and essay formats.

ExamView® Testing Software (ISBN 0-324-28835-2).   ExamView, South-Western's computerized testing program, contains all the questions in the printed Test

Bank. This easy-to-use test-creation program is compatible with both Microsoft® Windows and Macintosh systems and enables instructors to create printed tests, Internet tests, and LAN-based tests quickly. Blackboard- and WebCT-ready versions of the *Primer's* Test Bank are also available to qualified instructors. Contact your South-Western/Thomson sales representative for more information.

PowerPoint™ Presentation Slides (ISBN 0-324-28835-2). A set of PowerPoint presentation slides accompanies every chapter, providing instructors with a complete set of basic notes for lectures and students with a helpful set of review materials. These slides, which highlight and synthesize key concepts for greater recall, are available for download at **http://dumler.swlearning.com.** A duplicate set can also be found on the Instructor's Resource CD-ROM.

Product Support Site. The dedicated *A Primer for Management* site provides broad online support. Visit **http://dumler.swlearning.com** to view available video, download supplements, take a quiz, and find links to and repositories of related resources.

Instructor's Resource CD-ROM (ISBN 0-324-28835-2). This CD-ROM contains the Microsoft Office application files of various teaching resources (the Instructor's Manual with Test Bank and the PowerPoint slides), along with our ExamView testing program and test files.

ACKNOWLEDGMENTS

Throughout the development of the *Primer,* our work was aided by many helpful reviews. We gratefully acknowledge those who commented on early drafts of our manuscript and whose suggestions expanded our thinking and improved our presentations.

Tope Adeyemi-Bello	East Carolina University
Gene Marie Black	Arkansas Technological University
Paula Brown	Northern Illinois University
Ray Coye	DePaul University
Robert A. Donnelly, Jr.	Goldey-Beacom College
Lon Doty	San Jose State University
Jud Faurer	Metropolitan State College of Denver
Francis E. Hamilton	University of South Florida
Linda Hefferin	Elgin Community College
James Keebler	St. Cloud State University
Thomas Lloyd	Westmoreland Community College
Michael Mahler	Montana State University
Dan Moshavi	Montana State University
Donald C. Mosley, Jr.	University of South Alabama
Lisa Ritzler-Crawford	Wright State University
Linda B. Shonesy	Athens State University
Patricia Kramer Voli	University of North Carolina, Wilmington

The *Primer* benefited from the assistance of several anonymous reviewers as well. We would also like to acknowledge the writers who worked with us to prepare ancillary materials. Our special thanks go to Linda Hefferin (Elgin Community College), who wrote the Instructor's Manual and prepared the online quiz questions for student review and assessment; and to Charlie T. Cook, Jr. (University of West Alabama), who authored the PowerPoint slides. Finally, the authors would like to acknowledge that this book was supported in part by sabbatical leave programs at their respective institutions.

M. P. Dumler
S. J. Skinner
January 2004

ABOUT THE AUTHORS

Michael P. Dumler is a Professor of Management in the College of Business at Illinois State University. He has taught undergraduate, graduate, and on-site professional MBA courses for over twenty years. He previously taught at the University of Wisconsin—Eau Claire and worked for the University of Chicago at Argonne National Laboratory. Professor Dumler has been an active consultant to several health care organizations, facilitating organization change, compensation planning, and employee assessment.

Professor Dumler has been the recipient of the College of Business Research Award and the University Research Initiative Award; and he is a member of Beta Gamma Sigma. He has made more than 40 presentations to professional organizations, including the Academy of Management and the Decision Sciences Institute, and has published more than 25 articles in scholarly journals. His work has appeared in the *Journal of Occupational and Organizational Psychology, Psychological Reports, Administration and Society, Group and Organization Management, Journal of Managerial Issues, Journal of Educational Leadership, Journal of Business Communications, Journal of Management Systems,* and *Journal of Social Behavior and Personality,* among others.

Steven J. Skinner is the Rosenthal Professor in the Gatton College of Business and Economics at the University of Kentucky, where he has taught undergraduate and graduate courses in the School of Management for over twenty years. He was previously on the faculty at Illinois State University and was formerly a research administrator for State Farm Insurance Companies. He has also consulted with a variety of large and small organizations.

Dr. Skinner has authored or co-authored seven books, including the recently published *High Performers: Recruiting and Retaining Top Employees* (South-Western, 2004), part of South-Western's Professional Portfolio. Dr. Skinner's research has been published in a number of journals, including the *Academy of Management Journal, Journal of Marketing Research, Journal of Retailing, Journal of Business Research, Public Opinion Quarterly, Journal of the Academy of Marketing Science, Journal of Advertising Research, Journal of Risk and Insurance,* and *Journal of Personal Selling and Sales Management.* He has received the Mu Kappa Tau Award for the best article in *Journal of Personal Selling and Sales Management.*

Managing and the Environment

part one

Chapter One

Management and Managers

Have you ever overheard someone say this? "I work for a poorly run company; management is totally incompetent." Or have you heard the converse? "My boss stays on top of the details; really, this is a great place to work."

Perhaps you have voiced similar sentiments yourself. If so, what precisely did you mean? These statements, both the complaints and the compliments, underscore some important principles about management: (1) that management is a type of work; and (2) that management can be performed quite well sometimes and, at other times, quite miserably. When we charge that an organization is inadequately managed, how obvious are the mistakes that have been made? How easy would it have been to avoid them?

Don't let anyone fool you. Managing well is neither easy nor obvious. If it were, there'd be a lot less acrimony in the world and a lot more certainty associated with every business decision ever made.

But learning to be a better manager involves much more than just reading a few good books on the subject. It requires dedication of purpose, an advanced understanding of how organizations really work, and knowledge of human behavior. As a field of study, management draws on a vast array of accumulated research about organized activities and task-based human behavior, complemented with the applied experience and skills of people who actively strive to attain organizational goals. Managers are people who plan, organize, lead, and control organizations. A good manager, then, is someone with knowledge, skills, and experience who attains goals in an effective manner. Remember also, as you begin your formal study of management, that it is not a new concept. As long as humans have roamed the planet, some among us have made plans, organized activities, motivated others, and led them toward goal attainment. History is filled with stunning examples of human accomplishment achieved through management. The pyramids at Giza, the Parthenon in Greece, and the Great Wall of China would not have been possible without managers—people who understood the principles of management and applied them, sometimes relentlessly, for better or worse.

ORGANIZATIONS VERSUS MARKETS

Managers perform their work in organizations. **Organizations** are structural arrangements of people brought together to accomplish a goal or goals. Your local church, a large corporation, a police department, a prison, and a professional baseball team are all organizations. Each of them has a different membership and purpose. Some organizations are voluntary, such as a church; others, such as a prison, are coercive (forced membership); still others attract membership based on economic exchange, such as a business.

It almost goes without saying that organizations are important to society. Without them, how would we accomplish commerce, maintain social order, or gather together to worship? Well, the answer might surprise you. The alternative to an organization is a market, a place where buyers and sellers congregate to bid on products or services. Without organizations we would have to go to a market, like the farmer's market or eBay. While markets are useful, they may not be efficient for repetitive transactions. Imagine engaging in a bidding war every time you want to grab a sandwich for lunch. To solve this problem, organizations evolved. A distinct advantage of organizations over markets relates to **hierarchy.**[1] Through hierarchy, an organization classifies work into its component parts, assigning people with specialized skills to complete tasks necessary to the purpose of the organization. Organizations—by performing similar tasks faster, more accurately, or at lower cost than a market—provide an efficient means of exchange. Also, they are handy because they represent one-stop shopping. When we want lunch in a hurry, we go to McDonald's or a similar business whose goal is to quickly provide food to the public. In summary, *hierarchies* are adept at performing repetitive tasks where value and price are clear; they are thus useful facilitators of exchange. *Markets* also facilitate exchange, but they do so most advantageously in situations where a product is unique and its value and price are unclear.

Not all organizations are created equal. What makes some organizations better than others is the people who inhabit them. In the context of this book, we are particularly interested in managers. Their organizational success can be understood by evaluating how they work and what they accomplish. Similarly, we can gauge the quality of an organization in two basic ways: efficiency and effectiveness. **Efficiency** (i.e., productivity) is using the minimum resources necessary to produce a product or service. In other words, an efficient organization is not wasteful. Waste is a cost of production that should be minimized. **Effectiveness** is the ability of the organization to achieve a goal or goals. One goal might be to make a 5 percent profit after taxes; another might be to achieve a balance in hiring underrepresented groups; still another might be to expand business operations into a wider geographic area. Usually, organizations have multiple goals that they attempt to achieve simultaneously. The degree to which they are successful at goal attainment is a measure of their overall effectiveness. **Organizational performance** is an outcome that assesses the degree to which an organization is both efficient in using resources and effective in attaining stated goals.

ORGANIZATIONS AS SYSTEMS

Metaphorically speaking, an organization is a system. A metaphor is a figure of speech that describes one thing in terms of another. You can imagine how useful a metaphor might be in portraying a complex organization like Vivendi Universal. "An organization is a personal computer" is a metaphor commonly used to convey the idea that an organization is a network of specialized component parts (or processes) that creates, markets, and distributes products or services.

Envisioning the organization as a system creates opportunities for finding and solving organizational problems. In other words, a problem that might occur in just one part of the organization is seen as affecting the entire organization when that organization is viewed as a system. A poor-quality TV, for example, may be the result of purchasing inferior parts. Solve the problem of inferior input, and the whole system surges forward. With that in mind, a **system** can be defined as a collection of interrelated entities (subsystems) that operate interdependently to achieve common goals. The entities of a system achieve more by working together than by each entity working independently. As shown in Exhibit 1.1, a system consists of three subsystems: **input, processing, and output (IPO).** An input subsystem, such as purchasing, ensures that resources are available to produce the product or service. A processing subsystem creates the good or service. Manufacturing facilities build or construct the physical product for later sale. An output subsystem makes the product or service available to distributors or customers. Organization problems are normally associated with one of the three subsystems. So as you can see, understanding systems theory greatly helps the manager in visualizing situations and diagnosing problems.

It is useful to think of an organization as a system. Management scholars agree that organizations are open systems in which the organization receives inputs from the external environment, utilizes the input in the internal organization, and transmits organizational output back to the external environment. Systems theory helps us envision the organization as a series of specialized components. If one component is bad, the whole system is degraded. Think about the systems theory metaphor in the following situation.

A small organization consists of a sales force, a production facility, and a logistics department, all controlled by an accountant who happens to own the company. Salespeople generate business, production makes the good or service, and logistics delivers the product to the consumer while accounting ensures that costs are contained on the road to profitability. However, the production workers are sitting idle, and the logistics department has a truck at the loading dock, but there's nothing to load. What is the problem? Not enough information, you say. Well, more information might help, but systems theory leads us to examine the input side of the IPO model for answers. One explanation might be that the sales force needs to generate more business. Whether the demand for the product or service exists is another issue entirely. Either way, the systems theory metaphor helps diagnose, evaluate, and offer an explanation for the situation.

EXHIBIT 1.1
Organizations as Systems (the IPO model)

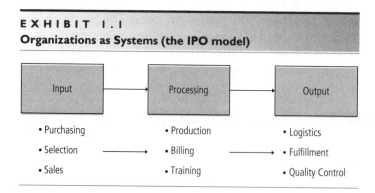

ORGANIZATIONS AND THE ECONOMY

Business organizations are embedded in a larger economic context. **Evolutionary activity** is economic activity that occurs over long periods of time. This gradual evolutionary activity allows the economy to expand or contract and organizations to become more efficient by weeding out the inefficient producers. We see market forces in action when a producer who charges more than his competitors for a comparable product is forced (i.e., by lack of demand) to lower price or lose sales and ultimately go out of business. **Revolutionary activity** occurs periodically to forever alter the nature of business transactions. Economic revolution occurs when a new innovation, such as new methods of production, are introduced into the economy. For example, desktop computing put the power of the computer at our fingertips and transformed many aspects of daily life. Desktop computers allowed small companies the same computing advantages as much larger companies.

All organizations require resources in the form of land, labor, and capital to support economic activity. However, the basis of worldwide economic activity has changed over time. Early **agrarian economies** (before 1830), characteristic of the post-revolutionary era, were based on small family-owned farms and small shop production. Craftsmen and trade workers created products to meet the needs of individual farms and shops. The agrarian form fit the demand of the time with the means of production. The **industrial economy** (1830–1950) was ushered in by technological revolutions, beginning with the invention of steam power. Steam power created the energy necessary for mass production. Coupled with the revolution in production, the influx of immigrants created the demand for more products and services than the craft system could provide. The economies of the industrial age built the world as we now know it. Post–World War II economies scurried to rebuild the world, supplying products and services to a growing population. The development of computer technology during World War II set the stage for the knowledge economies that we see in their infancy today. **Knowledge economies** are based on information and intangibles such as computer software, which is often referred to as vaporware because it is not a physical product in the traditional sense. Compared to the industrial economies of the post–World War II era, knowledge economies represent new challenges and opportunities that require special management skills. For a more detailed treatment of management history, see Appendix A.

ORGANIZATIONS WORLDWIDE

The three dominant world economies—the United States, Japan, and Germany—are propelled by organizations that are operated by managers. Each country has nurtured economic growth as the basis for a stable society. Economic stability requires a growing **gross domestic product** (**GDP,** a measure of the purely domestic output of a country), stable currency, and low unemployment. Each of these countries has seen the growth of major corporations that dominate trade in their respective industries: Sony in Japan, Microsoft and Exxon in the United States, and Siemens in Germany. Managers of these companies around the world have one thing in common—the goal of generating above-average economic returns for investors. According to Lester Thurow,[2] world economies have formed three trading coalitions to compete worldwide. To remain competitive, countries have developed trading partnerships to assure economic stability in their region of the world. The North American Free Trade Agreement (NAFTA), EEC (Eastern European Countries), and the Pacific Rim countries are three such partnerships.

Russia and the EEC and the Middle Eastern countries represent still other potential partnerships. However, they also demonstrate that economic stability is not possible without political stability. Politicians create the environment in which organizations can succeed or fail. Managers strategically respond to environmental conditions by aligning the organization's resources and capabilities with the environmental opportunities. Over the long run, organizations that survive fulfill consumer needs efficiently.

While organizations have been part of human existence from the beginning of time, organizations that emerged in the United States during the twentieth century relied on extensive investments in both machine and human capital. Managers helped to plan, organize, lead, and control these organizations that led to the urban industrial economy. Today, managers direct or oversee the work and performance of other individuals toward the attainment of organizational objectives.

MANAGEMENT AND MANAGERS DEFINED

Management as a Process

Management is a process of achieving organizational goals and objectives through the efforts and contributions of other people. The management process uses the functions of planning, organizing, leading, and controlling to accomplish organizational goals. For example, the planning function is used to identify goals and develop plans to attain the goals. The organizing function might include implementing human resource plans by developing a selection process to hire employees for a new plant opening. **Managers** are individuals who use principles of management to guide, direct, or oversee the work and performance of others.

Management as a Discipline, or Field of Study

Designating management as a discipline implies that it's an accumulated body of knowledge that can be learned by study. Thus management is a subject with principles, concepts, and theories. We study management to understand these principles, concepts, and theories and to learn how to apply them in the process of managing.

Management as People

Whether you say, "that company has an entirely new management team," or "she's the best manager I've ever worked for," you're referring to the people who guide, direct, and thus manage organizations. The word *management* used in this manner refers to the people (managers) who engage in the process of management. Managers are primarily responsible for guiding people toward the attainment of organizational goals and objectives. People are an organization's lifeblood. Without people, there's no such thing as a profitable firm or a successful new product launch.

Management as a Career

"Joe Cardenas is on the fast track in the marketing department. He has held three management positions and is now, after 10 years, being promoted to the vice president level." Joe has moved through a sequence of jobs on a career path. He has a management career.

The different meanings and interpretations of the term *management* can be related as follows: *People* who wish to have a *career* as a manager must study the *discipline* of management as a means of practicing the *process* of management. Thus, we define management as the process undertaken by one or more persons to coordinate the work activities of other persons and to allocate resources such as capital, materials, and technologies in order to achieve high-quality results not attainable by any one person acting alone.

THE PROCESS OF MANAGEMENT

As mentioned earlier, the process of management usually consists of basic management functions. The traditional management process identifies the functions as planning, organizing, and controlling, linked together by leading. Planning determines *what* results the organization will achieve; organizing specifies *how* it will achieve the results; and controlling determines *whether* the results are achieved.

Planning

The planning function is the capstone activity of management. **Planning** activities determine an organization's objectives and establish appropriate strategies for achieving them. The organizing, controlling, and leading functions all derive from planning in that these functions carry out the planning decisions.

Managers at every level of the organization plan. Through their plans, managers communicate expectations and specific actions necessary for success. Although plans may differ in focus, they are all concerned with achieving short- and long-term organizational goals. Taken as a whole, an organization's plans are the primary tools for managing changes in the business environment.

Strategic planning is a multidimensional concept that provides a firm with vision, direction, a sense of unity, and purpose. It's the integrative blueprint for the organization. Strategic planning assures that the right products are produced to meet or exceed customer expectations. An important aspect of strategic planning is to create a sustainable competitive advantage over competitors. Strategy serves to obtain a match between the firm's external environment and internal capabilities. If a competing firm lowers price, then the firm's strategy must address that environmental force.[3]

Organizing

After developing a strategy, objectives, and plans to achieve the objectives, managers must design and develop an organization that can accomplish the objectives. Thus the organizing function is used to create a structure of task and authority relationships that supports the attainment of organizational goals.

The **organizing** function takes the tasks identified during planning and assigns them to individuals and groups within the organization, so that objectives set by planning can be achieved. Organizing, then, involves turning plans into action. The organizing function also provides an organizational structure, enabling the organization not only to function effectively as a whole but also to achieve objectives.

Leading

Sometimes called directing or motivating, leading involves influencing organization members to perform in ways that accomplish the organization's objectives and goals. Leaders are responsible for the design, manufacture, and distribution of products and services. Successful leaders satisfy consumer needs while making a profit for the owners or stockholders.

The **leading** function focuses directly on the employees in the organization. Its major purpose is to channel human behavior toward organizational goals such as improved quality. Effective leadership is important in organizations. As we have seen in the Enron debacle,[4] not all leaders operate in the best interests of organizational stakeholders. In fact, questions of insider trading, personal arrogance, and downright greed often are the prime motivation of some leaders. But over the long run, these leaders are exposed and driven out of the organization.

Controlling

Finally, a manager must make sure that the organization's actual performance conforms to planned performance. This **controlling** function of management requires three elements: (1) established *standards* of performance, (2) *information* that indicates deviations between actual performance and the established standards, and (3) *action* to correct performance that fails to meet the standards. Simply speaking, the purpose of management control is to make sure the organization efficiently produces a product or service that meets or exceeds standards.

Over the long run, the four functions of management must be learned in the context of quality improvement and maintenance. Management functions and quality are related; they should not be separated. Performance of one function depends on the performance of the other functions. A plan requires leaders, an organization, and control to be properly carried out. If a plan fails to incorporate quality considerations, it will be only a matter of time until failure becomes the reality.

The Ford Edsel's failure, a classic case in mismanagement, highlights this point.[5] Plans for entering the Edsel into the medium-priced auto field were elaborate. The 1950s saw a growing trend toward medium-priced cars: Pontiac, Oldsmobile, Buick, and Dodge all targeted the middle-income car buyer. Marketing research led Ford to introduce the Edsel, with great fanfare, in 1958. But Ford's high expectations resulted in a $350 million loss. It was the biggest new-car failure in automotive history. Contributing to the loss were such factors as a recession, poor promotion, and changing consumer preferences for even smaller cars. However, lack of quality was the Edsel's true Achilles heel. In getting the Edsel to market on schedule, production was rushed; numerous defects were not cleared up. Brakes failed, oil leaked, there were rattles, and the car didn't start properly. Edsel owners were driving an inferior product. Before these defects could be corrected, the car became known as a lemon. The Edsel's poor quality became the butt of many jokes and the standard of poor quality for a generation of Americans.

Planning, organizing, controlling, and leading were all carried out at Ford. Its managers followed these functions to the letter—the Edsel was a textbook example of how to manage a product from an idea to the market. Unfortunately, quality was neither the primary objective nor the driving focal point in the management process. The Edsel case clearly illustrates the need to integrate the functions of management with an overriding quality umbrella. Failure to build in quality will result in an opportunity for the competition to gain advantage.

TYPES OF MANAGERS

For a good example of management evolution, consider Dell Computer Corporation in Austin, Texas. Since 1984, when Michael Dell started the company, its leadership has changed from a single entrepreneur to a team of many managers with many subordinates. The development of different types of managers is a further result of such evolution.

EXHIBIT 1.2
Vertical Specialization

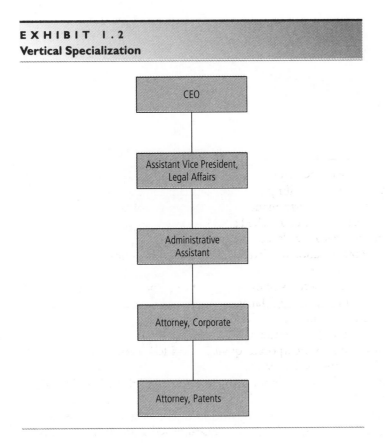

Now let's look at a more general case. Assume that a successful firm, led by CEO Rose Fernandez, decides to add some new products and sell them to new markets. As she becomes more overworked due to the increased complexity of her job, Fernandez may decide to specialize *vertically* (i.e., creating more levels from top to bottom in the organization) by assigning the task of supervising subordinates to other people (Exhibit 1.2). She may also choose to specialize *horizontally* by creating new areas within the organization—such as production, marketing, finance, and purchasing—and by hiring a manager to supervise each new area (Exhibit 1.3). Whichever method Fernandez chooses, the management process in her organization is now shared, specialized, and thus more complex. The various management levels are described in the following subsections.

First-Line Management

First-line managers coordinate the work of others—workers, who aren't themselves managers. People at the **first-line management** level are often called supervisors, office managers, or foremen. The first-line manager may oversee the work of blue-collar workers, salespeople, accounting clerks, or scientists, depending on the particular tasks carried out by that subunit of the business (for example, production, marketing, accounting, or research). First-line managers are responsible for the organization's basic work; they are in daily or near-daily contact with workers. They must work with their own workers and with other first-line supervisors whose tasks are related to their own.

EXHIBIT 1.3
Horizontal Specialization

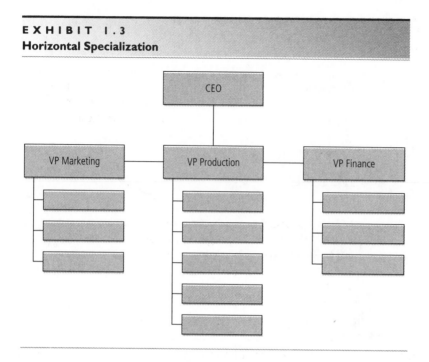

Middle Management

The middle manager is known in many organizations as the department manager, plant manager, or director of operations. Unlike first-line managers, those in **middle management** plan, organize, control, and lead the activities of other managers. Yet, like first-line managers, they're subject to the managerial efforts of a superior. The middle manager coordinates the work activity (for example, marketing) of a subunit.

Over the past ten years, firms such as Sears, General Motors, Xerox, IBM, and General Dynamics have laid off many middle managers. Organizations like these have downsized the management cadre, especially middle-level management. Changes in the environment, competitive pressures, cost overruns, lost market share, and operations inefficiencies have stimulated the move to downsize. Management reductions in large companies are expected to continue into the twenty-first century.

Top Management

A small group of senior executives (usually including a chief executive officer, president, or vice president) constitutes **top management.** Top management is responsible for the performance of the entire organization. These executives rely on middle management to carry their plans for action to each of their respective departments. Unlike other managers, the top manager is accountable to the board of directors and owners of the company or stockholders.[6] Of course, top-level managers depend on the work of all their subordinates to accomplish the organization's goals and mission.

The designations *top, middle,* and *first-line* classify managers based on their vertical rank in the organization. Completing a task usually requires completing several interrelated activities. As these activities are identified, and as the responsibility for completing each task is assigned, that manager becomes a functional manager.

As the management process becomes horizontally specialized, a functional manager is responsible for a particular activity. The management functions in a manufacturing firm could include quality and production, marketing, and accounting. Thus, one manager may be a first-line manager in quality and production, while another may be a middle manager in marketing. The function refers to what *activities* the manager oversees due to horizontal specialization of the management process. A manager's **management level** refers to the *right to act and use resources* within specified limits as a result of vertical specialization of the management process.

MANAGERIAL SKILLS

Regardless of the level at which managers perform, they must learn and develop many skills.[7] A **skill** is an ability or proficiency in performing a particular task. Various skills classifications are important in performing managerial roles. Managerial skills are described in the following subsections; Exhibit 1.4 illustrates the management skills required at each level of management.

Technical Skills

Technical skills are the ability to use *specific* knowledge, techniques, and resources in performing work. Accounting supervisors, engineering directors, and nursing supervisors need technical skills to perform their management jobs. Effective managers know the work they manage. Without task-specific knowledge, a manager will have neither the respect of workers nor the ability to solve technical problems. Technical skills are especially important at the first-line management level, since daily work-related problems must be solved quickly. The technical skill of measuring performance is especially important. As we will see in Chapter 13, managers have many control techniques at their disposal to ensure that plans come to fruition.

EXHIBIT 1.4
Management Skill by Level

Level	Primary Skills	Secondary Skills
First-Line Management	Technical Decision making People	Communication Computer
Middle Management	Analytical Decision making People	Communication Computer
Top Management	Analytical Conceptual Decision making People	Communication Computer

Analytical Skills

Analytical skills involve the ability to analyze or logically diagnose problems and develop solutions. Analytical reasoning powers help managers to gain a broad understanding of a complex situation or problem. Analytical techniques—in the form of computer software—are powerful tools that assist managers in logically assessing and solving specific problems. For example, techniques such as materials requirement planning, inventory control, activity-based cost accounting, forecasting, and human resource information systems help managers develop solutions to complex business problems. In short, analytical tools help the manager to identify key factors, understand how they interrelate, and develop alternative solutions for decision making. Analytical skills of diagnosis, evaluation, and solution are important management problem-solving tools. They help managers not only to understand problems better but also to develop action plans for overcoming the problems.

Decision-Making Skills

All managers must make decisions by choosing between several equally viable alternatives. The quality of these decisions determines that manager's effectiveness. A manager's **decision-making skill** in selecting a course of action is greatly influenced by her analytical skill. Poor analytical proficiency inevitably results in poor decision making. Some decisions are best made by an individual manager; others might best be made by a group. A wise manager knows when to allow a wider range of participation in the decision-making process. However, time pressures and preference for a course of action often drive him to an independent decision. If the manager hopes to gain support in the long term, he must then sell his decision to other members of the organization.

Computer Skills

Computer know-how is an important management skill. In many cases, computers can substantially increase a manager's productivity. In minutes, computers can perform tasks in financial analysis, human resource planning, and other areas; it can take hours, even days, to complete such tasks without a computer. The computer—which instantly places at a manager's fingertips a vast array of information in a flexible, usable form—is invaluable in decision making. Software enables managers to manipulate the data and perform "what-if" scenarios, looking at the projected impact of different decision alternatives.

Today, basic management literacy includes **computer skills** and knowledge of business software. But managers need more than the basics for success. Today, that means using essential desktop software in daily business transactions such as e-mail, forecasting, and budgeting. Additionally, knowledge of the Internet and Web-based business solutions can mean the differences between profit and loss. For example, L.L. Bean traditionally employed catalog sales as its medium for generating sales. Today, 30 percent of L.L. Bean sales are made through the company's website.[8] The L.L. Bean experience is not unique. In coming years, digital sales will continue to account for an increasingly larger percentage of all business sales. Additionally, business-to-business marketing, or B-to-B as it is commonly called, assures that supply chain management is fast and efficient.

As customer shopping patterns switch to Web-based transactions, managers must likewise develop the skills to manage this new technology. As part of the planning process, managers are often responsible for directing the development of websites and managing the website in support of strategic objectives. Because the technology is rapidly changing, managers need to understand how to use outsourcing versus in-house development to maximize their organizational objectives. Managers need the technical knowledge and a willingness to venture beyond their current technical abilities. Though embracing e-commerce can be a daunting and formidable obstacle for managers, the reward for the technically competent manager can be a competitive edge over the competition.

People Skills

Since managers must accomplish much of their work through other people, their ability to work with, communicate with, and understand others is vital. **People skills** are essential at every organizational level of management; they reflect a manager's leadership abilities.

Communication Skills

Effective communication—the written and oral transmission of common understanding—is important to success in every field. It is crucial to managers, who must achieve results through others' efforts. **Communication skills** involve the ability to communicate in ways that other people understand and to seek and use feedback from employees to ensure that you're understood.

Lewis Lehr, former chairman and CEO of 3M, emphasized open communication among managers and employees. Lehr spent six months of every year away from 3M headquarters in St. Paul, Minnesota, visiting the company's numerous plants. During the visits, he participated in question-and-answer sessions with employees. Lehr believed that frequent communication is the only way to build employee trust and cooperation, which are essential to 3M's success. He also required that executives who run 3M operations frequently visit with media, government, and education officials in their regions to talk about 3M.[9]

Conceptual Skills

Conceptual skills consist of the ability to see the big picture—the complexities and connections of the overall organization. To keep an organization's efforts focused, it is vital to conceptualize how each part of the organization fits and interacts with other parts in order to accomplish goals and operate in an ever-changing environment.

Warren Buffett, chief executive officer of the investment firm Berkshire Hathaway, is concerned with making decisions about creating wealth in the future for employees and stockholders. He looks at mergers, acquisitions, and investments that may occur several decades ahead. Buffett uses logic and a conceptual approach to predict future winners.[10]

Although the management skills just described are all important, the relative importance of each skill varies according to the level of the manager in the organization. Note in Exhibit 1.4 that technical and people skills are more important at lower management levels. First-line and middle managers have greater contact with the work being done and the people doing the work. In contrast, communication and computer skills are equally important at all levels of management. Analytical skills are slightly more important at higher levels of management, where the environment is less stable and problems are less predictable. Finally, decision-making and conceptual skills are critical to the performance of top-level managers. Top management's primary responsibility is to make decisions that are implemented at lower levels.

The Management Highlight for this chapter lists and defines some competencies and skills that managers need for success in today's complex organizations. At one time or another in the workplace, a manager will use all these competencies and skills. Yet the importance of one skill or competency over another depends on the situation as well as the level of management (top, middle, or first-line). Demands of the situation may dictate that a manager use compassion or understanding—people skills—when dealing with

---

MANAGEMENT HIGHLIGHT
Management Competencies and Skills

Personal	Organizational	Management	Decision Making
Conscientious Meet deadlines, arrive on time.	**Leadership** Understand the vision and direction of the CEO.	**Leader** Be willing to lead and prepared to assume responsibility.	**Access to information** Be able to use the Internet and other sources of information needed for decision making.
Outgoing Be willing to meet and work with other people. Take the initiative and don't wait for an introduction.	**Teamwork** Be willing to work on a self-directed team. Know how to be a good team member.	**Trust** Develop a sense of trust. Let people know that you can be trusted.	**Problem finding** Seek to identify problems. What decisions need to be made?
Courteous Be polite and respectful of the rights of others.	**Structure** Know how your company is organized.	**Learning** Be open to learning new skills.	**Finding options** Look for alternatives that reflect the varying interests of organization members.
Helping Be ready to help others find solutions to organizational problems.	**Political** Understand the political aspects of your organization and how they can influence decisions.	**Adaptability** Show a willingness to change.	**Acting strategically** Look for opportunities and avoid threats.
Open to new ideas Be willing to change.	**Performance** Know your job; know what is expected of you, and then do it.	**Network** Develop relationships across the organization.	**Being decisive** Make decisions and then stay the course.
	Focus energy Concentrate effort and prioritize your workload.	**Advocate** Champion your cause, selling it to inform others when necessary.	

an employee problem. At each level of management, some skills are more important than others. For top management, creating a vision for the organization and strategic thinking are important. For first-line managers, being fair and building trust far outweigh communicating a long-term vision of the company to employees.

MANAGERIAL ROLES

A **role** is a behavior pattern expected of an individual within a unit or position. One of the most frequently cited studies of managerial roles was conducted by Henry Mintzberg. For two weeks, Mintzberg observed and interviewed five chief executives from different industries. He determined that managers serve in ten different but closely related roles.[11] The ten roles can be placed into three more general categories: interpersonal roles, informational roles, and decisional roles.[12]

Interpersonal Roles

The three **interpersonal roles** of figurehead, leader, and liaison grow out of the manager's formal authority and focus on interpersonal relationships. By assuming these roles, the manager can also perform informational roles that, in turn, lead directly to performing decisional roles.

All managerial jobs require some duties that are symbolic or ceremonial in nature. The college dean who hands out diplomas at graduation, a manager who attends the wedding of a worker's daughter, and the mayor of Chicago formally meeting with Phil Condit, CEO of Boeing, in Boeing's new Chicago corporate offices, are all performing the *figurehead role*.

The manager's *leadership role* involves directing and coordinating subordinates' activities. This may involve staffing (hiring, training, promoting, dismissing) and motivating workers. The leadership role also involves controlling, or making sure that things are going according to plan.

The *liaison role* involves managers in interpersonal relationships outside their area of command. This role may involve contacts both inside and outside the organization. Within the organization, managers must interact with many other managers and individuals. They must maintain good relations not only with the managers who send work to the unit, but with those who receive work from the unit.

Informational Roles

The **informational role** establishes the manager as the central point for receiving and sending information. As a result of the three interpersonal roles just discussed, managers build a network of interpersonal contacts. These contacts aid them in gathering and receiving information as a monitor and transmitting that information as the disseminator and spokesperson.

The *monitor role* involves examining the environment to discover information, changes, opportunities, and problems that may affect the unit. Formal and informal contacts developed in the liaison role are often useful here. The information gathered may concern competitive moves that could influence the entire organization, such as observing young people at a mall wearing a new fashion that suggests a change in a product line.

The *disseminator role* involves providing important or privileged information to subordinates. During a lunch conversation, a firm's president learns that a major customer is upset because of quality defects in the firm's products. Returning to the office, the president asks the vice president of operations and quality about the quality problem. He also instructs the vice president to personally assure him of the quality of the orders sent to the customer.

In the *spokesperson role,* the manager represents the unit to other people. This representation may be internal, when a manager makes the case for salary increases to top management; it may also be external, when an executive represents the organization's views on a particular issue of public interest to a local civic organization.

Decisional Roles

Though developing interpersonal relationships and gathering information are important, they aren't ends in themselves. They serve as the basic inputs to the process of decision making. Some people believe that **decisional roles**—entrepreneur, disturbance handler, resource allocator, and negotiator—are a manager's most important roles.

The purpose of the *entrepreneurial role* is to improve the unit. Effective first-line supervisors continually seek new quality improvement methods to boost their unit's performance. A bank president is continually planning changes that will improve banking services. The effective marketing manager continually seeks new customer tastes.

In the *disturbance handler role,* managers make decisions or take corrective action in response to pressures beyond their control. Because decisions often must be made quickly, this role takes priority over other roles. The immediate goal is to bring about stability. When an emergency room supervisor responds quickly to a local disaster, when a plant manager reacts to a strike, or when a first-line manager responds to a breakdown in a key piece of equipment, they're dealing with disturbances in their environments. Their response must be fast, and it must return the environment to stability.

In the *resource allocator role,* a manager decides who gets which resources (money, people, time, equipment). Invariably, there aren't enough resources to go around; so the manager must allocate scarce goods in many directions. Resource allocation, therefore, is one of the manager's most critical decisional roles. A first-line supervisor must decide whether to set up overtime schedules or hire part-time workers. A worker with three projects must decide how much time to spend on each project daily. The president of the United States must decide whether to allocate more to defense and less to social programs.

In the *negotiator role,* managers must bargain with other units and individuals to obtain advantages for their unit. Negotiations may concern work, performance, objectives, resources, or anything else influencing the unit. A sales manager may negotiate with the production department over a special order for a large customer. A first-line supervisor may negotiate for new work schedules for workers. A top-level manager may negotiate with a labor union representative.

Henry Mintzberg suggests that recognizing these ten roles serves three important functions.[13] First, the roles help explain the job of managing, at the same time emphasizing that all the roles are interrelated. Neglecting one or more of the roles hinders the manager's total progress. Further, says Mintzberg, a team of employees can't function effectively if any one of the roles is neglected. Teamwork in an organizational setting requires that each role be performed consistently. Finally, the magnitude of the ten roles underscores the importance of managing time effectively, so that managers can successfully perform each role.

CONTEMPORARY PERSPECTIVES ON MANAGING

Many of the skills described are words of wisdom and reflect a somewhat static view of organizational life. Organizational downsizing in the 1990s resulted in fewer middle managers and far fewer employees. What we are left with is a well-educated workforce in which the line between the worker and the manager is often less clear. The manager's role has changed from that of a direct supervisor to more of an employee advocate, or simply a provider of resources for employees. Even Henry Mintzberg recognizes that his roles are more useful as guideposts that mark the manager's way.[14]

Mintzberg's current view is that all managers work both inside and outside the organization. *Managers influence by managing information, by managing people, and by managing action.* Internally, managers use information to communicate and control the behavior of people inside the organization. They manage people by leading their employees. They manage action by making decisions that create internal change. Externally, managers communicate information about the organization to people outside the organization. They manage people by linking with others outside the organization. Managers complete their work by making deals and negotiations outside the organization.

Successful managers learn to handle ambiguity. Most situations and problems in organizations have many possible alternatives. The right choice is never easy or clear. Today more than ever before, managers are accomplishing their goals through groups rather than individuals. In that process, building team skills is essential to managerial success. Finally, Peter Senge suggests that managers would do well to use systems theory for problem diagnosis. He believes that managers who use a systems approach to problem diagnosis and resolution are more likely to find and develop solutions for business problems.[15]

Conclusion
——Management and Managers——

Management is both a process and a discipline characterized by a constant state of change. As Mintzberg noted, managers at all levels perform three key roles—interpersonal, informational, and decisional. The dynamic nature of management means that managers must understand and apply the principles of management in daily activities. We believe that students of management should understand how management principles and managers shape the success of their organizations. Management principles are tools and techniques that can make this linkage between process and discipline successful as well as productive.

However, we believe that knowledge and appreciation of management fundamentals is the important point. As you read, analyze, and discuss the chapter content, think about how change occurs in organizations. Remember, change seldom occurs because a manager tells employees to do something. Rather, managers set the direction and then stand back and let employees use their discretion, education, experience, and common sense to effectuate change.

SUGGESTED READINGS

Bossidy, Larry, Ram Charan, and Charles Burck. *Execution: The Discipline of Getting Things Done.* New York: Crown Group, 2001.

Bunker, Kerry A., Kathy E. Kram, and Sharon Ting. "The Young and the Clueless." *Harvard Business Review,* December 2002.

Walker, Carol A. "Saving Your Middle Managers from Themselves." *Harvard Business Review,* April 2002, 3–7.

ENDNOTES

1. Oliver Williamson, *Markets and Hierarchies* (New York: Free Press, 1975).

2. Lester Thurow, *Head to Head* (New York: Morrow, 1992), 56–57.

3. Charles Hill and Gareth Jones, *Strategic Management Theory,* 5th ed. (Boston: Houghton-Mifflin, 2000).

4. *Washington Post,* "Timeline of Enron's Collapse," November 14, 2002.

5. Robert F. Hartley, *Marketing Mistakes* (Columbus, OH: Grid, 1976), 59–70.

6. Charles M. Farkas and Phillippe De Backer, "There Are Only Five Ways to Lead," *Fortune,* January 15, 1996, 109–12.

7. Robert L. Katz, "Skills of an Effective Administrator," *Harvard Business Review,* September–October 1974, 90–102.

8. "L.L. Bean Leverages Net.Commerce to Launch the Great Outdoors in Cyberspace," *E-business Solutions,* IBM Corporation, 1997.

9. Del Marth, "Keeping All the Lines Open," *Nation's Business,* October 1984, 85–86.

10. Bill Gates, "What I Learned from Warren Buffett," *Harvard Business Review,* January–February 1996, 148–152.

11. Henry Mintzberg, *The Nature of Managerial Work* (Englewood Cliffs, NJ: Prentice-Hall, 1980).

12. Henry Mintzberg, "The Manager's Job: Folklore and Fact," *Harvard Business Review,* July–August 1975, 49–61; Jay W. Lorsch, James P. Baughman, James Reece, and Henry Mintzberg, *Understanding Management* (New York: Harper & Row, 1978), 220; Neil Synder and William F. Glueck, "How Managers Plan—The Analysis of Managers' Activities," *Long-Range Planning,* February 1980, 70–76.

13. Mintzberg, *The Nature of Managerial Work.*

14. Henry Mintzberg, "Covert Leadership: Notes on Managing Professionals," *Harvard Business Review,* November–December 1998.

15. "Three Skills for Today's Leaders," *Harvard Management Update,* November 1999, 1–4. Peter Senge, *The Fifth Discipline: The Art and Practice of the Learning Organization.* New York: Currency Doubleday, 1990.

Chapter Two

The Management Environment

Organizations are affected by a host of internal and external environmental factors, ranging from the choices their employees make to the new, technologically sophisticated products their competitors bring to market. We begin this chapter with a discussion of some of the most significant environmental forces, both internal and external, that managers face in making decisions. Next we examine different ways that managers monitor the environment, since managers must analyze many environmental forces to ensure the success of an organization. We end with a strategic approach to environmental analysis and action, focusing on the actions organizations can take to deal with uncertainty and change.

THE INTERNAL ENVIRONMENT

An organization's **internal environment** refers to the factors within an enterprise that influence how work is done and how goals are accomplished. Employees, work flow, office or plant layout, managers' styles, and reward systems are some of the factors affecting an organization's internal environment. Taken together, these factors create a culture within an organization. **Culture** refers to the system of behavior, rituals, and shared meanings that distinguish a group or an organization from other similar units.[1] Managers act to define and energize an organization's culture by training employees, setting goals, and rewarding good performance in specific ways. It's one thing to say that every member of an organization, from the chief executive officer to the newly hired office clerk, shares responsibility for the firm's products and services. It's an altogether different beast to live and breathe that conviction. A unique culture that drives employee actions and attitudes and distinguishes successful employees from also-rans can contribute to higher sales growth, higher return on assets, higher profits, higher product-service quality, and higher employee satisfaction. To perpetuate culture, each employee is expected to pass valued knowledge along to new employees. Behavioral expectations such as this underpin a company's cultural mind-set and serve as guidelines for what's appropriate and acceptable. Culture gives employees an organizational identity and establishes the rules that they follow.

> Culture by definition is elusive, intangible, implicit, and taken for granted. But every organization develops a core set of assumptions, understandings, and implicit rules that govern day-to-day behavior in the workplace. . . . Until newcomers learn the rules, they are not accepted as full-fledged members of the organization.[2]

Quality improvement efforts and activities have become an integral way of life for many organizations around the globe. The attempt to achieve system-wide quality changes, and to maintain them, is generally considered to depend on cultural transformation.[3] According to some studies, however, there is no clear causal chain from organizational culture to overall performance.[4] Other research has linked elements of organizational culture to innovation. For example, researchers Francis Gouillert and James Kelly found that the following seven characteristics of organizational culture are related to innovation:

1. A stated and working strategy of innovation.

2. The use of workplace teams.

3. Rewards and recognition for employee creativity and innovation.

4. An environment in which managers allow people to make mistakes and take risks.

5. A setting in which training in creativity is provided to employees.

6. A carefully managed organizational culture.

7. An atmosphere in which new opportunities are actively created.[5]

When a strong organizational culture emerges, the organization reaps the benefits of organizational commitment, loyalty, and cooperation. But culture can be a liability when employee behaviors and work patterns don't match the values and actions that enhance performance. Changes in the external environment may require rapid responses and adaptation. However, a culture that obstructs change may inhibit or block organizational growth. IBM developed a strong culture that simply wouldn't budge when new competitors created the need for rapid changes in product design and development. Its resistance to change slowed IBM's ability to respond to strong competitors like Apple and Compaq, which were able to capture market share. In an attempt to become more responsive and regain some of the market share it lost to competitors, IBM revised its culture.

Multiple Cultures

Research suggests that most organizations have a dominant culture and a set of subcultures.[6] **Dominant culture** refers to the core values shared by most of the employees in an organization. Think of the distinct characteristics of a firm such as Disney, which emphasizes quality goods and services. In a dominant culture, subcultures are most likely to develop in a unit, group, or section where employees routinely face common situations or problems. The finance department, for example, might create a subculture shared by its members.

Dominant cultures can be weak or strong.[7] In a strong culture, core values are intensely held and widely shared. Employees and role models can dramatically affect the behavior of other employees or members. In the early days at Apple Computer, employees routinely worked long after their shift was over to complete a job. The clock at Apple meant very little, especially when a group was attempting to solve a problem.

Cultures vary from organization to organization. Southwest Airlines has a strong dominant culture, reflecting the personality of its legendary founder and current chairman Herbert Kelleher. Frequent flyers on Southwest get birthday cards, and passengers who write letters get personal responses, sometimes several pages long. Both services are part of the culture that Kelleher established and that Chief Executive James Parker and President Colleen Barrett are continuing. With a culture characterized by "keen intelligence, a deep devotion to Southwest and its employees, and a taste for a good party,"[8] the airline remains the most profitable of the major carriers.

In contrast, newly appointed General Motors CEO Rick Wagoner's major challenge is to energize the firm's dormant culture.[9] Wagoner broke with tradition by hiring two outsiders for top-level positions—head of product development and chief financial officer—and giving them more than the usual authority to solve the company's problems. Wagoner's low-key style seems to be working in tearing down the warring factions inside GM and fostering a culture of cooperation among diverse units such as design, marketing, engineering, and manufacturing.

Building Culture

Many of the firms on *Fortune* magazine's list of "100 Best Companies to Work For" exhibit common values—camaraderie, loyalty, low turnover, and no secrets, to name but a few.[10] Management success in building an effective culture involves selecting, motivating, rewarding, and retaining high-performing employees. Managers must continually work at instilling commitment to a common philosophy and service, developing and rewarding competence, and finding and retaining the right people. Through the **organizational socialization** process, managers and co-workers offer consistent help to newcomers in developing skills and evolving into accepted team members who understand and are committed to the firm's culture.

Values represent convictions that a specific mode of conduct is personally or socially preferable to another mode of conduct. Knowing the values held by individuals is important in helping managers to interpret workers' attitudes and motivations.

The values employees bring to the workplace were largely established in their early years by parents, teachers, relatives, and friends. The discussions a young person hears at home, in the street, or at school provide a basis for values later in life. Values are relatively stable and enduring. A workforce that includes recent immigrants, Hispanics, African Americans, Asian Americans, Caucasians, and other ethnic groups will possess a variety of values spanning economic, social, religious, and political issues.

Managers today deal with a workforce that holds an array of values. Some employees value economic recognition for performance; others value time off to be with their families. Some value making a career commitment to their organizations; others value making a commitment to their profession. Often, what people lack—respect, autonomy, power, or the opportunity for promotion—by its absence becomes the thing most highly valued. Values can also shift with age, significant life experiences, increased education, and achievement of success. Since values differ, managers should not assume automatically that they know what employees value. As the Management Highlight on page 22 shows, research has a role in shaping managerial knowledge regarding what employees value in the workplace.

MANAGEMENT HIGHLIGHT
Nine Values Important to Employees

1. *Recognition*—Employees want to be recognized for their accomplishments.
2. *Respect and dignity*—Employees want to be treated with respect.
3. *Autonomy*—Employees want the freedom to do the job in the way they think is best.
4. *Involvement*—Employees want to be kept informed, included, and involved in important decisions at work.
5. *Pride in one's work*—Employees want to do a good job and exercise good-quality workmanship.
6. *Lifestyle quality*—Employees want time for family and leisure.
7. *Financial security*—Employees want some security in their retirement years from inflation, economic cycles, or catastrophic financial events.
8. *Self-development*—Employees want to personally improve in order to further themselves.
9. *Feedback*—Employees want to be well informed about how they are performing.

Sources: David Jamieson and Julie O'Mara, *Managing Workforce 2000* (San Francisco: Jossey-Bass, 1991), 28–29; Daniel Yankelovich and Associates, *Work and Human Values* (New York: Public Agenda Foundation, 1983), 23; and Edward E. Lowler III, *High-Involvement Management* (San Francisco: Jossey-Bass, 1991), 88.

THE EXTERNAL ENVIRONMENT

Managers must deal not only with internal culture and subcultures but also with factors outside the organization. The **external environment** includes those forces outside the organization that have a direct or indirect impact on the firm's activities. Any one of these forces can dramatically influence the course taken by an organization. Some of these forces are under the organization's control; some are uncontrollable, and their impact is difficult to predict. Exhibit 2.1 depicts the various forces comprising the external environment. In the following subsections, we examine each of these forces.

Direct Forces

Direct forces exert an immediate and daily impact on the organization. These forces include competitors, employees, customers, and suppliers.

Competitors.   In the business world, organizations that produce similar goods or services are generally referred to as **competitors.** They are usually rival firms competing for the same group of customers. Failing to recognize its competition can spell disaster for an organization. At Nissan, it was high prices that led to the demise of the original Z line of cars: when the price of a fully loaded 300ZX reached nearly $50,000 in the late 1990s, the car was thrust into direct competition with models from Mercedes-Benz and Jaguar.[11] When introducing the new 350Z in 2002, Nissan managers recognized that competition was intense among sports cars in the medium-priced range. Although demand had fallen during the previous decade, Nissan believed competitive pricing would determine the success or failure of the new Z.

Organizations must constantly assess their competition and differentiate themselves in the marketplace. One consumer may buy her car from Volvo, which touts its reputation for safety. Another consumer may buy from Toyota because it advertises high-quality cars at reasonable prices. The critical issue for any organization is to maintain dominance in its selected market by staying a step ahead of competitors.

EXHIBIT 2.1
Forces in the External Environment

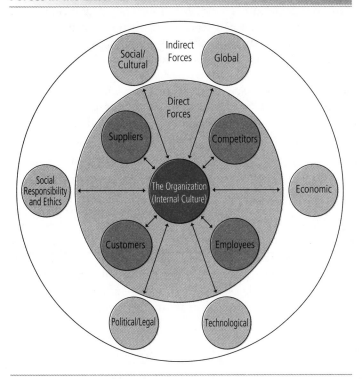

Managers must also monitor the changes their competitors are making, and determine what adjustments to make in maintaining their firm's position in the market. For instance, a manager should determine if—and why—major competitors are changing product designs, distribution methods, customer service policies, or promotional methods such as advertising. Managers can obtain information about competitors' activities through direct observation as well as by surveying customers, reading trade publications, talking with employees such as salespeople, and studying market research.

Employees.   Employees are an organization's most important resource; they do the work of the organization. By offering a pleasant, effective work environment and attractive compensation and incentive packages, successful firms recruit, train, and retain energetic, talented employees.

Organizations compete externally not only for customers, but for human resources. The organizations that attract and retain the most talented employees are likely in the best position to attract and retain customers. Thus management is faced with the dual challenge of designing programs—recruiting, compensation, training, career advancement, education—that bring the best people into the organization and keep them there.

Several trends in the U.S. workforce are influencing the managers' job. The workforce is more diverse, and managing these differences is a significant challenge. The diversity spans age, race, and gender. The median age of the workforce, now over 40, was 28 in 1970. By 2010, one quarter of the U.S. population will be at least 55.[12] A workforce that was once dominated by white males is now made up of African Americans, Hispanics, Asians, and individuals from an array of other ethnic groups. And today women comprise nearly 50 percent of the workforce. These changes require managers to develop new approaches to recruiting, training, promoting, and motivating a more diverse workforce.

Customers.   Customers are the lifeblood of an organization. They may include consumers who purchase an organization's goods and services, or organizational customers that purchase products for their own operations. Customers are perhaps the most critical of the direct environmental forces, because they ultimately determine whether the organization will succeed.

Most organizations make great efforts to stay close to their customers. They accomplish this goal by conducting research to identify the needs and wants of present and potential customers. Surveys typically address how satisfied the customers are with products and quality of service, and inquire about customer needs that are not being met.

Suppliers.   Organizations depend upon other firms to supply them with resources, including capital, raw materials, office supplies, parts, and so on. Suppliers are important to an organization because they can directly affect the quality of goods and services produced. The quality of a car, for example, is affected by the quality of the auto parts that a manufacturer purchases from a supplier.

Because suppliers affect product quality, it is important for organizations to have cooperative relationships with them. Many organizations use several suppliers to reduce their dependence on a single supplier. Other firms are partnering with supplier firms, in some cases investing directly in—and relying solely on—those firms for supplies. Some organizations even purchase the supplier organization in order to have greater control over the cost and availability of supplies.

Indirect Forces

Although they are not directly involved in daily operations, **indirect forces** in the external environment also influence an organization. Indirect forces are categorized as social-cultural, economic, global, technological, political-legal, and social responsibility and ethics (see Exhibit 2.1).

Social-Cultural.   Families share certain beliefs and values that make up their social and cultural systems. So do small and large organizations—even nations. The social-cultural environment is shaped and influenced by the learned and shared values of all the individuals and organizations within that system. Because social structures and cultures are in constant flux, managers must be aware of change and incorporate that knowledge into their decisions. Organizations and managers that consider the effects of their decision making on the social-cultural environment are among the most socially responsible.

Many businesses have created policies and programs to help employees manage their home and work roles. The heightened interest in an employer work-family agenda is fueled by changing workforce demographics as well as by a growing understanding of the bottom-line benefits to employers for acknowledging and supporting people's personal lives. In determining the organizational costs of failing to have family-friendly policies, studies have found that problems with dependent care arrangements affect productivity and job effectiveness for both men and women. The benefits are measurable. Dependent care assistance has been proven to increase staff availability; work-family programs affect employee retention and reduce related stress.

Employee health is another area of growing concern to managers. The United States has become an increasingly sedentary society. Our shift to postindustrial society means an increase in indoor working and living. Americans spend about 90 percent of their time indoors, usually sleeping, eating, dressing, or watching television. Bad habits associated with a sedentary lifestyle include smoking, snacking, and drinking soda and coffee. It's generally accepted that healthy workers lose less time and have fewer accidents than unhealthy ones.

The United States spends over $800 billion a year in health care—that's more than 13 percent of the gross national product. In the workplace, employees are responsible for their own personal health and safety as well as that of fellow workers. Every year, 2.2 million people in the United States suffer ill health either caused or aggravated by workplace activities.[13] More and more firms are trying to improve workers' knowledge about health, lifestyles, and disease prevention. Issues such as mental stress, substance abuse, eyestrain from computer use, and proper use of equipment are covered in training programs, employee assistance programs, and new employee orientation sessions.

These examples of social-cultural factors emphasize the uncontrollable nature of the external environment. To be prepared for changes in the mix of employees, preferences of consumers, and availability of skilled employees, managers need to be aware of social-cultural trends, values, and forecasts.

Economic.   The economic environment influences management decisions and plans in many areas. An expanding economy directly affects demand for a firm's goods or services. If demand increases, the workforce will probably need to be expanded, or new shifts added to the workday. In a recessionary economy, decisions may have to be made about layoffs, downsizing, cutting back on the size of the firm, or even plant and office closings.

Managers must monitor changes in economic indicators—inflation rates, interest rates, unemployment rates, productivity—and make appropriate adjustments. When the economy is on the upswing, managers may decide to expand operations. Conversely, during economic downturns, demand for products may fall, along with profits, as unemployment rises; managers must be prepared to adjust to this environment as well. During the economic slump at the turn of this century, most companies faced weak and falling revenues, and many firms responded by cutting jobs.

Global.   Throughout the world, managers are facing the same challenge—intense global competition. Large companies like IBM and AT&T as well as smaller ones like Bicknell Manufacturing and Lucerne Farms are fighting for customers by venturing beyond domestic borders, spurred on by deregulation, privatization, and rapid technological change. A study on the internationalization of firms with 500 or fewer employees reported that 50 percent of the firms were involved in international business.[14] Global fever has now reached the ranks of U.S. entrepreneurs as well as the huge firms of corporate America.

As a result of this intense scramble to enter foreign markets, companies around the world are at war. Any one company has no idea where its next challenge may originate. Car companies compete with banks in credit card wars, while software firms fight with cable companies over rights on the information highway. And the target in these wars, the competitor, is always moving. Giants like Coca-Cola and Pepsi have to fight off private-label brands sold in copycat cans, and Six Flags taunts Disney in television ads, claiming that "Disney is a great vacation destination. So is Australia."

Today, size and experience count for much less than they once did. Speed and execution are critical, and battles between firms are fierce. In the United States, perhaps nothing illustrates this point better than the war among the three major long-distance carriers—AT&T, MCI, and Sprint. In Thailand, the Japanese firms Sony and Matsushita are fighting for the electronics market. Whether they're trying to escape flat domestic markets or building on their successes, more and more companies are looking to foreign markets for growth opportunities.

Technology.   **Technology** can be broadly defined as all of the ways that people apply practical knowledge to provide comfort and human sustenance. Technology is a part of the human condition; we give it meaning, substance, and function. So it's hardly valid to think of technology itself as being the problem, or even the reason for other problems. Cartoon character Pogo's wry statement, "We have met the enemy and he is us," can apply to people misusing technology as much as to people electing a bad government. We can either help or hurt ourselves with technology. And, because technology enables organizations to meet consumer needs, we will almost certainly continue to expand it.

Technological innovation involves all those activities that people carry out in translating technical knowledge into a physical reality that can be used. The process of technological innovation progresses from the most basic research to wide-scale marketing. The automobile is a technological innovation that has had long-term effects on the mobility of society and the purchasing patterns of consumers. Other innovations such as the telephone, airplane, radio, television, computers, and various medical technologies have also significantly influenced society.

It takes time and money to carry out technological innovation and marketing. Years may pass before an innovation in biomedicine, energy, or any other sector reaches the marketing stage. A significant environmental force, technology drives change in industries, forges relationships between firms and customers, and creates new competitors. To continue in business, managers must use technology properly. Astute managers employ technology to improve their services to customers, find new customers, lower cost, and speed the introduction of new products.

Political-Legal.   The political-legal environment consists of government rules and regulations that apply to organizations. The very words *rules and regulations* often make managers uneasy and resentful. No one likes being regulated. For years, the American manager has generally been a staunch theoretical supporter of a hands-off government policy (a policy of not interfering with business activity). Yet most managers know that the business system can't work without some government rules and regulations to organize and monitor the external environment.

The number and variety of government regulations affecting business are huge. Some are directed toward goals as disparate as economic growth, job security, and environmental pollution control. These regulations and government programs can be divided into those designed specifically to support business and those intended to influence various business activities. For instance, the government supports business by providing subsidies in the form of guaranteed and insured loans, support to keep the airlines flying, and money to build highways to move people and products. Numerous laws and regulatory agencies influence virtually all business activities, including hiring practices, workplace safety, environmental impact of production, processes and products, and product safety, to name a few. The Securities and Exchange Commission (SEC) recently ruled that mutual fund companies, which had avoided the financial scandals that plagued many firms, must disclose how they vote in corporate proxy contests. The SEC is also looking into establishing tougher internal controls for the mutual fund industry.[15]

The political-legal environment can have an adverse effect on the organization. Firms may be fined severely for polluting the environment or engaging in other illegal practices. In some instances, the resulting negative publicity may damage the organization further. Although many organizations think they are overregulated, most observers believe government regulation will grow, especially as emerging technologies like the Internet present new avenues for abuses.

Social Responsibility and Ethics. In our society, federal and local laws set the minimum standards for responsible and ethical business practices and employer and employee behavior. In organizations, a philosophy that becomes part of the culture reveals the firm's approach to social responsibility. A firm's **social responsibility** is reflected in its practices with other parties such as customers, competitors, the government, employees, suppliers, and creditors. What it means to be socially responsible differs across industries and from firm to firm. There's no specific standard that a firm follows, since managers think quite differently about what constitutes socially responsible behavior.

Although social responsibility may sound like an abstract concept, it is an important part of the relationship between organizations and society. Society expects businesses to obey laws, act ethically, and contribute to the quality of life in the community—while making a profit. Thus most companies consider the expenses incurred for social responsibility, such as the cost of building a community playground, as the price of doing business. Determining the wants of customers, employees, government regulators, and society at large plays a key role in an organization's success.

Ethics refers to principles of behavior that distinguish between right and wrong. Managers' behavior is judged as ethical or unethical based on commonly accepted principles of behavior established by special interest groups, competitors, management, customers, and the expectations of society. Managers decide how to behave based on these principles, and the general public and various interest groups evaluate whether the actions are ethical.

Ethics is ultimately a function of mutual trust among individuals and organizations. An ethical violation makes continued trust difficult, and may cause irreparable damage to an organization. Public outcry and a great deal of litigation ensued when Enron, WorldCom, Qwest, and other firms were investigated for reporting phony earnings and inflated revenues, and forming off-the-book partnerships that yielded billions of dollars—millions of which went to corrupt executives. As a result, the public confidence in corporate America fell dramatically, along with a steep decline in the stock market.[16]

The following Management Highlight is a useful summary of the types of indirect forces that affect organizations.

MANAGEMENT HIGHLIGHT
Indirect Environmental Forces

Social-Cultural	Economic	Global	Technological	Political-Legal	Social Responsibility and Ethics
Lifestyle changes	Interest rates	Trade agreements	New products	Antitrust laws	Environmental protection
Life expectancies	Deficit	Exports	Patent laws	Product liability laws	Waste management
Birth rate	Gross domestic product	Trade deficits	Productivity measurement and growth	Tax laws	Public image regarding environmental responsibility
Population growth rate (immigration included)	Unemployment levels	Cultural environment	Industry R&D	Import-export trade	Product safety
Family arrangements	Energy sources and costs	Exchange rates	Federal support of R&D	Trade regulations	Packaging procedures
Consumer activism	Inflation rates	Infrastructure	Robotics	Investment tax credits	Ethical behavior
Shifts in population	Money supply	Competition	Computer technology	Corporate responsibility	
Changing women's roles					

Monitoring the Management Environment

The forces in the management environment can change; the rate of change varies depending on the specific environment. In *stable environments* the rate of change is relatively slow, while *dynamic environments* are characterized by more rapid change. Additionally, some environments are more complex than others. **Environmental complexity** refers to the number of forces in the environment that influence the organization. Some environments are relatively simple, comprised of a few factors, while others are more complex and include many factors.

Whether the forces in the environment change slowly or rapidly, and whether the forces are few or many, they create uncertainty for managers. **Environmental uncertainty** is the degree to which managers can predict how environmental factors will change and the impact these changes will have on the organization. If managers have a great deal of information about environmental forces and they are in a position to predict changes, they can reduce environmental uncertainty. Managers must constantly monitor the environment to capitalize on opportunities and minimize adverse effects that result from changes. Each element should be monitored, with special emphasis on those forces likely to have an impact on the organization. To effectively monitor changes in the environment, managers engage in environmental scanning and analysis.

Environmental scanning is the process of collecting information concerning forces in the management environment. Scanning involves gathering information through observation; reviewing business, trade, and government publications; and engaging in research efforts. Although this information is important to managers, they must be careful not to acquire so much information that its sheer volume makes analysis impossible.

Environmental analysis is the process of assessing and interpreting the information gathered through environmental scanning. A manager reviews the information for accuracy, tries to reconcile inconsistencies in the data, and interprets the findings. Analysis allows a manager to discern changes in the environment and, if possible, to predict trends and changes. By evaluating these changes, a manager should be able to determine possible threats and opportunities associated with environmental fluctuations.

Organizations should have a plan in place for responding to environmental forces. Managers use one of two general approaches. In the traditional approach, managers view the forces of the environment as uncontrollable. Thus they assume that organizations can do little to alter the influence of the various forces in the management environment. A well-managed organization taking this *reactive* approach tries to prepare itself to respond quickly to changes in the environment. For example, an organization has little power over external forces such as economic conditions and the actions of its competitors. But it can monitor the environment closely, adjusting its strategy to counter the effects of inflation and staying abreast of product improvements by competitors.

A second response to the management environment is to take a *proactive* or aggressive stance toward environmental forces. A growing number of professionals argue that the management environment can be controlled, at least to some extent. Organizations can choose to strategically manage elements of the environment to the benefit of the organization. Through lobbying, legal action, advertising of key issues, and public relations, organizations can alter some environmental forces. For instance, a firm can control its competitive environment by using aggressive pricing or competitive advertising strategies to influence the decisions of rival firms. It can lobby political officials to repeal legislation that it believes will restrict its business. Likewise, a firm can use its political skills and public relations activities to create opportunities by opening foreign markets to American businesses. Let's examine a strategic approach to environmental management.

STRATEGIC MANAGEMENT OF THE ENVIRONMENT

Strategic management of the environment is the process of identifying environmental uncertainties and developing strategies to manage or reduce those uncertainties. Successful organizations pay particular attention to critical unknowns, such as market demand and intermediate product cost. To ensure profitability, they take necessary actions both to control uncertainties and to better estimate demand and control cost. James D. Thompson, the distinguished organizational sociologist, noted that "uncertainty is the fundamental administrative problem." He suggests several environmental management strategies for reducing uncertainty in his landmark book, *Organizations in Action.*[17]

Internal Strategies

Organizations can use internal strategies in order to benefit from environmental opportunities and avoid threats. **Internal strategies** are tactical actions that organizations can choose in adapting the organization to, reducing, or at least managing environmental uncertainty.

Changing Domain.   Organizations can decide where they will do business and what they will produce and market. When the competition heats up or profitability evaporates, an organization can change its domain and compete in a different market. In response to the passage of more restrictive laws regulating automobile insurers by some states, several automobile insurers stopped writing new policies in those states (New Jersey is a notable example). Likewise, in areas of the country where natural disasters such as flooding, fires, and hurricanes occur most often, insurers have substantially limited their risk by ceasing to write new policies. After the devastation caused by Hurricane Andrew, many home insurers simply stopped writing homeowner insurance in Florida. Uncertainty is thus managed by moving to a more accommodating, perhaps even friendly, environment.

Recruiting.   One way to manage uncertainty is by hiring top employees from a major competitor. It is not unusual to see an executive leave General Motors for a major promotion at Volkswagen. In other situations, recruitment can mean hiring a former government official who had responsibility for regulating your industry.

Buffering.   The strategy of buffering is a common way to maintain steady production. Organizations can buffer on either the input side or the output side of the production process. *Input buffering* manages the fluctuations caused by the interruption of supplies of materials needed to manufacture the product. This strategy often takes the form of stockpiling materials or the outright purchase of suppliers. In *output buffering,* finished goods are warehoused until they can be absorbed by the environment. Automobile manufacturers usually have big, fenced parking lots for storing vehicles until shipment. Yet even when shipped, the vehicles might be stored at a railhead facility until final delivery to the dealer. The buffering process can move fast or slow, depending on the demands of the environment.

Smoothing. Smoothing is a method of maintaining continuous demand for a product or service. Pricing is a mechanism that is often used to smooth customer demand. Price increases soften demand; price reductions increase demand. In the communications industry, providers often charge more during peak hours and discount prices at off hours to attempt to influence usage patterns. Smoothing results in efficient use of assets, reducing costs by eliminating the need to buy more equipment.

Rationing. We know what's likely to happen when we show up at our favorite restaurant without a reservation—no table. Restaurants and many other service providers often use rationing as a way of ensuring that all their time is productive. Without rationing, too many people to process may arrive at once, resulting in disgruntled customers who will seek service elsewhere.

External Strategies

External strategies are organizational attempts to change environmental circumstances, thereby reducing environmental uncertainty.

Advertising. We are all familiar with the effects of advertising on human behavior. Indeed, we often catch ourselves repeating familiar slogans or whistling jingles that are designed to stimulate demand for a product or service. Most organizations use advertising to signal price changes, new product features, or new locations. Organizations use advertising to provide information, create brand recognition, and encourage consumer demand: "Buy our new and improved product now—prices may never be this low again!"

Contracting. Seasonal products such as natural gas are often sold to consumers on contract. Contracting is a mutually beneficial arrangement. The purpose of the contract is to reduce the uncertainty on both sides of the buyer-seller relationship. The buyer is assured a set price for the contract, and the seller has a guaranteed buyer. In rural communities, propane is often sold on contract in the spring and delivered the following fall. While prices are guaranteed to the buyer, actual commodity prices may increase or decrease between the spring and fall, thus defining who benefits most from the contract deal—the propane company or its customers.

Co-opting. *Co-optation* represents an attempt to influence an external party. Concerned consumers or consumer groups who complain about product design features or functions might be asked to join a customer design team. They are thereby effectively co-opted into the organization. Once an external group becomes part of the organization, their resistance to organizational actions dissipates rapidly.

Coalescing. A *coalition* is an alliance of several organizations, bound by common purpose, taking a united action. Coalition building is based on the idea that there is power in numbers. When selling commodity items, vendors often grant substantial discounts for volume purchases. In healthcare, it's common for several hospitals to form an alliance to purchase common hospital supplies or share a laundry facility.

Lobbying. *Lobbying* is an attempt to influence a decision maker. In business-government relations, lobbying is the act of influencing a public official to understand and appreciate an organization or industry's perspective on an issue of mutual concern. Businesses often attempt to influence the direction of legislation in their favor. Interested business community members often write first drafts of the law, hoping that their vision of the pending legislation will be enacted into law. This form of uncertainty reduction is a way to affect or change the environment. Obviously, only the largest companies can hope to use this powerful external management strategy.

Conclusion
The Management Environment

In this chapter we introduced the various forces in the management environment, both direct and indirect. Because these forces can have a major impact on organizations, managers must monitor the environment and take action as needed. Ignoring the management environment can lead to a host of problems and may even destroy an organization.

SUGGESTED READINGS

Brook, Manville, and Josiah Ober. "Beyond Empowerment: Building a Company of Citizens." *Harvard Business Review,* January 2003, 48–53.

Makower, Joel. *Beyond the Bottom Line: Putting Social Responsibility to Work for Your Business and the World.* Carmichael, CA: Touchstone Books, 1995.

Pava, Moses. *The Search for Meaning in Organizations: Seven Practical Questions for Ethical Managers.* Westport, CT: Quorum Books, 1999.

Salmon, Robert, and Yolaine de Linares. *Competitive Intelligence: Scanning the Global Environment.* Oxford: Economica, 1999.

Schein, Edgar H. *Organizational Culture and Leadership.* San Francisco: Jossey-Bass, 1997.

Tichy, Noel, Andrew R. McGill, and Lynda St. Clair (eds.), *Corporate Global Citizenship: Doing Business in the Public Eye.* Lanham, MD: Lexington Books, 1998.

Wei Choo, Chun. *The Knowing Gap: How Organizations Use Information to Construct Meaning, Create Knowledge, and Make Decisions.* New York: Oxford University Press, 1998.

ENDNOTES

1. Edgar H. Schein, *Organizational Culture and Leadership* (San Francisco: Jossey-Bass, 1997), 58.
2. T. A. Deal and A. A. Kennedy, "Culture—A New Look through Old Lenses," *Journal of Applied Behavioral Science* (November 1983): 50.
3. Peter F. Drucker, *Post-Capitalist Society* (New York: Harper-Collins, 1993), 72.
4. Bruce Brocka and M. Suzanne Brocka, *Quality Management* (Burr Ridge, IL: Business One Irwin, 1992), 64–71.
5. Francis J. Gouillert and James N. Kelly, *Transforming the Organization* (New York: McGraw-Hill, 1995), 4–5.
6. Lyndall Urwick, *The Golden Book of Management* (London: Newman Neame, 1956), 72–79.
7. Frederick W. Taylor, *Principles of Scientific Management* (New York: Harper & Row, 1911), 36–37.
8. Wendy Zellner and Michael Arndt, "Holding Steady," *Business Week,* February 3, 2003, pp. 66–68.

9. David Welch and Kathleen Kerwin, "Rick Wagoner's Game Plan," *Business Week,* February 10, 2003, pp. 52–60.

10. Robert Levering and Milton Moskowitz, "100 Best Companies to Work For," *Fortune,* January 20, 2003, pp. 127–52.

11. Chester Dawson, "Nissan," *Business Week,* July 22, 2002, pp. 47–49.

12. *Statistical Abstracts of the United States,* 2002, p. 20.

13. Rowena Rees, "Commonsense Campaign Tackles Work-Related Illness," *Works Management,* July 1995, pp. 18–19.

14. Tatiana S. Manlova et al., "Internationalization of Small Firms: Personal Factors Revisited," *International Small Business Journal,* February 2002, pp. 9–31.

15. Amy Borrus and Mike McNamee, "Why It's Open Season on Mutual Funds," *Business Week,* February 10, 2003, p. 69.

16. "System Failure," *Fortune,* June 24, 2002, pp. 62–74.

17. James D. Thompson, *Organizations in Action* (New York: McGraw Hill Book Company, 1967), chapters 2–3, p. 159.

Planning

part two

Chapter Three

Decision Making

Every day and in every organization, managers are constantly making decisions. Some decisions are unimportant in the larger scheme of things; others may affect the lives of many people for years to come. While we generally think of decision making as an individual action, in organizations many decisions are made by groups, teams, or committees. For example, a hiring decision might be made by a personnel committee, a purchasing decision by a procurement group, and product design by a design team. Empowerment, education, democratic organizations, and advances in information technology have made group decision making quite common in organizations today. This trend toward group decision making is not likely to change in the future.

Regardless of its magnitude and ultimate outcome, decision making in organizations is about choosing from among several competing alternatives. A key component in the decision-making process is the amount of information that is available to the decision maker. Generally speaking, the more information the decision maker has, the better the decision will be. More information also means less risk for the decision maker and increases predictability of the outcome. Decision making is not easy. It involves a complex mixture of information, knowledge, experience, creativity, and risk taking.

An important measure of the effectiveness of an individual manager, a management team, or a worker team is the quality of decisions reached. Indeed, some have argued that the primary function of management *is* decision making and that the essence of managerial behavior is found by studying the decision-making process.

A **decision** is a choice among competing alternatives and the implementation of the chosen alternative. All decisions have a time horizon or scope. *Strategic decisions* have a long-term perspective; they are related to an organization's overall strategy. *Tactical decisions* have a shorter time scope; they entail choices that must be made in the near term. However, tactical decisions must also remain consistent with the organization's strategy. Managers make many strategic and tactical decisions every day. Some decisions are inconsequential, representing merely an opinion or preference of the decision maker. Other decisions can affect an organization for many years to come.

Decision making requires information, but the decision maker rarely has complete information. This lack of information is referred to as uncertainty. As author James Thompson notes, "Uncertainty appears as the fundamental problem for complex organizations, and coping with uncertainty, as the essence of the administrative process."[1]

Decision making involves one of three situations:

- **Certainty** The decision maker has complete information of the probabilities of the outcomes of each alternative.

- **Uncertainty** The decision maker has absolutely no knowledge of the probabilities of the outcomes of each alternative.

- **Risk** The decision maker has some probabilistic estimate of the outcomes of each alternative.

Obviously, the best situation for a manager is one of certainty. Where certainty exists, the decision is clear and the outcome is known. How can you lose? The worst case for the manager is uncertainty. With little information and the inability to assign probabilities to outcomes, a manager is operating in the dark. However, most managerial decisions are made with some degree of risk. The advantage of risk is that it can be managed when alternatives are known and probability of occurrence can be assigned to outcomes.

For example, if a university knows that on the first day of the fall semester it wants to have an incoming class of three thousand students, how many students should it accept? One factor we must take into account is that although students apply to many schools, they attend only one. In this hypothetical case, say the administrators use a rational decision-making model that includes many years of past admissions data to predict a probabilistic answer. In fact, the answer might be that only 42 percent of all applicants actually attend the university. So, if the university wants three thousand students to attend the university beginning in the fall semester, its admissions office must admit 7,143 students ($3,000 \times 1/.42$). Of course, the process is more complicated than what we've just described, but the point is the same. In this example, using a rational admissions model significantly reduces uncertainty about how many students will actually attend the university for the fall semester.

So managerial decision making entails both a process and subsequent action. A **decision-making process** is a series of related steps or stages leading to an action, an outcome, and assessment. As we noted earlier, as a process a decision is a choice among alternative courses of action. From a managerial perspective, a decision is also an action that someone takes, and that individual is subsequently held accountable for the outcome of the action (decision). In today's complex, information-rich organizations, the managerial decision-making process is often fragmented and rapid. In the modern work environment, it's becoming less likely that a single individual can process enough information to make the best decisions for the organization. Besides dealing with the vast amount of data available for most nonroutine decisions, managers must respond to interruptions and unexpected events. As they often find, the decision-making process occurs over time rather than as a single event. Managers must learn to deal with a decision-making environment that emphasizes oral communication, brief meetings, incomplete information, and close approximations. Their decisions are often based on impressions, estimates, and personal experience. Decision making often reflects a manager's effort to make sense of the complicated environment, to attain some control over the uncontrollable, and to achieve some sense of order.

Managers are fundamentally decision makers. An organized approach to decision making—including a clear understanding of the current state of affairs, the historical basis for improving decisions, and the possible errors that can be made—enables managers to make better decisions and to reach personal and organizational goals. Management theorists have investigated decision making from many different perspectives and have developed a set of useful concepts to understand the phenomenon. To increase your awareness of the complexity of this highly social process that involves reason and emotion, risk and uncertainty, and imagination and knowledge, in this chapter we will explore several important concepts.

TYPES OF MANAGERIAL DECISIONS

Decision making is an entirely human process; like human beings themselves, it is fraught with complexities and ambiguities. By gaining some understanding of the different concepts that researchers have used to understand decision making, the practicing manager can often avoid difficulties. For example, a manager who is used to making decisions based on intuition may notice that many of his recent decisions are less effective than they used to be. If he is aware of the distinction between *intuitive* and *rational* decision making, he may understand that his intuitions are based on personal experiences that may no longer be appropriate in a changed environment. Switching, at least temporarily, to a more rational approach may very well lead to more effective decisions.[2]

Programmed versus Non-Programmed Decisions

Decision making in an organization occurs during routine operations and in unexpected situations alike. Herbert Simon[3] has identified two distinct categories of managerial decisions.

- **Programmed decision** If a particular situation occurs often, a solution is designed in the form of a routine procedure. Decisions are programmed to the extent that they are repetitive and routine, and a definite procedure has been developed for handling them.

- **Non-programmed decision** Decisions are non-programmed when they are unstructured, novel, or unique. They often represent one-time situations that require a choice among existing alternatives. There is no established procedure for handling the problem. These decisions deserve special attention and treatment due to their importance or complexity.

Managers in most organizations face many programmed decisions in their daily operations. Such decisions should be treated without expending unnecessary organizational resources. On the other hand, the non-programmed decision must be properly identified as such since this type of decision can involve significant risk and uncertainty.

Despite some managers' efforts to place all organizational processes under rigorous and invariant control regimens, variation, complexity, and ambiguity in the workplace are the rule rather than the exception. Much day-to-day variation can be accommodated with routine responses, yet a creative response or non-programmed decision of some sort is often needed.

Non-programmed decisions involve searching for information and alternatives that lie out-side the routine decision-making process. These decisions are often time-consuming and (unlike routine decisions) demand that workers be prepared to create alternative solutions, analyze them critically, and choose a course of action.

Many organizations now use computers and software to assist with complex, non-programmed decisions. Boeing transformed the process of manufacturing commercial air-liners when it created an online CAD/CAM system that integrated individual component designs with the final subassembly. For example, the manufacturer of a screw would design it online and submit the design, and be able to view his product used on a soft-ware model of the final assembly. The designer receives an error message for any design parameter defects (e.g., screw was too long) immediately. The error can be corrected before the component is ever manufactured.

Programmed decisions, which don't allow for flexibility, aren't always useful for work-ers in manufacturing jobs. Product design engineers are still often directed by manage-ment to create product assembly processes so simple that they require no input from assemblers on the factory floor. Such a simple design may be valuable to an untrained cus-tomer when assembling a product at home (e.g., a piece of home exercise equipment). But for a trained assembly worker, ordering such simple assembly processes reflects con-tempt for the worker's ability to make non-programmed decisions.

One company that has succeeded in employing an innovative form of Frederick Taylor's scientific management principles on the factory floor (see Appendix A for a discussion of scientific management) is New United Motor Manufacturing, Inc. (NUMMI), of Fremont, California. NUMMI is a joint venture between Toyota and General Motors. NUMMI has used the principles of scientific management to create a highly programmed process flow and to increase quality, productivity, and employee motivation at the same time. How does the company manage this? It does so by allowing the workers themselves to design the formal work standards and establish the programmed decisions. As University of Southern California Professor Paul Adler stated following a two-year study of the com-pany, "Procedures that are designed by the workers themselves in a continuous, success-ful effort to improve productivity, quality, skills, and understanding can humanize even the most disciplined form of bureaucracy."[4]

Programmed and non-programmed decisions affect organizations daily. Sometimes managers need to react to events and make decisions. At other times they can anticipate changes and make decisions before events occur. This distinction is captured in the fol-lowing discussion of two more decision types: proactive and reactive.

Proactive versus Reactive Decisions

You may recall that earlier in this chapter, we defined the term *decision* as a choice among competing alternatives. A decision made in anticipation of an external change or other conditions is called a **proactive decision**. Managers who utilize a rational, proactive approach can prevent problems from developing.

A **reactive decision** is one made in response to external changes. Suppose that the ABC Router company (a manufacturer of woodworking routers) learns that their main com-petitor, XYZ Routing, is offering a free router accessory (a $30 value) with the purchase of their new TECH1 router. Using a reactive approach, ABC Router believes that they must respond by marketing their routers in a similar fashion. In fact, ABC Router raises the stakes by offering two free router accessories and quickly working the new offer into their holiday-season advertising campaign. The decision made by ABC Router is strate-gic, yet reactive. The point is that their response was not based on a plan, but in response to the plan of a competitor. Reactive decisions are not always inferior to proactive decisions, but over the long run, merely reacting to environmental stimuli is risky. Why? It suggests a lack of planning and strategy. In the next few chapters, we'll see that planning and strategy formulation create a decision context. In that context, managers can make decisions that support the strategy ("we stay the course") in relation to a competitive response. This is a different situation than a reactive decision.

Management history teaches us that whenever possible, it's better to be proactive than reactive. Wise managers recognize that one person alone doesn't make things happen; whether you're the boss or the worker out on the shop floor, success depends on a team. To help focus the endowed talents and virtues of their subordinates, managers must first provide a vision; otherwise, all decisions are reactive. Reactive decisions aren't necessarily made out of context, but rather without a context. The ABC Router example demonstrates this point. ABC Router's decision had more to do with the decision context of another organization than of its own. If ABC Router's decision increases costs with no increase in customer demand, the firm may lose money on every router it sells.

Managerial vision provides the context for proactive decision making. If the vision is strong enough and communicated effectively, many employees will intuitively make decisions in support of that vision. Intuitive decisions are based on experience, and they are usually made in situations that allow little time for analysis. Rational decision making should also conform to the managerial vision for the organization, but it involves more time and prior data gathering. We explore the intuitive and rational types of decision making next.

Intuitive versus Systematic Decisions

Intuitive decisions involve the use of estimates, guesses, or hunches to decide among alternative courses of action. Of course we assume that these actions are based on experience or reflection, rather than merely random responses to novel situations. Most managers will admit that many of their decisions are considerably influenced by flashes of insight, or intuition. Nonetheless, decisions based purely on intuition can be premature, unnecessary, and even counterproductive. For example, one common flaw with so-called merit pay systems is that managers may falsely assume they can determine meaningful individual differences among workers' performances. If these differences are determined more by personal opinion and human biases than by facts and logical analysis, the concept of merit may be lost. Such biased pay raise decisions can be destructive rather than productive in encouraging workers to perform at high levels. While intuition is part of the decision-making process, it may be more useful for selecting among several equally viable options. Ultimately the decision maker must be able to explain and sometimes sell the decision. For a manager to state that she just has a "gut feeling" that decision X is correct is not an acceptable business practice.

In contrast to intuitive decision making, **systematic decisions** are the result of a logical, organized analytic process. Systematic decision making requires developing a clear set of objectives, relevant information, rational and creative alternative generation, implementation and assessment.

Not all situations require systematic decision making. However, in all cases judgment is needed to determine when a decision is best made intuitively or rationally. Neither approach works in all situations; there will be some surprises. At times managers must react quickly, relying on their intuition. But where does that intuition come from? Sound intuition is developed primarily through experience and training, as well as from practice in rational decision making. For example, a service repair manager may have to react to an angry customer who is dissatisfied with a product. If the manager doesn't react quickly and appropriately, the customer may be lost. Yet the manager's reactive, intuitive decision will be better if it's based on training and experience with similar situations.

Business success demands constant attention to detecting and responding to changes in customer needs and competitive challenges. In responding effectively to changes in customer needs and the global marketplace, employees at all levels of an organization will use their knowledge and experience to make non-programmed decisions for the organization. In the next section, we examine strategic decisions, an important type of systematic, non-programmed decision-making. As we will see, strategic decisions will be either proactive or reactive.

Mintzberg's Strategic Decision Categories

Mintzberg[5] organizes strategic decisions into three categories: entrepreneurial decisions, adaptive decisions, and planning decisions.

- **Entrepreneurial decisions**—Inventive decisions that strategic managers make about the nature of the product and the future of the organization. These decisions are based on a higher degree of uncertainty because less information is available about customer preferences and material costs at the time of the decision.

- **Adaptive decisions**—Reactive responses to environmental conditions. Competitive actions often stimulate the organization to make a decision. A new product feature by a competitor requires a competitive product change.

- **Planning decisions**—Proactive as well as reactive decisions that develop specific reactions to reduce uncertainties related to growth, uniqueness, and efficiency. A new product launch introduces an organization's unique product, built in a "state-of-the-art manufacturing facility." The managers' goal is to increase market share in their industry segment.

DECISION MODELS

Rational Decision Model

The rational decision model is a *prescriptive model*—one that advises the decision maker how decisions should be made. The rational model bases a decision on a logical, factual analysis that leads the decision maker to an optimal decision. Though this model is often criticized for its somewhat simplistic assumptions, many decisions fit its context quite well. A simple example might be a gasoline purchase, where the objective is to get as much gas as possible for your money. Suppose that while driving home from work, you see two gas stations. One station advertises regular-grade gasoline for $1.50 per gallon; the other is selling the same grade for $1.45 per gallon. Based on the stated decision criteria, a decision maker using the rational model would choose the station with the lower price.

Rational decision models[6] assume that, in most cases, people attempt to make logical decisions. After analyzing the facts, the decision maker chooses the alternative that offers the greatest benefits. Rational models assume little uncertainty and risk in the decision. When using a rational model, the decision maker often relies on rules and procedures to reach a decision. A virtue of the rational decision model is its general appeal to logic; it's hard to argue with the results of a rational decision. However, in situations where the assumptions of the model are clearly inappropriate, the decision can suffer.

Rational decision models are most appropriate for:

- Programmed decisions
- Situations where all the alternatives are known
- Unambiguous decisions
- Situations where information is readily available
- Individual decision making

A key characteristic of the rational decision model is clear factual information. Rational decision making works best in a predictable, information-rich environment. Programmed decisions fit best with the rational approach. Intuitive decision making is characterized by a gut-level response to a decision context. The parameters of an intuitive decision may be less easily quantified than those of a rational decision. The decision maker relies more on instinct or a feeling, often basing the response on experience or familiarity with the situation.

Administrative Decision Model

The **administrative decision model** is a *descriptive model* of decision making—it makes more realistic assumptions about the decision context and human nature. Further, it describes how people actually make decisions, not how they *should* make them. **Bounded rationality**[7] refers to the fact that people have a limited ability to process information. We can't have available all the information needed for the decision, nor can we entirely understand the complexity of the information that might be brought to bear on the situation.

The administrative decision model makes these assumptions:

- Limited information processing ability
- Non-programmed decisions
- Preferences of individuals or group
- Alternatives unclear
- Greater participation through group decision making

Rather than seeking an optimal decision, the administrative model assumes that the decision maker satisifices. To **satisfice** (a term coined by Herbert Simon) is to seek a satisfactory decision, one that's good enough but not perfect. Often the search for information reviews familiar information or areas that we understand well. The information search culminates in a limited set of alternatives. *The first alternative that proves to be a satisfactory alternative is the one chosen.*

Think for a moment about a simple entertainment decision that you might make this weekend. You and a friend, Sam, want to go to a movie. The many different types of movies, locations, and show times are some considerations that influence your preference for a movie. You each have different viewing preferences, but you both agree on six movies you'd like to see. Together, you create a combined list of alternative movie options (see Exhibit 3.1). The first movie appeals to you but not to Sam, the second movie appeals to Sam but not to you, and the third movie appeals to both of you. For you and Sam, the decision is to see the third movie in your combined list. You choose the first satisfactory alternative available, and then stop your search. The sixth movie was also acceptable, but you never got that far. Remember, the two of you did not have complete knowledge of all movies available for viewing. You made a limited search and chose the first alternative that was satisfactory to both. The result of this process is a decision that both parties agree upon, though it might not be the best decision. With more time and a greater search, you and Sam might have found the best movie-going choice.

EXHIBIT 3.1
Movie Decision Model Matrix

Movie Preference	You	Sam
Movie 1	Y* .	N
Movie 2	N	Y
Movie 3	Y	Y
Movie 4	y	n
Movie 5	n	y
Movie 6	y	y

*Uppercase = movies evaluated; lowercase = not evaluated.

Political Decision Model

Unlike rational and administrative decision making, the **political decision model** involves non-programmed decisions. The decision is often ruled by political concerns rather than a logical analysis of the situation. The important question is not what is the best decision, but rather which alternative (decision) will be accepted by the groups involved in the decision. Most organizations have multiple goals and a variety of departments. When many different groups are empowered in the decision-making process, we can expect them to have different goal preferences—which obviously increases the potential for internal conflict in an organization. Building consensus and developing agreement among diverse groups are important to arriving at a decision that is accepted by all. The more diverse the participants in the decision-making process, the more political the decision will be.[8]

Political decisions require the decision maker to garner the support of the groups involved in the decision to form a powerful block or coalition of support for the final decision. On the international level in 2003, President George W. Bush and Secretary of State Colin Powell actively engaged in dialogue with Turkey and Russia, as well as with more traditional U.S. allies, to develop a strategy for disarming the Iraqi regime. The same process occurs in organizations when the CEO needs to rally employee support to accomplish goals. For example, the decision to build a new and innovative Harley-Davidson motorcycle with a liquid-cooled V-twin Porsche engine required CEO William Davidson to build political support inside Harley. The new bike, the V-ROD, represents the future for Harley-Davidson—a way to leapfrog over the competition. Internally, Harley was firmly locked into traditional motorcycle design and manufacturing. This new product challenged employees to go beyond their comfort zone. The V-ROD required new technology, innovative design, partnerships with Porsche and other suppliers, and the creativity of H-D employees to become a success in the marketplace. Was CEO Davidson successful at coalition building inside and outside H-D? Only time will tell, but early reports are that all constituents like the V-ROD.

Political decisions often:

- Are non-programmed
- Contain ambiguous information
- Entail low consensus on goals among stakeholders
- Involve groups that can influence the decision process

Exhibit 3.2 summarizes each type of decision model, indicating the decision outcome and the degree of objectivity among decision makers.

E X H I B I T 3 . 2
Decision-Making Models

	Rational Model	Administrative Model	Political Model
Decision Type	Programmed	Non-programmed	Non-programmed
Decision Outcome	Optimal	Satisficed	Negotiated
Degree of Objectivity	High	Moderate	Moderate to low

THE DECISION-MAKING PROCESS

The decision-making process is a manager's mechanism for seeking some desired result. The nature and structure of the process influence how effective the decision outcome is likely to be in solving or preventing the problem. But note again that decision making is a *process* rather than a single, fixed event. In most decision situations, managers go through a series of steps or stages that help them identify the problem, develop alternative strategies, analyze those strategies, choose one among the alternatives, implement the choice, and assess the results. These stages aren't always rigidly applied, and feedback is typically conceived to be a part of each step. Identifying steps in the decision process is valuable; it helps the decision maker to structure the problem situation in a meaningful, rational way. A variety of models can be used. The model shown in Exhibit 3.3 depicts a typical progression of the events leading to a decision. Steps 1 through 6 of this model are the **decision formulation** stages; steps 7 and 8 are the **decision implementation** stages. In the following subsections, we'll take a closer look at each step.

But first, it's important to understand that *decision making is always done in the context of goals and objectives.* We'll discuss the setting of goals and objectives in more detail in Chapters 4 (Planning) and 5 (Strategy). For now, just be aware that all behavior is basically goal oriented.[9] Especially in organizations, goals and objectives are needed in each area where performance influences effectiveness. If goals and objectives are adequately established, they will dictate not only what results must be achieved but also the measures indicating whether they have been achieved. Establishing goals and objectives brings people in the organization together. And a firm's system of drawing people together is a crucial factor in its success.

Step 1 Identify and Define the Problem

A **problem** is defined as the realization that a discrepancy exists between a desired state and current reality. When clear goals and objectives are established, problems become apparent. To determine how critical a problem is for an organization, its managers measure the gap between the level of performance specified in the firm's goals and objectives and the current level of performance. For example, a product defect rate of ten per million doesn't meet the famous "six-sigma" quality standard established by Motorola, which allows for only three defects per million.

It's easy to understand that a problem exists when there is a gap between desired results and actual results. But certain factors often lead to difficulties in precisely identifying the problem. These factors are as follows:

- **Perceptual inaccuracies** Individual attitudes, feelings, or mental models may prevent individuals from recognizing problems. For example, prior to 1968

EXHIBIT 3.3
Steps in a Typical Decision-Making Process

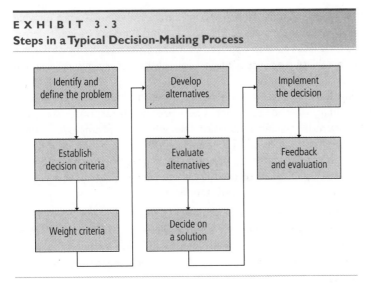

the Swiss dominated the world in the production of watches and clocks. They had continuously improved their products and were constant innovators. Yet by 1980 their market share had collapsed, dropping from 65 percent to 10 percent. Why? Because they didn't perceive that world demand was changing from mechanical to electronic inner works. The Swiss themselves had invented electronic quartz movement. But when Swiss researchers presented the revolutionary idea to Swiss manufacturers in 1967, it was rejected. The new movement didn't fit the watch makers' mental model of watches, so they couldn't see its potential for the future.

- **Defining problems in terms of solutions** This is really a form of jumping to conclusions. For example, before doing any research, a design engineer may state, "The excessive rework we're experiencing is due to bad supplies." The engineer is suggesting a solution before the problem has been adequately identified. The supplies may indeed be of low quality; but there are other potential explanations for excessive rework, including poor employee training, outdated technology, or cumbersome process flow. Research needs to be conducted to identify the problem before suggesting solutions.

- **Identifying symptoms as problems** Problems generally are of three types: opportunity, crisis, or routine. Crisis and routine problems present themselves; opportunities usually must be found. Opportunities await discovery; they often go unnoticed and eventually are lost by an inattentive manager. On the other hand, by their very nature, most crises and routine problems demand immediate attention. Thus a manager may spend more time handling problems than pursuing important new opportunities. Many well-managed organizations try to draw attention away from crises and routine problems and toward longer-range issues through planning activities and goal-setting programs that establish companywide priorities.

Step 2 Establish Decision Criteria

Common criteria for a decision might be initial cost, efficiency, and size. Analyzing cost criteria usually means that the decision maker seeks to minimize the cost associated with the initial decision. Efficiency criteria are related to the use of resources. The decision maker might specify that a decision must take into consideration the in-use cost, or what is often termed *efficiency*. Size implies there are space limitations to be considered. Generally, organizations have less space as opposed to more. Criteria limitations narrow the range of decision acceptability. An acceptable decision must meet specific criteria that the decision maker sets for the decision.

Also related to setting decision criteria is the magnitude of the problem. All problems aren't created equal. Deciding whether to launch a new product in response to a competitor's move is probably a more significant decision than whether the employee lounge should be repainted. The process of decision making and solution implementation requires resources. Unless an organization has unlimited resources, it must prioritize its problems. This means determining the significance of each problem, which in turn involves considering three issues: urgency, impact, and growth tendency.

- **Urgency** is defined as the amount of time available to solve a problem. Some companies have learned that urgent problems are best dealt with at their source.[10] Ford Motor Company realized early on that the problems with the Firestone Wilderness AT tires on the Explorer sport utility vehicle (SUV) could represent a major problem.

- **Impact** refers to the seriousness of a problem's effect. Effects may be on people, sales, equipment, or any number of other organizational variables. Whether problem effects are short or long term, and whether the problem is likely to create other problems, are also impact-related issues. Firestone failed to recognize that the Wilderness AT problem could undermine confidence in all Firestone tires.

- **Growth tendency** refers to the future consequences of a problem. A problem may currently be of low urgency and have little impact; but if it is allowed to go unattended, its consequences may become more severe over time. The case of Ford Motor Company and Firestone Tire exemplifies what can happen if a problem goes unrecognized or underestimated for too long. As the media focused daily on the rollovers caused by Firestone tires, it became clear that both Ford and Firestone were at substantial financial risk from lawsuits and lack of consumer confidence in their brands—for which equity was rapidly evaporating.[11] A critical part of effective decision making is determining the problem's cause. Another critical part is determining problem significance. The more significant a problem is—as determined by its urgency, impact, and growth tendency—the more important that it be addressed.

Step 3 Weight Criteria

Weighting criteria is the process of ranking the importance of decision criteria. More heavily weighted criteria are more important than those given lower weight.

Step 4 Develop Alternatives

Before reaching a decision, the decision maker needs to develop alternative solutions to the problem. This step involves examining the organization's internal and external environments for information and ideas that may lead to creative solutions to a problem. Alternatives should provide the decision maker with a range of acceptable alternatives, from which she will select only one.

Step 5 Evaluate Alternatives

Once alternatives have been developed, the decision maker must evaluate and compare them. In every decision situation, the objective is to select the alternatives that will produce the most favorable outcomes and the least unfavorable outcomes. In selecting among alternatives, the decision maker should be guided by the degree of uncertainty and/or risk associated with each alternative as well as previously established goals and objectives.

In evaluating alternative solutions, two cautions should be kept in mind. First, this phase of the decision-making process must be kept separate and distinct from the preceding step—especially in a group decision-making context. When alternatives are evaluated as they are proposed, fewer alternative solutions may be identified. If evaluations are positive, there may be a tendency to end the process prematurely by settling on the first positive solution. On the other hand, negative evaluations make it less likely for someone to risk venturing what may be the best solution.

The second caution is to be wary of solutions that are evaluated as being "perfect," especially when the decision is being made under conditions of uncertainty. If a solution appears to have no drawbacks—or if, in a group setting, there's unanimous agreement on a course of action, it may be useful to assign someone to be a devil's advocate. The role of the devil's advocate is to be a thorough critic of the proposed solution. Research supports the benefits of devil's advocacy and the conflict a devil's advocate may cause, thus forcing a decision maker to reexamine assumptions and information.[12]

Step 6 Decide on a Solution

The purpose of selecting a particular solution is to solve a problem in order to achieve a predetermined objective. This means that a decision isn't an end in itself, but only a means to an end. Although the decision maker chooses the alternative that is expected to result in achieving the objective, the selection of that alternative shouldn't be an isolated act. If it is, the factors that led to the decision are likely to be excluded. Specifically, the steps following the decision should include implementation and follow-up.

Unfortunately for most managers, situations rarely exist in which one alternative achieves the desired objective without having some impact on another objective. If one objective is optimized, the other is suboptimized. For example, if production is optimized, employee morale may be suboptimized, or vice versa. A hospital superintendent may optimize a short-term objective such as maintenance costs at the expense of a long-term objective such as high-quality patient care. Thus the interrelatedness of organizational objectives complicates the decision maker's job.

As we mentioned earlier in this chapter, the decision maker can't possibly know all of the available alternatives, the consequences of each alternative, and the probability of these consequences occurring. Thus, rather than being an optimizer, the decision maker is a satisficer, selecting the alternative that meets a satisfactory standard. A **satisficer** is a person who accepts a reasonable alternative that is good enough, but not necessarily the optimal alternative. This isn't a negative comment on managerial decision making. Rather, it's a frank acknowledgment that searching for optimal solutions is usually time and cost prohibitive. Managers must be prepared to act on decisions that may, in fact, have some negative implications along with the positive results they are intended to achieve.

Step 7 Implement the Decision

Any decision is little more than an abstraction if it's never implemented; further, it must be effectively implemented to achieve an objective. It's entirely possible for a good decision to be impaired by poor implementation. In this sense, implementation may be more important than the actual choice of the alternative.

In most situations, it is people who implement decisions. Thus the test of a decision's soundness is the behavior of the people who put it into action or are affected by it. Although a decision may be technically sound, it can easily be undermined by dissatisfied employees. A manager's job is not only to choose good solutions but also to convert such solutions into behavior in the organization. Managers often accomplish this transformation by empowering employees to make decisions that affect work processes.

Step 8 Feedback and Evaluation

Effective management involves periodic measurement of results. Actual results are compared with planned results (the objective). If deviations exist, changes must be made. If actual results don't meet planned results, changes must be made in the solution chosen, in its implementation, or in the original objective if it has been deemed unattainable. If the original objective must be revised, then the entire decision-making process will be reactivated. The important point is that once a decision is implemented, a manager can't assume that the outcome will meet the original objective. Some system of control and evaluation is necessary to make sure the actual results are consistent with the original objectives.

Sometimes a decision's outcome is unexpected, or it is perceived differently by different people. Dealing with this possibility is an important part of the follow-up phase in the decision process. Examining this feedback can result in different means of implementation, selection of different alternatives, or a revised evaluation of the various alternatives.

Summary of the Decision-Making Process

The eight-step decision-making process is an outline of how managers in the modern workplace spend much of their time. In an increasingly technological world, even in traditional industries like agriculture and manufacturing, work has become less a matter of physical effort and more a matter of processing information. However, making effective decisions requires more than just the ability to process information and then choose among and manage alternatives. Decision making requires effective post-decision implementation, usually involving employees from various levels and functions of the organization.

Regardless of the number of steps in the decision-making process, decision making always involves people. Some decisions are made by individuals acting alone. More often in today's organizations, decision making occurs in groups. In the next two sections, we'll explore how decision making by individuals differs from group decision making.

FACTORS THAT INFLUENCE INDIVIDUAL DECISION MAKING

In today's workplace, managers make a lot of decisions in groups, but many still must be made on an individual basis. Being an effective manager requires the ability to make individual decisions. This ability is enhanced by knowing some of the factors that influence individual decision making.

Several behavior factors influence the decision-making process. Some of these factors influence only certain aspects of the process; others influence the entire process. Each behavioral factor may affect decision making and, therefore, must be understood if managers are to fully appreciate decision making as a process involving individuals in organizations. Exhibit 3.4 lists the individual factors that influence the decision-making process, highlighting four key elements: values, personality, risk tolerance, and cognitive dissonance.

EXHIBIT 3.4
Influences on Decision Making

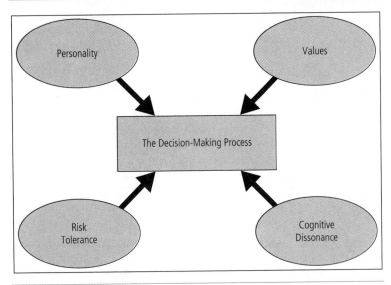

Individual Values

In the context of decision making, **individual values** are the guidelines a person uses when confronted with a situation in which a choice must be made. Most of an individual's enduring values are acquired early in life; they're a basic part of each person's personality. Other values can be acquired in adulthood and are usually associated with group membership. In a quality-based organization, for example, the group might value customer service, continuous improvement, and employee empowerment to make decisions. Values influence the decision-making process in the following ways:

- *Establishing goals and objectives* Value judgments must be made throughout the process of selecting opportunities and assigning priorities.

- *Developing alternatives* Value judgments are made while compiling the possible alternative solutions.

- *Selecting a solution* The decision maker's values influence which alternative is chosen.

- *Implementing* Value judgments are necessary in choosing the means for implementation.

- *Following up* Value judgments can't be avoided when corrective action is taken.

Because values play a role throughout the decision-making process, they need to be recognized by managers. As these values and beliefs are diffused and adopted throughout the organization, they become guidelines enabling individual employees to make decisions that are in the interest of the organization.

Personality

Decision makers are influenced by many psychological forces. One of the most important is the decision maker's personality, which is reflected in the choices made. Several studies have examined the effect of selected personality variables on the decision-making process.[13] These studies generally have focused on three sets of variables:

- *Personality variables* Dimensions of personality include introversion-extroversion, altruism, conscientiousness, ability to deal with new situations, and neuroticism.
- *Situational variables* These are variables related to the decision context or the external (physical and social) situation.
- *Interaction variables* These variables include the combined, unique effect of personality and the situation.

According to most researchers, the most important conclusions concerning the influence of these personality variables on the decision-making process are as follows:

- It's unlikely that one person can be equally proficient in all aspects of the decision-making process. Study results suggest that some people will do better in one part of the process, whereas others will do better in another part.
- Such characteristics as risk tolerance are associated with different steps of the decision-making process.
- Based on factors such as gender and social status, the relationship of personality to the decision-making process may vary from one person to another. Thus, a person's gender and social status combine with personality to influence decision making.

Significantly, this research has determined that the decision maker's personality traits combine with certain situational variables, and both factors interact to influence the decision-making process.

Risk Tolerance

Decision makers vary greatly in their willingness to take risks—their **risk tolerance.** The risk-tolerance aspect of an individual's personality influences decision making so strongly that researchers break it out from other personality variables and consider it separately. In the same situation, a decision maker with low risk tolerance will establish different objectives, evaluate alternatives differently, and select different alternatives from a decision maker who has high risk tolerance. The former typically avoids decisions where risk is high; the latter often seeks riskier alternatives. Many people are bolder, more innovative, and advocate greater risk taking in groups than when they're acting as individuals.

A person's risk propensity is also affected by whether potential outcomes are characterized as losses or gains. This, in turn, depends on how the decision maker frames the decision. *Framing* refers to the decision maker's perception of the decision's possible outcomes in relation to gains or losses.[14] Individuals display a greater propensity to take risks when a choice is perceived as being between losses than when it is perceived as being between gains.

Cognitive Dissonance

Historically, much attention has been focused on the decision itself, and on the forces and influences affecting the decision maker before the decision is made. Only recently has attention been given to what happens *after* a decision is made. Specifically, behavioral scientists are focusing attention on the occurrence of post-decision anxiety.

Such anxiety is related to *cognitive dissonance*.[15] **Cognitive dissonance** theory states that there is often a lack of consistency or harmony among an individual's various cognitions (attitudes, beliefs, and intentions) after a decision has been made. That is, there is often a conflict between what the decision maker believes and the consequences of a particular decision.

As a result, the decision maker will have doubts and anxiety about her choice. The intensity of the anxiety may be greater when any of the following conditions exists:

- The decision is important psychologically or financially.
- There are a number of foregone alternatives.
- The foregone alternatives have many favorable features.

Any or all of these conditions are present in many decisions, in all types of organizations. You can expect, therefore, that cognitive dissonance will affect many decision makers across many decision opportunities.

When dissonance occurs, individuals are likely to use any of the following methods to reduce their dissonance:

- Seek information that supports the wisdom of their decision.
- Selectively perceive (distort) information in a way that supports their decision.
- Adopt a less favorable view of the foregone alternatives.
- Minimize the importance of the negative aspects of the decision and exaggerate the importance of the positive aspects.

Although each of us may resort to some of this behavior in our personal decision making, a great deal of it could be extremely harmful to organizational effectiveness. The potential for dissonance is influenced heavily by our personality, specifically our self-confidence and potential to be persuaded. In fact, all of the behavioral influences are closely interrelated; they are isolated here only for purposes of discussion. For example, there's a close relationship between the kind of risk taker you are and your likelihood of experiencing dissonance following a decision. Both characteristics are strongly influenced by your personality, your perceptions, and your value system.

Decision-Making Styles

Research indicates that people develop and use different decision styles, based upon two factors: *tolerance for ambiguity* and *ways of thinking* about the decision context. Tolerance for ambiguity is a person's ability to reconcile a situation that may have multiple perspectives and interpretations. A person with a low tolerance for ambiguity has a propensity to see things in black and white, whether they are that way or not. A person with a high tolerance for ambiguity is more likely to recognize a lack of clarity and not be bothered by it. Ways of thinking range from rational to intuitive. Rational decisions are factual and analytic, whereas intuitive decisions are more emotional, gut-level responses to a situation. Exhibit 3.5 shows the relationship between these key dimensions and the four common decision-making styles.

- *Analytical* seeks a rational decision and has a high tolerance for ambiguity.
- *Directive* seeks a rational decision and has a low tolerance for ambiguity.
- *Behavioral* seeks an intuitive decision and has a low tolerance for ambiguity.
- *Conceptual* seeks an intuitive decision and has a high tolerance for ambiguity.

Analytical Decision Makers. **Analytical decision makers** use a logical, analytical approach to decision making. They gather facts and other information relevant to the decision situation. Ambiguous situations are seen as riskier due to lack of information. Analytical decision makers assess the opportunities and risks inherent in the decision and make a rational decision based on their analysis of the situation.

EXHIBIT 3.5
Decision-Making Styles

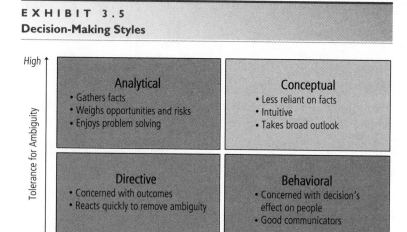

Source: Based on A. J. Rowe, J. D. Boulgarides, and M. R. McGrath, *Managerial Decision Making,* Modules in Management Series (Chicago: SRA, 1984), A. J. Rowe and J. D. Boulgarides, *Managerial Decision Making* (Englewood Cliffs, N. J.: Prentice Hall, 1994; G. M. Marakas, *Decision Support Systems in the Twenty-First Century,* 2nd ed. (Upper Saddle River, N. J.: Prentice Hall, 2002).

Directive Decision Makers.   **Directive decision makers** are rational and straightforward in their approach to decision making. They avoid making decisions in highly ambiguous situations, or gather more information to remove the ambiguity from the situation. The directive decision maker moves quickly to reach a final outcome.

Conceptual Decision Makers.   **Conceptual decision makers** are contemplative and tend to structure the decision situation as a mental model. They might review facts, but the focus of their thinking revolves around the cognitive assessment of the decision situation. Their assessments are often intuitive. In this process, the decision maker reviews his or her assumptions and develops alternative outcomes for different assumption sets.

Behavioral Decision Makers.   **Behavioral decision makers** are concerned with people and the implications a decision is likely to have on employees and customers. Behavioral decision makers talk to people and get their reaction to a proposed decision. They try to understand the people impact of similar decisions made elsewhere. For example, a company needs to reduce employment by 500 employees. How might they best go about the employee reduction in a manner that results in the least disruption to their employee's lives?

The concept of decision styles is important; there is no single best method of making a decision. Although decision makers follow similar steps to reach a decision, their decision style often dictates the final decision. Figuring out how to deliver what customers want is a complicated business, made worse by failures to accurately identify key dimensions of customer value. Look at the Management Highlight on page 51 to see the most important new-car characteristics as identified by *Business Week* in the early 1990s. If a similar survey were conducted today, would you change any of the characteristics to be ranked—adding city miles per gallon, perhaps?

> ### MANAGEMENT HIGHLIGHT
> #### Decision Making: Buying a Car
>
> First, rank each of the eight product attributes based on their importance to you. Then compare your rankings to those of actual survey respondents. What values influence your and others' decisions? How would you expect survey respondents who are ten years older than you to rank each attribute? People 20 years older than you?
>
> | | | Your Ranking | Survey Ranking |
> |---|---|---|---|
> | 1 | Price: dollar amount of purchase | | 3 |
> | 2 | Features: options (e.g., tape player, power controls, sports package) | | 7 |
> | 3 | Styling: exterior design and look | | 6 |
> | 4 | Foreign origin: model bears a non-U.S. nameplate (e.g., Honda) | | 8 |
> | 5 | U.S. origin: model bears U.S. (Big Three) nameplate | | 5 |
> | 6 | Reliability: record of absence of need for repair; low maintenance | | 1 |
> | 7 | Safety: crash, repair, and survival record of the make | | 2 |
> | 8 | Feel: interior features of the car (e.g., seating, controls) | | 4 |
>
> **Source:** "Detroit May Be Missing the Mark That Matters Most," Survey of 1,250 adults conducted July 13–18, 1990, for *Business Week* by Louis Harris & Associates, Inc. *Business Week,* October 22, 1990, p. 91. Reprinted from the October 22, 1990 issue of *Business Week* by special permission, copyright © 1990 by the McGraw-Hill Companies, Inc.

Judgment Errors or Bias in the Decision Process

We begin this discussion by defining the term *heuristic,* which is a set of rules (or a strategy) that is used to simplify a decision. Now we'll consider the kinds of heuristics that apply to judgment errors in decision making.

Our cognitive processing abilities can bias decision making in several ways.[16] One type of bias is based on our ability to recall facts. When we use the **availability heuristic,** we rely on how easily we can recall a set of facts from our memory to make a decision. For example, suppose someone asks you this question: "Are there more trucks on the roads today than ten years ago?" If you regularly travel a road that's heavily congested with trucks—and you just read an article that discussed several truck accidents—you might conclude that there are more trucks on the road than cars. But highway transportation data indicates that the percentage of cars and trucks on the highway has stayed about the same for the past ten years.

With the **representative heuristic,** we assess a decision situation by using a stereotypical response. Imagine you're in an aircraft that is about to depart from your city. As the plane takes off, you hear a female voice announcing that the weather is clear, destination temperature is 65 degrees, and arrival time at the destination is 5:30 p.m. After hearing the announcement, the man in the seat behind you asks a nearby flight attendant why another flight attendant made the announcement instead of the pilot. The attendant replies that the announcement was made by the pilot; she is a woman. Obviously, the man had a stereotypic response—that all pilots are males—because he had never seen a female pilot before. He generalized from his stereotype *that all pilots are males* to reach his conclusion that the voice must be that of a flight attendant.

A final decision-making bias is called escalation of commitment. **Escalation of commitment** is an increased commitment to a previous decision despite knowledge of contrary information. Cognitive dissonance theory holds that a person's desire to reduce dissonance is also related to the desire to appear consistent to oneself. The desire to reduce cognitive dissonance becomes dysfunctional when it leads to escalation of commitment. Research has shown that individuals will escalate their commitment to a failing course of action when they view themselves as responsible for the action. According to dissonance theory, this behavior results from the individual trying to demonstrate that the original decision was correct.

Before managers can fully understand the dynamics of the decision-making process, they must appreciate the effect that various biases can have on a decision. The availability heuristic, the representative heuristic, and escalation of commitment all have the potential of leading to flawed decisions.

GROUP DECISION MAKING

In many organizations today, group decision making occurs in teams, task forces, and committees. Group or team decision making occurs partly due to today's ever-increasing decision complexity and the volume of information needed to make effective decisions. Because group decision making involves more organizational members than simply one individual decision maker, group decision making also builds commitment to the decision through greater member participation. Managers often have to decide whether to make an individual decision or allow the group to make the decision.[17] This is especially true for the non-programmed decisions that typically have the greatest outcome uncertainty and require the most creativity. Additionally, most complex and important decisions are most often made by groups—not individuals. In many decision-making situations, problem complexity requires specialized knowledge in several different areas. Normally, the best way to get specialized knowledge in multiple areas is from an expert in each area. Further, decision acceptance is greater when a decision is made by a group.

Group decision making is not without risk. Here are several factors that contribute to increased risk and a lower-quality decision:

- **Groupthink** The tendency of the group to be swayed collectively can negate the benefits of group decision making.

- **Empowerment** While participation generally is seen as a good thing, it allows more people in the organization access to the decision-making process. Sometimes this makes for a lower-quality decision.

- **Corporate governance** dictates who can and should be part of the decision-making process. For example, corporate governance may require that a union representative be part of any decision-making committee.

- **Politics** can occur in situations where group participants have diverse views and preferences about the decision outcome. This may lead to a decision that favors the dominant political coalition in the organization.

Comparing Individual and Group Decision Making

Considerable debate has centered on the relative effectiveness of individual versus group decision making. Groups usually take more time to reach a decision than individuals do. But bringing together individual specialists and experts has its benefits; the mutually reinforcing effects of their interaction often result in better decisions. In fact, a great deal of research has shown that consensus decisions with five or more participants are usually superior to individual decision making, majority vote, and leadership decisions.[18]

On the other hand, research has also found group decision making to be negatively influenced by such behavioral factors as pressure to conform (sometimes called group-think), presence of a dominant personality in the group, "status incongruity" (whereby lower-status participants are inhibited by higher-status participants and acquiesce even though they believe that their own ideas are superior), and attempts by certain participants (who are perceived to be expert in the problem area) to influence others.

Certain decisions (such as non-programmed decisions) appear to be better made by groups; others appear better suited to individual decision making. Here are some advantages of group decision making:

- *Establishing goals and objectives* Groups probably are superior to individuals because of their greater collective knowledge.

- *Developing alternatives* Groups can ensure a broad search in the various functional areas of the organization.

- *Evaluating alternatives* The collective judgment of the group, with its wider range of viewpoints, seems superior to that of the individual decision maker.

- *Making a decision* Research has shown that group interaction and the achievement of consensus usually result in the acceptance of more risk than an individual decision maker would tolerate. In any event, the group decision is more likely to be accepted due to the participation of those affected by its consequences.

- *Implementation of a decision* When a group makes the decision, its implementation is usually carried out by individual managers. Thus, the group that made the decision can't be held responsible when an individual manager implements the decision in an ineffective manner. The responsibility for implementation rests with the individual manager.

Stimulating Creativity in Group Decision Making

If groups are better suited to non-programmed decisions than individuals are, then an atmosphere fostering group creativity must be developed. In this respect, group decision making may be similar to brainstorming, in that discussion must be free-flowing and spontaneous. All group members must participate; to encourage participation, the evaluation of individual ideas must be suspended in the beginning. Still, a decision must be reached, and this is where group decision making differs from brainstorming.

When properly utilized, three techniques—brainstorming, the Delphi technique, and the nominal group technique—increase a group's creative ability to generate ideas, understand problems, and reach better decisions. Raising a group's creative capability is especially necessary when individuals from diverse sectors of the organization must pool their judgments to create a satisfactory course of action for the organization.

Brainstorming.   In many situations, groups are expected to produce imaginative solutions to organizational problems. In such instances, brainstorming has often enhanced the group's creative output. **Brainstorming** includes a firm set of rules whose purpose is to promote the generation of ideas, at the same time diminishing the inhibitions among members that meeting face-to-face may cause. Here are the basic rules:

- *No idea is too ridiculous* Group members are encouraged to state any extreme or outlandish idea.

- *Each idea presented belongs to the group* Ideas are not tied to the person stating them, so that group members can utilize and build on the suggestions of others.

- *No idea can be criticized* The purpose of a brainstorming session is to generate ideas, not to evaluate them.

Brainstorming is considered effective in advertising and various other fields. In some other situations, it has been less successful. Because there is no evaluation or ranking of the ideas generated, the groups never really conclude the problem-solving process.

The Delphi Technique. The **Delphi technique** involves soliciting and comparing anonymous judgments on the topic of interest through a set of sequential questionnaires that are interspersed with summarized information and feedback of opinions from earlier responses.

This technique retains the advantage of having several judges, while removing the biasing effects that might occur during face-to-face interaction. The approach has been to collect anonymous judgments by mailing questionnaires to a specified set of individuals—members of a management team, for example. Staff members summarize the responses as the group consensus and feed this summary back to the original respondents, along with a second questionnaire for reassessment. Based on this feedback, respondents independently evaluate their earlier responses. The underlying belief is that the consensus estimate results in a better decision after several rounds of anonymous group judgment. Although it's possible to continue the procedure for several rounds, research has shown that, typically, no significant changes occur after the second round of feedback.

The Nominal Group Technique. The nominal group technique (NGT) has gained increasing recognition in health, social service, education, industry, and government organizations. Researchers adopted the term **nominal group technique** to refer to processes that bring people together but initially do not allow them to communicate verbally. Thus, at first, the collection of people is a group in name only (a nominal group). In its present form, NGT actually combines both verbal and nonverbal stages.

NGT typically takes the form of a structured group meeting that proceeds through the following stages. As the meeting opens, 7 to 10 individuals are seated at a table; but they don't speak to one another. Talking to each other isn't permitted. Rather, each person writes ideas on a pad of paper. After five minutes, a structured sharing of ideas takes place. Each person presents one idea. A person designated as recorder writes the ideas on a flip chart in full view of the entire group. This continues until all participants indicate they have no further ideas to share. There is still no discussion.

The output of the first stage is usually a list of ideas. The next stage involves structured discussion, in which each idea receives attention before a vote is taken. Discussion includes asking for clarification and stating the degree of support for each idea on the flip chart. In the next stage, independent voting, each participant privately selects priorities by ranking or voting. The group decision is the mathematically pooled outcome of the individual votes.

Both the Delphi technique and NGT have excellent success records. There are two basic differences between them: (1) In the Delphi process, all communication between participants is through written questionnaires and feedback from the monitoring staff; in NGT, communication occurs directly between participants. (2) NGT participants meet face-to-face around a table; Delphi participants are physically distant, never meet face-to-face, and are typically anonymous to one another. Practical considerations, of course, often influence which technique is used. These considerations can include the number of working hours available, costs, and participants' physical proximity.

We have included this brief overview of individual and group decision making to help you understand some of the forces that influence decision making. You should now have an appreciation of the differences between individual and group decision making, as well as an understanding of the different circumstances appropriate for each approach.

Conclusion
Decision Making

Managers are decision makers. The better we understand the process of decision making, the decision context, and factors that influence decision making, the better the decision quality will be. The trend in decision making is to encourage greater participation in decision making. Hence, we see more evidence of group decision making opportunities that empower more stakeholders with a voice in corporate governance. Managers will always make decisions, for better or worse. But the best decisions for a situation will be made by people who not only understand the decision process, but can apply it in achieving organizational goals.

SUGGESTED READINGS

Burke, Lisa A., and Monica K. Miller. "Taking the Mystery Out of Intuitive Decision Making." *Academy of Management Executive* 13, no. 4 (1999).

Garvin, David A., and Michael A. Roberto. "What You Don't Know About Decision Making." *Harvard Business Review,* September 2001, pp. 108–16.

Nutt, Paul C. "Surprising but True: Half of All Decisions Fail." *Academy of Management Executive* 13, no. 4 (1999).

ENDNOTES

1. James D. Thompson, *Organizations in Action* (New York: McGraw-Hill, 1967), 159.

2. E. Frank Harrison, *The Managerial Decision Making Process* (Boston: Houghton-Mifflin, 1981).

3. Herbert A. Simon, *The New Science of Management Decision* (New York: Harper & Row, 1960), 5–6.

4. Paul S. Adler, "Time-and-Motion Regained," *Harvard Business Review,* January–February 1993, pp. 97–108.

5. Henry Mintzberg, "Strategy-Making in Three Modes," *California Management Review,* Winter 1973, pp. 44–53.

6. Max Bazerman, *Judgment in Managerial Decision Making,* 2nd ed. (New York: Wiley, 1990), 3–4.

7. Herbert Simon, *Administrative Behavior,* 3rd ed, (New York: Free Press, 1976).

8. Edward C. Banfield, *Political Influence* (New York: Free Press, 1961).

9. Paul Hersey and Kenneth Blanchard, *Management of Organizational Behavior* (Englewood Cliffs, NJ: Prentice Hall, 1993), 19.

10. Joann Muller, "Ford: Why It's Worse Than You Think," *Business Week,* June 25, 2001, pp. 80–89; Muller, "Ford vs. Firestone: A Corporate Whodunit (safety crisis involving Explorer SUVs and Wilderness AT tires)," *Business Week,* June 11, 2001, pp. 46–47.

11. Richard A. Oppel Jr., "Bridgestone Agrees to Pay $7.5 Million in Explorer Crash," *New York Times,* August 25, 2001.

12. R. A. Cozier and C. R. Schwenk, "Agreement and Thinking Alike: Ingredients for Poor Decisions," *Academy of Management Executive* (February 1990): 69–74.

13. P. A. Renwick and H. Tosi, "The Effects of Sex, Marital Status, and Educational Background on Selected Decisions," *Academy of Management Journal* (March 1978): 93–103; A. A. Abdel Halim, "Effects of Task and Personality Characteristics on Subordinates' Responses to Participative Decision Making," *Academy of Management Journal* (September 1983): 477–484.

14. Glen Whyte, "Decision Failures: Why They Occur and How to Prevent Them," *Academy of Management Journal* (August 1991): 23–31.

15. Leon Festinger, *Theory of Cognitive Dissonance* (New York: Harper & Row, 1957), 10.

16. Bazerman, *Judgment in Managerial Decision Making,* chapter 2.

17. Victor H. Vroom and Arthur G. Jago, *The New Leadership: Managing Participation in Organizations* (Englewood Cliffs, NJ: Prentice Hall, 1988).

18. Richard A. Guzzo and James A. Waters, "The Expression of Affect and the Performance of Decision-Making Groups," *Journal of Applied Psychology* (February 1982): 67–74; D. Tjosvold and R. H. G. Field, "Effects of Social Context on Consensus and Majority Vote Decision Making," *Academy of Management Journal* (September 1983): 500–506; and Frederick C. Miner Jr., "Group versus Individual Decision Making: An Investigation of Performance Measures, Decision Strategies, and Process Losses/Gains," *Organizational Behavior and Human Decision Processes,* Winter 1984, pp. 112–124.

Chapter
Four

Planning

In the early part of the twentieth century management theorist Henri Fayol succinctly described the functions of management as planning, organizing, leading, and controlling.[1] As a business owner, he also believed that the burdens of management could be taught to non-owners; Fayol was thus among the first to envision the role of the professional manager. So began modern management. To this day the four core functions are rarely disputed; but not surprisingly, managers are continually challenged to change the way they plan, organize, lead, and control.

It is no accident that the first function of management is planning. Today, long after Fayol, leading management scholars continue to refer to the "primacy of planning."[2] Perhaps, since planning sets the course, common sense dictates that all other management functions must follow. Managers can then *organize* to create a structure for carrying out the plans, *lead* to motivate and engender plan participation, and *control* to ensure that plans are fulfilled as envisioned. Yes, in the final analysis, planning is seen to precede all. Likewise, we introduce it first among a series of chapters on the functions of management.

In this chapter we examine planning as it pertains to allocating the resources of an organization as well as to using its skills, competencies, and capabilities in achieving goals. Economic success requires planning to accomplish organizational goals and objectives; but we readily acknowledge that planning often occurs without full knowledge. Environmental uncertainty makes planning necessary. For an organization to achieve economic success, managers somehow must cope with, and adapt to, uncertainty and change. Planning is a manager's most valuable tool for adapting to change. An organization that doesn't plan for the future must constantly adjust to new circumstances. For managers to have any control over the organization's direction, they must plan. Planning is proactive, allowing the organization to select the best course of action for matching its competencies with existing and future environmental opportunities. Lack of planning compels organizations to react to the actions of others. Rather than anticipating a competitive move, the organization waits for directions from the marketplace. The reactive organization is not in control; it must respond to external pressures rather than act aggressively to achieve the organization's long-term goals.

Planning is the part of the management process that attempts to define an organization's future. There are different types of planning activities and different ways of putting plans together. In this chapter you will gain an understanding of strategic, tactical, and operational plans, and then learn a six-step planning process. We conclude the chapter with an overview of several planning methods, including those used in a quality-based organization.

WHAT IS PLANNING?

Planning is the process of developing action-oriented plans for achieving an organization's purpose, mission, goals, and objectives in the short term and the long term. As part of the planning process, strategic managers consider organizational, human, financial, and physical resources. They also explore opportunities and risks—including innovation, competition, and consumer demand—in the competitive marketplace. Good planning means asking tough questions about the company, customer needs, and the future. Planning guides employee behavior because it deals with future actions. In this way, planning helps organizations achieve specific results. The true test of any manager is ultimately his or her ability to achieve results (objectives and goals) consistent with the organization's values and mission. Without planning, it's impossible for organizational leaders to achieve specific outcomes.

Internally, planning is an analytical process in which organizational members chart a course of action for the organization in the years to come. Although not a flawless process, planning is necessary in order to schedule organizational actions that anticipate future needs. Even with new technological innovations, new markets, and changing consumer demographics, planning can help an organization be more competitive. Planning facilitates success by anticipating and responding to changing government demands, market conditions, and customer expectations. Effective organizational planning includes people from different areas and levels of the organization. Planning that is dominated by a few managers often lacks sufficient information and can be concerned more with the process of planning than with content or results.[3] Planning is a group activity; formal planning requires a team effort.

Systematic Planning Occurs at Several Levels

Planning occurs at all levels of the organization. *Corporate-level* planning focuses on resource allocation issues between several divisions within the same organization. *Business-level* planning concerns how to achieve business objectives within the context of overall corporate objectives. Finally, *functional-level* planning supports specific aspects of the business level strategy, such as advertising.

To drive the planning, all three organizational levels require a rational, analytic, and systematic process that everyone understands. Like decision making, planning is most effective when it's systematic. For example, formal planning for updating the organization's personal computers requires input from many different users. These computer users must consider costs and budgets, technical specifications, and software purchases and support. Next, they will develop a plan for the timely and cost-effective acquisition of personal computers. Once the final budgets are approved, financing arrangements, delivery schedules, and operating policies can proceed. The formal planning process begins at the top of the organization but ultimately moves through the organization to include more information. In the end, the resulting plan can be evaluated to determine how successful the planning process was in achieving organizational objectives.

Planning Involves Everyone

Effective planning requires as much information as possible to reduce uncertainty. By its very nature, planning is a complex process that must answer two questions: (1) what resources do we have, and (2) how should we use them to achieve our objectives? The first question is common across all levels; but the second question deals with allocation of resources at a much more specific level as we move down the organizational hierarchy. The time frame of the plan also varies, with the top level of the organization often looking five years into the future while the lower levels of the organization might be looking only six months ahead. Regardless of organizational level or time frame, the more people who are involved in the planning process, the more information is available to planners. Finally, greater involvement and participation in the planning process lead to greater acceptance of the plan in the long run.

WHY PLANNING IS NECESSARY

Planning puts purpose into action. Without planning, organizations can only react to changes in the environment, technology, and customer demands. With careful planning, an organization can both anticipate and influence upcoming events.

Three characteristics of the modern organization underscore the need for planning: (1) cycle time reduction, (2) organizational complexity, (3) global competition.

Cycle Time Reduction

Cycle time reduction (CTR) has become a key goal for organizations. *Cycle time* refers to the length of time required to complete a process and to be ready to begin anew. For example, automobile manufacturers compete fiercely to reduce cycle time for new product development. In the 1990s, Chrysler introduced many new products. One key to the company's success was cycle time. Of the big three U.S. automobile manufacturers, Chrysler had the fastest new product development cycle time, bringing new offerings to market in two and one-half years. By comparison, Ford and General Motors cycle times are more than three years. Toyota leads the way with a new product development cycle time of two years. These facts indicate that time and planning often go hand in hand. The first to market has a huge competitive advantage.

High-performing, competitive organizations have realized that although **economy of scale**—a decrease in per-unit manufacturing cost due to increased size of production facilities—was formerly the key to success, today **economy of time** is important. Sam Walton said that everyone thought the success of Wal-Mart was a result of placing large stores in small towns and evolving to superstores in large cities (economies of scale). In reality, he attributed Wal-Mart's success to having faster inventory turns (economy of time).

Like Wal-Mart, organizations of all types are putting significant planning effort into improving functionality, reducing cycle time, and accommodating the needs of people who interact with the organization.[4]

The rise of regional air carriers JetBlue and ATA, among others, casts an interesting light on the concept of economy of time when you consider that their success can be attributed, in part, to attracting to their ticket windows customers who might otherwise drive to their destinations. For a closer look at how planning has helped regional carriers outperform their industry, see the Management Highlight below.

Organizational Complexity

Mergers, acquisitions, restructuring, and strategic alliances all make organizations more complicated and difficult to manage. This complexity means that few organizational decisions can be made independently of other decisions. For example, design and development

---

MANAGEMENT HIGHLIGHT
Planning for Success: JetBlue, ATA, and Southwest Airlines

The recent problems of United Airlines and the demise of other air carriers such as Pan American and Eastern Airlines have caused financial ruin and disrupted air travel. Since the terrorist attacks of 9/11/2001, the airlines have struggled to rebuild consumer confidence while meeting strict security requirements imposed by the federal government. Airlines experiencing the most difficulty are the full-price, full-service, intercontinental air carriers. These giants have large fleets and high costs. They do business all over the world, but regularly lose money on many of the routes they serve.

Now some new airlines have emerged and are capitalizing on an opportunity that major air carriers missed—the regional low-cost market. Southwest Airlines was the first to enter this market; other carriers such as JetBlue and ATA have since carved out different market segments.

JetBlue, which began operations on February 11, 2000, attributes its success to sound financial backing, using new planes, hiring the best people, and focusing on customer service. JetBlue offers lower fares and uses point-to-point service (i.e., no layovers), operating mainly in the eastern United States. Services include in-flight entertainment with free direct TV in each seat, security cameras, bulletproof cockpit doors, and e-ticketing.

ATA follows a similar low-cost strategy, with several important differences. ATA services a select number of U.S. cities from its Chicago hub. ATA's feeder-service flights link Chicago with many smaller Midwestern cities, moving travelers to and from their Chicago hub. ATA also services profitable tourist destinations including Hawaii, Cancun, San Juan, and Aruba.

Southwest Airlines is the original innovator in low-cost regional air travel. With Dallas as its hub, Southwest pioneered low-cost, no-frills air service. Today it serves many cities in the continental United States. Unlike ATA routes, Southwest's are limited to the continental United States.

The 1978 deregulation of the airline industry was supposed to be a boon for air travelers. Deregulation has resulted in lower airfares; but low fares also mean less service and more restrictions. The airlines industry is complex. Yet the experiences of the major air carriers over the past quarter century and the after-effects of deregulation have created new opportunities. New airlines have emerged, with new plans for meeting consumer airline needs. The modern breed of air carriers offers consumers what they want—low air fares and on-time availability. Success in the airline industry for JetBlue, ATA, and Southwest began with a new plan.

Source: Adapted from ATA, AMTRAN Annual Report, 2001; JetBlue Prospectus, 2002; A Closer Look at Airlines; available at http://ata.com, http://jetblue.com, http://southwest.com, and ConsumerReport.org, 2003.

EXHIBIT 4.1
Global Competition Requires More Planning

Effect of Global Competition	Examples
New markets	Eastern European countries (such as Russia and Bulgaria); China, Korea, and Japan; India and Southeast Asia; and many Latin American countries all represent vast new markets.
Greater customer diversity	Customers in different countries have different needs and wants. The goal of the global organization is to compete globally, yet respond to local needs. Customers are no longer seen as one homogeneous group.
Increased quality and lower cost	New markets have an effect on costs. Sometimes they reduce costs with lower labor costs; at other times they increase costs with higher transportation costs. Increased information created a new awareness in customers to demand higher quality products, forcing corporations to respond.

decisions affect production, finance, and marketing. More products and more services increase the complexity of managing daily business activities. The more markets an organization competes in, the products it offers—and the more its competitors in the market all increase the internal complexity of their organization. For all practical purposes, before 1970 the Big Three auto organizations—GM, Ford, and Chrysler—competed among themselves. The Big Three held a commanding share of the automobile market in the United States. Now they compete among at least thirty major auto organizations worldwide. In his book *The Fifth Discipline,* Peter Senge observes that to remain competitive in the global economy, organizations must learn to be comfortable with uncertainty and complexity. Managers must develop a capacity for thinking clearly and continuously about the unknown future.[5] Planning helps organizations deal with complexity and uncertainty by providing a road map for change. With such a road map an organization can move with the forces of global competition without straying off course.

Global Competition

Change is constant. New rivals enter the global economy each year, often dramatically affecting the existing competition. For example, due to the increasing cost of labor in the United States, many U.S. manufacturers have developed strategic alliances with production facilities in mainland China. While it has increased profitability, the subsequent transfer of production to China has led to the loss of many high-paid manufacturing jobs in the United States. In our new global economy, new customers, new markets, and new competitors can come from across the hemisphere. They're no longer just in our own back yards, and they pose both opportunities and competitive threats for many organizations. Exhibit 4.1 summarizes the effects of global competition on the planning function.

BENEFITS OF PLANNING

Planning is beneficial for all organizations; specifically, planning (1) coordinates effort, (2) identifies priorities and creates action and change, (3) defines performance standards, and (4) develops managerial skills and talent. Formal planning charts a course and communicates strategic intent to employees and other external constituents.

Coordinates Effort

Management exists because the work of individuals and groups in organizations must be coordinated, and planning is one important technique for coordinating effort. An effective plan specifies goals and objectives for the total organization as well as each of its parts. Successful planning communicates to all levels of an organization their roles in attaining organizational goals and objectives. By working toward planned objectives, each level contributes to and is compatible with the entire organization's goals.

Identifies Priorities and Creates Action and Change

An effective plan prioritizes activities. What is most important? What is least important? What needs to be done first? Planning answers these questions and others. Next, planning creates action and prepares an organization for change. Plans create an expectation for results. When the plans have been in place for a reasonable amount of time, results are expected. Financial results are a typical outcome of a plan, for example, increased sales or increased profits. However, the longer the time between completion of a plan and accomplishment of an objective, the greater the necessity to include contingency plans. If management considers the potential effect of a change, it can be better prepared to deal with it. Most organizations recognize that change is inevitable; but not all of them succeed in negotiating change. History provides vivid examples of the result of failing to prepare for change. Over the past decade the collapse of many banks, savings and loans, and airlines has been largely due to lack of preparedness.

Defines Performance Standards

Plans create what the psychologists call behavioral expectations. In management parlance, expected behaviors are **performance standards.** As plans are implemented throughout an organization, the objectives and courses of action assigned to each person and group are the bases for standards that can be used to assess actual performance. In some cases the objectives provide the standards. Managers' performance can be assessed by how close their units come to accomplishing their objectives. In other cases the actions performed are judged against standards. A production worker can be held accountable for doing a job in the prescribed manner.

Competency-based performance is another way to ensure consistent employee response, by requiring that employees performing a particular job have certain competencies, meaning a set of skills, behaviors, or other job requirements. These job-specific competencies become the basis for human resource planning, including screening, hiring, training, and compensating employees. Competency-based performance requires managers to complete the following activities:

- Describe the purpose of the job.
- Identify job outcomes.
- Define performance standards for each outcome.
- Identify barriers to meeting performance standards.
- Use training to increase performance to standards.
- Train to achieve performance standards.[6]

Planning helps managers develop performance standards or competencies based on organizational goals and objectives. Without planning, performance standards are difficult to define, and those standards developed may be contrary to the organization's values and mission.

Develops Managerial Skills and Talent

Planning involves managers and workers in high levels of intellectual activity. Planning is conceptual and forward-looking; it requires intelligence, experience, and a risk-taking nature. Those who plan must be able to deal with abstract ideas and voluminous information. Planning requires contingency analysis and scenario development. Using all available information, managers need to integrate what is known and develop alternative scenarios about what is unknown. One way to think about it is that planning helps managers "learn the future" before it happens.

- *Planning creates action* Through planning, the organization's future can be improved if its managers take an active role in moving the organization toward that future. Thus planning implies that managers should be proactive and make things happen rather than being reactive and letting things happen.

- *Planning develops conceptual skills* The act of planning sharpens managers' ability to think as they consider abstract ideas and possibilities for the future, and it reinforces the planning cycle as objectives are met through systematic actions. Thus both the result and the act of planning benefit the organization and its managers. Through planning, managers can develop their ability to think futuristically. And, to the extent that their plans lead to effective actions, their motivation to plan is reinforced.

CRITICISMS OF PLANNING

Does planning work? Critics contend that the greatest output of formal planning is unused plans. For a variety of reasons, plans cannot always guide goal attainment. The external environment has a lot to do with the success of formal planning. Competition and the structure and dynamic nature of the industry may influence plans more than the formal planning process.

Competition

You can't always predict competitive actions. For instance, the introduction of a new product by a competitor may negate a year's worth of planning. In another wasteful situation, simply the lack of internal agreement among planners wastes time and resources that are better spent on other value-creating activities.

Dynamic Environment

According to the critics, another more ominous reason that planning won't work is the dynamic nature of the industry. A company may develop plans in one direction only to find the market is moving in a different direction. As the company quickly shifts production to follow the market, their planning is now driven by short-term market trends. While the company might be financially successful in the long term, its formal planning had nothing to do with its success.

Regardless of the criticisms of planning, it would be foolhardy to operate a business and forgo the potential benefits of planning. Lack of planning leads to a business failure more often than flawed planning does.

TYPES OF PLANNING

In this section we will examine the different types of planning. First we will discuss the scope and timing of plans. Then we will differentiate between strategic, tactical, and operational planning. The section concludes with a comparison of single-use and standing plans.

Scope and Timing

As we know, not all plans are created equal. Plans vary in three important ways: scope, time frame, and level of detail. For example, a fixed deadline makes the time frame a key facet. Each facet should be analyzed to determine its potential impact on the plan. The planning process takes into consideration these aspects of scope and timing:

- **Scope** refers to the range of activities (e.g., budgeting, human resources) covered by a plan.

- **Time frame** is the period considered by the plan that includes the short term, the intermediate term, and the long term.

- **Level of detail** concerns the specificity of the plan. All plans must be specific enough to direct actual decisions, but multiple contingencies and uncertain futures require some plans to be more general than, for example, a mattress factory's production schedule for the coming month.

Strategic, Tactical, and Operational Planning

The type of planning process followed is determined by the goals and/or objectives to be achieved through the plan. Broad, long-term goals require strategic planning, but short-term goals with more precise objectives call for greater operational planning. Tactical planning falls somewhere between strategic and operational planning, as described in the following list:

- **Strategic planning** (discussed in Chapter 5) is comprehensive, long-term (more than five years), and relatively general. Strategic plans focus on the broad, enduring issues for ensuring the organization's effectiveness and survival over many years. A strategic plan typically states the organization's mission and may describe a set of goals to move a company into the future. For example, it may establish a mission of market dominance in a particular product area, and set a goal to penetrate new markets based on targeted consumer research and development work.

- **Tactical planning** develops more specific actions or activities to implement parts of the strategic plan. It's more narrow, intermediate-term (two to five years), and specific than strategic planning. Tactics deal more specifically with a range of options available to implement a strategy. Tactical plans usually involve short-term methods of implementation such as advertising or new product introduction.

- **Operational planning** is focused, short-term (less than two years), and specific. Operational planning translates the tactical plan into clear numbers, specific steps, and measurable objectives for the short term. Operational planning requires efficient, cost-effective application of resources to solving problems and meeting objectives.

Single-Use versus Standing Plans

As we have discussed in earlier chapters, managers seek to reduce uncertainty. The planning process helps uncertainty reduction by developing a sequence for completing work. In general, work falls into two categories; it is either unique or repetitive. Work that is unique requires different planning considerations than work that is repetitive in nature. Plans are needed that consider both unique activities as well as repetitive or reoccurring activities.

The time frame for a plan typically takes the form of either single-use or standing plans. **Single-use plans** have a clearly specified time frame for their usefulness. For example, a task force may be established to plan the development of a new product. This single-use plan will include detailed goals and objectives, but it becomes obsolete when the product has been developed. Then the organization has no further need to consult that plan.

In contrast to the single-use plan, **standing plans** guide repetitive situations. A standing plan makes decision making faster, easier, and more consistent from one decision to the next. That's because individuals armed with the same information often make quite different decisions. For ethical, strategic, and legal reasons, organizations need to limit individual decision-making discretion. To do so, organizations use standing plans to limit human behavior by using the following:

- A *policy* is a guideline that describes expected behavior in a specific situation, or the rules that guide decision making. An example policy in a healthcare institution might be a policy for the proper retrieval and storage of medical records.

- *Procedures* help define rules that apply to a specific policy. In our healthcare example, the procedure used for medical records retrieval and storage might require that a digital copy of each paper document in the patient's file be maintained online for a period of five years; after five years, the patient's medical records may be archived to offline storage.

- A *method* describes a particular sequence of activities to accomplish an objective. Generally, a manager can pick one of several methods for accomplishing an activity. If the organization prefers using one method over another, then a policy manual will communicate which method to use in a specific situation.

Here's a good example of a standing plan for a hotel restaurant: For many travelers, hotels are homes away from home. Assume that a hotel's managers know their guests typically eat 50 percent of their dinners in the hotel restaurant. Based on an average occupancy rate of 65 percent, the hotel restaurant will need to prepare for a minimum of 350 meals each evening. The standing plan identifies the following allocation: 100 meals with a beef entrée, 100 with a turkey or chicken entrée, 100 low-calorie combination entrées, and 50 meals with a pork entrée. Remember that effective standing plans prove correct over the long term and can be modified if additional information becomes available.

STEPS IN THE PLANNING PROCESS

The **planning process** is very much like the decision-making process presented in Chapter 3. It consists of six steps: (1) identify current conditions, (2) determine goals and objectives, (3) create action plans, (4) allocate resources, (5) implement the plan, and (6) control. This six-step process does not distinguish among the different types of plans we've just discussed. Instead, it's generally applicable to all types of plans, differing in the issues considered as well as in specificity, scope, and time frame.

EXHIBIT 4.2
The Planning Process

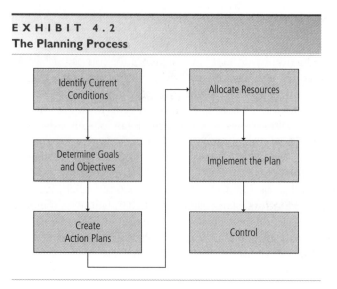

Step 1 Identify Current Conditions

Before goals and objectives can be established, the current state of the organization must be assessed. In strategic planning, for example, this includes the organization's resources as well as market trends, economic indicators, and competitive factors. Strategic planning takes a broad view of the organization's internal and external environments.

In operational and tactical planning, a manager's assessment of current conditions focuses less on trends and more on hard information about cash flow, market share, employee turnover ratios, and so on. In contrast to strategic planning, operational planning focuses on how to achieve specific goals and objectives.

Understanding the current conditions requires participation. That is, managers must seek out information from a broad base of organizational constituencies—for example, sales, engineering, manufacturing, and finance. Although each organizational unit may have a different perspective, managers must consider all viewpoints in order to accurately assess the organization's current situation.

Competitive benchmarking is another approach to assessing current conditions that's widely used among organizations. Benchmarking sets standards for performance based on what other successful organizations have been able to achieve. Benchmarking is one tool that provides insights into new opportunities.

Step 2 Determine Goals and Objectives

Once current conditions are assessed, goals and objectives can be set. Managers often use these two terms interchangeably, but it is useful to distinguish between them. **Goals** are defined as future states or conditions that contribute to the fulfillment of the organization's mission. Goals express relatively intermediate criteria of effectiveness. They can also be stated in terms of production, efficiency, and satisfaction. Customer satisfaction and productivity become workplace reality only when employees choose day-to-day behaviors that support the organization's ideals and goals. To achieve business goals, employees must understand those goals as a framework in which to perform their jobs, something that tells them which tasks are to be performed and at what level.

Objectives are short-term, specific, measurable targets that must be achieved to accomplish organizational goals. For example, an organization sets a goal of $1.2 million dollars in sales for the fiscal year. It also sets short-term objectives of $300,000 per quarter (every three months). The short-term quarterly objectives serve as benchmarks along the road to goal attainment. Failure to meet an objective signals that the goal may be unattainable. For objectives to be valuable they must be relevant, challenging, and direct employee action and behavior. Managers plan not only to determine the priority and timing of objectives but also to resolve any conflicts between objectives.

Priority of Objectives. It's entirely possible for an organization to have multiple goals and objectives contributing to its mission. In fact, some writers today insist that the old profit-centered enterprise needs to be replaced in a postindustrial society by "multipurpose" institutions that involve employees, customers, and the public as well as investors in establishing multiple goals.

Managers always face alternative objectives. To allocate resources in a rational way, a manager must establish priorities and distinguish between objectives that are mission critical (higher priority) and those that are not. Once this distinction has been made, the manager may still be faced with the need to prioritize among the *mission-critical* objectives, because time and resources will not allow all objectives to be accomplished at once. At that point, the manager may have to seek input from others in the organization. Ultimately, however, it's the manager who must set priorities for the organization and be prepared to carry them out.

Conflicts among Objectives. At any time, stakeholders—such as shareholders (owners), employees (including unions), customers, suppliers, creditors, and government agencies— are all concerned with different aspects of the organization. The process of establishing objectives and setting priorities must not overlook these interest groups, and plans must incorporate and integrate their interests. The form and weight to be given to conflicting objectives is a matter of managerial judgment. Common planning horizon trade-offs are displayed in Exhibit 4.3.

Managers must consider the expectations of the diverse groups on whom the organization's ultimate success depends. For example, present and potential customers hold power over the organization. If they aren't happy with the price and quality of the organization's products, they withdraw their support (stop buying). Suppliers can disrupt the flow of materials to express disagreement with the organization's activities. Government agencies can enforce compliance with regulations. Managers must recognize these interest groups and their power to affect the organization's objectives.

It's difficult to balance the concerns of dramatically different interest groups. However, it appears that successful organizations consistently emphasize profit-seeking activities that

E X H I B I T   4 . 3
Planning Horizon and Conflicting Objectives

Short term	Long term
Profit	Growth
Efficiency	Quality
Daily production	Future growth
Market penetration	Market development
Stability	Growth
Low risk	Risk
Cost	Greater service

maximize stockholder wealth. This is not to say that successful organizations seek only profit-oriented objectives, but rather that they are clearly more important than other objectives.

Measuring Objectives.   Objectives must be clear, achievable, and measurable to be effective. In fact, many people believe that specific, measurable objectives increase the performance of both employees and organizations, and that difficult objectives—if employees accept them—result in better performance than easier objectives. In practice, effective managerial performance requires establishing objectives in every area that contributes to overall organizational performance.

Here are some measurements used to quantify objectives in general business areas:

- **Profitability objectives** include the ratios of (1) profits to sales, (2) profits to total assets, and (3) profits to capital (net worth). Managers have a tendency to emphasize the ratio of profits to sales as an important measure of profitability. Both quantities in this ratio are taken from the income statement, which organizations generally regard as a better test of performance than the balance sheet. The measures are not mutually exclusive. All three ratios are profitability objectives because each measures, and therefore evaluates, different yet important aspects of profitability.

- **Marketing objectives** measure performance relative to products, markets, distribution, and customer service. They focus on prospects for long-run profitability. Thus well-managed organizations measure performance in such areas as market share, sales volume, number of outlets carrying the product, and number of new products developed.

- **Productivity objectives** are measured with ratios of output to input. Other factors being equal, the higher the ratio, the more efficient is the use of inputs. In this way, an organization's efficiency is measured directly. This measure of productivity is also used for comparisons across functional areas.

- **Physical and financial objectives** reflect the organization's capacity to acquire resources sufficient to achieve its objectives. Measurement of physical and financial objectives is comparatively easy since numerous accounting measures can be used. Liquidity measures—such as the current ratio, working capital turnover, debt/equity ratio, and accounts receivable—and inventory turnover can be used in establishing objectives and evaluating performance in financial planning.

- **Quality objectives** have become increasingly important in organizations. Quality can be a measure of physical characteristics of the product or service, or it can be assessed as a psychological customer perception of the physical product. To measure service quality, A. Parasuraman, Valerie Zeithaml, and Leonard Berry offer ten dimensions that define customer satisfaction: access, communication, competence, courtesy, credibility, reliability, responsiveness, security, tangibles, and knowing the customer.[7] In the final analysis, quality is the capability to meet or exceed customer expectations.

Planning Values.   **Planning values** are the underlying decision priorities used in determining planning objectives and making decisions. What is called for is a system-wide approach involving changes in a company's fundamental operations, beliefs, and values.[8] All departments act in unison to align department objectives with corporate goals. As we'll see in the next chapter, an organization's mission and core values should direct action at all levels.

Harvard business professor David Garvin identified eight planning values that make up a quality-based system: performance (primary operating characteristics, e.g., speed), features (supplements to performance), reliability (no malfunctioning or need for repair), conformance (to established standards), durability (product life), serviceability (speed and ease of repair, if needed), aesthetics (appeal to taste, looks, feel), and perceived quality (customer perception).[9]

It is also important that planning values reflect the realities of the internal and external environments. Internal considerations are people, processes, and practices that promote quality and continuous improvement. External considerations include customer satisfaction, supplier quality and cost, and government constraints.

Step 3 Create Action Plans

To achieve its objectives, an organization needs to create action plans. Actions need to be specified prior to implementation, as part of the planning process.

Actions are specific, prescribed means that are developed to achieve objectives. Such actions determine success or failure in meeting objectives. Planned courses of action, called strategies or tactics, are usually differentiated by scope and time frame (described earlier). In any case—and whatever your organization calls it—an action plan is directed toward changing a future condition; that is, achieving an objective.

Sometimes managers can choose among alternative actions. For example, productivity increases can be achieved in various ways, including improved technology, employee training, management training, reward systems, and improved working conditions. In such cases, managers must select the most effective alternative. Often, top managers who are planning for the total organization have before them several possible courses of action. As the plan becomes more localized to a simple unit in the organization, the pool of alternatives tends to decrease, yet become more familiar.

The future is fraught with uncertainty. To reduce uncertainty, managers develop forecasts for the future. **Forecasting** is the process of using past and current information to predict future events. Armed with a forecast, an organization attempts to determine the likely outcomes of alternative courses of action. For example, a sales forecast would include past and current information about the organization's product, price, advertising, and cost of goods sold. External conditions to be measured include product demand, price of competing products, consumer income levels, consumer credit card interest rates, and other measures of local economic activity. Forecasts can also be useful for predicting important internal conditions, including hiring requirements, factory space needs, employee training expenditures, and healthcare costs.

Step 4 Allocate Resources

The fourth step in the planning process is allocating resources. **Resources** are defined as the financial, physical, human, time, or other assets of an organization. Resources are also known as *factors of production*. In creating product value, highly productive organizations use their capital, human, and material resources more effectively than do less productive organizations.

Expenditure of resources is usually controlled by use of a budget. A **budget** is an allocation of resources to an activity, account, or unit in the organization. For example, as part of the plan to bring a new product to market, a budget is likely to include salaries, materials, facilities, travel, and other resources. A good budget recognizes and allocates the needed resources to meet an objective.

Budgeting is both a planning technique and a control technique. As a planning technique, budgeting serves to allocate resources among competing objectives. As a control

EXHIBIT 4.4
The Budgeting Process

Management Objectives

Sales Budget	Other Income
• Quantity	• Interest
• Dollar amount	• Misc. income

Less

Production Budget	Marketing Budget	Administrative Expense Budget	Misc. Budget
• Units produced	• Promotion costs	• Each department	• Interest on loans
• Cost of material	• Selling expenses		
• Direct labor	• Advertising		
• Factory overhead			

Results in

Financial Budget
• Balance sheet

Source: James H. Donnelly, Jr., James L. Gibson, and John M. Ivancevich. *Fundamentals of management,* 8th ed. Homewood, IL: Richard D. Irwin, 1992, p.157. Used with permission.

technique, budgeting compares initial allocations to actual expenditures. Often budget overruns occur that require corrective action by management.

To appreciate the complexity of the budgeting process, look at the flowchart in Exhibit 4.4. The sales budget plays a key role, as you can see by its location at the top of the chart. All other budgets are related to it either directly or indirectly. The production budget, for example, must specify the materials, labor, and other manufacturing expenses required to support the projected sales level. Similarly, the marketing budget details the costs associated with the sales level projected for each product in each sales region. Administrative expenses also must be related to the predicted sales volume. In the final step of the budgeting process, projected sales and expenses are combined to result in the financial budget, which consist of formal financial statements, inventory budgets, and the capital additions budget.

Flexibility in Budgeting.   Forecast data are based on assumptions about the future. If these assumptions prove wrong, the budgets are inadequate. So the usefulness of financial budgets depends mainly on how flexible they are regarding changes in conditions. Organizations can achieve flexibility in two principal ways: variable budgeting and moving budgeting.

• **Variable budgeting** provides for the possibility that actual output deviates from planned output. It recognizes that variable costs are related to output, while fixed costs are unrelated to output. Thus, if actual output is 20 percent less than planned output, it doesn't follow that actual profit will be 20 percent less than that planned. Rather, the actual profit varies, depending on the complex relationship between costs and output.

- **Moving budgeting** entails the preparation of a budget for a fixed period (say, one year) with periodic updating at fixed intervals (such as one month). For example, a budget is prepared in December for the next 12 months (January through December). At the end of January, the budget is revised and projected for the next 12 months (February through January). In this manner, the most current information is included in the budgeting process. Drawing from recent experience, managers constantly revise the premises and assumptions on which the budget is based. Moving budgets have the advantage of allowing for systematic reexamination; they have the disadvantage of being costly to maintain.

Although budgets are important instruments for implementing an organization's objectives, they must be viewed in perspective as one item on a long list of demands for a manager's time.

Criticisms of the Budgeting Process.   The major criticism of the budgeting process is its rigidity. Budgeting is often inflexible; once resource allocations are made, they are hard to change. This is largely due to the dual nature of budgeting as both a planning technique and a control technique. On the planning side, resource allocations can be changed; but on the control side, too much change in allocation makes control impossible. Further, by strictly adhering to a planning process that relies on budgeting to allocate numbers and dollars, companies tend to overlook critical variables such as quality, customer service, and technological change. This inflexibility makes it hard for an organization to adapt to change, which is necessary for long-term competitive success.

Information is a useful resource in the budgeting process and needs to be allocated or distributed to members of the organization. The best decisions are made with more rather than less information. Information is perhaps the most important resource in modern, knowledge-based organizations. Without full access to the company's information—cost and market data, product developments, and so on—employees cannot be expected to help in planning.

Step 5 Implement the Plan

Implementation concerns the activities involved in delegating tasks, taking action, and achieving results. Without effective implementation, the four preceding steps of the planning process are pointless. Implementation means using resources to put a plan into action. In small businesses and entrepreneurial ventures, the manager often carries out each step of the planning process, including implementation. In most large organizations, however, the manager must implement plans through others, by motivating them to carry out the plan, rewarding them for successful performance, and redirecting them when their actions lead to outcomes that differ from the objectives. Managers have three ways to implement plans through others: authority, persuasion, and policies.

Authority.   **Authority** accompanies the position, not the person. In an organization, those in authority have the right to make decisions and to expect that subordinates will comply with those decisions. A manager with authority can expect employees to carry out a plan so long as it doesn't require illegal or unethical behavior. Authority is often sufficient to implement simple plans, but a complex plan can seldom be implemented through authority alone.

Persuasion.   **Persuasion** is the process of selling a plan to those who must implement it, communicating relevant information so those individuals understand possible implications. Persuasion requires convincing others to accept a plan based on its merits, rather than on the manager's authority. Using persuasion has its drawbacks. What happens if persuasion fails? If the plan is crucial, management must then implement it by use of authority (pulling rank). Managers who have failed once in using persuasion may be well advised to limit its use in the future.

Policies.   **Policies** are written statements reflecting a plan's basic values and providing guidelines for selecting actions to achieve objectives. When plans are expected to be rather permanent, policies are developed to implement them. Standard operating procedures (SOPs) are a typical example of formal guidelines used by workers and managers to make consistent decisions across consistent situations. Effective policies have these characteristics:

- *Flexibility* A policy achieves a balance between rigidity and flexibility. In quality-based organizations, policies always leave some room for workers at all levels to exercise their discretion.

- *Comprehensiveness* A policy must cover multiple contingencies. The degree of comprehensiveness depends on the scope of action controlled by the policy itself. Narrow issues require narrow policies.

- *Coordination* A policy must readily coordinate among other decisions, teams, and departments. Activities must conform to the policy without building conflict across activities.

- *Clarity* A policy must be stated clearly and logically. It must specify the aim of the action, define appropriate methods, and describe the limits of discretion provided to those applying the policy.

- *Ethics* A policy must be ethical and responsive to cultural differences. This guideline may be most difficult to follow when an organization is doing business in a foreign country, where local standards may differ from the organization's standards as developed in another country or society. Again, judgment must often be applied.

Policies can sometimes be brief, enduring, and dramatic. Other policies, such as an organization's overall personnel policy, are longer, more detailed, and periodically updated. In any case, managers should seek to carefully define the process of policy development. For example, a key issue in personnel policy development is the question of who should be involved in developing the policy. Employee participation with management is essential in the drafting of such policies. Another issue in policy development is how and when to communicate new policies to employees. Managers must ensure that policy development processes, and the communication of policies to employees, are clear and allow for appropriate feedback.

Whereas a policy is a general guide to decision making, a **regulation** (or standard procedure) is a set of instructions for implementing a policy. For example, a policy of "employee empowerment" may translate into a procedure for team leaders specifying that work process changes can be instituted only after meeting with all affected employees and obtaining their approval of any changes. Team leaders may also be trained to follow specific procedures in initiating the discussion, recording employees' recommendations, and documenting the approved changes.

Step 6 Control

Control includes all managerial activities dedicated to ensuring that actual results conform to planned results and is the final step in the planning process. Note that the controlling step and the implementation step occur virtually simultaneously. As actions are undertaken to implement the plan, measurement of the effectiveness of those actions should provide immediate feedback. Managers should be careful not to make the mistake of waiting until their actions have been completed before measuring their effectiveness. Managers receive feedback, and take corrective action, by measuring actual performance and comparing it to the standard or original plan. The process of taking corrective actions based on measurement of actual performance is known as **feedback.**

Managers must obtain information—feedback—that reports actual performance and permits comparison of the performance against standards. Such information is most easily acquired for activities that produce specific and concrete results; for example, production and sales activities have results that are easily identifiable and for which information is readily obtainable.

We'll say more about control issues in a later chapter. For now, you should note that controlling is a necessary part of the planning function. The people responsible for taking corrective steps when actual results are not in line with planned results must know not only that they are indeed responsible, but that they have the authority to take action.

QUALITY APPROACH TO PLANNING

Organizations that take a quality approach to planning can choose from various specific planning methods. In this section we'll examine three of those methods: the plan, do, check, act cycle; time-based planning; and planning for continuous improvement. These approaches form the basis for quality planning. Noted consultant W. E. Deming described **quality planning** as the activity of (1) determining customer needs and (2) developing the products and processes required to meet those needs. Quality planning is required for every product and service within an organization, not only for goods and services sold to external customers. Total Quality Management (TQM) planning stresses employee involvement, teamwork, and focusing the entire company on the customer. Ultimately, these quality-conscientious companies develop strategies that use new and innovative processes to produce products or services that consistently meet or exceed customer expectations.

Each of the quality approaches to planning discussed in this section emphasizes exceeding customer expectations, maintaining continuous improvement, and practicing team-based problem solving. Although all of these planning approaches are based on a similar concept of quality, each one is developed by a different thinker and has some unique aspects. At the end of this section, we'll take a look at planning for continuous improvement in a quality management environment.

The Plan, Do, Check, Act Cycle

The **plan, do, check, act (PDCA)** quality planning approach is conceived as a planning cycle that forms the basis for continuous improvement (see Exhibit 4.5). In the PDCA cycle, the first step is to plan the quality improvement. Second, workers perform or produce a short version or a small batch of the procedure or product. Third, workers check the results of this pilot project for compliance with standards. Fourth, workers implement the tested process. The PDCA cycle is then repeated.

Employees at Cincinnati-based Procter & Gamble (P&G) use the PDCA cycle to manage environmental quality efforts. First, they develop a *plan* to remove pollutants from each stage of production, as well as from packaging and the final product. Next (*do*) they

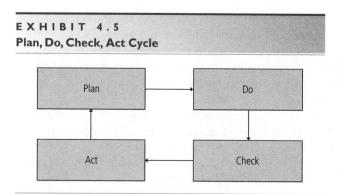

EXHIBIT 4.5
Plan, Do, Check, Act Cycle

reduce discharges to the environment and correct other potentially harmful environmental defects. Then they *check* the results, using statistics and other measurement tools. Once the results are assessed, employees (*act*) install permanent systems to maintain the quality improvement and to apply it to other aspects of the business. Using this technique, a P&G pulp mill cut landfill dumping by 75 percent; a coffee-processing plant in Missouri added a machine to compact chaff from coffee beans, cutting solids in sewage by 75 percent. New packaging cut 3.4 million pounds of waste in deodorant product cartons. As a result of PDCA, P&G's redesigned vegetable oil bottle uses 28 percent less plastic than the earlier bottle.[10]

Time-Based Planning

Speed can often determine the success or failure of a plan's implementation. The important period between the time a product is first considered and the time it's sold to the customer is called **concept to customer**. Speed in planning and delivering a product or service can be a strategic competitive advantage. All other things being equal, the prize (typically, market share) goes to the fastest organization. For example, DaimlerChrysler's new sports car, the Crossfire, completed the concept-to-customer cycle in a record-breaking twenty-four months using innovative methods for both design and production.[11] Further, paying attention to time usually forces the organization to look at other issues (e.g., design, staffing, and inspection) affecting product and service quality. For example, it's not uncommon for a product to lie untouched during 90 percent of the time allocated for its assembly. Paying attention to production speed can lead to reductions in these idle periods. Time-sensitive organizations are not only likely to deliver products to their customers faster than competitors but also likely to develop greater customer loyalty and learn more about improving the production process itself.[12]

One important initiative currently popular in many organizations is the concept of reengineering. **Reengineering** has been defined as "the fundamental rethinking and radical redesign of business processes to achieve dramatic improvements in critical, contemporary measures of performance, such as cost, quality, service, and speed."[13] Reengineering was largely responsible for the trend toward corporate downsizing, or "rightsizing," that swept organizations around the world during the early to mid-1990s. Many layers of management have been excised from organizations in the interest of reducing the time it takes for organizations to accomplish goals. From a reengineering perspective, this meant a reliance on a more highly educated workforce and greater use of technology to streamline the workflow which resulted in fewer errors and higher quality products and services. On the whole, however, reengineering efforts have failed to achieve the desired objectives. Senior managers still complain that middle managers are entrenched, blocking necessary changes. And middle managers complain that senior managers have neither the vision nor the fortitude to take the enterprise through changes. To survive, managers must be willing to challenge their assumptions. An entire pattern of thought, a whole set of ideas and expectations, must be let go. According to James Champy, a founder of the reengineering approach, to speed change in the organization, managers must:

1. Abandon the quest for perfection, with its notion of the universal right way of doing things;

2. Trade in the airy abstraction of authority that comes from their title or office, for the messier reality of authority based on competence and ability; and

3. Broaden their age-old devotion to growth to include an equally old, but only recently rediscovered, devotion to service.[14]

Time based planning requires new processes and structures that create the conditions for a faster cycle time. While reengineering works on the process changes needed for efficient production, new organizational structures are also needed. A new and innovative structural change that is consistent with the principles of reengineering is known as the **horizontal organization.** Unlike the more traditional vertical organizations based on a pyramidal hierarchy, the horizontal organization is flatter, more responsive, and affords better communication among participants. In the horizontal model, organization processes drive planning. Each process has fewer levels of complexity, which keeps decision making closer to the source of the decision. That is, resources and information are deployed when and where they are needed to support a core activity. In other words, unlike vertical hierarchies, horizontal organizations have resource and information needs that planning must take into consideration.[15]

Another important time-based initiative in current industry practice, as noted earlier, is called cycle time reduction (CTR). CTR is concerned with reducing the time it takes for completing organizational processes, reducing costs, and increasing customer service. A key concept in CTR is the **3 percent rule,** which states that only 3 percent of the elapsed time for a process is actually needed to complete the activity. Insurance claim filing and handling is a good example: physically completing the claim may take only five minutes, but processing the claim often takes thirty days.[16]

Reengineering and CTR are two techniques used by planners in attempting to reduce completion times of key organizational processes. However, as proponents of both techniques recognize, it's a never-ending challenge. That's why most organizations also use another form of planning that allows for the continuous improvement of the organization.

Planning for Continuous Improvement

Effective planning and plans lead to quality outcomes as well as continuous improvements in performance. Quality pioneer Joseph M. Juran notes three main negative outcomes resulting from a lack of attention to quality in the planning process:

1. *Loss of sales due to competition in quality* In the United States, this outcome affects almost every manufactured product, from TVs to lawn mowers to cars.

2. *Costs of poor quality, including customer complaints, product liability lawsuits, redoing defective work, products scrapped, and so on* Juran estimates that 20 to 40 percent of all costs of doing business are from redoing poor-quality work.

3. *Threats to society* These run the gamut from minor annoyances like home appliance breakdowns to global disasters such as the Three Mile Island nuclear emergency; the Bhopal, India, poison gas release; and the Chernobyl, Ukraine, nuclear reactor explosion and contamination.[17]

Outcomes of Quality Planning.   Managers can minimize the possibility of negative outcomes by using quality-based planning methods and by establishing quality goals. Quality means knowing what your customers, clients, or patients (in the case of health-care) want and then designing a delivery system (an organization) to provide the good or service. Customer-driven organizations closely and continually scrutinize their system's output for quality. Ultimately, the primary outcome of quality planning is customer satisfaction and delight. Many scholars have offered advice about how best to achieve these ends. Most notably, Juran's description of quality planning includes the following main points:

- Identify customers, both external and internal.
- Determine the customer's needs.
- Develop product features that satisfy customer needs.
- Establish quality goals that meet customers' and suppliers' needs at a low combined cost.
- Develop a process to produce the needed features.
- Prove that the process can meet the quality goals under operating conditions (i.e., prove process capability).[18]

Thus the focus of quality outcomes is on customers—both external (i.e., consumers) and internal (i.e., another department). Changes in the workplace have helped create systems for continuous improvement in many organizations. For example, American Express made a significant change when it adopted a system built on customer-based transactions. In response to its external customer requests, the company created a comprehensive delivery system that would support key customer transactions.[19]

Quality Planning Models.   Some quality planning models are revolutionary; others are evolutionary. **Revolutionary planning models** (e.g., traditional planning models) implement a massive, one-time change in the production process or product in order to reduce costs or improve the product in a significant way. Then no other changes or improvements are made until the next revolutionary change occurs at the end of another planning cycle. Between planning cycles, however, the original improvements tend to erode. Eventually, the improvements erode enough to initiate another plan for improvement. **Evolutionary planning models** make gradual and more continuous changes based on input from inside and outside the production system. Improvements typically are not dramatic, but they are consistent and incremental.

Planning is beneficial because it allows an organization to anticipate and respond to change in a systematic manner. Planning adds value by finding ways to reduce the overall cost of doing business while also anticipating and satisfying customer needs. We recognize today the importance of quality to the consumer when considering the purchase of goods and services. But not too long ago, quality was considered a cost. Exhibit 4.6 summarizes traditional and quality-based characteristics of planning. As you can see, quality-based planning emphasizes the system rather than the employees as the source of organizational problems. Quality-based planning regards the employee as an asset.

EXHIBIT 4.6
Traditional versus Quality Planning Characteristics

Traditional	Quality
Quality is an expense.	Quality decreases costs.
Quality through inspection.	Higher quality reduces the need for inspection.
Workers cause defects.	System causes defects.
Employ standards and quotas.	Eliminate standards and quotas.
Manage by fear.	Drive out fear.
Employees represent a cost.	Employees are an asset.
Focus on profit.	Focus on quality; profit will follow.

Conclusion
Planning

Planning is a fundamental management activity that covers any time span, from short to long term. In this chapter we examined various definitions of and justifications for planning, enumerated the benefits and criticisms of planning, surveyed the steps involved in planning, and looked at quality approaches to planning. These topics certainly don't cover all of the important issues associated with planning. But our purpose in this chapter is to emphasize that planning is an important management function. All organizational goals and objectives flow from planning. Without a formal planning process, organizations are subject to the vagaries of environmental circumstances; they have little recourse but to react to environmental changes. Planning is a proactive activity that enables an organization to take an offensive stance, creating circumstances that are most favorable to the organization.

SUGGESTED READINGS

Fisher, Marshall L., Janice H. Hammond, Walter R. Obermeyer, and Ananth Raman. "Making Supply Meet Demand in an Uncertain World." *Harvard Business Review*, May–June 1994.

Gajilan, Arlyn Tobias. "The Amazing JetBlue." *Fortune*, May 17, 2002.

Kenney, Jennifer. "Cleaning Up," *Fortune*, April 24, 2003.

Lorange, Peter, and Richard F. Vancil. "How to Make Strategic Planning Work." *Harvard Business Review*, September–October, 1976.

ENDNOTES

1. Henri Fayol, *General and Industrial Management* (London: Sir Isaac Pitman and Sons, 1949).

2. Harold Koontz and Cyril O'Donnell, *Management: A Systems and Contingency Analysis of Management Functions,* 6th ed. (New York: McGraw-Hill, 1976).

3. Henry Mintzberg, "The Rise and Fall of Strategic Planning," *Harvard Business Review,* January–February 1994, p. 107.

4. James C. Wetherbe, "Principles of Cycle Time Reduction: You Can Have Your Cake and Eat It Too," *Cycle Time Research,* 1995, pp. 1–24.

5. Peter Senge, *The Fifth Discipline: The Art and Practice of the Learning Organization* (New York: Doubleday, 1990).

6. Timm J. Esque and Thomas F. Gilbert, "Making Competencies Pay Off," *Training,* January 1995, pp. 44–50.

7. A. Parasuraman, Valerie A. Zeithaml, and Leonard L. Berry, "A Conceptual Model of Service Quality and Its Implications for Future Research," Working paper 84–106 (Cambridge, MA: Marketing Science Institute, 1984), 13–14.

8. For relevant discussions of these and related management problems, see M. L. Gimpl and S. R. Daken, "Management and Magic," *California Management Review* (Fall 1984): 125–136; R. T. Pascale, "The Paradox of Corporate Culture: Reconciling Ourselves to Socialization," *California Management Review* (Winter 1985): 26–41; and Frederick D. Sturdivant, *Business and Society,* 3rd ed. (Burr Ridge, IL: Irwin, 1985).

9. David A. Garvin, "Competing on the Eight Dimensions of Quality," *Harvard Business Review,* November–December 1987, pp. 101–109.

10. Karen Bemoski, "Carrying on the P&G Tradition," *Quality Progress,* May 1992, p. 24.

11. Alex Traylor, "Crossfire Just another Sexy Sports Car? Sure, but It's also a Whole New Way of Doing Business," *Fortune,* March 3, 2003.

12. George Stalk Jr. and Thomas M. Hout, *Competing against Time: How Time-Based Competition Is Reshaping Global Markets* (New York: Free Press, 1990).

13. Michael Hammer and James Champy, *Reengineering the Corporation* (New York: HarperCollins, 1993), 32.

14. James Champy, *Reengineering Management* (New York: Harper Business, 1995).

15. Frank Ostroff, *The Horizontal Organization* (New York: Oxford University Press, 1999).

16. James C. Wetherbe, "Principles of Cycle Time Reduction: You Can Have Your Cake and Eat It Too," *Cycle Time Research,* 1995, pp. 1–24.

17. J. M. Juran, *Juran on Quality Planning* (New York: Free Press, 1988), 1–2.

18. J. M. Juran, "The Quality Trilogy," *Quality Progress,* August 1986, pp. 19–24.

19. D. Keith Denton, "Creating a System for Continuous Improvement," *Business Horizons,* January–February 1995, pp. 16–21.

Chapter Five

Strategy

The origin of strategy, as a concept, is rooted in military planning. The word *strategy* comes from the Greek and means the "art of the general." In a business context, a company devises a strategy that anticipates what its opponents (competitors) will do and favorably positions itself in relation to its rivals. Modern corporate strategy owes much to this traditional view, which focuses on the external environment. In the last quarter of the twentieth century, researchers began giving equal weight to a firm's internal environment. As noted scholars Charles Hofer and Dan Schendel observed, strategy is the process of matching the competencies of the organization with opportunities that are present in the larger environment.[1] Through this process, strategy helps a company perform better than the competition by creating a sustainable advantage that competitors cannot easily duplicate.[2] In this chapter, we explore how strategy creates value for organizational stakeholders through a process of analysis, decisions, and actions to achieve and maintain competitive advantage.[3] *Strategy formulation* is concerned with analysis and decisions, whereas *strategy implementation* represents actions taken to implement strategic decisions.[4]

STRATEGIC PLANNING

Strategic planning is the process of developing a strategic orientation for an organization. Because it forces introspective questioning of purpose, customers, resources, and skills, strategic planning can benefit any organization. The process begins with the identification of the core competencies of the organization. **Core competencies** are activities done well, or skills that the organization possesses. For example, marketing expertise might be a core competency. The strategic planning process culminates in the formulation and implementation of a multilevel strategy for achieving organizational goals.

Exhibit 5.1 is an overview of the strategic planning process, with examples of each aspect of the strategic planning process included in the chapter. As you can see in Exhibit 5.1, step 1 in the strategic planning process focuses on articulation of the organization's *purpose, mission, goals, objectives, philosophy,* and *values.* The philosophy and values entail the organization's contribution to society, its moral and ethical beliefs, and the way it operates. Generally, the organization's CEO articulates these components, which often represent strong personal beliefs. (We'll cover the subjects of mission and goals shortly.) Step 2, *skills and resources,* relates to the people and assets at the disposal of the organization. While an organization may establish a goal, it may have neither the financial resources nor the personnel to achieve the goal. However, skills and resources can always be acquired or outsourced; that recognition must be an explicit part of strategic planning. *Environmental analysis,* step 3 of strategic planning, involves exploration of all the forces affecting the organization's ability to attain its goals. Largely, these are factors present in the environment that create opportunities for the organization or threats to the organization. Favorable demographic trends, emerging markets, and new technologies, as well as government regulations, legal requirements, and rising prices for raw materials, are all understood through environmental analysis. In step 4, *strategy formulation and implementation,* the organization's managers seek to develop and execute a multilevel strategy. Strategies represent the organization's plan for navigating the competitive environment. The early phases of strategic planning focus on developing (formulating) the strategy and fitting the strategy to the complexity present in the environment. In the later phases of strategic planning, strategy implementation locks in place specific organizational actions that support the strategy. Along the way, conceptual ideas are converted into action plans such as creating a TV commercial as part of an advertising campaign to support the strategy. An important part of the strategic planning process is to set target outcomes or expectations for performance. Finally, in step 5, *performance* represents the multiple outcomes of the strategic planning process. The most notable outcome of this step is profit. As you read through this chapter, the strategic planning process outlined in Exhibit 5.1 should serve as a context to help you understand the more detailed discussions of strategic management concepts and ideas that follow.

EXHIBIT 5.1
Strategic Planning Process

	Strategic Planning Component	Example
1	Purpose, mission, goals, objectives, philosophy, and values	States purpose, philosophy, and values and examines the long-term and short-term aspirations of the organization.
2	Skills and resources of the organization	Identifies employee skills, competencies, and other resources
3	Environmental analysis: external and internal	Identifies internal and external stakeholder requirements
4	Strategy formulation and implementation	Developing strategic intent and thinking. Also entails developing strategies to maximize organizational goals in light of available resources
5	Performance	Assesses financial performance as well as stakeholder satisfaction, market share, and so forth

Developing a Mission Statement

An organization's mission is its *raison d'être* (French for "reason for being"), the fundamental purpose it's designed to serve. The organizational **mission statement** answers the question, "What is this organization's purpose?" for employees, customers, and other constituents. Whereas a strategy represents the path toward the attainment of mission, goals, and objectives, the firm's mission statement describes an even more fundamental rationale for its existence.

Some organizational theorists assert that the organizational mission should be based on something even more abstract, an organizational vision. In other words, a mission statement should be related to vision. The vision, which usually implies the CEO's vision for the organization, is based on values, competencies of the organization, and opportunities in the future environment. The vision is important because it helps an organization to model strategic plans, and it provides a kind of touchstone for goal setting. In a constantly shifting industry environment, a vision helps avoid reactive decision making and keeps a firm focused on its long-term goals.

A visionary CEO in the automobile industry would be able to synthesize and integrate the impact of a new and emerging technology on vehicles of the future. As an example in the automotive industry, consider the fuel cell, which is expected to revolutionize commercial and personal transportation. A fuel cell is an electrochemical process that uses energy from a chemical reaction to create electricity. Unlike a battery, the fuel cell does not need recharging or replacing as long as it is supplied with fuel and an oxidizer. The fuel cell can be used to power electric motors that drive the wheels of the vehicle. Think of it! No oil tankers, no trucks hauling gasoline, no dependence on the Middle East, and no oil storage facilities wasting prime real estate. The question the CEO must answer is, "When will the fuel cell be commercially viable as a reliable and affordable source of power?" Hence, the CEO's vision of the future must be flexible enough to recognize that the fuel cell is coming and to prepare for integrating fuel cell technology into future products in a way that creates value for organizational stakeholders. A vision of the future probably includes the fuel cell, but the CEO has to hedge his bets on when and how it might be used in the organization.

Characteristics of an Effective Mission Statement

To establish a mission and vision for an organization, its CEO must take the company's history into consideration. For established firms, the mission should be consistent with what is known about the firm's history. This history includes accomplishments and failures, objectives and policies, decisions, employees, and more. An organization must assess its history to determine its current resource base, its image, and its various capacities. Odd as it may sound, many management consultants help organizations appreciate and use **organization stories**—tales about experiences and events that transpired where the storyteller works. Within an organization, stories serve to legitimize power, to rationalize group behavior, and to reinforce organizational values, identity, and commitment.[5] Before the invention of writing, human cultures relied on stories to convey the history of their culture to the young and to outsiders. Similarly, organizational stories convey the history of an organization to new employees and outsiders. Managers should review organizational stories when establishing a mission statement.

Start-ups and new ventures need a mission too, but have no history upon which to base a long-term vision. Instead, such firms can look to the history of the industry they are part of, or to the history of the human needs and expectations they hope to satisfy through organized activity.

The mission statement that results from the analysis of history, distinctive competence, and the environment must be (1) customer-focused, (2) achievable, (3) motivational, and (4) specific.

Customer-Focused.   Mission statements emphasize a customer focus. Many firms have faltered or failed because they continued to define themselves based on what they produced rather than on whom they served.

For enduring success, strategies must be based on the premise that customer satisfaction—and, better yet, customer delight and loyalty—is necessary. The reasons are many and fundamental. Finding new customers is far more expensive than keeping current customers. Dissatisfied customers not only fail to return and buy again, they are also likely (1) to decline to express the reasons for their dissatisfaction (which could be a source of learning and growth for the firm) and (2) to share their dissatisfaction with other potential customers. Customers, not employees, are a firm's best salespeople.

By relying too heavily on rental car and fleet markets to boost production numbers and reduce unit costs, Ford unwittingly created the perception in consumers' minds that the once-venerable Taurus had become little more than a drab vehicle suitable only for discounted bulk sales. At the same time Toyota, Ford's rival, focused on the consumer market and created a safe, reliable, and economical family car that sold without discounting and received rave reviews from automobile analysts. Ford finally admitted that it had lost sight of the real customer. Once the top-selling car in the United States, the Ford Taurus has gradually lost market share to the Toyota Camry. In speaking to reporters at the 2003 Chicago Auto Show, Jim O'Connor, who heads Ford's sales and marketing division for North America, said: "Very frankly, Camry is a better product than Taurus today."[6]

Achievable.   A mission statement should be challenging, and it must also be achievable. Unrealistic ambitions can exceed a firm's capabilities and lead to the squandering of resources. It's the CEO's role to shape and set the culture and tenor of the organization. But once all stakeholders embrace that culture, it's important to ensure that goals are implemented through strategic intent and execution. As noted management consultant Ram Charan advised Larry Bossidy, chairman and former CEO of Honeywell, "People think of execution as the tactical side of business, something leaders delegate while they focus on the perceived 'bigger' issues. . . . This idea is completely wrong. Execution has to be built into a company's strategy, its goals, and its culture. And the leader of the organization must be deeply engaged in it."[7]

Motivational.   At all levels of an organization, the mission must serve as a source of inspiration and motivation. Effective mission statements have meaning to every employee, allowing them to translate the words of the mission into their own motivation and serving as a guide for decisions and actions.

Motivation affects the enduring effort of employees. Employee conviction and commitment to the organization's mission and goals are necessary for long-term success. With conviction, employees show dedication to the mission; with commitment, they demonstrate behavioral expression of the psychological conviction.

Specific.   A mission statement should define in which industries the organization intends to compete—and in some cases, where it will not compete. A specific mission allows employees to focus their energy and to be more productive, making the entire firm more profitable. Broad statements of value or goodness (e.g., "the highest quality at the lowest price") do not make a good mission statement. By attempting to be all things to all people, a firm scatters its energy; doing so makes the firm less able to develop distinctive competence, which in turn makes it nearly impossible for the firm to please anyone.

Since the 1980s, mission statements have been developed by a growing number of organizations. From corporations to community groups, organizations are using these declarations to gain direction, purpose, perspective, and vision. Most mission statements are directed both inside and outside of the organization, ideally sending a strong, clear message to management, staff, clients, and prospects. While writing a mission statement, an organization needs time to reflect on what it's trying to accomplish. It needs to focus on the fundamentals: defining the business, identifying and serving stakeholders, and engendering in the employee a spirit of both loyalty and commitment.[8]

Establishing Goals and Objectives

In an organization, the mission statement sets the tone and direction for more specific goals and objectives. The mission helps strategists develop long-term goals and short-term objectives. Strategists then convert the goals into precise actions, thus creating a context in which to develop short-term objectives. Clear goals—those leaving no doubt about the firm's intentions—inform employees where to direct their efforts. With the mission and goals as context, organizational leaders can communicate not only what needs to be done but also how it should be done (i.e., consistent with the mission). Goals facilitate management control by helping employees track their progress toward goal attainment and by serving as standards against which to compare the firm's actual performance.

Strategic Terminology

What do strategists mean when they speak of concepts like distinctive competence, competitive advantage, and industry environment? In this section we define these key terms, along with several more that are commonly used in strategic management (see the Management Highlight on page 85).

Distinctive Competence.   Although an organization likely is capable of doing many things, strategic success stems from its ability to identify and capitalize on corporate strengths in order to satisfy customer needs. A **distinctive competence** is a unique strength that allows a company to achieve superior efficiency, quality, innovation, or customer responsiveness.[9] This capacity is unique to the firm and valued in the market. For example, Wal-Mart's distinctive competence is derived from efficiency. The company purchases goods in quantity and maintains the lowest price for the product. Efficiencies gained through the purchasing and distribution processes create value, which translates into the lowest price for consumers. From the Wal-Mart perspective, a superior distribution system optimizes availability and inventory cost to maintain consistent profit margins.

Competitive Advantage.   Competitive advantage in the marketplace allows an organization to attain greater profits than its competitors. Organizations can achieve competitive advantage in either of two ways: efficiency and differentiation. Efficiency allows the organization to be the **low-cost leader,** creating a lower cost structure and achieving greater profits than the competition. An organization uses **differentiation** to create a product that is unlike and, in some manner, superior to those offered by the competition.

MANAGEMENT HIGHLIGHT
Strategic Terminology

	Description	Focus	Examples
Planning	Analytical process that anticipates future requirements of the organization.	Affects the entire organization and takes a long-range perspective.	Indicates budgeting processes, acquisition, and merger activities.
Strategy	Describes how the organization will compete and create competitive advantage in the long run.	Exists at three levels: functional, competitive, and institutional.	Cost leadership is a competitive-level strategy.
Strategic Thinking	The ability to integrate complex information and apply that information to create greater value than competitors.	Strategic managers synthesize information about organization's core competencies, technical advances, and competitive information.	Dell's ability to create value by selling servers rather and commodity PCs. Dell created the direct-selling market for commercial file servers.
Business Model	Describes the way the organization will conduct business. New business models often rely on untested and sometimes flawed assumptions.	Processes that describe the business. Contains a *narrative test* that describes what the organization hopes to accomplish and a *numbers test* that projects financial information based on assumptions.	*Successful:* Wal-Mart used mass merchandising techniques and brand-name goods to sell in rural America. *Unsuccessful:* WebVan customers were unwilling to pay premium prices for Internet grocery shopping.

Source: Adapted from: Joan Magretta, "Why Business Models Matter" *Harvard Business Review,* May 2002, pp. 3–8; Richard Hammermesh, "Making Planning Strategic," *Harvard Business Review,* July–August 1986, pp. 3–9; and Henry Mintzberg, "The Rise and Fall of Strategic Planning," *Harvard Business Review,* January–February 1994, pp. 107–114.

That organization can then charge a premium price associated with a differentiated product, resulting in higher profits. Strategic management theorists Charles Hill and Gareth Jones propose that the four building blocks of competitive advantage are quality, innovativeness, efficiency, and customer responsiveness:[10]

1. *Quality*—an advantage is created by building a quality product. Lexus automobiles are known for quality as defined by fit and finish, reliability, and low level of reported defects.

2. *Innovativeness*—an advantage based on innovation creates a uniqueness that the competition does not possess. In 2003 Apple computer introduced the one-inch-thick PowerBook G4™ with a 17-inch monitor. Quite big, but very thin, for a laptop. Competitors have no similar products.

3. *Efficiency*—an advantage based on efficiency reduces products costs and gives the organization more room for price reduction. In the steel industry, clearly NUCOR™ created a lower cost base than competitors. Through efficiency they were able to increase market share by offering their products at a lower cost.

4. *Customer responsiveness*—an advantage created through customer responsiveness focuses on the needs of the product user. GM's ONSTAR™ satellite-controlled system can unlock vehicle doors, if you inadvertently lock your keys in the vehicle, or inform the police of a stolen vehicle's location in real time (i.e., during a police pursuit).

Industry Environment.   Management strategists define the **industry environment** as the competition, products, customers, and any unique characteristics of a particular industry. As you can imagine, the cosmetics industry has a different structure and customer base than those of the automobile industry. By understanding the opportunities and threats presented by its industry, an organization has a head start on developing and fulfilling an effective mission.

Strategic Intent.   **Strategic intent** is the overall meaning or interpretation of actions, behaviors, formal communications, and decisions of an organization's decision makers. Strategic intent is a signaling communication. Strategic intent informs organizational stakeholders about what to expect from the organization in the future. For example, GM executives may indicate, in several different forums, that they expect to increase the company's domestic automobile market share by 5 percent over the next decade. This information alone may not indicate true strategic intent. It is information about what they would like to see happen in the future. However, the perspective changes when we know that GM plans to form strategic alliances with Suzuki to manufacture diesel engines, carry out major redesign of many models by 2007, and eliminate the Oldsmobile division. It's the sum of all these actions, along with formal communication, that signals the true strategic intent of the organization.

Strategic Thinking.   Strategic thinking moves beyond formal planning methods and techniques. As critics have observed, formal planning is often more mechanical than truly insightful or innovative. **Strategic thinking** refers to the mental ability of a strategic manager to synthesize competitive implications of diverse information. To be useful, strategic thinking must produce strategies that create competitive advantage. Certainly, Michael Dell, Bill Gates, and Jack Welch are examples of people with this ability.

Business Model.   In many people's minds, the concept of a business model is synonymous with the Internet boom of the 1990s. Many Internet start-up companies had less than traditional approaches to business; during that period, investors often ignored business fundamentals in favor of wishful thinking. The **business model** describes the organizational processes an organization intends to use in conducting a viable business. Although it's no substitute for a strategy, the business model is a useful concept when applied appropriately. A reasonable business model should include two components: (1) a *narrative test* that describes what the organization hopes to accomplish; and (2) a *numbers test* that projects financial information based on assumptions about demand and costs. A good business model has a narrative that makes sense, along with the financial numbers that indicate profitability.

ENVIRONMENTAL ANALYSIS PROCESS

Strategic planning is the process of examining the organization's environment, establishing a mission, setting goals and objectives, and developing an operating plan. During the strategic planning process, strategic planners are concerned with the future of the industry and their place in it. In most organizations, strategic planning never ends. The organization is either formulating a new strategy or implementing an existing one, assessing progress, and revising current strategies.

Managers are involved in the strategic planning process in two important ways: (1) By providing information and suggestions relating to their particular areas of responsibility, they can influence the strategic planning process; and (2) by monitoring the process and responding to strategic planning documents, they help ensure not only that their department's role in the strategy is clear but also that their department has resources to support the strategy. Once the strategy has been approved, everything a department does—including the objectives established for its areas of responsibility—should be derived from the strategic plan.

Strategic planning is best conceived as a cyclical process governed by competitiveness, analysis, and innovation. Competitive organizations develop strategic scenarios of the future based on different contingencies. They attempt to anticipate the future and develop alternative responses based on a variety of competitive factors. For example, many firms have five-year strategic plans. If they are competitive, they probably revise the plan every eighteen months to two years.

SWOT Analysis

A strategy, plan, or mission for the future begins with an assessment of the organization's current situation. A systematic, thorough analysis requires attention to four factors: *internal* strengths and weaknesses, and *external* opportunities and threats. Such an analysis is often referred to as a **SWOT analysis** (SWOT is an acronym for Strengths, Weaknesses, Opportunities, Threats). Historically, the SWOT analysis has provided managers with useful signals for strategic change. Exhibit 5.2 is a partial SWOT analysis for Starbucks Corporation. What can you contribute to the breakdown of the four factors?

A company's **strengths and weaknesses** are usually derived from a realistic assessment of financial, human, and other internal resources. The firm's financial assets include cash, securities, receivables, and other tangible resources usually presented on its balance sheet and other accounts. Human resources are not easy to evaluate, yet they are a primary component of modern organizations. Human resources include the ideas, ingenuity, patents, and other intangible yet essential bases for competitiveness that only human beings can bring to an organization. An organization's current skills may not be useful if it makes a strategic move into a different industry requiring a different set of skills. For example, an engineering company that employs many older engineers to develop and design traditional electronics products may not be able to make the transition into the computer networking equipment industry, where electronics engineers have different skills, interests, and experience. In the end, the company may be forced to hire more engineers than originally anticipated in order to acquire the skills necessary for the industry.

EXHIBIT 5.2
SWOT Analysis for Starbucks Corporation

Internal	External
Strengths:	Opportunities:
1. Brand recognition	1. New channels of distribution
2. High-visibility outlets	2. Product extensions (ice cream, candy)
3.	3.
Weaknesses:	Threats:
1. Expensive	1. Saturated market
2. Limited drive-throughs	2. Caffeine product substitutes
3.	3.

Externally, the company's business environment presents both threats and opportunities. An **opportunity** is anything that has the potential to increase the firm's strengths. For example, a pending reduction of trade barriers may allow a firm to increase its business in another country. A **threat** is anything that has the potential to hurt or even destroy an organization. For instance, a change in tax laws may portend ruin for a firm that depends on the tax breaks that are to be eliminated by the change.

With all we've said here about SWOT analysis, there are other methods of strategy planning. A recent approach, called the resource-based theory, suggests that organizations can build on the concept of core competencies by basing their competitive strategy on utilizing their unique resources.[11] The resources should be hard to duplicate, long-lasting, and not substitutable; further, they should create value for the organization and be valued by the customer (e.g., some people like Fords better than Chevys).

Analyzing the External Environment

Key components of an organization's environment include the sociocultural environment, technological developments, economic conditions, political climate, and competitive environment. In the following subsections, we discuss each of these components in more detail.

Sociocultural Environment.   Modern societies are constantly changing. Strategic planners must therefore be able to identify the changing cultural and social conditions in the environment, especially those with potential to influence the organization. Unfortunately, many organizations still fail to consider the effects such changes will have, or underestimate their impact. As noted in Chapter 2, many organizations use a technique known as *environmental scanning* to stay abreast of these changes. This technique, which involves acquiring and using information about events and trends in an organization's external environment, helps managers plan the organization's future courses of action. Research has shown that organizations using this technique focus primarily on the competition, customer, regulatory, and technological sectors of their environment. Information is usually received from multiple, complementary sources.[12]

Another technique used by many firms is **issues management,** which focuses on a single issue. A manager in the organization is often assigned leadership on the issue, and he or she is responsible for making strategic decisions on that issue. In the battery industry, for example, a firm may assign a manager to consider the impact of the organization's product on the physical environment. The manager engaged in issues management will consider sociocultural factors like these: Strategically, how will the company respond to concerns of environmental groups that battery disposal should be regulated by the government? If government regulations were enacted, forecasts indicate that battery cost will double and consumer demand for batteries will decline.

Technological Developments.   Changes in technology can influence an organization's destiny, creating new industries or forever altering existing ones. Consider the impact of the personal computer and the Internet on business transactions over the past fifteen years. Communication and information technologies are also changing the rules of work. Telecommuting, for example, has led to "distributed work"—work activity conducted by teams of people separated from each other in time and space. Management of distributed work processes takes place using advanced communications technologies. Smart managers anticipate technological changes, adapt to their implementation in the workplace, and exploit them for competitive advantage.[13]

Economic Conditions.   Economic activity will be increasingly global and increasingly competitive. Every day, new players enter the worldwide economic game. New alliances form, new trading blocs come into existence, and new rules of fair competition are constantly being drafted and debated. The emerging global economy will create a more complex economic playing field than ever before. Around the world, stock markets run all night. Major investment banks can monitor and issue orders to buy and sell overnight on the international stock markets. Competitive advantage is gained by those firms with satellite and computer links to the world.

The dynamic economic environment further includes global economic considerations, downward cost pressures, and specialization based on resources, location, or knowledge. Due to these forces, managers will need to make a wide variety of strategic adjustments in order to remain competitive in the years ahead. New companies will emerge to satisfy new consumer needs, while other noncompetitive companies will go out of business. This era is based on fast-changing technologies and wireless instant communication making possible new products and services worldwide. It's also an era of employee empowerment and changing global relationships and structures. Traditional ways of doing business are gone forever. If companies are going to achieve success, they must stay abreast of and adapt to changing economic conditions.

Political Climate.   The political climate that propelled the United States to the status of a world superpower no longer exists. Nations of the world no longer need to align themselves with one of two opposing economic giants. The breakup of the former Soviet Union, the breakup of Yugoslavia, and the independence of former Soviet satellites have changed the meaning of the term *allies.* New trading partners and markets become available as politics breaks old bonds and presents opportunities to forge new ones. Business must be prepared for volatile, even revolutionary changes in geographic boundaries, contract and licensure regulations, and limitations on direct investment. As democracy rises around the world, expect much debate and even rancor as many long-oppressed nations finally get an opportunity to flex their political muscles.

Competitive Environment.   For any organization, the external business environment presents a mix of opportunities, constraints, and threats. Before articulating a mission, strategic planners must analyze and evaluate these conditions. The resulting mission statement should be responsive to the organization's competitive environment.

Stakeholder Analysis

An organization's success may be controlled by people outside the organization as much as by those within. For example, a well-designed product may fail in the marketplace if it does not meet the customers' needs. If customers don't buy the product, it really doesn't matter how well it was designed. Because an organization's success is thus affected by its customers, they are viewed as being among its stakeholders. Any group or individual having the potential to influence an organization's ability to achieve its goals and objectives is a **stakeholder.**[14]

Stakeholder analysis puts renewed emphasis on understanding the concerns of the numerous groups involved in achieving an organization's success or failure. All of these stakeholder groups make demands on the organization. In reacting to these demands, the organization develops strategies for managing each group. Many organizations have learned the hard way that ignoring a stakeholder can have disastrous consequences. Reverend Jesse Jackson and Operation PUSH in Chicago targeted Mitsubishi Motors of

America for advertising to African American consumers, yet having few dealerships owned by African Americans. In the end, Mitsubishi Motors agreed to establish more African American–owned dealerships, but not before considerable damage was done to consumer confidence in the company. Organizations have also learned that customers, or stakeholders, come in a variety of forms. There are internal and external stakeholders. One important internal stakeholder who has gone through cycles of neglect in American business is the employee.

Employees.   Whereas the traditional view of strategy suggests that managers and shareholders are a company's most important assets, a customer-focused organization directs attention toward the product user and nonmanagement employees. These stakeholders are critical in defining and adding value to the product or service. Increasingly, organizations are relying upon their own people as the source of new ideas, energy, and creativity.

The only sustainable competitive advantage for a firm in the global marketplace is its human resources. Although cash, equipment, facilities, and infrastructure can be quickly transferred, built, or acquired, human resources are not so easily or quickly developed. Strategic management of employees requires managers to dedicate time, money, and attention to employee training and development. This not only increases workers' value, but enhances their capacity for continuous improvement. In a global market, to allow a workforce to grow stagnant without ongoing training is to invite failure.

The prudent approach is to adopt a long-term strategy, and then build a sensible employee training program to develop skills that can be applied to problems throughout the organization. Employees want training that will help them make progress in their careers, but managers have to recognize that in modern organizations the meaning of *progress* has changed. Career paths in the modern organization often don't follow the traditional "corporate ladder."

Many jobs today involve collecting, organizing, and analyzing information. In short, professional work is knowledge work. To help the modern professional succeed requires not only training but also an organizational structure conducive to continuous learning. The main difference between training and learning is that training is often a group activity; learning is often more effective as an individual activity. Managers who provide both training and a learning environment for employees will create more innovation, better service, and more efficient operations than their competitors.

Customers.   **Customers** are the end users of the organization's products and/or services. For some companies, a variety of customers or groups may use its products and services. For example, a hotel may rent single rooms to walk-in customers, tourists in small groups, or the business manager of a professional organization who secures rooms for thousands of convention-goers. Similarly, a household-goods moving firm may sell its full range of services to corporate clients at a discount for large volume, and at regular rates to single households that use only some of the firm's services (e.g., shipping but not packing of household goods). Careful identification of the firm's customers is essential.

Customers use the goods and services produced by a firm. Many firms are themselves customers of suppliers. Working with suppliers to ensure a steady flow of high-quality raw materials is vital to a firm's overall success.

Suppliers.   Suppliers provide a firm with essential raw materials for its products. Strategic aspects of supplier management include focusing on developing long-term relationships with key suppliers, focusing on building partnerships, continuously improving product quality, and driving down costs. As part of strategic planning, managers devote special attention to eliminating defective parts and to involving the supplier in the design process for the firm's product(s). This type of relationship is the basis of such process innovations as just-in-time manufacturing.

The old purchasing departments have been replaced by a new business concept called supply chain management that treats inbound raw materials strategically. A **supply chain** is a network of suppliers and distributors that procures materials, processes materials into finished products (sometimes this means simply materials handling), and distributes products to customers. Supply chains function in both service and product companies. The supply chain process can be simple or quite complex, depending on the product and the industry. The value-added component of each step in the chain, and the cost of the chain, both need continual monitoring.

Stockholders.   **Stockholders** are those who own a firm's stock and hence own a portion of the company. The traditional view of business in the United States has placed highest priority on satisfying stockholder expectations. Because of the stockholders' exclusively financial interest, that usually meant paying close attention to the quarterly report. The upshot of this focus is a heavy emphasis on short-term profit improvements, often realized at the expense of long-term investment.

In Japan, by way of contrast, stockholders and senior management are the first to suffer in bad business times. The traditional U.S. approach to a downturn in the business cycle has been to lay off workers first while the firm waits for customer demand to return. A 1980 NBC News white paper, "If Japan Can, Why Can't We?" showed how Mazda of Japan, during a sales crisis induced by rising energy costs, assigned engineers to sales jobs—to learn more about the customer—without calling for layoffs.

A major responsibility of corporate management is communicating with stockholders. Perhaps the most effective communicator is the chairman of the investment firm Berkshire Hathaway, Warren Buffett, who is well known for his annual reports to shareholders. In fact, many people purchase Berkshire Hathaway stock just to have an opportunity to read Buffet's messages to stockholders. Good communication from managers to stockholders helps the latter understand a firm's long-term strategy, in turn helping to align stockholders' interests with the strategic interest of the organization.

Community.   The **community** consists of private citizens plus government and other public or regulatory agencies. Traditionally, the community is dependent on the firm; it is grateful for the salaries and taxes it pays and for its use of community suppliers and contractors. Many communities and states offer companies special inducements to bring their production to the community.

We have said that an organization must act in a legal, ethical fashion with each stakeholder; but the community also expects the firm to demonstrate a strong sense of social responsibility. Further, most communities view the firm as needing to make a positive contribution to the community—going beyond the firm's payroll, purchases, and taxes. The strategic quality-based view of the community as a stakeholder must also be considered for the long term.

Limits of Strategic Planning

Strategic planning has it limits due to unexpected events, randomness, and even the weather. Organizations develop elaborate forecasting models that produce information about future demand for a product. But then customer demographics change or a key component of the economy sours—and costs change. Forecasting the future is one method organizations use to reduce uncertainty.

Chaos theory has been applied to numerous scientific disciplines over the past decade, and it has recently been used to understand the dynamics of organizations. Essentially, **chaos theory** says that predictions of the future could be enormously inaccurate due to only slight imprecision in the measurement of existing conditions. Weather phenomena are a good example of chaotic systems. How often have you noticed your local weather forecasters being embarrassingly wrong? Usually, they're wrong because some weather conditions are just too complex to measure with great accuracy. The same is true in today's complex organizations and global economy. Managers like to be able to predict the future so they can better prepare for it; but chaos theory suggests there may be some inherent limitations in an organization's ability to forecast the future accurately. Some theorists have even argued that the long-term future is essentially unknowable. They think managers should view as fiction the elaborate computer-modeled forecasts presented to them. The purpose of such forecasts, these theorists claim, is to allay anxiety rather than perform any genuinely predictive function. On the other hand, chaos theory provides a useful framework for understanding the dynamic evolution of industries and the complex evolution of individual companies within industries. By understanding industries and organizations as complex—perhaps chaotic—systems, managers can build better strategies.[15]

Chaos theory has its advocates, but other less controversial ideas offer others ways of making the future better for the organization. New organizational strategies and structures enable organizations to deal with complexity through constant learning and creativity. As Harvard Business School professor Rosabeth Moss Kanter states, "New organizational models offer the best of both worlds—enough structure for continuity, but not so much that creative responses to chaos are stifled."[16] Changes in the way managers understand their competitive environment are rooted in how they see the business world. Peter Senge suggests that successful organizations are learning organizations. Building a learning organization requires a manager to develop new skills, such as building shared vision, testing mental models, and engaging in systems thinking.[17] Senge's advice may help managers to better adapt to competitive pressures as well as to design an organization that fits the needs of a complex competitive environment.

THREE LEVELS OF STRATEGY: CORPORATE, BUSINESS, AND FUNCTIONAL

No single strategy guides all aspects of organizational activity. Strategy falls into one of three categories: corporate, business or competitive, and functional. A corporate-level strategy is described as a **domain definition** strategy,[18] because corporate strategy integrates complex domains (often multiple industries) in which an organization competes. For example, Altria owns both Philip Morris and Kraft Foods. While the business was built in the tobacco industry, PM formed Altria after acquiring Kraft Foods. Clearly, the tobacco industry faces an uncertain future in the United States but is still quite profitable worldwide. The Kraft acquisition helps ameliorate the risks in the tobacco industry.

Business-level or competitive strategies are referred to as **domain navigational** strategies. Two of the most common strategies in this category are cost leadership and differentiation. Functional-level strategies describe how organizational resources are deployed in each functional area to support the business-level strategy. Common functional areas include production, marketing, accounting, and finance.

Corporate-Level Strategy: The Big Picture

Corporate-level strategy is concerned with how best to achieve an organization's goal consistent with its mission. Organizations often compete in multiple lines of business, with some lines in different industries calling for different strategies. Common corporate strategies are concentration on a single business, diversification, and vertical integration.

Concentration on a Single Business.   An organization using the strategy of concentration on a single business focuses, not surprisingly, on only one business. The surprise is that many organizations fall into this category. For example, Federal Express and Domino's Pizza are companies that focus on only one line of business. Federal Express is in the overnight shipping business, and Domino's is in the carry-out, freshly made pizza business. The benefits of concentration derive primarily from focusing all corporate energies in one area. But that same benefit can be a disadvantage, because all the company's "strategic eggs" are in one basket. Any economic downturn in the industry can immediately affect companies following this strategy.

Diversification.   **Diversification** strategies are employed when a firm competes in more than one industry. Each industry has it own structure and warrants a separate strategy. **Related diversification** occurs when an organization diversifies into similar industries, products, and/or infrastructures. Del Monte in the preserved food industry is a good example of related diversification. Del Monte owns vegetable processing facilities, a glass jar company, and a snack food company. All these industries are related to their core products. **Unrelated diversification** describes the situation where the organization moves into an industry unrelated to its core business. Large global conglomerates fall into this category. Hitachi Corporation makes consumer electronics, power tools, and computers. It diversifies either by acquiring or merging with another company.

Vertical Integration.   **Vertical integration** is a strategy that seeks to gain cost advantage by owning members of the supply chain; it occurs through acquisition. In an industry with few stages of production from raw material to finished goods, vertical integration makes sense. It affords greater access to limited raw materials, allows greater control over costs, and ensures a higher level of product quality. Because all stages of production are in-house, vertical integration also makes customizing the product easier. The major disadvantage is that the purchaser's own production process becomes obsolete.

The Portfolio Matrix Model.   Portfolio analysis—evaluating an organization's current mix of products and businesses—is useful in developing corporate-level strategy. The Boston Consulting Group (BCG) developed the Portfolio Matrix to help large diversified organizations strategically manage their holdings. For example, the Coca-Cola Company manufactures, markets, and distributes more than 300 beverage brands worldwide. Some brands will succeed; others will fail. Along the way, Coke's strategic managers must decide what to do with each brand.

The dominant business on which a company has built its success, for example Coke at Coca-Cola, may generate substantial cash that affords the opportunity to expand into other profitable areas. According to the BCG, organizations use portfolio analysis to make strategic decisions across multiple lines of business.

Strategic Business Units.   The first step in the BCG approach is to identify each division, product line, and so forth that can be considered a business. These are the **strategic business units (SBUs)**. An SBU is a product or service division within a company that establishes goals and objectives in harmony with the firm's overall mission and is responsible for its own profits and losses. Each SBU has four characteristics:

- SBU has a distinct mission.
- SBU has its own competitors.
- SBU is a single business or collection of businesses.
- SBU can be planned for independently of the other businesses of the total organization.

Thus, depending on the organization, an SBU could be a single product, product line, division, department, or agency. Once managers have identified and classified all the SBUs, they need some method of measuring their performance. This is the important contribution of the BCG approach.

An organization following the BCG approach would classify SBUs using the BCG Portfolio Matrix (see Exhibit 5.3). The matrix depends on two business indicators of strategic importance: market growth rate and relative market share. **Market growth rate** refers to the annual rate of growth of the market in which a product, division, or department is located. The **relative market share** indicates an SBU's market share. As you can see in the exhibit, this indicator ranges from a high to low relative share of the market. Based on these two indicators, BCG has identified four distinct SBU classifications:

- **Star** An SBU that has a high share of a high-growth market is considered a star. Stars need a great deal of financial resources because of their rapid growth. When growth slows, they become cash cows and important generators of cash for the organization. For example, Ford's acquisition of Jaguar and revitalization of the brand ultimately recreated the cachet of the old Jaguar nameplate. Although it's a high-profit star today, it could have easily been a failure without the proper strategic guidance, resources, and customer acceptance of the final Jaguar product.
- **Cash Cow** An SBU that has a high share of a low-growth market is labeled a cash cow. They produce a lot of cash for an organization; but, since the market isn't growing, they require less of a company's financial resources for growth and expansion. The company can thus use the money generated by its cash cows to satisfy current debt and to support SBUs in need of cash. The Coca-Cola soft drink is the cash cow of the Coca-Cola Company. The firm has been able to use the cash generated through Coke sales to buy Fruitopia, Minute Maid, Dasani, and so on.

EXHIBIT 5.3
BCG Portfolio Matrix

Market growth			
	High	STAR Build	QUESTION MARK Harvest/Divest
	Low	CASH COW Hold/Harvest	DOG Harvest/Divest
		High	Low

Relative market share

- **Question mark** When an SBU has a low share of a high-growth market, it is identified as a question mark in the Portfolio Matrix. The organization must decide whether to spend more financial resources to build it into a star, phase it down, or just eliminate it altogether. Such SBUs frequently require high amounts of resources just to maintain their share, let alone increase it. We mentioned Ford's purchase of Jaguar in the star example. Had the market for luxury cars faltered temporarily or had Ford made decisions that affected the profitability of Jaguar, the Jaguar might easily have been reclassified as a question mark.

- **Dog** When an SBU has a low share of a low-growth market, it's classified as a dog. A dog may generate enough cash to maintain itself, or it may drain money from other SBUs. The only certainty is that dogs are not great sources of cash. In the late 1990s, for example, Time Warner made a strategic move to acquire America Online. It was a disaster—in 2002, AOL lost a phenomenal $100 billion. For Time Warner, the AOL merger represented both a product and a distribution vehicle for the delivery of digital products to consumers. Following the old salesman's adage of "beating a path to the customer's door," Time Warner was buying a digital pathway to contemporary consumers. While their strategic intent was consistent with the time, the AOL component quickly became a continual cash drain; over the past year, their combined stock has lost most of its value.

Depending on whether an organization's SBUs are products, product lines, or entire divisions, its portfolio matrix will include various combinations of the preceding four classifications. After completing the relevant classifications, the organization faces some strategic choices.

Strategic SBU Choices.   Any organization that operates in multiple industries or has multiple products can be analyzed using the BCG Portfolio Matrix. This technique enables managers to subject each SBU to some tough questions. If you go back to Exhibit 5.3, you can see the four alternative strategies that can be selected for each category of SBU.

- *Build* If it seems that an SBU has the potential to be a star (it's probably a question mark at present), the organization would want to build that SBU. The organization may even decide to give up short-term profits to provide the necessary financial resources to achieve this objective. A firm should also build its current stars.

- *Hold* If an SBU is a successful cash cow, a key objective would certainly be to hold or preserve the market share, so that the organization can take advantage of the positive cash flow.

- *Harvest* This strategy is appropriate for all SBUs except those classified as stars. It focuses on increasing the short-term cash return without too much concern for the long-run impact. It's especially worthwhile when more cash is needed for investment in other businesses.

- *Divest* Getting rid of SBUs with low shares of low-growth markets is often a good move.

SBUs can, and often do, change their position in the portfolio matrix. As time passes, question marks may become stars, stars may become cash cows, and cash cows may become dogs. In fact, as the market growth rate changes, an SBU can move through every category. The industry's technology and competitiveness influence how quickly these changes occur. This market fluctuation underscores (1) the importance and usefulness of viewing an organization based on its SBUs and (2) the necessity of constantly seeking new ventures as well as managing existing ones.

With all we've said about the BCG approach, be aware that it's not perfect. Some critics have pointed out that although strategy exists at the corporate, business, and functional levels, the BCG model is most useful at the corporate level. Further, portfolio analysis often leads an organization to neglect some of its SBUs. For example, a cash cow seldom receives additional resources, because its primary purpose is to generate cash; and classifying an SBU as a dog may be a self-fulfilling prophesy when by its very definition there seems little reason to support it. Some critics are concerned that the portfolio matrix model may encourage bureaucratic aspects of planning rather than strategic thinking. Another major criticism of the model centers on its focus on market share and market growth as the primary indicators of profitability. One study found that using the BCG Portfolio Matrix actually decreased managers' ability to choose the more profitable project. Researchers Scott Armstrong and Roderick Brodie surveyed managers in six countries over a five-year period, and found that of those managers who used the BCG Portfolio Matrix in analyzing which SBUs to invest in, 87 percent selected the less profitable investment.[19]

Another criticism to bear in mind when using the BCG matrix is that it's a 2-by-2 matrix, which is the simplest form of array on which the value of more than one variable can be plotted on each of more than one axis. An important reason for the popularity of this matrix seems to be that any concept worth using in the world of business has to be reducible to a fairly brief and simple form. Thus, for simplicity's sake, many complex concepts are often reduced to a 2-by-2 matrix. But the apparent simplicity of the 2-by-2 matrix is both a strength and weakness. When it's used to display concepts thoughtfully distilled from the real world, it can be very powerful. When employed to explain a situation whose considerable complexity must fit into only four boxes, it can be dangerously misleading. All these criticisms are valid; but thanks to the power of the BCG model for assessing SBU strategic positioning, it is used extensively by managers across all industries.

For better or worse, many organizations today believe that they must be involved in e-commerce in one form or another. Firms typically achieve this objective by acquiring an Internet company. In the late 1990s, leveraged buyouts, mergers, and acquisition activity centered on Internet companies. Building an Internet presence seemed to many organizations paramount to future economic success. It turned out that many Internet companies never made a profit. Bookseller Amazon.com, for example, struggles to this day to maintain profitability. One solution offered by researchers is to use portfolio analysis when assessing the viability and fit of potential acquisitions to a portfolio of investments.[20] Portfolio analysis is still a viable strategic tool for achieving a balanced investment of corporate resources.

Business-Level Strategy: Competitive Strategy

Large organizations often compete in several industries or market segments. Each industry or market has its own competitive environment, each of which requires a unique strategy. To navigate its particular industry domain, a business needs its own competitive strategy.

Porter's Five Forces.   Harvard Business School economist Michael Porter[21] has developed several useful frameworks for developing an organization's strategy. One of the most often-cited is the **five competitive forces** that determine industry structure (Exhibit 5.4). Porter states that in any industry, the nature of competition is defined by five competitive forces: (1) threat of new entrants, (2) threat of substitute products or services, (3) bargaining power of suppliers, (4) bargaining power of buyers, and (5) rivalry among existing competitors.

The strength of these five forces varies from industry to industry. However, no matter the industry, these five forces determine profitability because they shape the prices firms can charge, the costs they have to bear, and the investment required to compete in the

EXHIBIT 5.4
Porter's Five Forces Model

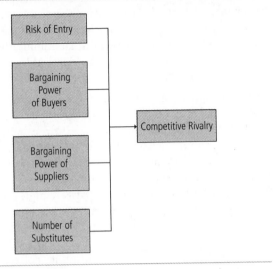

Adapted from: Michael E. Porter. *Competitive Strategy*. New York: Free Press, 1980.

EXHIBIT 5.5
Porter's Competitive Strategies

Cost Leadership	Differentiation
Wal-Mart	Outback Steakhouse products
Focus: Cost Leadership	**Focus: Differentiation**
Briggs & Stratton four-cycle engines	Porsche

industry. For example, the threat of new entrants limits the profit potential in an industry, because new entrants seek market share by driving down prices and thus driving down profit margins. Or, powerful buyers or suppliers bargain away profits for themselves. Before making strategic decisions, managers should use the five forces model to determine the competitive structure of an industry.

Competitive Strategies. According to Porter's competitive strategy model, which is illustrated in Exhibit 5.5, organizations can develop distinctive competence in three ways: cost leadership, differentiation, and focus (emphasizing either cost leadership or differentiation).

- *Cost leadership* Cost leadership is a common strategy for creating value while maintaining a lower than average cost structure. The **cost-leadership strategy** means lower prices for the customer with a higher volume of business, yet lower profit margins on each item for the producer. The cost leader seeks efficiencies in manufacturing or production to maintain a low-cost position. With every gain in efficiency, the cost leader gains the ability to lower prices further while maintaining the lowest cost base in the industry. Examples of cost leaders are Wal-Mart, Aldi (a low-cost wholesale food store), and Harbor Freight Tools.

- *Differentiation* In an effort to distinguish its products, an organization using the **differentiation strategy** offers a higher-priced product equipped with more product-enhancing features than its competitors' products. A firm using differentiation strategy seeks to charge a premium price for its products, and it attempts to maintain high levels of customer loyalty. The firm markets and sells the product to a relatively small group of customers who are willing to pay a higher price for the premium features. This differentiation strategy leads to relatively high cost structure, lower volume production, and a higher gross profit margin per item. The differentiator firm strives for product innovation to maintain its differentiation edge. Often advertising or marketing adds a perception of luxury that creates demand for the product due to the psychological value of buying and using it. Volvo automobiles, Starbucks coffee, and Outback Steakhouse products are marketed under a differentiation strategy.

- *Focus* A firm using the **focus strategy** creates a niche or target market for its product or service. The focus strategy can be achieved by either cost leadership or differentiation. An example of a successful focus strategy based on *cost leadership* is Briggs & Stratton, the ultimate low-cost producer for small, high-quality, four-cycle engines. In the low-cost lawn mower market, Briggs & Strattons appear to be the engine of choice. An equally successful focus strategy based on *differentiation* is Porsche. Porsche fills a niche in the high-end sports car market, sticking to that market with a product that differs significantly enough from their competitors to warrant a premium price.

Functional-Level Strategy: Creating Value

Functional strategies are needed for each value-creating area in the organization. Functional strategies create value by supporting competitive strategies. They are successful to the degree that they actually create value—by taking action that translates into efficiency in the case of cost leadership, or by supporting aspects of product differentiation in the case of a differentiation strategy. Functional strategies create value for the consumer in production, marketing, delivery to the consumer, and post sales service support. For example, the production functional strategy may require a cost-efficient production schedule, building a minimum of 100,000 units per manufacturing run to support cost leadership strategy.

Another competitive analysis framework developed by Porter[22] is known as the value chain. The **value chain** is the sum of all the activities an organization undertakes to create value for a customer. Value can be a measure of quality, speed, or uniqueness. The process of creating value needs to be understood and fostered. Value chain analysis identifies critical strategic processes of an organization that add value to the final product or service. According to Porter, components of the value chain include primary and secondary activities that create value. **Primary activities** include manufacturing the product (or creating the service) and the marketing functions of sales and service, and post sales support.

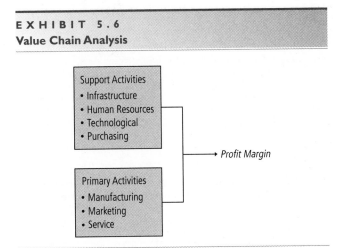

EXHIBIT 5.6
Value Chain Analysis

Support activities include infrastructure, human resources, R&D, and materials management. Exhibit 5.6 shows a typical value chain.

According to Porter, competitive advantage grows from the way firms organize and perform the various activities of their value chain. To gain competitive advantage over rivals, a firm must either provide comparable buyer value and perform the value chain activities more efficiently (reducing costs) than the competition, or it must perform the activities in a unique way that differentiates the product and creates greater value and commands a premium price.

Strategy guides the way a firm organizes its functional areas to support value chain activities. Some companies pursue a cost leadership strategy; others follow a differentiation strategy. Regardless of the strategy, value-creating activities are critical to an organization's success. Profitability follows when the value-creating functions cost less than the price of the product. Successful organizations understand that the value chain helps managers view the organization as an interrelated system. By improving the components of the value chain, managers are building a better organization that creates greater value for the customer. Improvements to the system are usually made by teams of individuals representing the various value-creating functions.

Ford Motor Company, for example, created value in the form of quality (making safety a standard component of quality) and service. The Ford Explorer/Firestone Wilderness AT tire situation altered the value chain. After both companies paid out millions of dollars in litigation, Ford undertook aggressive steps to recover brand equity. To repair the value chain, the auto maker established a bold strategy to reassure the public that Ford Explorer and Expedition vehicles are safe and not prone to rollover accidents. Ford totally redesigned the Explorer with a lower center of gravity and a more car-like responsiveness. To alleviate public concerns about safety, the Ford Expedition also received a makeover, with changes similar to those made in the Explorer. CEO Jac Nassar, and later William Clay Ford, took the lead in communicating the steps Ford was taking to rebuild both product and reputation. At the heart of the message was quality, innovativeness, concern for the customer, and new technology—all aspects of the value creation. Further, this program followed up on Ford's ongoing efforts to reduce excessive car and truck production costs. It's safe to say the Explorer/Firestone tire recall was in part due to the failure at Ford to recognize that the problem was escalating. Many Ford managers knew the Explorer had a tire problem. They knew that it was growing larger with each passing day

---

EXHIBIT 5.7
McKinsey's 7-S Model

Superordinate Goals	Goals should drive all organizational action. Clearly defined and realistic goals communicate strategic intent and serve as a basis for resource allocation and performance assessment.
Strategy	The organization must have a strategy or plan describing the actions that the organization will follow to achieve corporate goals. It should be clear and cause people to take specific action.
Structure	All organizations have a structure. But is the structure supportive of the strategy? The choice of structure should be based on the strategy chosen. Structure should fit the strategy. If it does not, the structure should be changed.
Systems	Systems are the infrastructure of the organization. These include accounting systems, information systems, and administrative systems that define the processing needs of the organization.
Staff	These are the people who work for the organization. Does the organization have the people it needs to achieve the goals of the organization? The organization's Human Resources area is responsible for planning and development needs that are supportive of organizational goals.
Skills	What are the organization's distinctive competencies? The organization should build on skills and competencies it already has in the market. It is less risky for an organization to build successes than to venture into uncharted waters.
Style	Style is a euphemism for culture. Remember that the culture of the organization is created by the CEO. The CEO values and philosophy are reflected in the culture that is created by the policies, decisions, and behavior of the CEO and the top management staff.

but were afraid to speak out for fear of losing their jobs and retirement packages. Ford wants that managerial culture to change. They know now, it is better to catch the problem early in the cycle. Once broken, the value chain can be expensive to fix.

STRATEGY IMPLEMENTATION

Strategy formulation develops a plan for competitive action. Strategy implementation commits the organization's resources, activities, people, and structures to supporting the strategy. Exhibit 5.7 details the 7-S Model developed by McKinsey and Company, a group of international consultants. This model proposes that successful implementation takes the form of a *strategic fit* among the seven key organizational elements outlined.

STRATEGIC PLANNING FOR THE INTERNET

The Internet has transformed business, and no discussion of strategy should ignore this increasingly important technology. Our knowledge economy depends on information and time. Organizations need current information fast and the Internet provides both. Organizations use the Internet in two ways. First, the Internet is *supportive* of ongoing business activities. In a sense, organizations use the Internet to do the same old things. L. L. Bean uses the Internet for an online catalog, order entry, and order fulfillment monitoring. L. L. Bean has merely automated its traditionally manual processes. Second, the Internet is *formative* to the creation of core business activities using the Internet. E*Trade Financial is an example. This firm uses information and software to make stock trades and complete other financial transactions. They have no full-service brokers; all activities are software driven, only rarely requiring human intervention. Most organizations fall into the first category mentioned, where the Internet is supportive of ongoing business activity.

Regardless of how an organization uses the Internet, three criteria drive successful e-commerce: reach, richness, and affiliation.[23] *Reach* means access—who can access your site? *Richness* is a measure of the depth of information available on the site. *Affiliation* concerns who benefits from the site. Increasingly, e-commerce is affiliating with customers rather than taking the more traditional path of affiliating with suppliers. The Internet can be a vital component of an organization's strategy if it integrates each of these three criteria into the sale of its product or service.

Michael Porter takes a more traditional view of the strategy for Internet integration.[24] He believes that the fundamentals of competition remain unchanged. In some cases the Internet may facilitate business, and in others it may be the prime mode of business activity, but it is not likely to create a fundamental shift in competition. Organizations should begin with an e-strategy for the Internet, but ultimately, they must integrate the Internet into a multilevel strategy.

Conclusion
Strategy

Strategic planning helps an organization to reduce risks and efficiently use its resources to achieve organizational goals. Strategic planning is a systematic, rational process of allocating resources in pursuit of organizational goals. The result of the strategic planning process is a *planned strategy*, though not all strategies come to fruition according to plan.[25] Critics note that strategic planning is more than a set of analytical techniques; it must be deeply ingrained in managers charged with the task of developing strategies.[26] Contrary to the very premise of strategic planning, many strategies—rather than following a formal process—actually emerge through a process of interaction between strategic planners, stakeholder negotiations, and environmental pressure from consumer, government, and special interest groups. Strategists might plan for a specific product design; but a competitive response, changing demographics, and societal trends may alter the actual strategy implemented. This emergent strategy makes the strategic management process evolutionary. Because the strategic management process is far more complex and filled with pitfalls than most business analysts care to admit, strategic thinking is a critical skill for successful corporate leaders.

SUGGESTED READINGS

Ghosh, Shirkir. "Making Business Sense of the Internet." *Harvard Business Review*, March–April 1998.

Peng, Mike W. "Institutional Transitions and Strategic Choice." *Academy of Management Review* 28(2): 2003.

Porter, Michael E. "Strategy and the Internet." *Harvard Business Review*, March 2001.

ENDNOTES

1. Charles W. Hofer and Dan Schendel, *Strategy Formulation: Analytical Concepts* (St. Paul, MN: West Publishing, 1978), Chap. 1.

2. Michael E. Porter, "What Is Strategy?" *Harvard Business Review,* November–December 1996, 62.

3. Gregg Dess and G. T. Lumpkin, *Strategic Management: Creating Competitive Advantages* (Burr Ridge, IL: McGraw-Hill-Irwin, 2003), 3.

4. Ibid.

5. Mark L. McConkie and R. Wayne Boss, "Using Stories as an Aid to Consultation," *Public Administration Quarterly,* Winter 1994.

6. "Ford Exec: Camry Better than Taurus; Ford Sales and Marketing Executive Offers Simple Reason Toyota's Sedan Outsells Ford's," Reuters wire, February 13, 2003.

7. Ram Charan, "Execution: The Discipline of Getting Things Done. How Did Honeywell Chairman Larry Bossidy Turn the Company Around? By His Maniacal Focus on Just One Thing," *Fortune,* May 28, 2002.

8. "This Month's Focus: The Mission Statement," *Manager's Magazine,* February 1995, pp. 30–31.

9. C. K. Prahalad and G. Hamel, "The Core Competence of the Corporation," *Harvard Business Review,* May–June 1990, 79–91.

10. Charles Hill and Gareth Jones, *Strategic Management Theory: An Integrated Approach* (Boston: Houghton-Mifflin, 1998), 113.

11. David J. Collis and Cynthia A. Montgomery, "Competing on Resources," *Harvard Business Review,* July–August, 1995.

12. Ethel Auster and Chun Wei Choo, "How Senior Managers Acquire and Use Information in Environmental Scanning," *Information Processing & Management* (September–October 1994): 607–618.

13. Samuel Fromartz, "Extreme Outsourcing: How One Business Owner Set Out to Avoid Having Employees—and Stumbled onto the Way Americans Really Want to Work," *Fortune Small Business,* May 31, 2001.

14. R. Edward Freeman, *Strategic Management: A Stakeholder Approach* (New York: Free Press, 1984), 25.

15. David Levy, "Chaos Theory and Strategy: Theory, Application, and Management Implications," *Strategic Management Journal* (Summer 1994): 167–178.

16. Rosabeth Moss Kanter, "The Best of Both Worlds," *Harvard Business Review,* November–December 1992, pp. 9–10.

17. Peter Senge, "The Leader's New Work: Building Learning Organizations," *Sloan Management Review,* Fall 1990, 7–23.

18. L. J. Bougeois III, "Strategic Management and Determinism," *Academy of Management Review* 9 (1984): 586–596.

19. J. Scott Armstrong and Roderick J. Brodie, "Effects of Portfolio Planning Methods on Decision Making: Experimental Results," *International Journal of Research in Marketing* (January 1994): 73–84. For criticism of this research, see Robin Wensley, "Making Better Decisions," *International Journal of Research in Marketing* (January 1994): 85–90. For Armstrong and Brodie's reply to this criticism, see J. Scott Armstrong and Roderick J. Brodie, "Portfolio Planning Methods," *International Journal of Research in Marketing* (January 1994): 91–93.

20. Anthony Tjan, "Finally, a Way to Put Your Internet Portfolio in Order," *Harvard Business Review*, February 2001.

21. Michael E. Porter, *Competitive Strategy* (New York: Free Press), 1980.

22. Michael Porter, *Competitive Advantage* (New York: Free Press), 1985.

23. Phillip Evans and Thomas S. Wurster, "Getting Real About Virtual Commerce," *Harvard Business Review*, November–December 1999.

24. Michael E. Porter, "Strategy and the Internet," *Harvard Business Review*, March 2001.

25. Richard Hammermesh, "Making Planning Strategic," *Harvard Business Review*, July–August 1986, 3–9; and Henry Mintzberg, "The Rise and Fall of Strategic Planning," *Harvard Business Review*, January–February 1994, 107–114.

26. Henry Mintzberg, "The Rise and Fall of Strategic Planning," *Harvard Business Review*, January–February 1994, 107–114.

Organizing

part three

Chapter Six

Organizational Structure and Design

Organizations are emerging today with much different structures from those of yesterday. Leading the way are organizations offering quality products, adapting quickly to their customers' demands, and accommodating environmental concerns. Although management theorists don't agree on exactly what is the best type of organizational structure, a picture of a flat, lean, high-performance workplace is emerging. Today the average company is smaller and employs fewer people; the traditional hierarchical organization is giving way to other forms, such as the network of specialists; the model of doing business is shifting from making a product to providing customer service; and work itself is being redefined to include constant learning and more high-order thinking.

In this chapter we present the basic elements of organizing. We'll begin by discussing the concept of organizing and organizational structure. Then we examine four decisions managers make in determining organizational structure: specialization of jobs, delegation of authority, departmentalization, and span of control. Next, we explore the dimensions of organizational structure—formalization, centralization, and complexity. In the final section we cover organizational design, including mechanistic and organic models, the contingency approach, and other systems.

ORGANIZING AND ORGANIZATIONAL STRUCTURE

Organizing is the process of structuring both human and physical resources to accomplish organizational objectives. Thus organizing involves dividing tasks into jobs, delegating authority, determining the appropriate bases for departmentalizing jobs, and deciding the optimum number of jobs in each department.[1]

Developing a responsive organizational structure is one of the most critical challenges facing managers today. Large companies like Home Depot, Southwest Airlines, and Microsoft, despite their size, have succeeded because their organizations are nimble and respond quickly to changes in the market. Many managers recognize that their organization is not responsive or flexible, that it doesn't move quickly when it must. But these same managers often attribute this problem to people—departments that cannot get along, uncommitted or unmotivated employees, or the inability to develop quality products in a timely fashion. These are clear symptoms of problems with organizational structure.

Organizational structure is the framework of jobs, departments, and divisions that directs the behavior of individuals and groups toward achieving the organization's objectives. The contribution of organizational structure to an organization's performance is demonstrated each time a customer is satisfied. When customers are not satisfied, chances are great that the fault is with the organizational structure. Thus organizational structure provides an orderly arrangement among functions, so that an organization's objectives can be accomplished effectively. Although the organizing function refers to decisions managers make, organizational structure reflects the outcomes of these decisions.

Organizational structure must be consistent with an organization's strategy. Strategic planning specifies *what* the organization will accomplish and *when;* organizational structure specifies *who* will accomplish what, and *how* it will be accomplished. Many organizations, unfortunately, try to implement a new strategy with an obsolete organizational structure. The result becomes the failed "initiative of the month." For instance, an organization may recognize a need to be "more market driven" or "more quality conscious." The result is a new program for customer satisfaction or quality improvement. But an organization doesn't become quality conscious simply by deciding to. Rather, it must develop an organizational structure that results in the behaviors that the strategy calls for.

Strategy Supports Organizational Structure

An effective organizational structure does not result from chance, luck, or historical accident. It is the responsibility of management to deliberately develop a structure that enhances the organization's overall strategy, taking into consideration factors such as competition and the environment. Managers, in attempting to implement a new program or directive, often encounter resistance to change. Over time, organizational structures become quite ingrained and resistant to change. This behavior is not consistent with an environment that is constantly changing, and it can place an organization in a weak position relative to competitors. To keep in step with the constantly changing environment, many organizations find themselves reorganizing on a regular basis.

Managers must also recognize that there is no single best structure for an organization. What works at IBM may be different from what works at Apple or Compaq. The challenge managers face is to design the best structure for a specific organization—the structure that facilitates getting work done well. If structure actually impedes employees from completing work and hence helping to achieve the organization's objectives, the structure may be incompatible with the strategy. If a bank teller cannot respond to a customer's request due to lack of authority, there is a problem in the bank's structure. Likewise, if an assembly line worker does not have the knowledge or ability to perform a job effectively, the company has a problem in its structure. Often employees can't do their best work because the organization's structure gets in their way.

Detecting Problems in Organizational Structure

When is organizational structure a problem? Ultimately, whenever work is not getting done well, there's likely to be a problem with organizational structure. Many factors or circumstances account for such problems. Conflicts between departments or groups within an organization suggest a structure problem. These conflicts may result from personality differences, but more often they are attributable to differences in the departments' goals. For example, the marketing department is most concerned with sales and introducing new products, whereas the production department is concerned with quality control. Difficulty in coordinating work between departments, slowness in adapting to change, and ambiguous job assignments also indicate problems with organizational structure. If employees are asking which goals are most important or what work to concentrate on, organizational structure may be the underlying problem.

Structure problems can be disastrous for an organization. First, the organization becomes a collection of departments or independent groups pursuing their own goals rather than a coherent organization with a common goal. Second, the organization's structure begins to dictate its strategy rather than strategy dictating structure; in short, its structure is determining what the organization does. This situation violates an important principle of management: strategy should dictate structure. Finally, if structure is allowed to determine strategy, only strategies compatible with the existing organizational structure are acceptable. This approach severely limits the strategies that an organization can pursue effectively; it especially limits efforts toward innovation and change.

Perhaps the greatest influence on how workers perceive their work and how they behave is organizational structure. It is management's job to design an organizational structure that enables employees to do their best work and achieve the organization's objectives. In the next section we'll examine the fundamental considerations or decisions that determine organizational structure.

DETERMINING ORGANIZATIONAL STRUCTURE

Most of us have worked in some type of organization, and we tend to think of structure in narrow terms: What is our own job task? To whom do we report? How much responsibility do we have? Managers responsible for designing organizational structure must think in much broader terms that describe the entire structure itself, not just the jobs that comprise it. Structure is a strategic choice; in determining which type of structure enables people to do their best work, managers make many decisions. The four major decisions pertain to specialization of jobs, delegation of authority, departmentalization, and span of control.

Exhibit 6.1 summarizes the choices managers can make regarding these decisions. In general, the structure of an organization falls on the same part of each continuum. In other words, an organization structured for workers to do highly specialized jobs will also tend to group jobs according to homogeneous or common functions, and assign to managers

---

EXHIBIT 6.1
Designing Organizational Structure

Specialization of jobs

High _____ Low

Delegation of authority

Centralized _____ Decentralized

Departmentalization

Homogeneous _____ Heterogeneous

Span of control

Narrow _____ Wide

---

only a few workers with little authority. In the following sections we examine each of these decisions in greater detail.

Specialization of Jobs

One of the manager's major decisions is determining how specialized jobs will be. Most organizations consist to some degree of specialized jobs—work is divided into specific jobs having specific tasks. By dividing tasks into narrow specialties, managers gain the benefits derived from division of labor: minimum training is required for jobs consisting of only a few tasks, economic gains are obtained when employees become highly efficient in those tasks, and the result is better-quality output.

Scientific Management versus Craftsmanship.   Frederick W. Taylor, a leading proponent of specialization, did much of his work in the late 1800s and early 1900s.[2] For further discussion of this period in management history, refer to Appendix A. The environment then was characterized by a smokestack economy of assembly lines and blue-collar workers—many of whom were unskilled and could not speak English. Taylor's system, the catalyst for the scientific management movement, required that tasks be broken down into their smallest elements and that problem solving be elevated to managers. Taylor, through his time and motion studies, identified basic movements that minimized effort and maximized the output of lathe operators, ironworkers, and bricklayers. This system has permeated our entire society. Specialization now applies to employees as diverse as airline pilots, nurses, and accountants. People learn a job routine and repeat the tasks over and over. If they experience problems, they must consult a supervisor or manager. Work, or execution, is clearly separate from thinking or planning.

Craftsmanship is basically the opposite of scientific management. The craftsman produces a product from start to finish, by working alone or cooperatively in a small group; management provides only the means and facilities. Craftsmanship produces high-quality products but is expensive and results in low output. It's not hard to understand why scientific management replaced the craftsmanship system, which for many years was considered its only alternative. According to quality expert Joseph Juran, "Taylor's concept of separating planning from execution fitted our culture and, at the time, was very logical. You had a lot of immigrants . . . some of them were completely illiterate. And they were in no position, in his [Taylor's] opinion, to make decisions on how work should be done."[3]

The strengths and weaknesses of scientific management versus craftsmanship are summarized in the following Management Highlight.

MANAGEMENT HIGHLIGHT Scientific Management versus Craftsmanship		
	Scientific Management	**Craftsmanship**
Strengths	High productivity	High skill
	Lower cost	High-quality output
	Higher wages	Pride in work
	Unskilled workers	High job interest
	Predictable scheduling	Control by worker
Weaknesses	Low morale and boredom	Low productivity
	Poor quality	Higher cost
	Lack of pride	Lower wages
	Low job interest	Poor control
	Control by managers	Scheduling problems

As we noted earlier, many people think of organizational structure in relation to their own jobs. Specialization has in some instances inspired a "that's not my job" attitude, which has seriously hurt some organizations. The system that worked so well after World War II—when America flooded the world market with affordable domestic products—is not as effective in today's complex global economy. Many organizations are searching for alternative approaches.

Teams and Quality Circles.   Japan was the first nation to realize that the scientific management approach to specialization would work only in an expanding market. Once markets began to shrink, Japanese firms made quality an issue and invaded markets that for years were thought to be untouchable. Basically the Japanese approach was to attack what they called *Taylorism*. It seems somewhat unfair to give Taylor sole credit for the entire system of scientific management since others took part in its development. But the Japanese identified Taylor's concepts of time and motion with their failures: high absenteeism, low morale, and poor-quality output. While some parts of the world were experiencing the benefits of specialization, Japan was experiencing its disadvantages. Other nations are now experiencing these same disadvantages and will also have to make changes if they hope to prosper.

Many organizations are modifying and redesigning jobs so that they can be performed by teams.[4] The most popular type is a **problem-solving team,** comprised of knowledgeable workers who gather to solve a specific problem and then disband. A **work team** is a group of employees who work closely together to pursue common objectives.[5] Some organizations become team-based, using teams throughout the organization on a regular basis; others use teams more selectively. Some teams are directed by a manager, whereas others are self-managed. The idea behind self-managed work teams is for workers to become their own managers, which increases reliance on their creative and intellectual capabilities besides their physical labor. At W. L. Gore & Associates—a manufacturer of a wide range of electronic, medical, fabric, and industrial products—"associates" (the term *employee* is not used) work on self-directed teams without managers or bosses.[6] Regardless which kind of team is used, teams can move swiftly, flexibly, and effectively to produce innovative products. Team members learn each others' jobs and bring their ideas together, capitalizing on workers' creativity. When truly empowered, a work team can change bored and demoralized workers into innovative and productive partners.

Quality circles are based on the belief that the people who work with the process are best able to identify, analyze, and correct the problems in any given situation. The quality circle concept originated in Japan in 1962, and Japanese firms expanded it into a highly developed system. A **quality circle** is a small group of people, usually fewer than ten, who do similar work and meet about once a week to discuss their work, identify problems, and present possible solutions.[7] Participation in the circle is voluntary, and the workers establish a moderator or team leader to lead discussions. The group's findings and proposals are forwarded to management.

American firms began using quality circles in the mid-1970s, and the concept grew in popularity over the next fifteen years. Unfortunately, because they were merely adaptations of the scientific management system, some efforts to use quality circles failed. The aim of managers in some cases was to increase the productivity of workers, who refused to cooperate. But these failures resulted from how the approach was used rather than from flaws in the approach itself. Quality circles cannot simply be "installed" in an organization. The concept has been most successful when used as part of an organization-wide improvement effort.

The extent to which jobs are specialized is a critical managerial decision. The important point here is that jobs vary considerably along the dimension of specialization. By changing the degree to which jobs are specialized, managers change the structure of the organization. In Chapter 7 we'll discuss job design in further detail.

Delegation of Authority

When designing an organizational structure, managers must also consider the extent to which authority will be distributed throughout the organization. **Authority** is the organizationally sanctioned right to make a decision. Managers delegate (assign) certain tasks to others, simply because one person cannot get all the work done. When delegating authority, managers must weigh the pros and cons of decentralization and centralization and strike an appropriate balance for the organization.

Decentralization and Centralization.   Authority can be distributed throughout the organization—or held in the hands of a few. **Decentralization** is the process of distributing authority throughout the organization. It delegates an organization member (historically a manager) the right to make a decision without obtaining approval from a higher-level manager. The authority to identify problems or issues and recommend solutions is delegated as well. In the strictest sense, decentralization represents one end of a continuum (Exhibit 6.1) in which the authority to make decisions is shared with all members of the organization. At the other extreme, **centralization** is the process of retaining authority in the hands of high-level managers, who make all the decisions.

Decentralization has several advantages. Managers develop their own decision-making skills and are motivated to perform because advancement is related to performance. Managers can also exercise more autonomy, which increases job satisfaction and motivation, contributing to the organization's profitability. Hewlett-Packard attributes much of its success to decentralization, through which people and power were moved away from headquarters. Some experts think Nike's recent turnaround—for the first time in a decade, the firm experienced double-digit profit growth—began when cofounder Philip Knight delegated day-to-day control of the company.[8] Decentralization also has some disadvantages. It requires costly management training, and organizations can end up employing highly paid managers. Delegation also leads to extensive (and often stifling) planning and reporting procedures. Some managers find it difficult to make decisions, even though they have the authority, because the methods used to measure accountability are time-consuming and instill fear in the managers.

Some organizations have begun to empower workers to make decisions that typically have been made by superiors. **Empowerment** involves giving employees who are responsible for hands-on production or service activities the authority to make decisions or take action without prior approval.[9] For instance, a machine operator can stop production when a problem is detected, or a ticket agent can give a customer a refund without calling the supervisor. Earlier, in talking about decentralization, we referred to delegating authority to other managers. Empowerment means that production, process control, and quality assessment become part of everyone's job: all individuals are given the ability and authority to take positive actions that will lead to high quality and performance. At Federal Express, for example, "all workers are routinely expected to take whatever initiative is required to fix problems and/or extend first-rate service to a customer."[10]

Chain of Command.   The delegation of authority creates a **chain of command,** the formal channel that defines the lines of authority from the top to the bottom of an organization (Exhibit 6.2). As you can see, the chain of command is a series of superior–subordinate relationships from the highest position in the organization to the lowest.

EXHIBIT 6.2
Chain of Command

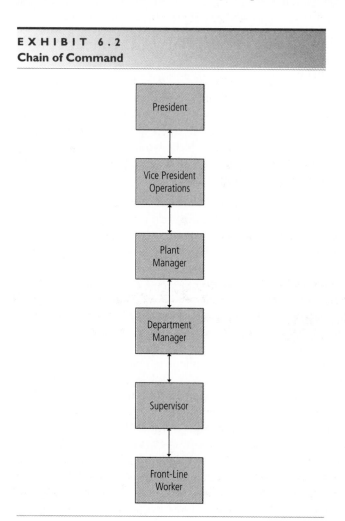

EXHIBIT 6.3
Differentiating between Line and Staff Positions

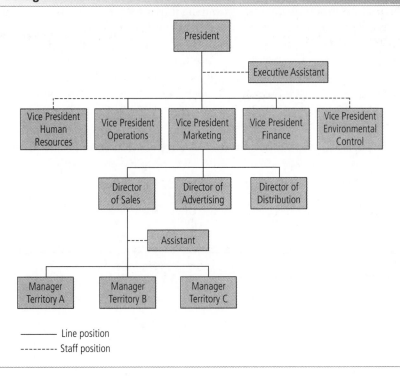

The chain of command is the communication link among all positions in the organization. It specifies a clear reporting relationship for each person in the organization and should be followed in both downward and upward communication. Generally, no individual should report to more than one supervisor.

Line and Staff Positions.   The chain of command includes both line and staff positions. A **line position** is in the direct chain of command and contributes directly to achieving the organization's goals. In Exhibit 6.3 the president; the vice presidents of operations, marketing, and finance; the directors; and the sales managers are in line positions. **Staff positions** facilitate or provide advice to line positions. In Exhibit 6.3, the executive assistant, the vice presidents of human resources and environmental control, and the assistant to the director of sales are considered staff positions because they provide support to others.

Departmentalization

Departmentalization is the process of grouping jobs according to some logical arrangement. As organizations grow in size and as job specialization increases, it becomes more complex to determine how jobs should be grouped. In a very small organization like a mom-and-pop grocery store, the owner can supervise everyone. In a large grocery chain, managerial positions are created according to some plan so that the organization can run smoothly. As we said earlier, some jobs are so specialized that they are unhealthy; this issue, as we will see, is changing the way organizations group jobs. The most common bases for departmentalization are function, product, customer, and geographic.

Functional Departmentalization.   Grouping jobs together according to organizational functions is called **functional departmentalization.** Generally, businesses include functions such as production, finance, marketing, research and development, and human resources (Exhibit 6.4). The major benefit of this approach is that it establishes departments based on experts in a particular function, taking advantage of specialization. But specialization does not encourage communication across departments. Functional departmentalization works best when an organization faces a stable environment, and when tight control over processes and operations is desired.

Product Departmentalization.   **Product departmentalization** groups jobs associated with a particular product or product line. It enables people working with a particular product to use their skills and expertise. Exhibit 6.5 illustrates how an organization groups jobs on this basis. Large organizations such as General Motors and Procter & Gamble have used this approach. The product manager may also draw on the resources of other organization

EXHIBIT 6.4
Functional Departmentalization

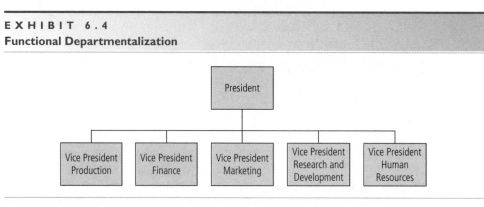

EXHIBIT 6.5
Product Departmentalization

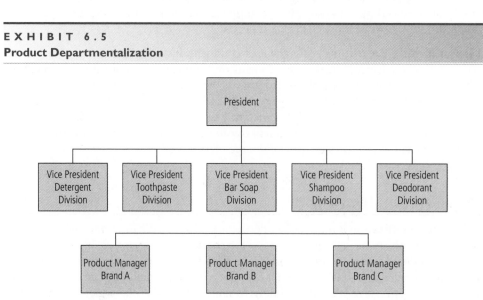

members. Product departmentalization gives an organization the flexibility to develop specific strategies for different products and to grow or make acquisitions with relative structural ease. It has also been used by managers of multinational corporations with diversified product lines. But this type of grouping is expensive because it requires a manager for each product and runs the risk of duplicating effort among divisions.

Customer Departmentalization.   Organizations using **customer departmentalization** (Exhibit 6.6) group jobs in a manner that will serve customers' needs. Organizations that have extremely large customers, or those serving diverse groups, are most likely to use this approach. For example, a firm that sells defense systems to the government may group jobs based on customers. Banks typically departmentalize on the basis of consumer and commercial accounts. Customer departmentalization can be a costly method of grouping jobs if a large staff is required to integrate the activities of several different departments.

Geographic Departmentalization.   Grouping jobs based on defined territories is called **geographic departmentalization** (Exhibit 6.7). Such a structure is useful when an organization is widely dispersed and its customers' needs and characteristics vary greatly; organizations can respond to unique customer needs in the various regions more quickly. Geographic departmentalization is the most common form used by multinational corporations (MNCs). Its major drawback is that it usually necessitates a large headquarters staff to manage the dispersed locations.

Mixed Departmentalization.   As an organization evolves over time, it may use more than one method to group jobs. **Mixed departmentalization** involves grouping jobs using more than one basis. Exhibit 6.8 illustrates how a bank might mix product, customer, and geographic departmentalization. In reality, most organizations group jobs using multiple bases.

The Matrix Organization.   The matrix design attempts to capture the strengths and reduce the weaknesses of both the functional and product designs. A **matrix organization** is a cross-functional organization overlay that creates multiple lines of authority and places people in teams to work on tasks for a finite period of time.[11] The functional departments are the foundation, and a number of products or temporary departments are

EXHIBIT 6.6
Customer Departmentalization

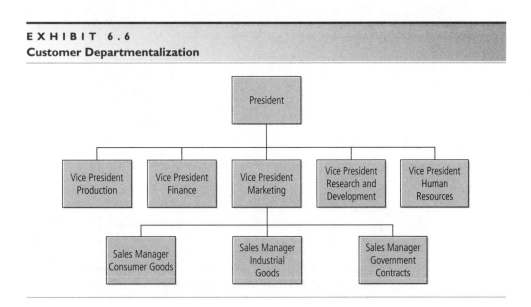

EXHIBIT 6.7
Geographic Departmentalization

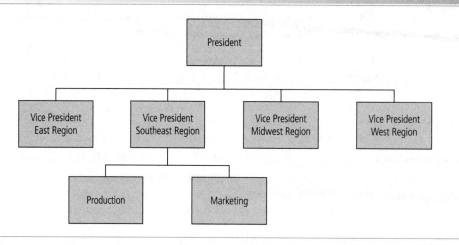

EXHIBIT 6.8
Mixed Departmentalization

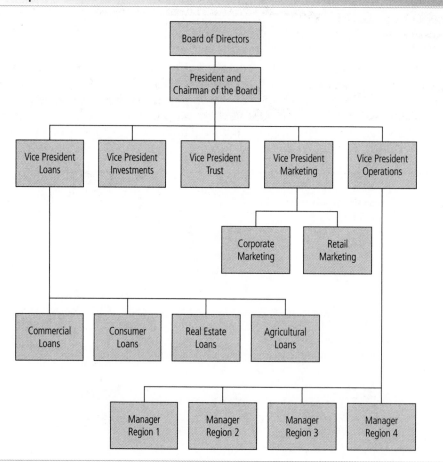

superimposed across the functional departments. The result (Exhibit 6.9) is a dual, rather than singular, line of command. Although the matrix organization was first developed in the aerospace industry, it is now used in all types of organizations, both private and public.

As Exhibit 6.9 shows, individuals or groups in each cell report to two managers. For instance, someone working in marketing on Product A would report to the Vice President of Marketing and Product Manager A. This arrangement is useful in speeding up innovation because each person's primary responsibility is to help produce what the organization sells. The key is to free people from bureaucratic constraints by empowering them to create winning ideas and products, while at the same time providing the structure needed to be successful.[12] Frigidaire Co., owned by Swedish-based Electrolux since 1986, uses a matrix organization that functions as a team and focuses attention on the consumer. The matrix organization has helped Frigidaire to become increasingly competitive, flexible, and market-driven.[13]

Matrix organizations have increased in popularity as organizations have decentralized and adopted project management concepts. They are most appropriate when coordination is needed in complex and uncertain environments.[14] Matrix organizations lead to efficient use of a specialized staff, offer timely response to a changing environment, enable technical specialists to interact with each other, free top-level management from day-to-day activities to spend more time planning, and encourage individual growth and development.[15] Since product or project groups are often employed with the matrix design, many organizations using teams and quality circles adopt this form of organization because of its flexibility and adaptability.

The matrix design has several drawbacks. The matrix can lead to confusion because individuals or groups report to more than one superior. Several bosses may place conflicting

---

EXHIBIT 6.9
The Matrix Organization

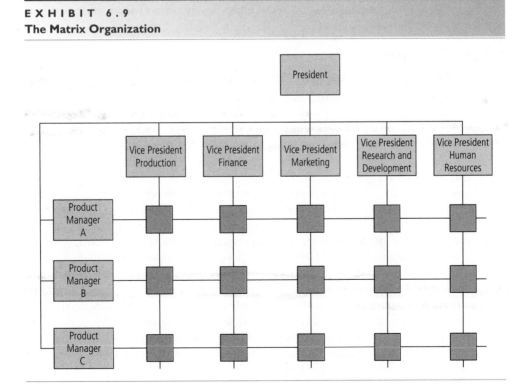

demands on subordinates or struggle with each other for power, placing workers in a compromising position. In some cases, organizations find that groups take longer to make decisions than individuals. The matrix is also costly because additional managers and staff may be needed.[16]

Alternative Forms of Departmentalization.   Because departmentalization reinforces specialization, some organizations are trying to involve everyone in the decision process by breaking down the barriers that often divide departments. Steelcase, Inc., a large manufacturer of office furniture, actually did away with formal departments. People work in multidisciplinary teams that encourage interaction. The physical facilities are also void of departments; they contain areas for teams to work and space for working on special projects. Executives are located in the center of the building, where everyone has equal access to them. This complex change took several years to implement but has been credited with cutting delivery cycles in half and dramatically reducing inventory.[17]

Some firms are abandoning departmentalization altogether and organizing around processes, as opposed to function, product, customer, or geography. **Process organization** involves basing performance objectives on meeting customer needs and identifying the processes that meet those needs. For instance, the processes that meet customer needs may be service quality or new product development. These processes, not departments, are used to organize the company. At Hallmark Cards, jobs are organized around the new product development process, according to specific holidays. There are teams for Christmas, Valentine's Day, and so on. Each holiday team includes artists, writers, lithographers, merchandisers, and accountants. Guided by project management principles, team members come from all over a 2-million-square-foot building so they can work together. Now only one team works on a Mother's Day card; previously the card had to go from one large department to the next. The time it takes to develop new cards is cut in half. Between projects or teams, workers return to their "center of excellence" for training or brief work assignments. Hallmark hopes any remaining signs of department structures eventually will disappear.[18]

Span of Control

Span of control refers to the number of people who report to one manager or supervisor. This is the final decision managers must make in designing organizational structure. The objective is to determine the optimal span of control—wide or narrow. A wide span of control (or flat organization) results in a large number of workers reporting to one supervisor; a narrow span (or tall organization) results in a small number. Exhibit 6.10 compares the two structures. In the first case, two supervisors each direct eight workers; the maximum span of control is eight. There are two levels of management: a president and the two supervisors. In the second case, two department heads each direct four supervisors, and each supervisor directs four workers. The maximum span of control is four, and there are three levels of management: a president, two department heads, and four supervisors.

Although there is no formula for determining the ideal span of control,[19] in the Management Highlight on page 119 we present a set of factors to consider when establishing span of control. Be aware that spans of control could be different for managers at the same level in the same organization, depending on their experience or the nature of the jobs they are supervising. Consistent with some of the trends in organizational structure we have already discussed (teams, quality circles, empowerment, and process organization), many firms are widening their spans of control, with the objective of developing flatter, more responsive organizations in which decisions can be made without needing approval by several levels of management.

MANAGEMENT HIGHLIGHT
Factors to Consider in Determining Span of Control

1. *Competence of both the manager and the subordinates*—the more competent they are, the wider the span of control can be.

2. *Degree of interaction required among the units to be supervised*—the more extensive the required interaction, the narrower the span of control must be.

3. *Extent to which the manager must carry out nonmanagerial tasks*—the more technical and job-related work the manager has to do, the less time is available to supervise others; thus the narrower the span of control must be.

4. *Relative similarity or dissimilarity of the jobs being supervised*—the more similar the jobs, the wider the span of control can be; the less similar the jobs, the narrower it must be.

5. *Extent of standardized procedures* The more routine the subordinates' jobs are and the more each job is performed by standardized methods, the wider the span of control can be.

6. *Degree of physical dispersion*—if all the people assigned to a manager are located in one area and are within eyesight, the manager can supervise relatively more people than if people are dispersed throughout the plant or countryside at different locations.

EXHIBIT 6.10
Wide versus Narrow Span of Control

a. Wide span of control

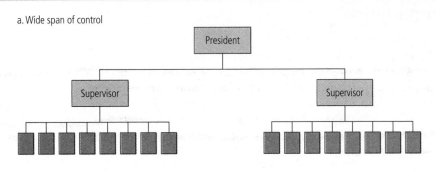

b. Narrow span of control

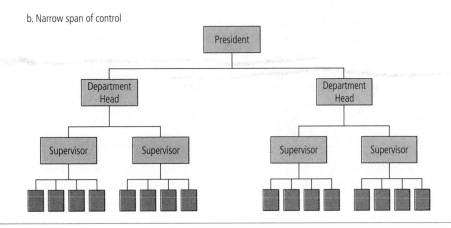

DIMENSIONS OF ORGANIZATIONAL STRUCTURE

The four organizational design decisions we have just discussed—specialization of jobs, delegation of authority, departmentalization, and span of control—determine the structure of organizations. Organizational structure provides the foundation upon which the organization functions. It also dramatically influences performance. Therefore, managers must be concerned with the entire structure and how it influences the organization. Three dimensions have been identified that enable managers to describe and understand the organizations' structure and measure differences between different organizations: formalization, centralization, and complexity.[20]

Formalization

Formalization refers to the extent to which an organization's communications and procedures are written down and filed. A highly formalized organizational structure would be characterized by rules and procedures to prescribe members' behavior. Simple and routine tasks lend themselves to formalization; more complex and nonroutine tasks don't.

In general, organizations characterized by high specialization, little delegation of authority, functional departments, and narrow spans of control are more formalized. Scientific management, then, results in a high degree of formalization, whereas craftsmanship leads to less formalization. In this sense, organizations that empower workers reduce formalization.

Centralization

Centralization, as we said earlier, refers to how much the authority to make decisions is dispersed throughout the organization. In a highly centralized organization, top-level managers retain decision-making authority; in contrast, a highly decentralized organization disperses decision-making authority throughout the operation. Most organizations are neither centralized nor decentralized, but somewhere in between the two extremes.

In relation to the four organizational structure decisions, centralization is the result of high specialization, low delegation of authority, the use of functional departments, and narrow spans of control.

Complexity

High specialization, product departmentalization, customer departmentalization, geographic departmentalization, high delegation of authority, and narrow spans of control result in high complexity. **Complexity** is defined as the number of different job titles and the number of different departments in an organization. As firms grow, divide work, and create more departments, they become more complex. Because of the dissimilarities in the jobs of both individuals and departments, a complex organization is more difficult to manage than one with few job titles and departments.

Organizations differ in how much they're formalized and centralized as well as in their degree of complexity. These differences result from managers' decisions concerning the organization's structure. No single structure is best for a particular organization. The purpose of structure is to reward and encourage behaviors that lead to accomplishing organizational objectives. Regardless of differences in how formalized, centralized, and complex organizations are, the critical issue is whether the organizational structure enables employees to do quality work. Perhaps the most important point is that managers must manage organizational structures over time and make changes in response to the changing environment.

ORGANIZATIONAL DESIGN

In this chapter we have noted that organizational structure is the framework of jobs and departments that directs the behavior of individuals and groups toward achieving an organization's objectives. Structure provides the foundation within which the organization functions, and managers must design an organizational structure that enhances the organization's overall strategy. Managers have many alternatives in developing an organizational structure. **Organizational design** is the process by which managers develop an organizational structure. Since organizational structure is determined by specialization of jobs, delegation of authority, departmentalization, and span of control (see Exhibit 6.1), organizational design includes coordinating these dimensions of organizational structure and deciding the extent to which the organization will be specialized, centralized, and so on.

Two extreme models of organizational design—the mechanistic model and the organic model—have provided much of the framework for understanding organizational design.[21]

The Mechanistic Model

In the early part of the twentieth century, much theory and practice in management was guided by the nature of the work and the existing organizational structure at that time. That is, many organizations, seeking a high production level, relied on unskilled workers. Factory workers were highly specialized, and little authority was delegated. Thus the term **mechanistic organization** describes a rigid organization that attempts to achieve production and efficiency through rules, specialized jobs, and centralized authority.

German sociologist Max Weber used the term *bureaucracy* to describe an organization based on a formal system of legitimate authority.[22] The major characteristics of Weber's bureaucracy describe the mechanistic model:

- Tasks are divided into highly specialized jobs.
- Each task is performed according to a standardized set of rules that ensures uniformity.
- Each member of the organization is accountable to a single manager.
- Business should be conducted impersonally, and managers should maintain a social distance from workers.
- Employment and advancement should be based on technical qualifications, and workers should be protected from arbitrary dismissal.

As you can see, this represents an extreme type of organization—perhaps not the kind in which you have worked or would like to work. It is important, though, to view the mechanistic model as one end of a continuum, with the organic model at the other end. Neither model is the ideal form of organizational design, and most organizations change over time. Later in this chapter we'll look at other forms of more or less bureaucratic organizational design.

The Organic Model

In sharp contrast to the mechanistic model, the **organic organization** seeks to maximize flexibility and adaptability. Whereas the mechanistic model is rigid and bureaucratic, the organic model encourages greater utilization of human potential. The organic model deemphasizes specialization of jobs, status, and rank. Horizontal and lateral relationships are as important as vertical relationships.[23]

The organic organization provides individuals with a supportive work environment and builds a sense of personal worth and importance.[24] Thus managers in this organization encourage and motivate employees to reach their potential. This type of organization tends to be decentralized, and communication flows throughout the organization rather than through the chain of command. Departmentalization would be based on product and customer rather than on function.

The organic model describes a more human organization. You may have already decided that this is the best type of organization, and it may look that way. Earlier in the chapter, however, we said that the best structure is one that facilitates getting the work done well. We also said that structure sometimes interferes with quality work. But this doesn't mean that everything about the mechanistic model is bad in all situations, or that everything about the organic model is good in all situations. Remember, we're describing a continuum. Between these two extremes are many organizational designs—some yet to be discovered.

Contingency Approach

In reality, there is no single best organizational design; you may remember that we identified this myth earlier. Many different circumstances influence the design decision. In some instances the mechanistic design may be more effective, while the organic design may work best in other situations. The **contingency approach** suggests that different organizational designs are more effective in different situations. Managers must examine the different contingencies or circumstances surrounding the situation and select the particular approach that is most effective. The contingencies that influence this decision include technology, environment, and strategy.

Technology and Organizational Design.   **Technology** refers to how tasks are accomplished using materials, equipment, and human resources to develop an organization's output. The organizational design is contingent on the type of technology that is used to convert inputs into outputs. Many studies have examined the relationship between technology and effective design. In general, the mechanistic organization is appropriate for organizations using more routine technologies. Conversely, organizations using more nonroutine technologies generally find the organic structure more appropriate.[25] For example, organizations employing simple technologies such as assembly line manufacturing can be managed through mechanistic design. Organizations that employ more complex technology to customize products for each order can be managed through organic design.

Environment and Organizational Design.   As we noted in Chapter 2, every organization operates in the context of a larger environment. If the environment is considered stable, there is little change in the forces that make up the environment. Some environments are characterized by forces that are changing constantly. If these changes are unpredictable, the environment is considered turbulent. Research has shown that mechanistic organizations are most effective in stable environments, while organic structures are best in changing and turbulent environments.[26]

Strategy and Organizational Design. The strategy an organization pursues also influences the decision regarding its structure. In fact, strategy precedes structure; the organization should first develop strategy and then design a structure compatible with its strategy.[27] If the converse is true—structure determines strategy—only those strategies compatible with the existing structure are pursued. This can limit innovation and the organization's ability to cope with change. Finally, organizations producing a single good or service will find the organic design more compatible. As firms move away from a single product through expansion and diversification, they adopt the mechanistic design.

Other Forms of Organizational Design

Many other forms of organizational design have been developed or are emerging in response to the rapidly changing environment. Increased global competitiveness, decentralization, buyouts and hostile takeovers, and the quality revolution are just a few of the factors causing organizations to search for new designs. In this section, we look at two additional forms of organizational design.

The Multidivisional Organization. The multidivisional (M-Form) organization has emerged in western Europe and the United States during the past fifty years.[28] The multidivisional organization is a high-performance organization whose operating units or divisions are partially interdependent. Thus each division's product is different from that of the other divisions, but all divisions share common endowments such as technology, skill, and information. Hewlett-Packard is divided into fifty semiautonomous divisions, one manufacturing hospital instruments, a second computers, a third handheld calculators, and so on. Each division sells to slightly different customers and uses different manufacturing methods, but all share a common foundation in electrical engineering, use similar manufacturing methods, and depend on a central laboratory to supplement their research.

The M-Form design attempts to strike a balance between autonomy for the divisions and control over them. Its structure represents the ambiguity common in many organizations; that is, each division is partially independent yet partially dependent on the entire organization. IBM found that as a huge, centralized organization it simply could not react fast enough to changes in the competitive marketplace. With the M-Form, each division is expected to operate independently to maximize profits and is sufficiently autonomous to make timely decisions. But the M-Form succeeds only if divisions cooperate on things they share in common. The key is to make sure this cooperation does not stifle a division's creativity and performance. This is the delicate balance between centralization and decentralization.

The Network Organization. A network organization is a flexible, sometimes temporary, relationship between manufacturers, buyers, suppliers, and even customers.[29] The design is dynamic in that the major components can be assembled or reassembled to meet changing competitive conditions. A major advantage of networks is that each member can concentrate on those activities it performs best. In the auto industry, everything from building factories to producing cars is getting cheaper as auto companies quit making parts and concentrate on designing cars. Members are held together by contracts and pursuit of common goals, not by the more traditional hierarchy. The term *virtual corporation* has been used to describe a temporary network of independent organizations, linked by information technology, that come together quickly to exploit fast-changing opportunities.[30] A virtual corporation has neither a central office nor an organization chart; rather, it is a series of partnerships that will more than likely terminate once an opportunity is met. Similarly, a *modular corporation* consists of a hub surrounded by a network of the best suppliers in the world. The hub is the center of activities, such as research and development; the network is made up of outside specialists that make the parts, handle deliveries, and perform accounting activities.

The network organization design is gaining popularity not only in the United States but globally. Part of its appeal, in the global context, is that network members can be added as needed. For example, a firm entering a foreign country for the first time may add a broker or a trading company to the network. Members that are not performing or are no longer needed can be removed. Since members pursue their distinctive competencies, quality is enhanced. Organizations can also eliminate those activities or operations that can be done better by other organizations.

Conclusion
——Organizational Structure and Design——

In this chapter, we introduced the concepts of organizational structure and design. Organizational structure is determined by specialization of jobs, delegation of authority, departmentalization, and span of control. We also discussed the three dimensions of organizational structure: formalization, centralization, and complexity. Organizational design is the process by which organizational structure is developed. The two extremes of organizational design are the mechanistic model and the organic model. The contingency approach to organizational design incorporates technology, the environment, and strategy into the design decision, suggesting that different organizational designs are more effective in different situations.

SUGGESTED READINGS

Coutu, Diane L. "Creating the Most Frightening Company on Earth." *Harvard Business Review,* September–October 2000, 143–150.

Davis, Margaret R., and David A. Weckler. *A Practical Guide to Organizational Design.* Menlo Park, CA: Crisp Publications, 1996.

Galbraith, Jay R. *Designing Organizations: An Executive Guide to Strategy, Structure, and Process.* San Francisco: Jossey-Bass, 2001.

Gibson, Cristina B., and Susan G. Cohen, eds. *Virtual Teams That Work: Creating Conditions for Virtual Team Effectiveness.* San Francisco: Jossey-Bass, 2003.

Hackman, J. Richard *Leading Teams: Setting the Stage for Great Performances.* Boston: Harvard Business School Press, 2002.

Mintzberg, Henry. *Structure in Fives: Designing Effective Organizations.* Upper Saddle River, NJ: Prentice Hall, 1992.

Walker, Carol A. "Saving Your Rookie Managers From Themselves." *Harvard Business Review,* April 2002, 97–102.

ENDNOTES

1. Hugh C. Willmott, "The Structuring of Organizational Structures: A Note," *Administrative Science Quarterly,* September 1981, 470–474.

2. Frederick W. Taylor, *Principles of Scientific Management* (New York: Harper & Row, 1911).

3. Scott Madison Paton, "Joseph M. Juran—Quality Legend: Part III," *Quality Digest,* March 1992, 49–58.

4. Marshall Sashkin and Kenneth J. Kiser, *Total Quality Management* (Seabrook, MD: Ducochon, 1991), 118.

5. Charles Garfield, *Second to None* (Homewood, IL: Business One Irwin, 1992), 164.

6. Frank Shippes and Charles C. Manz, "Employee Self-Management without Formally Designated Teams: An Alternative Road to Empowerment," *Organizational Dynamics,* Winter 1992, 48–61.

7. "The Quality Glossary," *Quality Progress,* February 1992, 20–29.

8. Stanley Holmes and Christine Tierney, "How Nike Got Its Game Back," *Business Week,* November 4, 2002, 129–131.

9. Sashkin and Kiser, 67.

10. Tom Peters, *Thriving on Chaos* (New York: Knopf, 1988), 292.

11. Robert C. Ford and Alan W. Randolph, "Cross-Functional Structures: A Review and Integration of Matrix Organization and Project Management," *Journal of Management,* June 1992, 267–294.

12. Martin K. Starr, "Accelerating Innovation," *Business Horizons,* July–August 1992, 44–51.

13. Richard Jaccoma, "Smart Moves in Hard Times," *Dealership Merchandising,* January 1992, 164–167.

14. Paul R. Lawrence, Harvey F. Kolodny, and Stanley M. Davis, "The Human Side of Matrix Organizations," *Organizational Dynamics,* September 1977, 4.

15. Stanley M. Davis and Paul R. Lawrence, *Matrix* (Reading, MA: Addison-Wesley, 1977).

16. Stanley M. Davis and Paul R. Lawrence, "Problems of Matrix Organizations," *Harvard Business Review,* May–June 1978, 131–142.

17. Garfield, *Second to None,* 4–5.

18. Thomas A. Stewart, "The Search for the Organization of Tomorrow," *Fortune,* May 18, 1992, 92–98.

19. Robert D. Dewar and Donald P. Simet, "A Level-Specific Prediction of Spans of Control Examining the Effects of Size, Technology, and Specialization," *Academy of Management Journal,* March 1981, 5–24.

20. Richard S. Blackburn, "Dimensions of Structure: A Review and Reappraisal," *Academy of Management Review,* January 1982, 59–66.

21. Tom Burns and G. M. Stalker, *The Management of Innovation* (London: Tavistock, 1961).

22. Max Weber, *The Theory of Social and Economic Organization,* trans. A. M. Henderson and Talcott Parsons (New York: Oxford University Press, 1947).

23. C. R. Gullet, "Mechanistic vs. Organic Organizations: What Does the Future Hold?" *Personnel Administration,* 1975, 17.

24. Rensis Likert, *The Human Organization* (New York: McGraw-Hill, 1967).

25. C. Chet Miller, William H. Glick, Yau-De Wang, and George P. Huber, "Understanding Technology-Structure Relationships: Theory Development and Meta-Analytical Theory Testing," *Academy of Management Journal,* June 1991, 370–399.

26. Paul R. Lawrence and Jay W. Lorsch, *Organization and Environment* (Burr Ridge, IL: Irwin, 1967).

27. Alfred D. Chandler, *Strategy and Structure* (Cambridge, MA: MIT Press, 1962); Robert E. Hoskisson, "Multidivisional Structure and Performance: The Contingency of Diversification Strategy," *Academy of Management Journal,* December 1987, 625–644.

28. Much of this discussion is based on William G. Ouchi, *The M-Form Society* (Reading, MA: Addison-Wesley, 1987), 23–25.

29. Charles C. Snow, Raymond E. Miles, and Henry J. Coleman, "Managing 21st Century Network Organizations," *Organizational Dynamics,* Winter 1992, 5–19.

30. John Byrne, Richard Brandt, and Otis Port, "The Virtual Corporation," *Business Week,* February 8, 1993, pp. 98–102.

Chapter
Seven

Job Analysis, Design, and Redesign

In Chapter 6 we discussed how some organizations are designing structures that empower workers to make their own decisions. Workers in America have changed greatly over the past century. They are more literate and they have different objectives in their work. People want interesting work, recognition for good work, the chance to work with others who respect them, an opportunity to develop skills, and a voice in the design of their jobs—they want to be heard. They are no longer satisfied to simply have a job, for few of today's independent-minded workers remember what it was like to be out of work during the Great Depression of the 1930s. In those days, people had no choice but to work, and do as they were told.

Work itself is also changing. Robots do much of the work in factories, replacing many traditional blue-collar jobs. And white-collar workers, once thought to be indispensable, now lose their jobs regularly as firms decentralize. Many firms have cut jobs through restructuring and by closing plants. Organizations are being told that the front-line workers need more autonomy to make decisions. Organizations are struggling to design—or redesign—jobs more suited to today's worker and the current work environment.

In this chapter we examine job design. First we'll discuss the steps involved in job analysis, including developing job descriptions and job specifications. Then we present three different aspects of job design: job specialization, job range, and job depth. Next, we explore approaches to job redesign, including job rotation, job enlargement, and job enrichment. Finally, we discuss the team-based approach to job design.

JOB ANALYSIS

Before actually designing a job, an organization must determine the description of the job itself. **Job analysis** is the process of gathering, analyzing, and synthesizing information about jobs.[1] This time-consuming, complicated task is a vital input to job design decisions. The purpose of job analysis is to provide an objective description of the job itself.[2] This involves gathering information about all aspects of the job and pushes the organization to answer some fairly fundamental questions, as suggested by the Management Highlight below.

Job analysis is an ongoing process. As organizations evolve over time, missions and objectives change, as do conditions in the environment and the nature of the work. By analyzing and redesigning existing jobs, organizations can adapt to those changes and remain competitive. Many jobs have changed as a result of technology, global competition, and the pressure to produce quality products. Managers are learning that organizations are a collection of human beings that need to be developed and nurtured, not a collection of assets to be traded, manipulated, and motivated by fear.

Job analysis applies to all types of jobs. Job analysis began with factory jobs, an integral part of the scientific management movement. The purpose was to use objective data to determine the single best way to design work. But eventually job analysis made its way into office and clerical jobs, and today applies to management jobs as well. Job analysis is used to help design work that enhances employee performance, not to limit workers by determining the single best way to do things. In many instances, those directly involved in doing the work are participating in the job analysis. They are closest to the task and can provide excellent information about the job.

Steps in Job Analysis

A typical job analysis involves several steps (Exhibit 7.1). First, the job analyst must examine how each job fits into the overall organization. An overview of the organization and jobs provides a working picture of the arrangement of departments, units, and jobs. During this step, organization charts are used to examine the formal relationships among the firm's departments and units. The relationships among jobs are also examined. For example, when analyzing an assembly-line job, the analyst would be interested in the flow of work to and from the assembly-line worker. Since analyzing each job would be too costly and time-consuming, the second step involves determining which jobs in the organization will be analyzed.

The third step involves collecting data on the jobs to be analyzed. Data are collected on the characteristics of the job, the behaviors and activities required by the job, and the employee skills needed to perform it. Several methods are used to collect job analysis data.

MANAGEMENT HIGHLIGHT
Questions Answered by Job Analysis

Question	Possible Answers
What activities are required in a job?	Hand and body motions, use of equipment, services, communication with others.
What skills are needed to perform the activities?	Education, previous experience, licenses, degrees, or other personal characteristics.
What are the working conditions of the job?	Physical demands, degree of accountability and responsibility, extent of supervision, and other job environment factors.

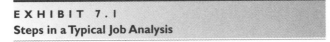

EXHIBIT 7.1
Steps in a Typical Job Analysis

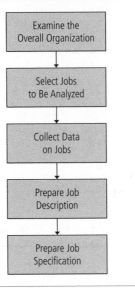

Examine the
Overall Organization

Select Jobs
to Be Analyzed

Collect Data
on Jobs

Prepare Job
Description

Prepare Job
Specification

Observation is used to collect data for jobs that require manual or standardized activities, such as assembly-line work. Conducting interviews with workers, often along with observation, is probably the most widely used data collection method. Questionnaires and logs or diaries pertaining to job tasks, frequency of tasks, when the tasks are accomplished, and so on are also used to collect information. A questionnaire called the *Job Analysis Information Format* (Exhibit 7.2) can provide basic information for use with any method employed to collect analysis data. Information collected by the job analyst is then used to prepare job descriptions and job specifications, steps four and five (see Exhibit 7.1).

Job Descriptions and Job Specifications

The major output of job analysis is the job description. The **job description** is a written summary of the job: its activities, equipment required to perform the activities, and working conditions of the job. A job description helps the organization with a variety of activities, including planning, recruiting, and training. It also helps workers understand what a specific job entails, and what jobs fit their particular skills and interests. Exhibit 7.3 shows a job description for a human resource manager.

Traditionally, a human resource manager was responsible for writing job descriptions. These job descriptions usually emphasize what employees should do, how they should think, and so on. In other words, they were for the most part prescriptive. Many organizations, in an effort to encourage more participation, now involve workers in developing their own job descriptions. By teaching workers how to write their own job descriptions and then having the employees and supervisors discuss and agree on a job description, workers must think about the best way to achieve desired outcomes. Rather than being prescriptive, this is an outcome-oriented approach to developing job descriptions. It is used by organizations interested in empowering workers to take control of their own jobs.

The **job specification** is a written explanation of skills, knowledge, abilities, and other characteristics needed to perform a job effectively. The job specification evolves from the

EXHIBIT 7.2
Job Analysis Information Format

Your Job Title _____   Code _____ Date January 1, 2004

Class Title _____   Department _____

Your Name _____   Facility _____

Supervisor's Title _____   Prepared by _____

Superior's Name _____   Hours Worked _____ AM _____ to AM
                                                                                PM   PM

1. What is the general purpose of your job?

2. What was your last job? If it was in another organization, please name it.

3. To what job would you normally expect to be promoted?

4. If you regularly supervise others, list them by name and job title.

5. If you supervise others, please check those activities that are part of your supervisory duties.

_____ Hiring	_____ Coaching	_____ Promoting
_____ Orienting	_____ Counseling	_____ Compensating
_____ Training	_____ Budgeting	_____ Disciplining
_____ Scheduling	_____ Directing	_____ Terminating
_____ Developing	_____ Measuring performance	_____ Other _____

6. How would you describe the successful completion and results of your work?

7. *Job duties.* Please briefly describe what you do and, if possible, how you do it. Indicate those duties you consider to be most important and/or most difficult.

   a. *Daily duties:*

   b. *Periodic duties* (Please indicate whether weekly, monthly, quarterly, etc.):

   c. *Duties performed at irregular intervals:*

   d. How long have you been performing these duties?

   e. Are you now performing unnecessary duties? If yes, please describe.

   f. Should you be performing duties not now included in your job? If yes, please describe.

8. *Education.* Please check the blank that indicates the educational *requirements* for the job, not your *own* educational background.

   a. _____ No formal education required   d. _____ 2-year college certificate or equivalent

   b. _____ Less than high school diploma   e. _____ 4-year college degree

   c. _____ High school diploma or equivalent   f. _____ Education beyond undergraduate degree and/or professional license

9. *Experience.* Please check the amount needed to perform your job.

   a. _____ None.   e. _____ One to three years

   b. _____ Less than one month   f. _____ Three to five years

   c. _____ One month to less than six months   g. _____ Five to 10 years

   d. _____ Six months to one year   h. _____ Over 10 years

10. *Skill.* Please list any skills required in the performance of your job. (For example, amount of accuracy, alertness, precision in working with described tools, methods, systems, etc.)

    Please list skills you possessed when you were placed on this job.

11. *Equipment.* Does your work require the use of any equipment? Yes, No. If yes, please list the equipment and check whether you use it rarely, occasionally, or frequently.

Equipment	Rarely	Occasionally	Frequently
a. _____	_____	_____	_____
b. _____	_____	_____	_____
c. _____	_____	_____	_____
d. _____	_____	_____	_____

EXHIBIT 7.3
Job Description of a Human Resource Manager

JOB TITLE: HUMAN RESOURCE MANAGER   Department: HRM
                                                          Date: Jan. 1, 2004

General Description of the Job

Performs responsible administrative work managing personnel activities of a large state agency or institution. Work involves responsibility for the planning and administration of an HRM program that includes recruitment, examination, selection, evaluation, appointment, promotion, transfer, and recommended change of status of agency employees, and a system of communication for disseminating necessary information to workers. Works under general supervision, exercising initiative and independent judgment in the performance of assigned tasks.

Job Activities

Participates in overall planning and policymaking to provide effective and uniform personnel services.

Communicates policy through organizational level by bulletins, meetings, and personal contact.

Interviews applicants, evaluates qualifications, classifies applications.

Recruits and screens applicants to fill vacancies and reviews applications of qualified persons.

Confers with supervisors on personnel matters, including placement problems, retention or release of probationary employees, transfers, demotions, and dismissals of permanent employees.

Supervises administration of tests.

Initiates personnel training activities and coordinates these activities with work of officials and supervisors.

Establishes effective service rating system, trains unit supervisors in making employee evaluations.

Maintains employee personnel files.

Supervises a group of employees directly and through subordinates.

Performs related work as assigned.

General Qualifications Requirements

Experience and Training

    Should have considerable experience in area of HRM administration. Six-year minimum.

Education

    Graduation from a four-year college or university, with major work in human resources, business administration, or industrial psychology.

Knowledge, Skills, and Abilities

    Considerable knowledge or principles and practices or HRM selection and assignment of personnel; job evaluation.

Responsibility

    Supervises a department of three HRM professionals, one clerk, and one secretary.

job description. The key difference is that the job description describes factors about the job, while the job specification describes factors about the person. The job specification is useful in recruiting and selecting workers.

JOB DESIGN

After job analyses, job descriptions, and job specifications have been prepared, an organization can use their information to design and redesign jobs. **Job design** determines exactly what tasks must be performed to complete the work. Job design should structure job elements and duties to increase performance and satisfaction.

There is no one best way to design jobs. Managers enjoy an array of choices. The choice of job design involves making trade-offs based on different characteristics of the job. Some job designs emphasize structuring jobs so they are broken down into simple, repetitive tasks; others emphasize enjoyment of the work. In this section we'll discuss three characteristics of job design: job specialization, job range, and job depth.

Job Specialization

Scientific management and Taylor's work stimulated a great deal of interest in **job specialization,** which breaks down work into smaller, more discrete tasks. The task specifies what is to be done, how it is to be done, and the exact time allowed for doing it.[3] Although specialization has been criticized because it leads to boredom and dissatisfaction, it made sense during the early twentieth century, and some of its principles are still relevant today. When Henry Ford developed the moving assembly line for manufacturing cars in 1913, job specialization led to production efficiencies. Many products made today—ranging from children's toys to this textbook to sophisticated computers—simply cannot be made by one individual; some degree of specialization is necessary.

Thus specialization is not the culprit it is often made out to be; the problem for organizations is identifying their appropriate degree of specialization. As we have noted in other chapters, the problems of boredom and absenteeism have plagued some companies and industries. It has long been assumed that managerial or white-collar jobs do not lend themselves to specialization—managers must think, create, and communicate. Many service organizations also are finding negative consequences associated with one person performing one specialized task.[4] On the other hand, more and more organizations are designing jobs that enable all workers, including nonmanagerial or blue-collar staff, to be creative and enjoy their jobs. Later in the chapter, we'll discuss strategies for redesigning jobs to overcome the problems associated with job specialization.

Job Range and Depth

Two other job characteristics are range and depth. **Job range** refers to the number of tasks a worker performs. A greater number of tasks takes longer for one individual to complete than fewer tasks. **Job depth** refers to the amount of discretion a worker has in performing tasks. Jobs designed with little depth are generally at lower levels of the organization.

Job specialization is closely related to the range and depth of jobs. Generally, more specialized jobs (e.g., assembly-line workers or bookkeepers) have low range and depth. People with such jobs perform only a few tasks and have little discretion in performing them. On the other hand, less specialized jobs (e.g., teachers or scientists) have high range and depth. In service industries such as hotel and banking, the front-line workers who actually face the customers also have jobs with high range and depth, and they can make or break the business.

Job range and depth can be used to differentiate jobs within and between organizations. Within an organization, jobs can be designed with different ranges and depths. Generally, as a person moves higher up in the organization and assumes more responsibility, job range and depth increase. But even at the same level, a machine mechanic may have higher range and depth than a machine operator. And an assembly-line job at a Ford plant may not have the same range and depth as an assembly-line job at a Toyota plant.

As is the case with specialization, it is the manager's responsibility to design jobs with optimal range and depth. If an employee has too many tasks or too much discretion, the job will not be accomplished efficiently and performance will suffer. Conversely, workers performing a single task with no discretion become bored, which may also lead to poor performance.

JOB REDESIGN

In response to the limits of specialization, organizations began to redesign jobs to give workers more autonomy, while at the same time meeting organizational objectives for performance. **Job redesign** refers to an organization's attempts to improve the quality of work and give workers more autonomy. Typically, job redesign attempts to improve coordination, productivity, and product quality, while at the same time responding to workers' needs for learning, challenge, variety, increased responsibility, and achievement.[5] Many firms are finding that workers with creativity are their greatest asset. Job specialization, associated with the scientific management movement, gives employees the least amount of autonomy and may stifle creativity. In this section we cover several approaches to redesigning jobs (job rotation, job enlargement, job enrichment, and flextime) that give workers more autonomy. In the final section of this chapter, we'll examine team-based approaches, which provide workers with the most autonomy.

Job Rotation

The **job rotation** approach involves systematically moving employees from one job to another. Job rotation increases job range by introducing workers to more jobs and therefore more tasks. The goal is not only to reduce worker dissatisfaction caused by job specialization but also to increase their interest and motivation.[6] For instance, workers in a tool factory may work on a machine one week, conduct stress tests the next week, pack orders the next, and so on. Ford, Bethlehem Steel, and Western Electric are some companies that have used this approach.

The major drawback of job rotation is that it does little to change the nature of the work itself. Rather than performing one task over and over again, a worker performs a variety of tasks; but in either case, the jobs are highly specialized so workers may grow bored or dissatisfied. Inefficiencies may also result since workers must be trained for several jobs. Because of these limitations, job rotation has not been entirely successful. However, it's often used along with other approaches we will now discuss.

Job Enlargement

Job enlargement was the first attempt by organizations to actually redesign work. In a study of mass production jobs in auto assembly plants, researchers found that workers were dissatisfied with highly specialized and repetitive tasks.[7] Based on this assumption, the **job enlargement** approach increases the worker's number of tasks. For example, a job may be redesigned so that a worker responsible for performing four tasks is given eight tasks to complete, thereby increasing the job range. While job rotation involves moving employees from one job or task to another, job enlargement seeks to increase job satisfaction by increasing the number of tasks the worker performs, thereby reducing boredom and monotony.

Many organizations have implemented job enlargement programs, including American Telephone & Telegraph (AT&T) and Maytag. Although job enlargement requires additional training and may not remove all the boredom, many such programs have increased satisfaction. Unfortunately, job enlargement isn't always successful. If workers simply end up doing four boring tasks instead of two, their job satisfaction is unlikely to rise.

Job Enrichment

Based on Frederick Herzberg's two-factor theory of work motivation (see Chapter 10), much work has been directed at changing jobs in more meaningful ways than either job rotation or job enlargement could accomplish. Herzberg's basic theory is that workers are motivated by jobs that increase their responsibility and feeling of self-worth.[8] **Job enrichment** attempts to give workers more control of their activities, addressing their needs for growth, recognition, and responsibility. Job enrichment increases not only the number of tasks performed (job range) but also job depth by giving workers more opportunity to exercise discretion over their work.

There are several approaches to job enrichment. Some managers redesign jobs to delegate more authority to workers, while others remove controls and assign new tasks to make the work as interesting as possible. Job enrichment can be accomplished by redesigning jobs with some additional features, providing learning opportunities, giving workers control over resources and tasks, and letting workers schedule some of their own work.

One widely known method of job enrichment is the job characteristics approach, which looks at the job from the jobholder's perspective and not the organization's.[9] The **job characteristics approach** (Exhibit 7.4) suggests that jobs should be redesigned to include important core dimensions that increase motivation, performance, and satisfaction, and reduce absenteeism and turnover.[10] These core dimensions include:

- *Skill variety:* The degree to which the job requires a variety of different activities in carrying out the work, which involves a number of skills and talents.

- *Task identity:* The degree to which the job requires completion of a "whole" and identifiable piece of work—that is, doing a job from beginning to end with a visible outcome.

- *Task significance:* The degree to which the job has a substantial impact on other people's lives or work—whether in the immediate organization or in the external environment.

- *Autonomy:* The degree to which the job provides substantial freedom, independence, and discretion to the individual in scheduling work and in determining the procedures to be used in carrying it out.

- *Feedback:* The degree to which carrying out work activities required by the job results in individuals obtaining direct and clear information about the effectiveness of their performance.[11]

Presence of these core dimensions in a job is expected to create in workers three critical psychological states that are necessary for motivation and satisfaction:

1. *Experienced meaningfulness:* The degree to which jobholders experience work as important, valuable, and worthwhile.

2. *Experienced responsibility:* The extent to which jobholders feel personally responsible and accountable for results of their work.

3. *Knowledge of results:* Jobholders' understanding of how effectively they are performing their jobs.[12]

The more workers experience these three states, the higher their motivation, performance, and satisfaction and the lower their absenteeism and turnover.

As Exhibit 7.4 shows, three of the core job dimensions we listed earlier—skill variety, task identity, and task significance—contribute to a sense of meaningfulness. Skill variety is influenced by individual differences in the strength of growth needs.[13] Autonomy is

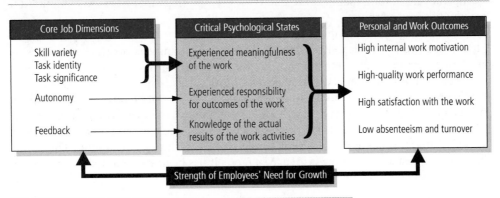

EXHIBIT 7.4
The Job Characteristics Approach

Core Job Dimensions	Critical Psychological States	Personal and Work Outcomes
Skill variety	Experienced meaningfulness	High internal work motivation
Task identity	of the work	
Task significance		High-quality work performance
Autonomy	Experienced responsibility	
	for outcomes of the work	High satisfaction with the work
Feedback	Knowledge of the actual	
	results of the work activities	Low absenteeism and turnover

Strength of Employees' Need for Growth

Source: Adapted from J. Richard Hackman and G. R. Oldham, "Motivation through the Design of Work: Test of a Theory," *Organizational Behavior and Human Performance* 16 (1976), 256.

directly related to feelings of responsibility. The more control workers feel they have over their jobs, the more they feel responsible. Feedback is related to knowledge of results. For workers to be internally motivated, they must have a sense of the quality of their performance. This sense comes from feedback.

Since different people have different capabilities and needs, managers need to be aware of the potential for individual differences to affect how the job characteristics approach works. The final part of the job-enrichment model, called employee growth-need strength, suggests that people with a strong need to grow and expand their potential are expected to respond more strongly to the core job dimensions than those with low growth-need strength. Thus job enrichment will probably have less effect on a person without a strong need for personal growth than on someone who values personal growth.

Managers must realize that job enrichment might change a job's skill requirements. Thus not everyone will necessarily be able to perform the enriched job, especially without additional training. And the organization may need to adjust its compensation rates for the enriched job because of the higher skill levels required.[14]

Before beginning a job-enrichment effort, managers should complete at least two actions. First, they need to thoroughly understand the job in question. Enrichment might not be feasible due to costs or other technological constraints. Second, they should consider individual preferences about enriched work. Do the employees want the work to be enriched? Obviously, accurate job descriptions and job specifications can greatly facilitate assessing these issues.

Flextime

Another approach to redesigning jobs lets employees have input in establishing their work schedules. **Flextime** is a schedule that allows workers to select starting and quitting times within limits set by management.[15] Rather than working the traditional eight-hour day, workers are given greater flexibility in deciding exactly when they will work. A person may work ten hours one day and six another. Jobs designed using flextime include bank tellers, data entry clerks, lab technicians, engineers, and nurses.

Flextime programs have reportedly been successful in many instances. Over half the firms using them report such improvements as increased productivity, lower labor costs, and higher morale.[16] One study found that flextime increases performance and job satisfaction and decreases absenteeism.[17] Another study reported that satisfaction with the work schedules and with interactions improved significantly for both managers and nonmanagers.[18] Companies are finding that flextime builds loyalty, and that employees are committed to making flextime work.

Flextime is difficult to implement for production units with assembly lines and multiple shifts. Since work is largely machine controlled, planning flexible work schedules is a challenge. Flextime is also difficult to arrange for jobs that must be continuously covered, like those of bus drivers or retail sales clerks. A firm can also experience increased costs of heating and cooling buildings for longer workdays. It may not be possible to coordinate supervisor and subordinate work schedules, resulting in lack of supervision part of the time. Most workers may prefer similar hours—say 9 a.m. to 5 p.m.—leaving other times understaffed. Without supervision, some employees may abuse flexible scheduling. Thus, while flextime is appealing and some evidence suggests it has been successful, proper administration is needed to ensure success.

TEAM-BASED APPROACH TO JOB DESIGN AND REDESIGN

Throughout most of Europe, Asia, and more recently the United States, the concept of job design is being revolutionized. The thrust of this new approach is to place greater emphasis on worker autonomy and to delegate increased decision-making responsibility. This new form of job design goes beyond traditional job-enrichment programs aimed at empowering workers, often members of teams, to make their own decisions. As noted in Chapter 6, a team is a group of employees who work closely together to pursue common objectives. Recall also that a team cannot be effective unless it is supported by the organization's basic structure. Team-based approaches to job design and redesign provide workers with the greatest autonomy. One of the most important benefits of the team-based approach is improved communication and coordination. People learn how other jobs are done and how to coordinate efforts to work together better.[19]

The use of teams has implications not only for organizational structure but also for the design of specific jobs. Working as a member of a highly motivated, self-directed work team is much different from performing several specialized tasks or performing jobs redesigned through job-enrichment programs. While job enrichment gives workers more responsibility, they are still part of a large group. Work flows from one person to another, each doing a specific job. As a member of a work team, an individual participates in small-group decisions. The group decides when to perform tasks, who will perform them, and so on. The Management Highlight on page 137 provides a useful consolidation of the various approaches to job design and redesign that we have explored in this chapter.

Teams also motivate workers by moving them sideways (laterally) instead of up. With fewer promotions to give out due to decentralization, many organizations are redesigning jobs and developing teams that enable employees to transfer back and forth among teams that make different products. This approach replaces the assembly-line structure in which employees worked on one product. For instance, American Greetings Corporation redesigned 400 jobs into teams and asked workers and managers to reapply. All employees were guaranteed a job without a pay cut, and many moved laterally into a new type of work.[20] This process unleashes creativity by giving workers a change in tasks and a chance to work with different people without having to deal with the uncertainty of changing jobs or organizations.

MANAGEMENT HIGHLIGHT
Approaches to Job Design and Redesign

	Job Specialization	Job Rotation	Job Enlargement	Job Enrichment	Teams
Description	Breaks work down into small, more discrete tasks.	Systematically moves workers from one job to another.	Increases the number of tasks the worker performs.	Increases the number of tasks and gives workers more control over activities.	Group works together to complete an entire task.
Assumptions	Production efficiencies can be achieved through division of labor.	By providing more variety, specialization reduces worker dissatisfaction.	Workers are dissatisfied with highly specialized and repetitive tasks.	Giving workers more control meets their needs for growth, recognition, and responsibility.	Teamwork reduces boredom and increases satisfaction and quality.
Setting	Assembly-line and mass production jobs.	Assembly lines and settings that can entail several different jobs.	Mass production, office, and clerical jobs.	Mass production, office, clerical, and managerial jobs.	Mass production, office, clerical, and managerial jobs.
Strengths	Workers master one job; training is minimized; useful if workers are unskilled or illiterate.	Can increase interest and motivation in the short run.	Can increase satisfaction and decrease boredom and monotony.	Provides growth and learning opportunities; redesigning jobs based on dimensions is important to workers.	Provides the most autonomy and opportunity for growth; empowers workers to make their own decisions.
Weaknesses	Can lead to boredom and absenteeism; little variety, responsibility, or growth.	Requires more training; doesn't change the nature of the work itself.	Requires more training; may not remove all the boredom from jobs.	Can change skill requirements, necessitating additional training; everyone may not be able to perform the enriched job.	Very difficult to implement; must overcome resistance; may be costly and time-consuming before benefits occur.

When an organization decides to build teamwork into its structure, it must design or redesign jobs accordingly. It is easy to talk about team-based approaches, but difficult to actually involve members of the organization in teamwork. Typically, developing teams involves redesigning jobs so that workers' (or teams') activities make up a whole or more complete task.[21] Although knowledgeable workers are critical to successful teams, individual skills are substantially leveraged through teamwork. Thus managers must ensure that employees have the knowledge and skills needed to perform tasks, but more importantly, they must create an atmosphere in which teamwork can prosper. For the most part, this attitude or philosophy flows from the top down and creates a sense of group pride, good relations with coworkers, and a spirit of teamwork that brings out the best in worker performance.[22] Training team members within this context eliminates old, counterproductive ideas and signals workers that a spirit of teamwork permeates the organization.

Perhaps the most important aspect of designing jobs for teams is empowering workers, giving them greater control over their work. This basically means that jobs must be designed so that authority equals responsibility. When individuals are made accountable for their actions, they become challenged to take responsibility for thinking, for implementing ideas, and for investing themselves in the organization.[23] Empowerment involves several conditions:

- Workers must believe their efforts can result in positive outcomes.
- Workers must have the knowledge and skills to do their jobs effectively.
- Work must be designed to form a "whole" job that is meaningful to the worker.
- Workers must have the authority to make decisions about the work on their own.[24]

Although much has been said—and many have written—about teams, organizations have been hesitant to adopt this approach for several reasons. Many executives and managers are simply reluctant to empower workers. Even workers themselves have been reluctant to participate in teams, fearing that teams will reduce their freedom when, in fact, they should do just the opposite. Some workers—opting for an easier, yet more mediocre, job experience—simply do not want to accept accountability for their work. The large bureaucratic structures of some organizations are not conducive to designing jobs in which workers set their own schedules and production goals, have access to formerly confidential information, vote on such issues as pay raises and new hires, and make other critical decisions. Some organizations try to implement teams, but either don't go far enough in empowering workers or don't give the concept long enough to work. When truly empowered, teams can turn bored employees into productive partners. In any case, it appears that teams will continue to be an integral part of contemporary organizations.[25]

Conclusion
—Job Analysis, Design, and Redesign—

Job design is an important function of management. Before designing a job, managers use analysis to determine job descriptions and job specifications. This information is used to design and redesign jobs. The three characteristics of job design include job specialization, job range, and job depth. Approaches to job redesign are job rotation, job enlargement, and job enrichment. Finally, some organizations use team-based approaches to design and redesign jobs.

SUGGESTED READINGS

Cusumano, Michael A. "How Microsoft Makes Large Teams Work Like Small Teams," *Sloan Management Review*, Fall 1997, 9–20.

Hartley, Darin E. *Job Analysis at the Speed of Reality*. Amherst, MA: Human Resource Development Press, 1999.

Herzberg, Frederick "One More Time: How Do You Motivate Employees?" *Harvard Business Review*, January 2003, 87–96.

Purser, Ronald E., and Steven Cabana, *The Self-Managing Organization: How Leading Companies Are Transforming the Work of Teams for Real Impact*. New York: Simon & Schuster, 1998.

Senge, Peter, et al. *The Dance of Change: The Challenges to Sustaining Momentum in Learning Organizations*. New York: Doubleday, 1999.

ENDNOTES

1. John M. Ivancevich, *Human Resource Management* (Burr Ridge, IL: Irwin, 1992), 172.

2. Frederick P. Morgeson and Michael A. Campion, "Social and Cognitive Sources of Potential Inaccuracy in Job Analysis," *Journal of Applied Psychology*, October 1997, 627–655.

3. Frederick W. Taylor, *The Principles of Scientific Management* (New York: Harper & Row, 1911), 21.

4. Greg L. Stewart and Kenneth P. Carson, "Moving Beyond the Mechanistic Model: An Alternative Approach to Staffing for Contemporary Organizations," *Human Resource Management Review*, Summer 1997, 157–184.

5. J. Barton Cunningham and Ted Eberle, "A Guide to Job Enrichment and Redesign," *Personnel*, February 1990, 56–61.

6. Allan W. Farrant, "Job Rotation Is Important," *Supervision*, August 1987, 14–16.

7. Charles R. Walker and Robert H. Guest, *The Man in the Assembly Line* (Cambridge, MA: Harvard University Press, 1952).

8. Frederick Herzberg, B. Mausner, and B. Snyderman, *The Motivation to Work* (New York: Wiley, 1959).

9. J. Richard Hackman, "Work Design," in *Improving Life at Work*, eds. J. Richard Hackman and J. L. Suttle (Santa Monica, CA: Goodyear, 1976), 96–162.

10. J. Richard Hackman and Greg R. Oldham, *Work Redesign* (Reading, MA: Addison-Wesley, 1980), 77–82.

11. Juan I. Sanchez, Alina Samora, and Chockalingam Viaweavaran, "Moderators of Agreement between Incumbent and Non-Incumbent Ratings of Job Characteristics," *Journal of Occupational and Organizational Psychology* (September 1997): 209–218.

12. Hackman and Oldham, *Work Redesign*, 72–77.

13. Robert P. Steel and Joan R. Rentach, "The Dispositional Model of Job Attitudes Revisited: Findings of a 10-Year Study," *Journal of Applied Psychology* (December 1997): 873–879.

14. Michael A. Champion and Chris J. Barger, "Conceptual Integration and Empirical Test of Job Design and Compensation Experiments," *Personnel Psychology*, Autumn 1990, 525–554.

15. Edward E. Lawler, *Pay and Organization Development* (Reading, MA: Addison-Wesley, 1981).

16. David A. Ralston, William P. Anthony, and David J. Gustafson, "Employees Love Flextime, But What Does It Do to the Organization's Productivity?" *Journal of Applied Psychology* (May 1985): 272–279.

17. Boris B. Baltes, Thomas E. Briggs, Joseph W. Huff, Julie A. Wright, and George A. Neuman, "Flexible and Compressed Workweek Schedules: A Meta-Analysis of Their Effects on Work-Related Criteria," *Journal of Applied Psychology* (August 1999): 496–513.

18. Randall B. Dunham and John L. Pierce, "The Design and Evaluation of Alternative Work Schedules," *Personnel Administrator*, April 1983, 67–75.

19. Edward E. Lawler, *High-Involvement Management* (San Francisco: Jossey-Bass, 1991), 37.

20. Joan E. Rigdon, "Using Lateral Moves to Spur Employees," *Wall Street Journal*, May 26, 1992, pp. B1, B5.

21. Marshall Sashkin and Kenneth J. Kiser, *Total Quality Management* (Seabrook, MD: Ducochon, 1991), 140.

22. Joseph A. Petrick and George E. Manning, "How to Manage Morale," *Personnel Journal*, October 1990, 83–88.

23. Stephen L. Perlman, "Employees Redesign Their Jobs," *Personnel Journal*, November 1990, 37–40.

24. Kenneth W. Thomas and Betty A. Velthouse, "Cognitive Elements of Empowerment: An 'Interpretive' Model of Intrinsic Task Motivation," *Academy of Management Review* (October 1990): 666–681.

25. George S. Easton and Sherry L. Jarrell, "The Effects of Total Quality Management on Corporate Performance: An Empirical Investigation," *Journal of Business*, April 1998, 253–307.

Chapter

Eight

Human Resource Management

People are the key resource in creating a successful organization. Companies that do not hire wisely will find it almost impossible to create a culture required to compete effectively. In large, formal organizations such as General Motors and Procter & Gamble, a department usually guides the human resource program. But even small organizations must take an action-oriented approach to people and their needs, goals, expectations, skills, knowledge, and abilities. When a strong human resource management function is in place, it facilitates the most effective use of employees to achieve an organization's goals.

For an organization to flourish, people must be the driving force; thus human resources practices, principles, and programs are the focus of this chapter. We discuss **human resource management (HRM)** in relation to the activities needed to acquire, develop, retain, and utilize human resources. In doing so we examine eight human resource management activities: equal employment opportunity, human resource planning, recruitment, selection, training and development, performance evaluation, compensation, and benefits and services. The chapter concludes with a discussion of some special issues in human resources.

EQUAL EMPLOYMENT OPPORTUNITY

Equal employment opportunity (EEO) refers to the employment of individuals in a fair and unbiased manner. EEO has slowly become a societal priority that has needed legal and administrative guidelines to encourage action. Although EEO is usually couched in legal terminology, it is also an emotional issue.[1] Employers have been ordered to develop employment policies that incorporate laws, executive orders, court decisions, and regulations to end job discrimination.

One approach used to reach the goal of fair employment is **affirmative action.** The goal of affirmative action is to urge employers to make a concerted effort to promote the hiring of groups of employees who were discriminated against in the past. Employers are asked under affirmative action to use—at least in part—the race, sex, or age of a person in reaching an employment decision. Opinions regarding the impact of affirmative action are many and varied. Research has shown that affirmative action programs have enabled a significant number of African Americans to obtain well-paying managerial positions.[2] Women, people with disabilities, and minorities other than African-Americans also have benefited from affirmative action programs. Research also has shown that workers hired through affirmative action may be viewed negatively by others, regardless of their qualifications. Some white males have claimed they are victims of *reverse discrimination*. The jury is still out regarding the long-term impact of affirmative action.[3]

The Management Highlight that follows itemizes the major federal employment legislation whose intent is to eliminate discrimination in the American workplace. This body of laws continues to evolve through the courts. The Civil Rights Act of 1991 has long been characterized as strengthening earlier civil rights legislation and increasing the likelihood that employees will sue employers by making actionable discrimination cases subject to jury deliberation and potential damages more substantial.[4] Therefore it is in the

---

MANAGEMENT HIGHLIGHT
A Selected Sample of Federal Employment Laws

Law	Provisions
Equal Pay Act of 1963	Requires all employers covered by the Fair Labor Standards Act and others to provide equal pay for equal work regardless of sex.
Title VII of Civil Rights Act of 1964 (amended in 1972, 1991, and 1994)	Prohibits discrimination in employment on the basis of race, color, religion, sex, or national origin; created the Equal Employment Opportunity Commission (EEOC) to enforce the provisions of Title VII.
Age Discrimination in Employment Act of 1967	Prohibits private and public employers from discriminating against persons 40 years of age or older in any area of employment because of age; exceptions are permitted where age is a bona fide occupational qualification.
Equal Employment Opportunity Act of 1972	Amended Title VII of Civil Rights Act of 1964; strengthens EEOC's enforcement powers and extends coverage of Title VII to government employees, faculty in higher education, and other employers and employees.
Americans with Disabilities Act of 1990	Prohibits discrimination in employment against persons with physical or mental disabilities or the chronically ill; enjoins employers to make reasonable accommodation to the employment needs of the disabled; covers employers with 15 or more employees.
Civil Rights Act of 1991	Provides for compensatory and punitive damages and jury trials in cases involving intentional discrimination; requires employers to demonstrate that job practices are job related and consistent with business necessity; extends coverage to U.S. citizens working for American companies overseas.
Family and Medical Leave Act of 1993	Requires all employers with 50 or more employees to provide 12 weeks of unpaid leave for family and medical emergencies.
Uniformed Services Employment and Reemployment Rights Act of 1994	Protects the employment rights of individuals who enter the military for short periods of service.

organization's best interest for managers to develop policies and procedures that comply with the law. The best way to begin studying the relationship between HRM functions and the law is to devote time and attention to EEO. No other regulatory area has so thoroughly affected HRM as EEO; it has implications for almost every activity in HRM, including hiring, recruiting, training, terminating, compensating, evaluating, planning, disciplining, and collective bargaining.[5] Employers set up EEO programs to prevent employment discrimination in the workplace and/or to take remedial action to offset past employment discrimination.

The Americans with Disabilities Act of 1990 (ADA) requires firms to make reasonable accommodations to the needs of present and future employees with disabilities. Nearly 20 percent of the U.S. population is disabled.[6] The ADA was enacted to provide equal employment opportunities and reduce the high unemployment rate—nearly 70 percent—among this group of people. To date, the ADA has not fulfilled its promise.

HUMAN RESOURCE PLANNING

Human resource planning is a two-step process that involves forecasting future human resource needs and then planning how to adequately fulfill and manage these needs. Exhibit 8.1 points out the activities involved in needs forecasting and program planning.

As its major objective, human resource planning seeks to determine the best use of the talent and skills available to accomplish what's best for the individual and the organization. As Exhibit 8.1 shows, needs forecasting involves four specific activities. The external market conditions must be studied, as well as the firm's future human resource requirements. The firm must determine if talented and skilled human resources are available.

Human resource planning also involves paying attention to the performance of the organization and the individual. Thus evaluation, developing compensation and reward programs, and coaching are important planning activities. There's also the need to select, assign, develop, and manage the careers of individuals.

Human resource planning requires the linking of external analysis and scanning with human resource management. Techniques and activities must be carefully employed to accomplish the quality and competitiveness outcomes that a firm seeks. These techniques include the use of:

- *Human resource inventories*—the skills, abilities, and knowledge that exist within the firm already.

- *Human resource forecast*—the firm's future requirements based on numbers available, skill mix, and external labor supply.

- *Action plans*—the recruitment, selection, training, orientation, promotion, development, and compensation plans used.

- *Control and evaluation*—the monitoring system used to determine the degree of attainment of human resource goals.

Human resource planning involves the necessary activities that help managers reduce uncertainty about the future. For human resource plans, managers can make forecasts, plan so that change can be managed more efficiently, and display the role they play in properly managing human resources.

EXHIBIT 8.1
The Human Resource Planning Process

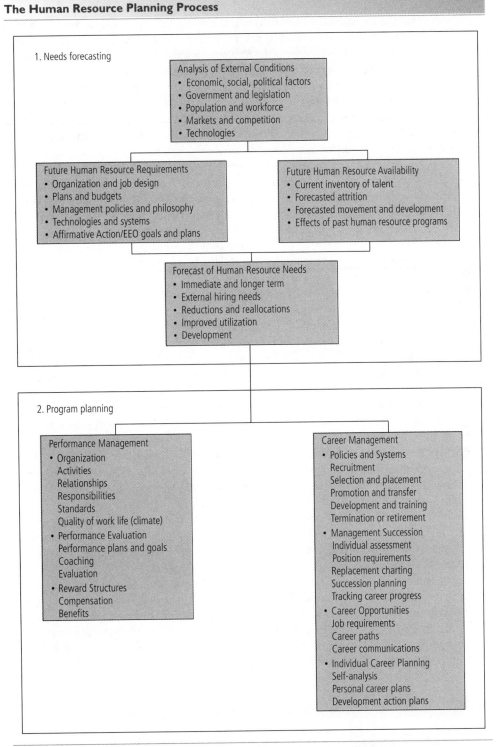

RECRUITMENT

Whenever an organization's human resources must be expanded or replenished, a recruitment plan must be established or set in motion. **Recruitment** is the set of activities used to attract job candidates with the abilities and attitudes needed to help an organization achieve its objectives. Recruitment requires a sound human resource planning system that includes personnel inventories, forecasts of the supply and demand of human resources, action plans, and control and evaluation procedures. The first step in recruitment is a clear specification of needs: number of people, skills mix, knowledge, and experience level. This information is especially important so that affirmative action goals and timetables for the recruitment and hiring of minorities can be met.

If human resource needs cannot be met within a company, outside sources must be tapped. Advertisements in newspapers, trade journals, and magazines notify potential applicants of openings. Because responses to advertisements will come from both qualified and unqualified individuals, occasionally a company will list a post office box number rather than use its company name. Such advertisements, called blind ads, eliminate the need to contact every applicant, but they don't allow a company to use its name or logo as a form of promotion. Some organizations effectively use their own employees in newspaper and magazine ads.

The college campus is a major source for recruiting lower-level managers. Many colleges and universities have placement centers that work with organizational recruiters. Applicants read ads and information provided by the companies, and then they sign up for interviews. The most promising applicants are invited to visit the companies for more interviews.

To find experienced employees in the external market, organizations use private employment agencies, executive search firms, and/or state employment agencies. Some private employment agencies and executive search firms are called no-fee agencies—meaning the employer pays the search fee instead of the applicant. An organization is not obligated to hire any person referred by the no-fee agency, but the agency usually is informed when the right person is found.

The employees responsible for recruiting are faced with legal requirements. These requirements are enforced by laws administered by the Equal Employment Opportunity Commission (EEOC). The federal government attempts to provide equal opportunities for employment without regard to race, religion, age, sex, national origin, or disability, through Title VII of the Civil Rights Act of 1964 and the Equal Employment Opportunity Act of 1972.[7] These laws have broad coverage and apply to any activity, business, or industry in which a labor dispute would hinder commerce. The laws also cover federal, state, and local government agencies.

Legal procedures regarding equal employment opportunities and recruitment are important to employers. Organizations must adjust to and work with these laws. Although adjustments are sometimes difficult, they seem to be a better alternative than long, costly court battles. Providing equal opportunities to all qualified job applicants makes sense both legally and morally. The vast majority of managers believe that all citizens have a right to any job they can perform reasonably well after a sufficient amount of training.

SELECTION

Selection is the process by which an organization chooses from a list of applicants the person or persons who best meet the criteria for the position available, considering current environmental and financial conditions. The selection process involves screening applicants and making decisions about which applicants to interview and which ones to hire. Firms such as Fairfield Inn and Holland America spend time and energy on their selection programs. After applicants are screened and interviewed, the firm decides whether to extend a job offer. Job candidates also enter into the decision-making process by deciding whether the job offer fits their needs and goals. Traditionally, through the selection process the organization is attempting to accurately assess the probability that a particular candidate will succeed in the job. As noted earlier, federal mandates and legal standards affect how business selects employees. For a list of legal versus illegal activities associated with employee screening, see the Management Highlight below.

The actual selection process is a series of steps. It starts with initial screening and ends with the hiring decision. Exhibit 8.2 presents each step in the process. A candidate can be rejected at any one of the nine steps. Recognizing human resource needs through the planning phase of staffing is the point at which selection begins. Preliminary interviews are used to screen out unqualified applicants. This screening often is an applicant's first personal contact with an organization. Applicants who pass the preliminary screening usually complete an application.

Screening Interviews

Interviews are used throughout the selection process. Interviewers usually first acquaint themselves with the job analysis information. Second, they review the application information. Third, they typically ask questions designed to give better insight into the applicants, and they add this information to that on the application.

Three general types of interviews are used: structured, semistructured, and unstructured. In the structured interview, the interviewer asks specific questions of all interviewees. In the semistructured interview, only some questions are prepared in advance. This approach is less rigid than the structured interview and allows the interviewer more flexibility. The unstructured interview allows interviewers the freedom to discuss whatever they think can be important. Comparing answers across interviewees is rather difficult, however. According to a recent study, the situational interview, in which job candidates role-play in mock job scenarios, is the most accurate of any type of interview in predicting job performance (54 percent compared to 7 percent for the standard structured interview).[8]

Some firms now use online selection services to administer structured employment interviews. Although this activity does not replace the face-to-face interview, an Internet consulting service can provide a low-cost base of information about each applicant before

---

MANAGEMENT HIGHLIGHT
Some Legal Guidelines for Staff Selection

Selection Screening Steps	Legal Activities	Illegal Activities
Tests	Can be used if they have been validated	Cannot be used when there is no relationship between test results and performing the job
Interview information	To ask if a person is a U.S. citizen	To require citizenship or to ask proof of citizenship
	To ask about convictions for crime	To ask if a person has ever been arrested
Age	To require proof of age after hiring	To require a birth certificate
Racial identity	To keep records on racial and ethnic identity for purposes of reporting	To ask for race, creed, or national origin in application or interview

EXHIBIT 8.2
Typical Selection Decision Steps

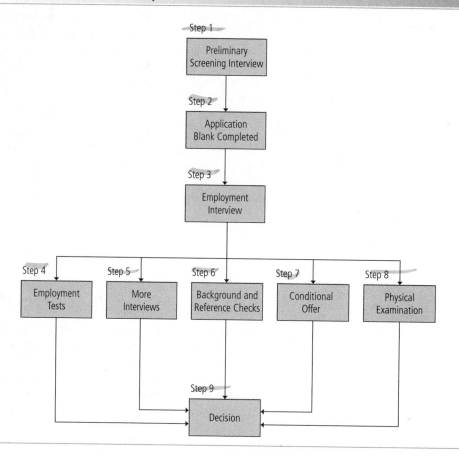

the interviewer meets him or her. An applicant can typically complete a 100-question computer-aided interview in less than twenty minutes.[9]

Tests

Managers often complain that they have a problem hiring and retaining successful employees. Relying solely on intuition, rather than finding objective procedures to select employees, is not adequate. Subjective procedures are not very accurate in predicting how employees actually will perform the job. One method to improve upon intuition and subjective judgments is testing. A **test** is a means of obtaining a standardized sample of a person's behavior.

Here are some advantages of valid selection tests (how well a test score predicts job success) and reliable selection tests (those that provide consistency of measurement):

- *Improved accuracy in selecting employees* Individuals differ in skills, intelligence, motivation, interests, needs, and goals. If these differences can be measured, and if they're related to job success, then performance can be predicted to some extent by test scores.

- *An objective means for judging* Applicants answer the same questions under test conditions. Then their responses are scored. One applicant's score then can be compared with those of other applicants.

- *Information on present employees' needs* Tests given to present employees provide data on their training, development, or counseling needs.

The U.S. Supreme Court made a landmark ruling relating to tests in the *Griggs* v. *Duke Power Company* case in 1971.[10] Six years earlier, Duke Power had established a policy requiring job applicants to pass a number of tests and have a high school education to qualify for placement and promotion. A group of African American employees challenged these requirements, arguing that they were denied promotions because of the company's testing policy. The Supreme Court ruled that neither the high school requirement nor the test scores showed a relationship to successful job performance.

Organizations using any test now must carefully examine how the scores are used, and test results must be validated. There must be statistical proof that test scores are related to job performance. But testing still can be an important part of the selection process. It is also a major tool for making decisions.

The Hiring Decision

When the human resources department has completed the preliminary screening steps—evaluation of the job application information, interviewing, and testing (if it is used)—a reference check should be conducted. Checking with previous employers can provide important information. However, fear of defamation lawsuits has caused a growing number of organizations to provide no relevant information. Courts in most states have held that former and prospective employers have a "qualified privilege" to discuss an employee's past performance. In exercising the privilege, a previous employer must follow three rules: (1) determine that the prospective employer has a job-related need to know; (2) release only truthful information about the former employee; and (3) do not release EEO-related information such as race, age, or ethnic background.[11]

TRAINING AND DEVELOPMENT

The training and development of human resources involves change: change in skills, knowledge, attitudes, and/or social behavior. For an organization to remain competitive, it needs to stay abreast of such changes. Maintaining technological superiority, teamwork, world-class quality performance, and social harmony among individuals with differing ethnic backgrounds and skills depends on the organization's ability to cope with change. For example, due to technical and software advances, computer specialists have to be continually retrained.

Training is, in short, an attempt to improve current or future employee performance. In most organizations, training is done in problem solving, problem analysis, measurement and feedback, and team building. Here are some important points about training:

- **Training** is the systematic process of altering employees' behavior to further organizational goals.

- **Development** is the acquisition of knowledge and skills that employees may use in the present or future. Development focuses more on the long term.

- A **formal training program** is an effort by the employer to provide opportunities for the employee to acquire job-related skills, attitudes, and knowledge. At IBM, Motorola, and Xerox, all employees go through a formal training program.

- **Learning** is the act by which individuals acquire skills, knowledge, and abilities that result in a relatively permanent change in their behavior.

- A **skill** is any behavior that has been learned and applied. Therefore, the goal of training is to improve skills. Motor skills, cognitive skills, and interpersonal skills are targets of training programs.

PERFORMANCE EVALUATION

Performance evaluation is the systematic review of individual job-relevant strengths and weaknesses. Two processes are used in reviewing an individual's job performance: observation and judgment. Both processes are subject to bias or human error. It would be ideal to eliminate evaluation bias and measure only objective indicators of performance, such as number of units produced, cost of completing a unit, or the time to finish a unit. But objective indicators often measure factors beyond an individual employee's control. Therefore organizations often use subjective criteria, such as a manager's rating of a subordinate. And it's here that bias enters the picture, since every rater is asked to observe and then make a judgment on the observations.

Performance evaluation is a difficult process to implement, and the problems of bias are hard to overcome. The evaluation itself appears to be uncomfortable for raters as well as those being rated. But for HRM, formal evaluations can serve the following purposes:

- Make decisions easier involving promotion, transfer, pay raises, and termination.

- Help establish training and development programs and evaluate their success.

- Provide employees with feedback about strengths and weaknesses.

- Predict whether recruitment and selection activities lead to attracting, screening, and hiring the best-qualified human resources.

- Help determine what type of individual can be successful within the organization.

These five purposes can be accomplished only if the evaluation system used satisfies two requirements. It must be relevant to the job(s) being evaluated, and it must be accepted by the raters and ratees. Raters must believe in the importance of evaluation and feedback. To motivate human resources, raters must view performance evaluation as a significant part of their job. From the ratee's perspective, performance evaluation must be relevant, fair, conducted by raters familiar with ratees' job performance, and open to modification if flaws are detected. Evaluation systems also must be able to discriminate between good, average, and poor performers.

Managers usually attempt to select a performance evaluation procedure that will minimize conflict, provide ratees with relevant feedback, and help to achieve organizational objectives. Basically, managers must try to develop and implement a performance evaluation program that also can benefit other managers, the work group, and the organization.

As with most managerial procedures, there are no universally accepted methods of performance evaluation to fit every purpose, person, or organization. What is effective at IBM might not work for General Mills. In fact, what is effective within one department or one group in a particular organization might not be right for another unit or group within the same company.

Graphic Rating Scales

The oldest and most widely used performance evaluation procedure, the graphic scaling technique, has many forms. Generally, the rater is supplied with a printed form for each subordinate to be rated. The form lists various job performance qualities and characteristics to be considered. Rating scales are distinguished by: (1) how exactly the categories are defined, (2) the degree to which the person interpreting the ratings (e.g., the ratee) can tell what response was intended by the rater, and (3) how carefully the performance dimension is defined for the rater.

Each organization devises rating scales and formats that suit its needs. Exhibit 8.3 is an example of the type of rating form used in many organizations.

EXHIBIT 8.3
Typical Graphic Rating Scale

Name _____ Dept. _____ Date _____

	Outstanding	Good	Satisfactory	Fair	Unsatisfactory
Quantity of work Volume of acceptable work under normal conditions Comments:	☐	☐	☐	☐	☐
Quality of work Thoroughness, neatness, and accuracy of work Comments:	☐	☐	☐	☐	☐
Knowledge of job Clear understanding of the facts or factors pertinent to the job Comments:	☐	☐	☐	☐	☐
Personal qualities Personality, appearance, sociability, leadership, integrity Comments:	☐	☐	☐	☐	☐
Cooperation Ability and willingness to work with associates, supervisors, and subordinates toward common goals Comments:	☐	☐	☐	☐	☐
Dependability Conscientious, thorough, accurate, reliable with respect to attendance, lunch periods, reliefs, etc. Comments:	☐	☐	☐	☐	☐
Initiative Earnest in seeking increased responsibilities; self-starting, unafraid to proceed alone Comments:	☐	☐	☐	☐	☐

Ranking Methods

Some managers use a rank-order procedure to evaluate all subordinates. Subordinates are ranked according to their relative value to the company or unit on one or more performance dimensions. This procedure usually identifies the best and worst performers, who are placed in the first and last positions on the ranking list. The next best and next poorest performers then are noted. This continues until all subordinates are on the list. The rater is forced to discriminate by the rank-order performance evaluation method.

Some problems are associated with the ranking method. First, ratees in the central portion of the list likely will not be much different from one another on the performance rankings. A second problem involves the size of the group of subordinates being evaluated. Large groups are more difficult to rank than small groups.

Descriptive Essays

The essay method of performance evaluation requires that the rater describe each ratee's strong and weak points. Some organizations require each rater to discuss specific points, whereas others allow raters to discuss whatever they believe is appropriate. One problem with the unstructured essay evaluation is that it provides little opportunity to compare ratees on specific performance dimensions. Another limitation involves variations in raters' writing skills. Some simply aren't very good at writing descriptive analyses of subordinates' strengths and weaknesses.

Rating Errors

The numerous traditional performance evaluation methods each have problems and potential rating errors. In some situations, raters are extremely harsh or easy in their evaluations. These are called strictness or leniency rater errors. The harsh rater tends to give lower-than-average ratings to subordinates. The lenient rater tends to give higher-than-average ratings. These kinds of rating errors typically result because raters apply their own personal standards to the particular performance evaluation system being used. For example, the words *outstanding* or *average* may mean different things to various raters.

Rating errors can be minimized if:

- Each dimension addresses a single job activity rather than a group of activities.

- The rater can observe the ratees' behavior on a regular basis.

- Terms such as *average* are not used on rating scales, since different raters react differently to such words.

- The rater does not have to evaluate large groups of subordinates. Fatigue and difficulty in discriminating among ratees become major problems when large groups of subordinates are evaluated.

- Raters are trained to avoid leniency, strictness, stereotyping, and other rating errors.

- The dimensions being evaluated are meaningful, clearly stated, and important.

COMPENSATION

Compensation is the HRM activity that deals with every type of reward that individuals receive for performing organizational tasks. It is basically an exchange relationship. Employees exchange their labor for financial and nonfinancial rewards. Financial compensation is both

EXHIBIT 8.4
Types of Compensation

Direct	Indirect
Base Pay	Education Programs (e.g., paying for course tuition and fees)
Merit Pay	Protection Programs (e.g., insurance)
Incentives Group Individual	Time Away from Work (e.g., vacation)
Cost-of-Living Adjustments	Perks (e.g., company car)

direct and indirect. **Direct financial compensation** consists of the pay an employee receives in the form of wages, salary, bonuses, and commissions. **Indirect financial compensation** (also called benefits) consists of all financial rewards, such as vacation and insurance, that are not included in direct financial compensation. Exhibit 8.4 presents a number of direct and indirect forms of compensation.

Compensation Objectives

The objective of the traditional compensation function is to create a system of rewards that is equitable to employer and employee alike. The desired outcome is an employee who is attracted to the work and motivated to do a good job for the employer. Compensation policy has seven criteria for effectiveness:

- *Adequate.* Minimum government, union, and managerial pay levels should be met.
- *Equitable.* Everyone should be paid fairly, in line with their effort, abilities, and training.
- *Balanced.* Pay, benefits, and other rewards should provide a reasonable total reward package.
- *Cost-effective.* Pay should not be excessive, considering what the organization can afford to pay.
- *Secure.* Pay should be enough to help employees feel secure and aid them in satisfying basic needs.
- *Incentive-providing.* Pay should motivate effective, productive work.
- *Acceptable to the employee.* Employees should understand the pay system and feel that it is reasonable for the enterprise and themselves.[12]

Pay can be determined absolutely or relatively. Some people have argued that the best procedure would be a pay system set by a single criterion for the whole nation or the world (i.e., the absolute control of pay). Since absolute pay systems are not used, however, the pay for each employee is set relative to the pay of others. Pay for a particular position is set relative to three groups:

- Employees working on similar jobs in other organizations (Group A)
- Employees working on different jobs within the organization (Group B)
- Employees working on the same job within the organization (Group C)

The decision to examine pay relative to Group A is called the *pay-level decision*. The objective of the pay-level decision is to keep the organization competitive in the labor market. The major tool used in this decision is the pay survey (discussed later in this chapter). The pay decision relative to Group B is called the *pay-structure decision*. The pay structure involves using job evaluation to set a value on each job within the organization relative to all other jobs. The decision involving pay relative to Group C is called *individual pay determination*.

Compensation and Performance

Due to increasing payroll costs and competition in the global marketplace, managers throughout the world are searching for ways to increase productivity by linking compensation to employee performance.[13] High performance requires much more than employee motivation. Employee ability and health, adequate equipment, good physical working conditions, effective leadership and management, safety, and other conditions all help raise employee performance levels. But employees' motivation to work harder and better is obviously an important factor. A number of studies indicate that if pay is tied to performance, the employee produces a higher quality and quantity of work.[14] Not everyone agrees with this finding; some researchers argue that if you tie pay to performance, you destroy the intrinsic rewards a person gets from doing the job well.[15] The importance of money varies from one employee to the next. If the organization claims to have an incentive pay system but in fact pays for seniority, the motivation effects of pay will be lost. The key to making compensation systems more effective is to be sure that they are directly connected to expected behaviors. An increasing number of organizations are tying pay and bonuses to the achievement of goals and individual performance.[16]

In sum, theorists disagree over whether pay is a useful mechanism for increasing performance. Because of individual differences in employees and jobs, it seems more fruitful to redirect this research to examine (1) the range of behaviors that pay can affect positively or negatively, (2) the amount of change in worker behavior that pay can influence, (3) the kinds of employees that pay influences positively and negatively, and (4) the environmental conditions present when pay leads to positive and negative results.

Selected Methods of Compensation

Employees can be paid for the time they work (flat rates), the output they produce (individual incentives), or a combination of these two factors.

Flat Rates.　In the unionized firm, where wages are established by collective bargaining, single *flat rates* rather than different rates are often paid. For example, all clerk-typists might make $6.50 per hour, regardless of seniority or performance. Flat rates correspond to some midpoint on a market survey for that job. Using a flat rate doesn't mean that seniority and experience do not differ. It means that employers and the union choose not to recognize these variations when setting wage rates. Unions insist on ignoring performance differentials for many reasons. They contend that performance measures are inequitable. Jobs need cooperative effort that could be destroyed by wage differentials. Sales organizations, for example, pay a flat rate for a job and add a bonus or incentive to recognize individual differences.

Choosing to pay a flat rate versus different rates for the same job depends on the objectives established by the compensation analyst. Recognizing individual differences makes the assumption that employees are not interchangeable or equally productive. By using pay differentials to recognize these differences, managers try to encourage an experienced, efficient, and satisfied workforce.

Individual Incentives.   Perhaps the oldest form of compensation is the **individual incentive plan,** in which the employee is paid for units produced. Individual incentive plans take several forms: piecework, production bonuses, and commissions. These methods seek to achieve the incentive goal of compensation.

Straight piecework usually works like this. An employee is guaranteed an hourly rate (often the minimum wage) for performing an expected minimum output (the standard). For production over the standard, the employer pays so much per additional piece produced. This is probably the most frequently used incentive pay plan. The standard is set through work measurement studies as modified by collective bargaining. The base rate and piece rate may emerge from data collected by pay surveys.

A variation of the straight piece rate is the *differential piece rate*. In this plan, the employer pays a smaller piece rate up to the standard and then a higher piece rate above the standard. Research indicates that the differential piece rate is more effective than the straight piece rate, although it is much less frequently used.[17]

Production bonus systems pay an employee an hourly rate. Then a bonus is paid when the employee exceeds the standard, typically 50 percent of labor savings. This system is not widely used.

Commissions are paid to sales employees. Straight commission is the equivalent of straight piecework and is typically a percentage of the item's price. A variation of the production bonus system for sales is to pay salespeople a small salary and commission or bonus when they exceed standards (the budgeted sales goal).

Individual incentives are used more frequently in some industries (clothing, steel, textiles) than others (lumber, beverage, bakery) and more often in some jobs (sales, production) than others (maintenance, clerical). Individual incentives are possible only in situations where performance can be clearly specified in terms of output (sales dollars generated, number of items completed). In addition, so that individual incentives can be applied equitably, employees must work independently of each other. Digital Equipment Company (DEC) uses an incentive system to reward whistle blowing.

Gainsharing Incentive Plans.   **Gainsharing plans** are companywide group incentive plans. Their goal is to unite diverse organizational elements behind the common pursuit of improved organizational effectiveness by allowing employees to share in the proceeds. The system has proven to be exceptionally effective in enhancing organization-wide teamwork. Gainsharing plans that use cash awards and have been in place for at least five years have shown productivity ratio improvements resulting in labor cost reductions of 29 percent.[18]

More and more companies have been implementing gainsharing plans using a formula that establishes a bonus based on improved productivity. Gainsharing rewards are normally distributed either monthly or quarterly.[19] Factors dictating a gainsharing plan's success include (1) company size, (2) age of the plan, (3) the company's financial stability, (4) unionization, (5) the company's technology, and (6) employees' and managers' attitudes. Because a gainsharing plan is expensive to administer, organizations considering it must weigh the projected benefits against costs.

Linking pay to group performance and inspiring team spirit are two reasons cited for the rising popularity of gainsharing.[20] For gainsharing to succeed, it must be supported by management. To optimize this type of group-based incentive program, management must also understand what gainsharing can and cannot accomplish.

The Equal Pay Act

The Equal Pay Act (1963) amending the Fair Labor Standards Act is the first antidiscrimination law relating directly to women. The act applies to all employers and employees covered by the Fair Labor Standards Act, including executives, managers, and professionals. The Equal Pay Act requires equal pay for equal work for men and women. It defines *equal work* as employment requiring equal skills, effort, and responsibility under similar working conditions.[21]

Under the Equal Pay Act, an employer can establish different wage rates on the basis of (1) seniority, (2) merit, (3) performance differences (quantity and quality of work), and (4) any factor other than sex. Shift work differentials are also permissible. But all these exceptions must apply equally to men and women. Since passage of the act, the female–male earnings gap has narrowed slightly. In an effort to close the remaining earnings gap, over the past few years there has been a growing movement to expand the widely accepted concept of equal pay for equal jobs to include equal pay for comparable jobs. Thus, for young people entering the workforce today, there is practically no difference between wages for men and women within a single job; the male–female wage discrepancy is heavily generational.

Comparable Worth

The doctrine of comparable worth (sometimes called pay equity) does not stipulate that women and men be paid equally for performing equal work. **Comparable worth** is a concept that attempts to prove and remedy the allegation that employers systematically discriminate by paying women employees less than their work is intrinsically worth, relative to what they pay men who work in comparable professions. The term *comparable worth* means different things to different people. Comparable worth relates jobs that are dissimilar in their content (for example, nurse and plumber) and contends that individuals who perform jobs that require similar skills, efforts, and responsibilities under similar work conditions should be compensated equally.

Advocates of comparable worth depend primarily upon two sets of statistics to demonstrate that women employees are discriminated against by employers. First, they point to statistics showing that women earn less than men overall.[22] Second, women have tended to be concentrated in lower-paying, predominantly female jobs. Although more women are entering the workforce, about one-fourth of all women employed in 1988 worked in three job categories: secretarial/clerical, retail sales, and food preparation and service.[23] *Child care*

BENEFITS AND SERVICES

Indirect financial compensation, which many organizations refer to as **benefits and services,** consists of all financial rewards that are not included in direct financial compensation. Unlike pay-for-performance programs and incentive plans, benefits and services are made available to employees as long as they are employed by the organization. Annual surveys suggest that about 75 percent of all U.S. workers say that benefits are crucial to job choice. If limited to only one benefit (beyond cash), 64 percent say that healthcare is most important.[24] Employee benefits and services are part of the rewards of employment that reinforce loyal service to the employer. Major benefits and services programs include pay for time not worked, insurance, pensions, and services like tuition reimbursement.

This definition of benefits and services can be applied to hundreds of programs. There is a lack of agreement among organizations on what is or is not to be included, the purposes to be served, responsibility for programs, the costs and values of the various elements, the units in which the costs and values are measured, and the criteria for decision making.

Compensation decisions regarding indirect compensation are more complex than decisions concerned with wages and salaries.

Benefits Required by Law

Benefits programs offered by organizations today are the product of efforts in this area for the past sixty years. Before World War II, employers offered a few pensions and services because they had the welfare of employees at heart, or they wanted to keep out a union. But most benefit programs began in earnest during the war, when wages were strictly regulated.

The unions pushed for nonwage compensation increases, and they got them. Court cases in the late 1940s confirmed the right of unions to bargain for benefits: *Inland Steel* v. *National Labor Relations Board* (1948) over pensions, and *W. W. Cross* v. *National Labor Relations Board* over insurance. The growth of benefit programs indicates how much unions have used this right. In 1929 benefits cost employers 3 percent of total wages and salaries; by 1949 the cost was up to 16 percent, and in the 1970s it was nearly 30 percent. By 1990 costs of benefits and services totaled about 50 percent.[25]

Additional Benefits and Retirement Plans

In addition to benefits required by the law (such as unemployment insurance, social security, and workers' compensation), many employers provide other kinds of benefits: compensation for time not worked, insurance protection, and retirement plans. There are many differences in employers' practices regarding these benefits. The most widely used benefits include paid vacations, holidays, and sick leave; life and medical insurance; and pension plans.

Childcare.   Two fairly recent additions to benefits packages are childcare and eldercare. Nearly 50 percent of today's workers are women, and as many as 70 percent of these women have children under age six at home. The Bureau of the Census reports that working mothers pay about $15.1 billion per year for childcare while they work. The U.S. Department of Labor states that in 1995, more than 80 percent of the women between the ages of 25 and 44 will be working outside the home at least part-time. This suggests that childcare programs will become a necessity.

Eldercare.   People age sixty-five or older will comprise 23 percent of the U.S. population by 2050.[26] Recent research shows that at least 20 percent of all employees already provide assistance to one or more elderly relatives or friends. On average, these employees spend between 6 and 35 hours per week providing this care. At least 50 percent of these employees also have children at home. The burden falls most heavily on the working woman, who traditionally cared for elderly relatives and did not work outside the home. Employees who are also caregivers to seniors experience the following problems: missed work (58 percent), loss of pay (47 percent), and less energy to do their work well (15 percent).

SPECIAL ISSUES IN HUMAN RESOURCES

The HRM activities already discussed are important and must be properly managed to ensure the efficient use of human resource abilities, skills, and experience. In addition, however, three special issues—AIDS, sexual harassment, and substance abuse—have become significant in the workplace.

AIDS in the Workplace

There are many reasons why a company should be knowledgeable about and have a plan to deal with acquired immunodeficiency syndrome (AIDS). First there is the moral reason, that people are dying and organizations are likely to be involved simply by being a part of society. The law of probability suggests that eventually AIDS will enter every workplace. Individuals, work groups, and departments will feel the tragedy of AIDS.

The 1992 Americans with Disabilities Act (ADA) protects individuals with AIDS from being discriminated against in the areas of hiring, advancement, compensation, training, or other conditions of employment. Under the ADA, employers may require employee physicals only if the exams are clearly job specific and consistent with business necessity, and then only after an offer of employment has been made to a job applicant.[27] A major concern of organizations is finding a balance between the rights of a person with AIDS and the rights of their coworkers to a healthy, safe environment. Education, counseling, and safety are the keys to minimizing the impact AIDS will have on an organization.

Sexual Harassment

According to public opinion polls, most American women believe they have experienced sexual harassment on the job. As the law has evolved, two types of conduct have been found to constitute sexual harassment in violation of Title VII of the Civil Rights Act. The first type, originally identified in 1977, is the designated *tangible job benefit,* also known as *quid pro quo harassment*. This form of harassment occurs when an employee's career path is directly affected by a supervisor's unwelcome requests for sexual favors or other sexual advances.

A second type of sexual harassment is a *hostile work environment*. The elements necessary for proving a sexual harassment claim related to a hostile work environment are stated by a New York State case:

> A person would have to show that (1) he or she belongs to a protected group (i.e., female or minority group); (2) he or she was subject to unwelcome sexual harassment as defined above; (3) the harassment complained of was based upon his or her membership in the protected class; and (4) the harassment complained of affected the terms, conditions, or privileges of his or her employment.

The creation of a work environment in violation of Title VII can occur in many ways, depending on the size of the workforce, managers' sensitivity to sexual harassment, and the dynamics of the workplace.

The number of sexual harassment complaints filed with the Equal Employment Opportunity Commission (EEOC) has soared by 150 percent—going from 6,127 in 1990 to 15,342 in 1996.[28] Since most victims don't file with the EEOC, these figures represent only some of the incidents. As the problem continues, managers are advised to develop a program to combat sexual harassment. Typically a company-based program involves (1) developing a sexual harassment policy and complaint resolution procedure, (2) training managers to implement the policy and procedure, (3) educating employees to recognize and confront harassment, (4) providing follow-up care after harassment incidents, and (5) monitoring the workplace for awareness of and compliance with sexual harassment policies.[29]

The seriousness of sexual harassment and why it must be dealt with through policies, increased awareness, and training are captured in this statement by the U.S. Merit Protection Board:

> Victims pay all the intangible emotional costs inflicted by anger, humiliation, frustration, withdrawal, dysfunctional family, and other damages that can be sexual harassment's aftermath. Victims of the most severe forms of harassment, including rape, can face not only severe emotional consequences, but also the possibility of a life-threatening disease. Some victims may leave jobs for one with a lower career path in order to escape the sexual harassment.[30]

Because of its trauma and potential impact, sexual harassment demands prompt managerial action. It is impossible for a worker to pay attention to the quality of production or service when harassment is occurring. Corrective action is required because of the need to protect the rights of every worker. It is also required because the law (although it's gray in some areas) indicates that employers are liable for sexual harassment. In fact, employers may also be responsible for the acts of their employees. For example, where an employer (or an employer's agent) knows—or should know—of the harassment and fails to take immediate and corrective action, the employer may be held liable. Sending a clear message that sexual harassment of any form will not be tolerated is a recommended course of action.[31]

Substance Abuse

Substance abuse is a major problem that may affect the safety, productivity, and image of organizations.[32] An American Management Association (AMA) survey indicates that about 75 percent of major U.S. companies now engage in drug testing.[33] Most major corporations also conduct preemployment substance abuse testing. Like many forms of testing, substance abuse screening has passionate opponents. Claims that it is inaccurate, an invasion of privacy, and demeaning are well articulated. But so long as substance abuse remains a problem, testing is likely to continue. It is estimated that substance abuse costs U.S. industry over $140 billion annually because of lost productivity.[34] Clearly, programs and policies are needed to reduce the burden of substance abuse.

Management's most powerful tool to combat substance abuse is an informed, educated workforce. Detecting substance abuse or a related problem requires careful observation and proper training. Here are some signs of possible substance abuse:

- Difficulty in recalling instructions
- Frequent tardiness and absence
- Numerous restroom breaks
- Difficulty in getting along with coworkers
- Increased off- and on-the-job accidents
- Dramatic change in personality[35]

The controversy about substance abuse detection and testing is likely to continue unabated. The need is for a policy and program that (1) explains the company's philosophy on substance abuse, (2) describes the firm's policy on testing, (3) implements a discipline and rehabilitation program, (4) communicates the program to all employees, and (5) educates managers on how to enforce a fair substance abuse policy and program.[36] The foundation of an effective approach to preventing substance abuse is a clear, coherent program.

Conclusion
——Human Resource Management——

People are the most important asset of an organization. To succeed in today's competitive global markets, organizations must recruit, retain, develop, and manage human resources. Many factors—laws, compensation, and benefits—must be considered in developing an effective human resource program.

SUGGESTED READINGS

Antilla, Susan. *Tales from the Boom-Boom Room: Women vs. Wall Street* (Princeton, NJ: Bloomberg Press, 2002).

Becker, Brian E., Mark A. Huselid, and Dave Ulrich. *The HR Scorecard: Linking People, Strategy, and Performance* (Boston: Harvard Business School Press, 2001).

Falcone, Paul. *96 Great Interview Questions to Ask Before You Hire* (New York: AMACOM, 1997).

Gupta, Kavita. *A Practical Guide to Needs Assessment* (San Francisco: Jossey-Bass, 1999).

Kirkpatrick, Donald L. *Evaluating Training Programs: The Four Levels* (San Francisco: Berrett-Koehler, 1998).

Pfeffer, Jeffrey. "Seven Practices of Successful Organizations," *California Management Review,* Winter 1998, 96–124.

Stolovitch, Harold D., and Erica J. Keeps. *Telling Ain't Training* (Alexandria, VA: American Society for Training and Development, 2002).

ENDNOTES

1. David P. Twomey, *Equal Employment Opportunity Law* (Cincinnati, OH: South-Western Publishing, 1994).

2. Alfred Edmond Jr., "25 Years of Affirmative Action," *Black Enterprise,* February 1995, 156–157.

3. D. Murry and James C. Wimbush, "Perceptions of Workplace Affirmative Action Plans," *Group and Organization Management,* March 1998, 27–47.

4. Ann C. Wendt and William M. Slonaker, "Discrimination Reflects on You," *HR Magazine,* May 1992, 44–47.

5. *Equal Employment Opportunity Manual for Managers and Supervisors* (Chicago: Commerce Clearing House, 1992).

6. Joel Schettler, "Equal Access to All," *Training,* January 2002, 44.

7. Twomey, *Equal Employment Opportunity Law,* 1–4.

8. Jennifer Merritt, "Improv at the Interview," *Business Week,* February 3, 2003, 63.

9. "HR Managers Have the Most Common Causes of Poor Candidate Selection," *Personnel Journal,* July 1995, 25.

10. Bently Baranabus, "What Did the Supreme Court Really Say?" *Personnel Administrator,* July–August 1971, 22–25.

11. M. Brown, "Reference Checking: The Law Is on Your Side," *Human Resource Measurements* (supplement to *Personnel Journal*), December 1991, 4–5.

12. Thomas Patton, *Pay* (New York: The Free Press, 1977).

13. B. J. Dewey, "Changing to Skill-Based Pay," *Compensation and Benefits Review,* January–February 1994, 38–43.

14. Peter V. Leblanc, "Pay for Work: Reviving an Old Idea for the New Customer Focus," *Compensation and Benefits Review,* July–August 1994, 5–14.

15. Joel M. Stern and G. Bennett Stewart III, "Pay-For-Performance: Only the Theory Is Easy," *HR Magazine,* June 1993, 48–49.

16. Michelle Conlin, "Now It's Getting Personal," *Business Week,* December 16, 2002, 90–92.

17. Carla O'Dell, *People, Performance, and Pay: America Responds to the Competitiveness Challenge* (Scottsdale, AZ: American Compensation Association, 1986), 108.

18. Jerry McAdams, "Alternative Rewards: What's Best for Your Organization?" *Compensation and Benefits Management,* Winter 1990, 133–139.

19. Dennis Collins, Larry Hatcher, and Timothy J. Ross, "The Decision to Implement Gainsharing: The Role of Work Climate, Expected Outcomes, and Union Status," *Personnel Psychology,* Spring 1993, 79.

20. Steven E. Markham, K. Dow Scott, and Beverly L. Little, "National Gainsharing Study: The Importance of Industry Differences," *Compensation & Benefits Review,* January–February 1992, 34–45.

21. A. L. Otten, "People Patterns," *Wall Street Journal,* April 15, 1994, A1.

22. Barry Gerhart, "Gender Differences in Current and Starting Salaries: The Role of Performance, College Major, and Job Title," *Industrial and Labor Relations Review* April 1990, 418–433.

23. "Women in Sales are Closing the Earnings Gap," *Personnel Journal,* July 1995, 28.

24. "Controlling the Costs of Employee Benefits," *The Conference Board,* 1992, 8.

25. J. E. Santora, "Employee Team Designs Flexible Benefits Program," *Personnel Journal,* April 1994, 30–39.

26. "Stride Rite Halts Its Elder-Care Program," *Personnel Journal,* September 1995, 11.

27. Helen Elkiss, "Reasonable Accommodation and Unreasonable Fears: An AIDS Policy Guide for Human Resource Personnel," *Human Resource Planning,* March 1992, 183–189.

28. Larry Reynolds, "Sexual Harassment Claims Surge," *HR Focus,* March 1997, 8.

29. Kelly Flynn, "Preventive Medicine for Sexual Harassment," *HR Focus,* March 1991, 17.

30. Jeffrey P. Englander, "Handling Sexual Harassment in the Workplace," *The CPA Journal,* February 1992, 14.

31. Jonathan A. Segal, "Seven Ways to Reduce Harassment Claims," *HR Magazine,* January 1992, 84–86.

32. Nicholas J. Caste, "Drug Testing and Productivity," *Journal of Business Ethics* (April 1992): 301–306.

33. Eric Rolfe Greenberg, "Test-Positive Rates Drop as More Companies Screen Employees," *HR Focus,* June 1992, 7.

34. "Report Finds Economic Cost of Substance Abuse Exceeds $143 Billion," *Alcoholism and Drug Abuse Weekly,* January 28, 2002, 1, 4.

35. Laura A. Lyons and Brian H. Kleiner, "Managing the Problem of Substance Abuse . . . Without Abusing Employees," *HR Focus,* April 1992, 9.

36. Martha Zetlin, "Corporate America Declares War on Drugs," *Personnel,* August 1991, 1, 8.

Leading

part four

Chapter
Nine

Groups, Processes, and Teams
in Organizations

Collective action is an integral part of all organizations. Without groups, organizations would have to rely solely on individuals to complete both daily tasks and longer-term assignments. As you can imagine, many activities would be impossible without the collective efforts of two or more people. Actions as simple as tying a shoe might be near impossible if someone wasn't around to show you how. Be thankful, then, that collective action is a natural extension of individual effort. Our prehistory suggests that hunting in groups for food and communal living increased chances of survival for all. Armies, sporting teams, bridge clubs, and church choirs are everyday examples of collective behavior known as groups. As we all recognize, in group behavior there is a power unmatched by individual action. Any organization may ignore an individual's demand for a salary increase; but the same demand, when made by a union, could cripple the organization's productive capacity if ignored. For these reasons and others, it is natural and important for future managers to learn the dynamics of group behavior.

In this chapter we describe types of groups, how they function, and what factors are likely to turn any group into a highly effective component of the organization. We'll end the chapter with a discussion of team-driven enterprises, whose notions of work and how work is managed continually challenge the status quo. But first we need to draw the distinction between a group and a team, and so we begin this chapter with a few key definitions.

Groups and *teams* are terms often used interchangeably to represent the same idea. However, there is a clear distinction; *group* is a general concept, whereas *team* is more specific. A **group** is defined as two or more people who act together to accomplish a goal. Groups often occur naturally, to accomplish a goal such as moving a log or pushing a car from a ditch. In an organization, a naturally forming group might be people who were all hired in the same department at about the same time and attend the same training session. A **team** is also a group, but it holds membership in a larger organization, and its purpose is related to the goals of that organization. While a group might be part of an organized activity, a team has a task, resources, leadership, and a goal. Further, a team is a self-managing collective that experiences synergy through shared information, interaction, interdependence, and the bond of a common goal. Teams often have resources at their disposal and have greater decision-making autonomy than a conventional group. The integrated work of several teams makes larger goals attainable.

In this chapter we consider the roles of both groups and teams, with an eye on the performance or outcomes of the group or team. As you read, bear in mind that most of the ideas that apply to groups also apply to teams.

GROUPS

Groups are a common fixture of organizational life. Much of the daily work of organizations is performed by groups. But not all groups work to achieve the goals of the organization. From an organizational perspective, there are two categories of groups: the informal group and the formal group. All other types of groups or teams are variants of these two basic forms of collective behavior.

Informal Groups

An **informal group** arises when two or more people engage in voluntary collective activity for a common purpose. Friendship groups and interest groups are two types of informal groups commonly found in organizations.

- **Friendship groups** A friendship group is a collection of people with similar values or beliefs who get together for a common purpose—possibly just to have fun.

- **Interest groups** An interest group is a collection of people addressing a specific subject. An example would be five people from different walks of life who meet regularly to discuss art and attend plays.

Informal group actions generally aren't recognized by the organization. However, work associations are often springboards into friendship groups and interest groups such as quilting, woodworking, Habitat for Humanity, or shopping excursions. Membership in an informal group provides the individual with new ways of understanding daily life experiences. These new worldviews often translate into action at work. For example, working in a quilting circle at church on Sunday might lead to the idea that the best way to accomplish a work task is by using a group rather than assigning a single person to complete the task. While not directly related to work organizations, informal groups are found in all organizations. Our ability to join one or more informal groups is greatly enhanced when we regularly interact with diverse groups of people. Most large organizations fit this description quite well. Membership in large organizations increases our exposure to different informal groups that we might join. With an informal group, the "joining" part is often rather casual.

Formal Groups

Groups are formal to the extent that membership is based on the employee's position in an organization. **Formal groups** consist of two or more people who engage in organizationally required actions for a common purpose. These groups are a permanent part of the organization. A marketing department is an example of a formal group. The role definition and membership requirements for a formal group are quite explicit. Thus to maintain membership in the marketing department, a marketing manager may have to reach targeted sales goals for assigned products.

Work Groups

Within a formal group, such as a customer relations department, there are many work groups. A **work group** is defined as two or more people in a work organization who share a common purpose. This common purpose is usually the completion of a task. The work group is the smallest formal organizational personnel arrangement. As such, a work group represents the most basic level of collective work activity. To govern the relationship between the group and the organization, the group has assigned reporting relationships, a formal leader, and, often, specific instructions to guide task completion. For many years the formal work group with external supervision was the mainstay of productive effort in organizations.

Characteristics of Effective Groups

An effective group is one that fully utilizes the abilities of its members in the attainment of group goals. A group continues to be effective as long as it can elicit contributions from members. Another way of thinking about the relationship between a member and the group is as a type of exchange. The group member gives time, energy, knowledge, and ability; in exchange, the group gives the member need satisfaction. Group membership holds the potential to satisfy several basic human needs. Individual member needs that are met through group involvement include need for achievement, need for affiliation, and need for power.[1] When a group has successfully attained a specific goal, its members are often encouraged to know that goal attainment would have been impossible without their efforts. Likewise, successful group members interact. For many individuals, group membership at work is their primary attachment to other people. Group interaction is an important part of human interaction as well as a necessary component of work.

An effective group doesn't just happen by accident; it is created, managed, and developed over time by managers and group members. Yet, not all groups will be effective. Managers are responsible for periodic group evaluation (even self-managing groups have a manager who is responsible for that group). Managers can use the qualities or characteristics of effective groups (Exhibit 9.1) as a basis for diagnosing problems in poorly performing groups.

Like the need for affiliation, the need for power can be fulfilled in a socially acceptable way at work. Work-group hierarchy allows some group members a degree of control over other group members' activities. People are accepted into the group, their behavior is scrutinized, and they are encouraged or discouraged based on group members' evaluation of them. The group leader or a designated leader may derive a real sense of personal power from these types of value-adding activities. But beyond these issues of group functioning are other, more enduring issues. For example, how does an effective group continue to function at high levels over time? What mechanisms sustain the group when high-performing members leave?

EXHIBIT 9.1
Characteristics of Effective Groups

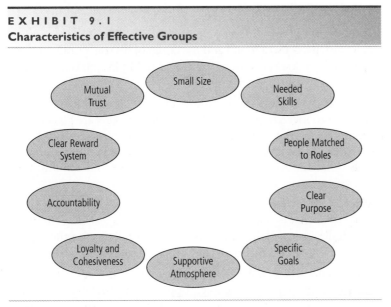

Source: Adapted from R. Likert, *New Patterns of Management* (New York: McGraw-Hill, 1961), 166.

Role Making in Groups

All work groups are defined not only by the roles that their members perform, but also by the hierarchy or status of these roles. As discussed in Chapter 1, a *role* is a set of shared expectations regarding a member's attitude and task behavior within the group. At the most basic level, a group will have available two roles: leader and member.

The greater the group's task complexity, the more roles will emerge. Group member agreement about the role to be performed is referred to as the **sent role.** Essentially, the sent role embodies the formal requirements of the role within the group. The **received role** is the role recipient's individual translation of what the sent role means to him or her. In other words, the sent role may be received differently by different people. The **enacted role** is the manner in which the received role is expressed or redefined by the individual assuming the role.[2] This role is defined by how formal group expectations are transmitted, filtered, and processed for action by the role occupant. We all have different backgrounds, values, education, and beliefs about how the job should be done. All these factors are brought to the forefront during the role creation and enactment processes.

Problems in Role Making

Role creation within groups is not without its share of problems. Common problems include role conflict, role ambiguity, and role overload.[3]

Role Conflict. **Role conflict** represents the incompatibility between the role's requirements and the individual's own beliefs or expectations. Remember, we all assume multiple roles in many different aspects of our lives. For example, a worker could simultaneously hold the roles of mother, wife, devoted church leader, manager, and engineer. It is easy to see that many of these different roles have required behaviors that may conflict with one another.

Such internal conflict can come from a variety of sources.

- **Interrole conflict** occurs when two different types of roles collide. A manager may have to fire an employee who is also a friend and the coach of his son's Little League team. The friend part of him doesn't want to fire the man, but his job requires him to do so.

- **Intrarole conflict** occurs when two similar roles come in conflict, for example, when your boss tells you to increase productivity and your workers are pushing for better working conditions. In this example, you are simultaneously a subordinate and a superior. Further, you believe not only that the organization needs greater productivity, but also that the work rules make for dissatisfied and unmotivated workers.

- **Intersender conflict** occurs when contradictory messages come from the same source. Your boss preaches that quality is the most important aspect of your work. However, he insists on hiring low-skilled workers who can't fully utilize the robotics that are a major determinant of quality in the company.

- **Person-role conflict** occurs when an individual's beliefs are in direct conflict with the requirements of his or her role. For example, suppose you know that a product batch is defective and that shipping the products could possibly cause consumer injury and increase liability for the firm. You've also received a memo from your boss, who insists your job is to help build sales volume by expediting the shipment of as many products as possible. You know shipping the product is wrong, but you feel compelled to make your volume quota.

Role Ambiguity.   In **role ambiguity,** the requirements of a role are not clear. In general, role ambiguity results when the role occupant is not sure how to fulfill role requirements. Simple, routine roles rarely generate ambiguity. In a routine role, for instance, an assembly-line job, role requirements are specific or decision criteria are simple. Professional roles present a greater chance of role ambiguity. Managers often face technical situations that they are not trained to fully understand. In such situations, managers may experience ambiguity in choosing between two courses: Should they consult a staff specialist (which might waste time), or go with the subordinate's judgment? Whether the outcome is positive or negative, managers know full well that they'll be held responsible.

Role Overload.   **Role overload** is a condition in which a task's demands overwhelm the role occupant's ability to perform the task. Too much, too little, or conflicting information may surpass the role occupant's ability to perform the task at a satisfactory level. With the emphasis on "lean organizations" and the corresponding reduction of America's white-collar workforce, it's very likely that role overload will be a common contributory symptom of role stress reported by those who remain employed.

Role conflict, role ambiguity, and role overload are all potential problems that can decrease a group's effectiveness. Managers must recognize these problems, which can undermine a group's overall performance.

Group Norms

Group norms define the borders of acceptable member behavior. Usually, intergroup behavior is thought of as a positive force in group productivity. But norms can actually have a negative effect on group output. Take, for example, the restriction of output. A work group might easily produce twenty-five units in an hour. Yet if the group's strategy is to suppress output, then the norm enforces lower effort and lower output. Norms represent

EXHIBIT 9.2
Typical Group Norms

Group Norm	Purpose	Example Situation
Rotate leadership	Avoid dominance of one person.	Mary is an accountant and has a low tolerance for ambiguity.
Timeliness	Make deadlines.	The product launch will be a week later than expected; the product testing group missed their deadline.
Loyalty	Maintain confidential information.	When asked by the head of another department to divulge a new employee's salary, John referred the question to his boss, thus maintaining confidentiality.
Fairness	Share rewards equally among the group.	In our department, vacation requests are based on rotation. The last person to request last year gets first pick this year.

a form of control over intermittent or random behaviors by group members—be they positive or negative behaviors. However, norms are not developed for all situations or circumstances that the group might encounter, only for those that hold some importance for the group. The group uses rewards and sanctions to encourage acceptance of the norm. Group members who adhere to the norm may receive praise or recognition for their devotion to group norms. Completing a project ahead of schedule may be rewarded with a Friday afternoon off.

Member acceptance of a norm is referred to as **conformity.** Because it creates a system of shared values among veteran group members as well as newcomers to the group, conformity is important. On the one hand, newcomers may be amazed by group performance or behavioral expectation.[4] But new members quickly learn to meet group expectations if they want to maintain a good standing in the group. On the other hand, veteran members of the group help create and enforce group norms. Without group norms, the group's expectations would be vague at best. For this reason, groups with clear normative expectations are more effective at attaining group goals—and in the process, creating greater member satisfaction—than are groups with comparatively limited normative guidance. Exhibit 9.2 presents some common group norms and their purposes, with example situations in which the norms are enforced.

Group norms are communicated in one of four ways:

- Explicit statements by the group leader
- Explicit statements by group members
- Critical events in the group's history
- Past group experiences[5]

Most often, group norms develop through efforts of the group leader. The leader communicates the group's wishes and values to new members and reinforces them with existing members. But the leader may not always be present in a norm-signaling situation. In this instance, coworkers may communicate the conformity to the group norm. For example, suppose a member of the counter crew at a fast-food restaurant observes a coworker's negative attitude toward customers. He might quickly take the worker aside and remind her that if the customer complained, the entire crew could be reprimanded for her poor attitude. If the rude worker fails to alter her inappropriate customer behavior, she might be shunned by other crew members until her behavior improves.

Another impetus for the development of group norms might be a critical event in the group's history. Say, for instance, that a group representative has been outmaneuvered in a staff meeting to the group's disadvantage. This could force a group norm to develop regarding how ideas are presented to other groups to ensure a successful outcome for the group.

Cohesiveness

A group has **cohesiveness** to the extent that (1) the group can do its work effectively, attract new members when necessary, and maintain the group over time; and (2) group members are able to influence one another.[6] Cohesiveness is a way of describing how well the group functions. Highly cohesive groups are good problem solvers. Further, in both work and social situations, members of cohesive groups interact more than people in less cohesive groups do.

By developing interaction skills, cohesive groups set the stage for greater success in their attempts to gain social influence. Social influence regulates deviation from accepted norms.[7] Group members can gang up on an individual member who is acting in ways the group believes are in conflict with group norms. For example, over a period of weeks, task group members on an auto assembly line might notice that one group member's "quality emphasis" is slipping. Each group member may pick a different time or approach to encourage the deviant worker to rethink how he does his job. This type of positive social influence may well make the deviant worker aware of his actions and bring him closer to the group norm. But if the worker's behavior is intolerable to the group, the social influence may be shifted toward the group leader—perhaps even forcing the leader to fire the worker for nonconformity to the quality norm.

Groupthink

Group decision making is not without some degree of risk. Group norms and conformity tendencies may actually suppress opposing or contrary perspectives. Irving Janis calls this concept groupthink. **Groupthink** is "a mode of thinking that people engage in when they are deeply involved in a cohesive in-group, when members' strivings for unanimity override their motivation to realistically appraise alternative courses of action."[8] Groupthink has been given as an explanation for the decision-making process that led to the Kennedy administration's disastrous 1961 Bay of Pigs invasion of Cuba. In essence, groupthink means suppressing or ignoring countervailing ideas that represent a threat to group consensus or unanimity. Unfortunately, when the group is wrong, group consensus doesn't mean very much in the long run. It is important to note, however, that within the same group, groupthink can occur during one decision-making situation and not another.[9]

Cultural Diversity

Groups are increasingly characterized by cultural diversity. Whether at work, at school, or during leisure time, cultural diversity exists in groups whose members differ by gender, age, ethnic background, disability status, religious affiliation, and lifestyle. Changing demographics and greater immigration bring greater diversity to the labor pool and ultimately to work. Over time, this means greater cultural diversity in work groups. Growing globalization and the addition of more women and minorities to the workforce mean that by 2020, a culturally diverse workforce will be the norm in most organizations.

Managing diverse groups has become a critical challenge in corporate America; firms that do not include diversity as part of their business plan will be at a competitive disadvantage.[10] For instance, one study found that firms receiving Department of Labor recognition for exemplary affirmative action programs are better able to recruit, develop, and maintain human resources, providing a competitive advantage.[11] Several approaches have been used to enhance cooperation and communication among culturally diverse groups, including multicultural workshops; female and minority support groups and networks; managerial reward systems based on managers' ability to train and promote women and minorities; fast-track programs targeted at women and minorities who demonstrate exceptional potential; and mentoring programs pairing women and minorities with senior managers.[12] At Ameritech, for example, a black advocacy panel was formed to review corporate policy on affirmative action and works to improve diversity at top levels.[13]

THE GROUP DEVELOPMENT PROCESS

Now that we've reviewed the different kinds of groups, we can examine how groups develop in a four-stage process of forming, storming, norming, and performing. **Group development** describes the progression from a collection of people literally tossed together for a common purpose to a well-functioning whole whose effectiveness stands the test of time.

Stage 1 Forming

Forming refers to the actual beginning of the group, when members get to know one another and start to understand each other's abilities and deficits. In the formation stage, the collection of people quickly comes together as a functioning unit. Members temporarily accept formation rules and orders in an effort to initiate the group. With the process under way, formal group functions are defined, and the beginnings of a hierarchy emerge. Sometimes, formal organizational task requirements dictate group purpose. A formal leader is often appointed to facilitate group development.

Stage 2 Storming

As the name suggests, this is the most tumultuous stage in the group development process. **Storming** refers to the group's coming to grips with inherent conflicts and developing solutions that keep the group focused on its work. During this stage, members learn to accept one another's individual differences. With this acceptance comes the beginning of a collective "group personality" that reflects their similarities and minimizes their differences. This collective viewpoint is the result of sharing common work, values, and purpose. Along with personality emergence comes informal vying for power or control of the group. Specialization through subgroups also begins to develop. Group members negotiate roles that are needed for effective group functioning, and members adopt those roles.

Stage 3 Norming

During the **norming** stage, the group charts its long-term vision of group purpose and how it will function over time. The process of achieving all members' agreement on the group's long-term vision is referred to as developing **shared values.** The group's norms are the unwritten guides to behavior. Conformity to norms is enforced through rewards and sanctions. Members who adhere to norms reap the benefits the group has to offer—such as status, affiliation, and personal growth. Deviance from group norms may subject the member to punishment, humiliation, or ostracism.

Stage 4 Performing

The group is now at the **performing** stage, in which the group functions as a highly effective unit. During this stage, a group that has remained together for a long time is fine-tuning group functioning. Group members carefully redefine group roles as needed. They decide how best to balance needs of the group and the organization. At this stage the group is most able to develop the skills of current members, recruit new members, and perform the group's work at a high level. By the time the group reaches the performing stage, all individuals have learned their roles in the group. The faster the group reaches the performing stage of development, the more effective the group.

Often short-term groups have to disband and merge their membership into other task groups. Some authors consider this "ungrouping" process a separate stage.

At each new stage in the group development process, the group is confronted with increasingly difficult decisions. One of the greatest challenges is how best to reward individual contribution and still maintain the group's integrity. In fully mature groups, individual efforts have been well integrated into specific group functions. Over time, the group's success or failure becomes evident. This is largely determined by how well the group performs its assigned functions and contributes to the organization's overall effectiveness.

TEAMS

Teams have become a widespread business phenomenon in recent years. Success stories of the team concept include Chrysler's initial product development of the Viper sports car as well as the use of cross-functional and cross-national work teams at Ford and Mazda.[14] These examples highlight the advantages of using self-managing, cross-functional teams to decrease product development time and/or increase overall product quality. Because effective work teams can be valuable assets to a firm, people who can successfully facilitate team interactions play an increasingly important role in organizations throughout the world.[15]

Although historically the use of teams has tended to be most prevalent in Japanese firms, the team approach seems to be gaining momentum in the United States as well.[16] More than twenty years ago management expert and college professor Edward Lawler estimated that about 150 (less than 1% of all organizations) manufacturing plants in the United States used some sort of self-managing team approach. In 1990 he estimated about 7 percent of the manufacturing firms in the United States used a team approach.[17] Today the consensus is that 15 percent of all manufacturing involves the use of teams. In fact, corporate leaders are increasingly relying on self-managed teams in all aspects of their businesses.[18] New hires are evaluated on their ability not only to work effectively within a team, but to direct the work of multiple teams. Project management skills have become essential to the upwardly mobile manager in dealing with time and cost, which are critical aspects of project management. All projects of any consequence have a deadline and limited resources.

We'll begin this section by examining the characteristics of teams and the advantages of teamwork. Other topics include team effectiveness, implementing work teams, and developing team-driven companies. We conclude by looking at how organizations can overcome employees' resistance to teamwork.

Characteristics of Teams

A good team has many hands, all helping to shoulder an otherwise individual burden. Teams are often responsible for all aspects of their work; they are given a goal or goals, a budget, and a deadline. The team is expected to perform the task and produce the output in accordance with the workflow of the organization. The result is efficiency, increased reliability, and innovation. For example, during recruitment, product design teams, creative advertising teams, and human resource management teams might each be charged with the responsibility of interviewing and recommending a prospective employee.

Generally, three characteristics can be used in describing the work of a team:

- Teams have a specific task.

- Teams are self-managing.

- Teams have decision-making autonomy.

As we mentioned earlier, two other factors are common to the team—resources and time. Resources mean a budget, and time takes the form of a deadline for task completion. Additionally, teams have to struggle with the concept of establishing a team reward for successful task completion.

However, not all teams are the same; a few distinctions are in order.

- **Work teams**—describes a special type of organizational work group, which is self-managed and has considerably more decision-making autonomy than some work groups. The primary difference between a work team and a work group is the way in which a team is governed and the special bond among team members.

- **Task teams**—are less permanent than a work team. Task teams are a formal group of people working on a temporary job. When its work is completed, a task team disbands.

- **Management team**—composed of several people from different functional or operating areas, brought together to plan, implement, and manage ongoing organizational activities.

Effective teams need members with the requisite skills to help the team achieve their goals. Regardless of the type of team, all team members need problem solving skills, interpersonal skills, and technical skills. Exhibit 9.3 lists the qualities of each skill team members need to possess or acquire to be effective team members.

EXHIBIT 9.3
Skills of Effective Team Members

Problem Solving	Interpersonal	Technical
• Thinking	• Facilitating	• Discovery
• Creativity	• Influencing	• Organization
• Discussion	• Listening	• Analysis
• Decisiveness	• Supporting	• Synthesis
• Implementation	• Visioning	• Clarification

Adapted from: Eileen K. Aranda, Luis Aranda with Kristi Conlon. *Teams: Structure. Process. Culture, and Politics* (Upper Saddle River, NJ: Prentice Hall, 1999), 18; and Jon R. Katzenbach and Douglas Smith. "The Discipline of Teams." *Harvard Business Review*, March–April 1992, 112–120.

Virtual Teams

The term **virtual team** refers to the collaborative activities of several people, working together on computer networks, using common software and sharing common data. Expensive office space and the environmental impact of increased automobile usage and automobile parking make virtual teams practical. As a cost-saving measure, Allstate Insurance in Northbrook, Illinois, encourages employees to telecommute to minimize parking problems and the cost of office space.

The advent of personal computers and **groupware** (group-based software) made possible the collaborative work by geographically dispersed users. Using groupware, virtual team members can interact in real time, modifying and updating designs or other elements in a database. Virtual teams are common in the publishing industry, in new product design, and in many other applications. Boeing Aircraft developed the 777 aircraft on a computer network that linked in-house services as well as all external subcontractors. Many participants in the development process were members of virtual teams. Design team members shared information and used virtual-space renderings of design elements to ensure that parts from different vendors fit together. The result is a high-quality, high-reliability product that airlines and air travelers can count on for safe, reliable, and economical service.

Here are some benefits of the virtual team:

- Geographically dispersed people can work together online
- Reduces employee cost per transaction
- Decreases time to complete a project
- Reduces transmittal and paper costs
- Increases work quality
- Allows greater work integration from several people

Advantages of Teamwork

Though teamwork is not a panacea, it does allow for more input from a variety of perspectives. A major advantage of teamwork is quick response time. While in the past group decision making has been criticized for slow response, teams are more likely charged with a sense of urgency. In the same sense, teams usually are given "hard target" deadlines that they must meet as a condition of effective performance. Another advantage of a team is higher quality output at every step of the production process. Whether the product is an advertisement, software, or an automobile, teamwork enhances the outcome. Generally, when more people are involved in a task, they make better decisions. Employee participation through team membership means greater commitment, motivation, and ultimately satisfaction with the final outcome of team effort. Finally, self-directed teams typically handle job assignments, plan and schedule work, make decisions that affect the team, and take action on problems, all with minimal direct supervision.

The self-regulating nature of the team allows for greater error detection and correction on the spot rather than at projection completion. Even in today's highly automated assembly facilities, almost every workstation has a switch within easy reach that the worker can use to stop the assembly line when something is wrong. Stopping the assembly line was far more difficult twenty years ago; it required managerial intervention. Because it was more trouble then to correct errors on the spot, most errors just slipped through. Immediate error correction means that fewer defects make it through final assembly, which yields higher-quality products. Thus procedures, methods, and practices of both the organization and its work groups must be physically and psychologically attuned to production requirements. In doing so, teams have become a focal component in, for example, delivering quality medical services, solving sales problems, and making factories more productive.

Teamwork affords many benefits, such as allowing one employee to compensate with his or her strength for another employee's weakness. Everyone on a team has a chance to contribute ideas, plans, and figures; but anyone on a team may expect to find some of his or her best ideas vetoed by team member consensus. However, a good team also has a social memory. As a collective, the team should be able to "remember" the contributions of individuals for the good of the group. Over time, contributing members play a major role in shaping the group's activities. In summary, teams:

- Provide a quick response time and focused energy
- Offer better-quality decisions
- Engender greater member commitment and acceptance of ideas
- Allow greater employee participation
- Afford workers greater autonomy and self-governance

But teams are not without their problems; the team-building process is often flawed from the start. Employees need time to get accustomed to working in teams. Team members need to know not just why teams are being used, but where each team fits into the larger picture. If employees feel teams are being used to reduce the size of the workplace or to make them do more work, they will sabotage the process. The team approach is certain to fail when managers do not create a supportive environment for the team. And all too often, organizations find that team leaders eventually resort to human nature and refuse to share authority with the rest of the team.[19] To overcome the pitfalls of teamwork, external leadership of the team-building process is needed to create an infrastructure that allows teams to thrive. If teamwork is successful, the rewards are lower costs and higher-quality products or services.[20] In the Management Highlight on page 174, you can try your hand at deciding when a team is a bad idea.

TEAM EFFECTIVENESS AND TEAM INTERACTION

In the same way that organizational effectiveness is a measure of organizational success, team effectiveness is a measure of team success. It follows, then, that moving from understanding the social psychology of groups to building successful teams is not such a large leap. In this section, we'll examine the topics of implementing work teams and overcoming resistance to teamwork.

A team is a work group with a common goal. **Team effectiveness** represents the outcomes or results of the team's efforts such as efficiency, satisfaction, and goal attainment. Assuring team success requires that the team has a common purpose, that specific goals flow from that purpose, that team members have complementary skills, that the team has a shared agreement about how the work will be done, and that there is mutual accountability for team action.[21] Research from cardiac response teams suggests that the team

---

MANAGEMENT HIGHLIGHT
When Is a Team a Bad Idea?

Are teams always the right way to organize people to attain organizational goals? After reading these three scenarios, you make the call—which team is a bad idea?

Team Scenario 1.   Physician Management Services Inc. manages five healthcare offices. Each office has five physicians and a staff of fifteen nurses, technicians, and clerical workers. Each office receives a budget based on a per capita (known as capitation) dollar amount for each patient under its care. In other words, each office has only so much money to spend on each patient. All physicians meet monthly to decide how best to treat each patient and allocate their budget on patient care. While an expensive new treatment might be available, if it cannot be provided in-house, it is against corporate policy to prescribe the treatment. Further, any physician can propose a less-expensive treatment than that called for in the attending physician's plan. *A binding vote by all physicians is taken based on cost and other factors.*

Team Scenario 2.   Provident Health Care, a struggling HMO, has been ordered by the board of directors to cut costs in order to increase profits. The organization's two-pronged strategy for success is to sign new patients and keep service costs low on existing patients. Dr. Henry wants to schedule a surgical procedure for a patient covered by Provident Health Care. Although the procedure is not common, it is well accepted and offered at most hospitals. Provident's care manager discusses the request with a team of administrators, area clerical specialists, and their in-house physician; but finally authorizes only a less-expensive procedure. *Dr. Henry believes that his patient is being afforded inferior service.*

Team Scenario 3.   PanJen Corporation has a team of employees that reviews all new-hire applicants who seek posted jobs. The team's role is advisory to the HR department, but its wishes are rarely disregarded. Each member of the team represents a different group in the company, and each member has a different agenda. In team decision making, politics often rules the day. Sometimes the techies rule; sometimes those calling for diversity are heard; sometimes the team bases its decision solely on an applicant's qualifications. *The trouble is, managers never know if (or when) they will get the best person for the job.*

---

leader plays an important role in a team's success. Successful teams have a team leader who's willing to be accessible; doesn't try to "go it alone," but asks for input from other team members when necessary; and isn't afraid to be "human," admitting mistakes and then moving forward.[22] Further, team effectiveness can be enhanced by building teams with greater emotional intelligence.[23] Team-based emotional intelligence is rooted in the group processes described earlier in this chapter.

Research on group dynamics suggests that team effectiveness is best understood using a systems model that describes the inputs (or context), processes, and outputs (or outcomes) of group interaction (Exhibit 9.4).[24] **Context** consists of structure, strategies, leadership, and rewards. Structure includes the members' personalities and abilities as well as the overall size of the group. Structure dictates what the team can accomplish. Strategy clarifies, among several action plans, the one that the team intends to use in achieving its goals. For example, a team wanting to increase quality may use a strategy that intentionally slows down the production process, thus allowing workers more time to complete their tasks. The final inputs to context are leadership and rewards. Team leadership must facilitate the team's overall strategy and goals, provide resources, communicate vertically, and reward performance.

Team rewards are one motivation for a team member to work in unison. Although extrinsic rewards such as money and promotions are important on an individual level, team

EXHIBIT 9.4
System's Model of Team Effectiveness

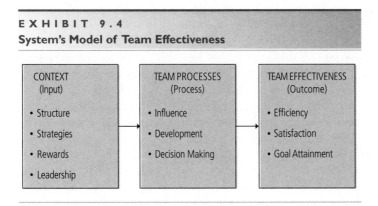

rewards serve as a powerful motivating force. Team recognition may be equally important to an individual. We have all seen sporting events where a player on the winning team reports an incredible feeling of accomplishment, even though her individual contribution to winning the final game was minor. And at NASA mission control, the images of a successful spacecraft landing tell a similar story of taking pride in team membership and achieving a difficult goal. Similarly, on an everyday level, work teams revel in their daily successes, knowing that their contributions made a difference. A supportive team environment that is fair to all engenders trust. Research indicates that employees view a process as fair if they are involved in the process early on, have the process clearly explained to them, and hold realistic expectations for the outcomes to follow from the process.[25]

By looking again at Exhibit 9.4, you can see that the inputs define how the team processes of the work group will unfold. Three separate **processes** occur in all work teams: influence, development, and decision making. The process of influence is a necessary and important part of the overall well-being of the team. Particularly in autonomous work teams or self-managing work teams, mutual influence allows all members access to change other members' minds or challenge unrealistic assumptions. But not all influence is productive. "Social loafing" and "free riding" occur when one group member does less work than others, knowing full well that his or her contribution will be hidden in the group effort.[26] Mutual influence should be viewed as inevitable and healthy. Team development involves the process of activities, interactions, and sentiments that occur as time passes. A major part of team development involves its members' attachment to and identification with the team. For example, wearing union jackets or company clothing outside the work environment indicates pride and group identity. Further, members quickly learn that not all groups are equal. Those groups that provide an opportunity for enjoyable and productive work are valued by members and nonmembers alike.

Goal attainment, efficiency, and member satisfaction are all team **outcomes** (see Exhibit 9.4). From a managerial perspective, it's important to think about the human component of the team. In an environment where teams are the primary productive unit, managers need to understand how well the team interacts on a continuous basis. Similarly, a team that has successfully attained an important goal is also likely to experience a high level of job satisfaction and feel a unique sense of inter-team loyalty. For all practical purposes, the highly effective team is one that experiences high levels of expected work outcomes such as quality, productivity, or reliability.

Implementing Work Teams

Management theorists have continually emphasized the importance of teamwork to the overall success of an organization. If we recall from Chapter 1 the open systems input, output, and processing (IPO) model, which characterizes the organization as consisting of three subsystems, we can see that teams are essential in the operation of each subsystem. One strong theme that runs throughout the management literature is the need for teams and teamwork. At every level, companies need teamwork. The aim of a team is to improve the input and the output at any stage of operations.

Three main features of effective self-managed teams are (1) extensive worker control over operating decisions, especially those traditionally made by supervisors, foremen, and quality inspectors; (2) high levels of feedback from the work itself (e.g., self-charting, online computerized reports); and (3) cross-training, so that each worker can perform many functions (i.e., job de-specialization).

As described in the Management Highlight on page 177, in a team-driven organization, work is designed around customers, not tasks. Senior managers are responsible for processes that are critical to satisfying customers. Self-directed work teams make decisions regarding hiring, scheduling, and so on. Fewer people are needed between senior managers and work teams, and their job is to facilitate, not control. This, in part, explains why so many mid-level management positions are being phased out in companies today.

Overcoming Resistance to Teamwork

The transition to teams isn't always easy. Following are some of the many problems encountered when building teams: confusing team building with teamwork, haphazard team planning, starting teams before assessing team needs, training team members individually, and not making teams accountable. Team members also have a tendency to become so intent on some of the group's issues that they forget to use effective team processes. Team members have to be trained not only to get along but also to work together as a team. Organizations must develop a system for planning teamwork. First, team needs must be defined; then team members should be trained as a team. Teams must also be accountable for what they've learned in training and what they do at work. Teams flourish when managers make room for spontaneity, value speaking out, encourage intellectual exchange, and select self-motivated people.[27]

Teams are not without their opponents. Often, teams mean fewer managers. Middle management is often the primary target for staff reduction when the team approach is implemented. A shift to teams and flatter organizations may reduce managers' opportunities for advancement. Unions are also opponents of work teams, whose self-regulating nature threatens the unions' traditional power and roles. Teams, they claim, threaten a union's very existence by posing a long-term threat to workers' job security and other union benefits. Through self-governance, teams resolve grievances, discipline workers, and award pay raises. Traditionally, these functions were part of the union's contractual relationship with the organization.

Teamwork is an important part of today's work environment. But team success comes only if workers are empowered to solve problems and make decisions, cultivate a natural sense of pride in their work, are self-managed, and receive group-based rewards and recognition for their accomplishments. If these elements are all present, teams can make important contributions to providing their customers with high-quality products or services.

MANAGEMENT HIGHLIGHT
Rules for Creating Effective Self Managed Teams

Team Development	Description
Organize around processes rather than tasks.	Organize around core processes, identify the critical processes, and assign teams responsibility related to process, not their functional area.
Create horizontal structures by grouping sub-processes.	Create cross-functional, project-based teams with clear objectives, diverse membership, and limited external management.
Reengineer the process.	Develop customer responsive processes and teams to support them. Healthcare intact of patients require clerical, nursing, physician, technicians, and administrative team members.
Give self-managed teams greater control over processes and process performance.	Self-managed teams are responsible for multiple tasks and have discretion over the methods of work, task schedules, assignment of members to different tasks, compensation, and feedback about performance for the group as a whole.
Link team performance to customer satisfaction.	Everything should be driven by the customer; successful performance also means customers have been satisfied.
Assign performance objectives to teams, not individuals.	Successful attainment of objectives must be a group effort and not the result of one or two individuals. Multiple member involvement is critical developing a sense of the collective.
Assign managerial tasks to the team where feasible.	Self-managed means just that—limited external leadership. Teams should be responsible for activities such as hiring, evaluating, and scheduling
Train team members to develop cross-functional skills and competencies.	Team members need multiple skills that support the work of the team or replace team members lost to illness, turnover, or reassignment.
Empower team members with information.	Information should go directly to those who can use it in their jobs. Trained and empowered workers know how to use information.
Put team members in touch with customers.	Know your customers, both internal and external. Visit them and understand their problems. Problem-solving teams can bring team members closer to customers. Knowledge of customer needs is then reflected in team work.
Reward skill development and team performance.	Performance evaluation should focus on team achievements rather than individual achievements. It is counterproductive to talk about teamwork while evaluating and rewarding individuals.

Adapted from Frank Ostroff, *The Horizontal Organization,* Oxford University Press, 1999; Daniel Goleman, Leadership that gets results, *Harvard Business Review,* March–April, 2000, 80–90, and, Charles C. Manz and Henry P. Sims, Jr., *The New Superleadership: Leading Others to Lead Themselves,* San Francisco, Berrett-Koehler, 2001, and Richard Hackman as cited in Charles C. Manz and Henry P. Sims, Jr., "Leading Workers to Lead Themselves: The External Leadership of Self-Managing Teams," *Administrative Science Quarterly* (March 1987), p. 106.

Conclusion
—Groups, Processes, and Teams in Organizations—

Organizations will increasingly utilize teams as they continue to reduce costs and downsize. After years of reorganizing and outsourcing, organizations are left with a lean core of knowledgeable employees. By necessity, many of these organizations are forced to rely on greater worker participation in the decision-making process through empowerment. With job security increasingly tenuous and new compensation plans encouraging less reliance on salary and greater compensation in the form of stock options than in the past, employees need to adapt to the changing work world. Upgrading skills in their teamwork, technology, and management education will all be essential for career success.

In the years ahead, workers will also be evaluated more and more as a group. Performance will be based on group productivity, and group members will be expected to improve their skills and help others perform better. Rewards will be based on group rather than individual performance, and the entire group will be held accountable for its actions. Teams will establish their own identity by devising their own name and by promoting personal relationships. In short, the emphasis in groups will be promoting cooperative teamwork.

The workplace of tomorrow will be even more diverse than today's. This will make the management of teamwork an even greater challenge for organizations than it is today. As corporate leaders begin to understand the impact of diverse groups on their organizations, their commitment to diversity will become much stronger. This means increased resources allocated for diversity training—for recruiting, training, and retaining qualified workers with diverse backgrounds. Managers will learn that a diversified workforce is a major asset in the twenty-first century.

SUGGESTED READINGS

Katzenbach, Jon R., and Douglas Smith. "The Discipline of Teams." *Harvard Business Review*, March–April 1992, 112–120.

Thompson, Leigh. "Improving the Creativity of Organizational Work Groups." *Academy of Management Executive* 17, no. 1 (2003): 96–109.

Wageman, Ruth. "Critical Success Factors for Creating Superb Self-Managing Teams." *Organizational Dynamics*, Summer 1997, pp. 49–61.

ENDNOTES

1. David McClelland, *The Achieving Society* (Princeton, NJ: Van Nostrand, 1961). Also see David McClelland and David H. Burnham, "Power Is a Great Motivator," *Harvard Business Review,* March–April 1976, pp. 100–110.

2. George Homans, *The Human Group* (New York: Harcourt, Brace, 1950).

3. Robert L. Kahn, D. M. Wolfe, Robert P. Quinn, J. D. Snock, and R. A. Rosenthal, *Organizational Stress: Studies in Role Conflict and Role Ambiguity* (New York: Wiley, 1964).

4. Meryl Reis Louis, "Surprise and Sense-Making: What Newcomers Experience in Entering Unfamiliar Organizational Settings," *Administrative Science Quarterly* (June 1980): 226–251.

5. Daniel Feldman, "The Development and Enforcement of Norms," *Academy of Management Review* 9, no. 1 (1984): 47–53.

6. Dennis Organ and Thomas Bateman, *Organizational Behavior* (Plano, TX: Business Publications, 1986), 473.

7. Marvin Shaw, *Group Dynamics: The Psychology of Small Group Behavior* (New York: McGraw-Hill, 1971), 192–204.

8. Irvin Janis, *Groupthink,* 2nd ed. (Boston: Houghton Mifflin, 1982), 9.

9. Christopher P. Neck and Gregory Moorhead, "Groupthink Remodeled: The Importance of Leadership, Time Pressure, and Methodical Decision-Making Procedures," *Human Relations,* May 1995, pp. 537–557.

10. James B. Strenski, "Stress Diversity in Employee Communications," *Public Relations Journal* (August–September 1994): 32–35.

11. Peter Wright, Stephen P. Ferris, Janine S. Hiller, and Mark Kroll, "Competitiveness through Management of Diversity: Effects on Stock Price Valuation," *Academy of Management Journal* (January 1995): 272–287.

12. Catherine Ellis and Jeffrey A. Sonnenfeld, "Diverse Approaches to Managing Diversity," *Human Resource Management,* Spring 1994, pp. 79–109.

13. Michele Galen and Ann Theresa Palmer, "Diversity: Beyond the Numbers Game," *Business Week,* August 14, 1995, pp. 60–61.

14. David Woodruff, "The Racy Viper Is Already Winning for Chrysler," *Business Week,* November 4, 1991, pp. 36–38; and James B. Treece, "How Ford and Mazda Share the Driver's Seat," *Business Week,* February 10, 1992, pp. 94–95.

15. Greg Burns, "The Secrets of Team Facilitation," *Training & Development,* June 1995, pp. 46–52.

16. James P. Womack, Daniel T. Jones, and Daniel Roos, *The Machine That Changed the World* (New York: HarperCollins, 1991), 92.

17. Edward E. Lawler, "The New Plant Revolution Revisited," *Organizational Dynamics,* Autumn 1990, pp. 5–14. Lawler estimated the number of plants as "somewhere between 300 and 500" (p. 9).

18. C. C. Manz, "Self-Leadership: Toward an Expanded Theory of Self-Influence Processes in Organizations," *Academy of Management Review* 11 (1986): 585–600.

19. Kenneth Labich, "Elite Teams," *Fortune,* February 19, 1996, pp. 90–99.

20. C. C. Manz and H. P. Sims Jr., *The New SuperLeadership: Leading Others to Lead Themselves* (San Francisco: Berrett-Koehler, 2001).

21. John Katzenbach and Douglas Smith, "The Discipline of Teams," *Harvard Business Review,* March–April 1993.

22. Amy Edmondson, Richard Bohmer, and Gary Pisano, "Speeding Up Team Learning," *Harvard Business Review,* October 2001, pp. 1–12.

23. Vanessa Urch Druskat and Stephen B. Wolff, "Building the Emotional Intelligence of Groups," *Harvard Business Review,* March 2001, pp. 80–90.

24. Marilyn Gist, Edwin A. Locke, and M. Susan Taylor, "Organizational Behavior: Group Structure, Process, and Effectiveness," *Journal of Management* 13, no. 2 (1987): 237–257.

25. W. Chan Kin and Renee Maurborgne, "Fair Process: Managing the Knowledge Economy," *Harvard Business Review*, July–August 1997, pp. 66–74.

26. S. G. Harkins, B. Latane, and K. Williams, "Social Loafing: Allocating Effort or Taking It Easy?" *Journal of Experimental Social Psychology* 16 (1985): 457–465.

27. Michael Pacanowsky, "Team Tools for Wicked Problems," *Organizational Dynamics,* Winter 1995, pp. 36–51; and see Harold J. Leavitt and Jean Lipman-Blumen, "Hot Groups," *Harvard Business Review*, July–August 1995, pp. 109–116.

Chapter Ten

Motivation

Why does he work so hard? Why does she go to law school at night after working all day? The actions that others take and the choices they make give us plenty to feed our curiosity. It's natural for us to want to understand the reason for human behavior. We expect people to behave rationally, we seek to understand the logic of their actions, and we judge them accordingly. The fundamental question we ask ourselves in this chapter is what motivates behavior? At work the answer to the motivation question is especially important, since all work is presumably voluntary. So we begin this chapter with the basics of motivation and then cut a path through the major theories of work motivation.

At work, managers are confronted with how best to encourage work-related behaviors, yet we know that two people in the same situation often behave quite differently. Why is that? Most motivation theorists believe that the answer is based on need. A **need** is a drive to achieve a specific outcome. Hedonism and Thorndike's Law of Effect[1]—the pursuit of pleasure and the avoidance of pain—inform us that people seek rewarding outcomes and avoid punishing consequences. For example, hunger is a need. When your body needs food, you act to satisfy your hunger. You break for lunch, or you hit the vending machine. Once your stomach is full, hunger no longer drives your behavior, leaving you free to attend to other things. In other words, a deficit in need causes a person to seek satisfaction of that need; but once the need is satisfied, it no longer motivates behavior. We know that eating satisfies our hunger need. From previous gastronomic experiences, we also know that some foods are enjoyable and others disagreeable to us. We seek out the enjoyable foods and avoid the disagreeable foods. In the need-satisfaction process, we make choices toward some outcomes and away from others.

MANAGEMENT HIGHLIGHT
What Motivates a Worker?

Intrinsic Rewards	What Organizations Can Do	Extrinsic Rewards	What Organizations Can Do
The work itself	Create interesting jobs that people enjoy and seek out.	*Compensation*	Explore new alternative compensation plans. For example, accumulation of paid time off rather than overtime.
Work environment	Create spaces that are natural and easily facilitate the work.	*Promotion*	Encourage promotion from within; let workers know when a move to the next level can be expected. Develop career paths within a set of jobs.
Jobs with greater autonomy	Allow workers greater control over the pace and outcome of the work.	*Corporate perks*	Provide use of company cars, golf course memberships, and other corporate facilities such as corporate parks.
Social interaction among workers	Design more group-based tasks that bring people together and encourage greater diversity.	*Stock ownership*	Create opportunities for workers to invest and share the wealth.
Creative expression	Allow workers greater freedom to change and explore new concepts and techniques.	*Funded retirement plans and 401k contributions*	Help workers build retirement assets that encourage commitment and tenure.

Failure to understand human motivation can mean wasted time, resources, and careers. We know different people have different needs. Managers must elicit effort from workers with often vastly different levels of interest, ability, and motivation. Not all workers are motivated by the same thing (see the Management Highlight above). For some workers, money is a motivator; for others, it's the opportunity to help people. Managers are constantly seeking ways to motivate people in order to increase productivity or increase the greater expression of workplace creativity. To do so, managers must motivate different types of people so they will all contribute to the attainment of organizational goals.

In a modern society, work means economic freedom. Work allows us the benefits that money can buy, but not everyone is motivated by money. People work for many different reasons—to survive, to achieve personal goals, to feed their families, to be respected. For other reasons—due to pride of workmanship; because of ability; from a sense of obligation; for personal, peer, and social recognition; or to make a customer happy—they may excel at their jobs. Just as there are many reasons for motivation, there are also many theories to explain it. Before beginning a discussion of motivation, it is important to define what we mean by motivation. **Motivation** is the set of forces that initiate behavior and determine its form, direction, intensity, and duration. At work these forces might be based on a need deficit (to become a lead engineer) and directed toward a goal (promotion to lead engineer). So what should a manager know about motivation? For one thing, most theories of work performance include motivation as a central concept. If managers are concerned with increasing worker commitment and productivity, they must be concerned with motivation.[2]

Motivation is defined in relation to a set of forces that drive behavior. Many theorists believe that motivation is driven by unsatisfied needs that people seek to satisfy. Exhibit 10.1 describes a model of motivation based on the concept of need satisfaction. For example, you have a need for greater importance in your work. With a sense of increasing tension,

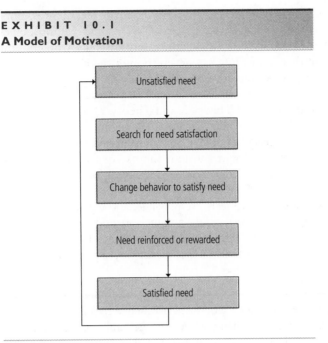

EXHIBIT 10.1
A Model of Motivation

you become dissatisfied with your current job. This tension drives you to thoughts of returning to school and finishing your college degree. Next, you search for the best way to attend college and complete your degree program. Once you graduate and get the job you wanted, your feelings of tension are reduced. The process of motivation never ends; it is just replaced by a different need. An unsatisfied need and its associated tension cause the process to begin anew. This model helps us understand that motivation is a lifelong process driven by satisfying unmet needs.

THE IMPORTANCE OF MOTIVATION

Why focus on worker motivation? The once popular view that computers and technology would make workers obsolete has been replaced by a realization that business still needs an educated workforce. Rather than seeking input and a competitive edge from a small number of key, top-level workers, companies must find ways to actively elicit the participation of all employees, and to motivate all employees to greater levels of quality performance.

To achieve organizational goals, managers must understand basic human nature. What motivates a person to work hard? What does a person want or need from work? Once this central question is answered, a reward system can be designed to satisfy these wants and needs. Although this may sound easy, it is not.

Assumptions about Human Nature

Before beginning our discussion of motivation, let's review several important assumptions about human nature. Managers, like most of us, have very specific attitudes and beliefs about what makes people tick. As in most other aspects of life, different people have different assumptions about human nature. **Assumptions** are a theoretic frame of reference against which we compare our daily human interactions. To a large degree, these assumptions dictate what we expect to see and what we actually see. If we assume that most blue-collar workers are disinterested in their work, we might interpret some workers' low performance as confirmation of this lack of interest—even though the correct interpretation might be that they were poorly trained. Douglas McGregor's two contrasting explanations of human nature have been widely used to understand and shape managerial practices. His sets of assumptions (called Theory X and Theory Y) describe diametrically opposed views of managerial direction and control.[3]

Theory X states that workers are passive (if not lazy) and in need of direction and control. Thus workers need external management through the use of force, persuasion, rewards, and punishment. McGregor described Theory X as the traditional view of direction and control.

Theory Y asserts that workers are eager to learn, responsible, and creative. McGregor believed that workers' capacities to learn are great and their abilities are underutilized. If given the autonomy, workers are quite capable of self-direction and self-control. In addition, an organization's reward system must be supportive of increased employee participation.

The Motivation Process

According to behavioral scientists, effective worker performance requires motivation, ability, and a reward system that encourages quality work.[4] In a general sense, Exhibit 10.1 describes the psychological relationship between motivation, behavior, reward, and feedback. A person's motive or motivation is characterized as a need-based state of arousal. **Need deprivation** increases our state of arousal or search to reduce the need deficit. At work, the term *behavior* refers to the specific work or task actions that result from a need-deficit-induced arousal. And finally, rewards are the direct consequence of our behavior. Feedback is knowledge produced about the cause-and-effect sequence that either stimulates or suppresses future states of arousal, depending on our level of need satisfaction. A **reward** is an attractive or desired consequence that can be either intrinsic or extrinsic. **Intrinsic rewards**—the intangible psychological results of work that are controlled by the worker—are inherent in the job and occur during performance of work. A task might be intrinsically motivating because it results in a feeling of accomplishment. Intrinsic rewards can have significant, yet often underestimated, impacts on job satisfaction, which as we'll see is closely linked to motivation. **Extrinsic rewards** are administered by another party and occur apart from the actual performance of work. An example of an extrinsic reward is a paycheck.

To be motivated, workers must also be able to do the job. **Ability** refers to the physical and mental characteristics that a worker requires in order to perform a task successfully. Management must do everything it can to continually develop each worker's ability through training.

Over the years, many people have developed theories describing how motivation affects work behavior. Theories of worker motivation attempt to explain people's inner workings, initiatives, and aspirations. Next, we'll examine the three basic types of motivation theories—content, process, and environmental.

CONTENT THEORIES OF MOTIVATION

Content theories (also called *need theories*) are based on the idea that people are driven to meet basic needs that produce satisfaction when they're met. These theories include Maslow's hierarchy of needs, Alderfer's ERG theory, Herzberg's two-factor theory, and McClelland's learned needs theory.

Maslow's Hierarchy of Needs

Abraham Maslow's motivation theory, commonly referred to as the **hierarchy of needs** (Exhibit 10.2), is based on two key assumptions. First, different needs are active at different times, and only needs not yet satisfied can influence behavior. Second, needs are arranged in a fixed order of importance called a *hierarchy*.

According to Maslow's theory, behavior is triggered by a need *deficit* that drives the individual to reduce the tension it creates. Tension leads to behavior that will potentially satisfy the need. For example, a new baby in the family means a greater financial burden. As a result, the worker increases work effort to ensure a promotion and an increase in pay (raise). In Maslow's theory, the idea that the most basic unsatisfied need (in the hierarchy) influences current behavior is called the prepotency (i.e., priority or order) of the need. This **prepotency** creates an urgency exerted by an unmet need that influences human behavior. In our example, the as-yet-unmet need for a promotion and raise has high prepotency. The need for greater security motivates the current behavior of the worker. Until the need is satisfied, the unmet need is said to influence behavior. Furthermore, as soon as a lower-order need is satisfied, a higher-order need emerges and demands satisfaction.

As Exhibit 10.2 illustrates, Maslow identified five categories of needs:

- *Physiological needs*, such as food, sleep, and physical movement
- *Safety needs*, such as freedom from fear or harm, stability, predictability
- *Social needs*, such as friendship, love, camaraderie, and teamwork
- *Self-esteem needs*, such as status and reputation
- *Self-actualization needs*, such as the fulfillment of human potential and personal growth[5]

The hierarchy of needs gives managers a straightforward way of understanding how various work conditions satisfy employee needs. Certain basic conditions of employment (such as pay) satisfy physiological needs. Safety needs are met by safe work conditions and job security. Social needs are satisfied by interaction and communication with fellow workers. And finally, work that is fulfilling can satisfy self-esteem and self-actualization needs.

EXHIBIT 10.2
Maslow's Needs Hierarchy

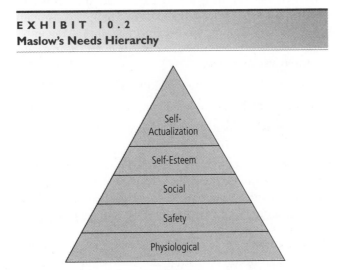

Source: Abraham H. Maslow, *Motivation and Personality* (New York: Harper & Row, 1954).

Although Maslow's ideas were a welcome relief from the emphasis on abnormal behavior that dominated the psychology of the day, they are not without some potential pitfalls. Maslow himself recognized that the hierarchy is not a stair-step approach. Humans have multiple needs that often occur simultaneously in modern society. It may make more sense to think about higher-order needs (such as esteem and self-actualization) as one set and lower-order needs (such as physiological, safety, and social needs) as another set. Using just these two categories, we can see that it is certainly possible for several needs to influence our behavior at once.

In addition, we have to consider the relative intensity of the need that we feel at a given time. Being thirsty is a relative concept. If you're in a desert and have no water, the prepotency of the need will influence 100 percent of your behavior. If you're mildly thirsty all morning but you're writing the weekly report, your behavior may be more determined by a deadline than your thirst.

Finally, Maslow's theory describes needs as internal; it says nothing about the environment's effect on behavior. How are needs determined? For example, the need for new clothes may be determined by comparing our clothes with those worn by friends, models, or prestigious people. Functionally our clothes may be fine; but in contrast to our friends' clothes, they might look old or out of style. So what might be considered a lower-order need for clothing becomes translated into a higher-order need for self-esteem. The referent for our need deficit is not internal, but external. In other words, the definition of need for new clothing is determined through other people, society, education, and religion—the external environment.

To a large degree, Maslow's ideas help us understand that everyone has basic needs that must be satisfied. One way to satisfy these needs is through work. But the complexity of the need-satisfaction process makes simple prescription problematic. Although Maslow's needs hierarchy describes a model of basic human needs, it offers little practical guidance for motivating workers.

Alderfer's ERG Theory

In response to several gaps in Maslow's needs hierarchy theory, Clayton Alderfer[6] developed a need-satisfaction theory of motivation that better describes human behavior. His theory is a modification of Maslow's earlier work, but it attempts to simplify Maslow's theory by including three basic needs rather than five. In addition, Alderfer introduced the concept of *frustration regression* to describe how we deal with our unmet needs. His **ERG theory** includes three primary needs:

- **Existence**—basic needs for survival, food, shelter, and clothing.

- **Relatedness**—needs that are part of building and maintaining social relationships.

- **Growth**—intrinsic desires for knowledge, creativity, and ability to learn new and different things.

Like Maslow, Alderfer recognized a hierarchy of human needs, beginning with our most basic needs for safety and sustenance. Once our existence needs are satisfied, we progress to the next need in the hierarchy—relatedness. Once we have satisfied our relatedness needs, we become more concerned with our needs to grow and achieve whatever goals we set for ourselves—our need for personal growth.

Overall, Alderfer's theory sounds a lot like Maslow's theory, but with some unique differences. Alderfer believed that people can become frustrated in their ability to fulfill a need. **Frustration regression** describes the situation where we find ourselves unable to satisfy a need and, in reaction to the unsatisfied need, we regress toward a lower need.

For example, in our quest to satisfy a relatedness need (i.e., becoming a member of a group), we regress toward seeking satisfaction in an existence need. Similarly, an unsatisfied growth need causes us to regress toward a desire to satisfy a relatedness need.

ERG theory offers another attempt to explain motivation in relation to need satisfaction. In his theory, Aldefer describes a hierarchy of needs and our ability to move up or down the hierarchy, depending on whether a need is satisfied or not. ERG theory suggests that existence and relatedness needs can be met at some point, but meeting a growth need only causes us to set higher growth goals.

Herzberg's Two-Factor Theory

Before Frederick Herzberg's research was published, most people viewed job satisfaction and dissatisfaction as opposite ends of a single continuum. Thus many managers believed that the greater the amount of any good condition, the greater the amount of worker satisfaction. Managers further believed that eliminating undesirable working conditions would result in job satisfaction. But Herzberg believed that not being satisfied is different from being dissatisfied.

Herzberg and his colleagues were interested in identifying those factors that caused workers to be satisfied with their work. To investigate this idea, Herzberg designed a study in which data were gathered from accountants and engineers. Herzberg asked participants in the study to think of times when they felt especially good and especially bad about their jobs. Each participant was then asked to describe the conditions or events that caused those good or bad feelings. Of particular interest was the finding that participants identified different work conditions for each of the two feelings. That is, although the presence of one condition (e.g., fulfilling work) made participants feel good, the absence of that condition (fulfilling work) did not make them feel bad. Consequently, Herzberg postulated that motivators lead to satisfaction, but their absence does not necessarily lead to dissatisfaction.

Herzberg identified two factors, hygiene and motivators, that he asserts can separately explain satisfaction and dissatisfaction. Factors whose presence prevents dissatisfaction are called **hygiene factors** or maintenance factors. Hygiene or maintenance factors refer to aspects of work that are peripheral to the task itself and more related to the external environment (the **job context**). The term *hygiene factor* is linked to the finding that the absence of readily available rest rooms led to worker dissatisfaction. Hygiene factors include

- Company policy and administrative practices
- Technical supervision by the manager
- Interpersonal relations with the supervisor
- Worker salary, job status, and job security
- The worker's personal life
- Physical conditions of the work setting (e.g., air conditioning)

Factors whose presence leads to satisfaction are called motivators. These factors can produce high levels of motivation when they're present. Motivator factors relate directly to the **job content** (the specific aspects of a job). They include

- Achievement
- Recognition
- Advancement

- The task or work itself
- The worker's potential for personal learning or growth
- The worker's responsibility for results[7]

Exhibit 10.3 illustrates Herzberg's two-factor theory. The distinction between motivational and maintenance factors is often clarified by the observation that motivational factors are *intrinsic,* whereas maintenance factors are *extrinsic.*

At the time of his study, Herzberg's ideas were considered groundbreaking. He and his colleagues challenged traditionally accepted ideas about the causes and nature of job satisfaction. But when the two-factor theory was tested in other organizations, researchers found little support for the theory. Controversy over Herzberg's findings centers on three areas:

- *Method of data collection.* The information was collected via a potentially biased, structured interview format.

- *Individual differences.* Individual differences were discovered to affect the two factors. For example, some workers avoid advancement.

- *Limited sample.* Conclusions were based primarily on studies of professionals (i.e., engineers and accountants), whose tasks differ significantly from other kinds of workers.[8]

Herzberg's motivational factors correspond to Maslow's higher-order needs, while his maintenance factors correspond to lower-order needs. Interestingly, Maslow, Alderfer, and Herzberg all provide evidence that the value of the work itself can contribute to worker motivation. While the work of Maslow and Herzberg has its limitations, these researchers have shaped the direction of subsequent work in the field of motivation.

EXHIBIT 10.3
Herzberg's Two-Factor Theory

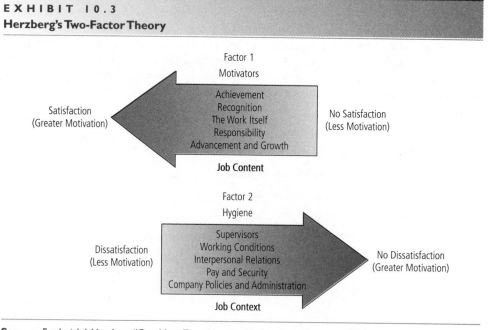

Source: Frederick I. Herzberg, "One More Time: How Do You Motivate Employees," *Harvard Business Review,* January–February 1968, 53–62.

McClelland's Learned Needs Theory

Another psychologist, David McClelland, paid further attention to the potential of work itself to motivate.[9] While McClelland is best known for research on achievement motivation, he also identified several other motives that have application to the work. McClelland's approach differs from Maslow, Alderfer, and Herzberg in the origin of human needs. McClelland believed that basic needs are transmitted or learned through culture and that the need for achievement was a powerful motivator. But how do you determine what these needs are, and what is the mechanism that results in motivation? McClelland sought the answers to these questions. McClelland believed that a person's unconscious mind is the key to unlocking his or her particular needs. Once an individual's dominant need is identified, it then becomes a matter of understanding how best to satisfy that need.

Identifying the Need.   McClelland showed subjects a picture and then asked them to write a story describing what was happening in the picture and what the probable outcome would be. He believed the story would reveal the writer's needs and motives.

Measuring the Need.   To measure an individual's need for achievement, McClelland used the Thematic Apperception Test (TAT), which was developed by H. A. Murray, another psychologist. Following Murray's work on need for achievement, McClelland and John Atkinson developed the scoring system for the Thematic Appreciation Test and McClelland used the TAT to measure need for achievement and other needs. The TAT contains pictures and asks the test taker to write a story (theme) about the picture. McClelland believed that a person's dominant needs are expressed in their description of the picture. The TAT is assessed by a trained evaluator who converts the verbal description into a numeric value suitable for analysis. McClelland contributed both a theory and a way to measure the need across people. In his later years he drew a link between the need for achievement and success at work.

Motivating the Individual.   Once the dominant need of the individual is identified, a strategy can be developed to satisfy the need. This may involve moving an individual to an intrinsically rewarding job rather than one that relies exclusively on pay or external recognition. It could involve recognizing the need for social contact. Or finally, it might mean a career path into management. Next we will explore the three primary needs identified by McClelland.

Three Dominant Needs.   Three dominant needs identified by McClelland are the need for achievement, need for affiliation, and need for power. If the dominant need identified in the individual was for achievement, then a manager should put the individual in a position where he or she can fulfill that need. If the dominant need is a need for affiliation, then a situation that provides more interaction with people might allow the person to fulfill his or her dominant need.

The **need for achievement** is a measure of a person's desire for clear, self-set, moderately difficult goals, with feedback given based on goal achievement. High achievers are seen as self-starters, goal-oriented, or full of task initiative, all traits that firms typically value.

The **need for affiliation** is the desire to work with others, to interact with and support others, and to learn the lessons of life through the experiences of others. A pronounced desire for social acceptance can be a powerful motivating force in our daily lives. Work organizations are important social institutions, bringing people into regular contact with one another. The need for affiliation is Maslow's social need, applied to the individual.

The **need for power** is a desire to have influence and control over others. This need can be an important determinant of behavior. People dominate one another in many socially acceptable ways. People are submissive to the dominance of police, managers, tour guides, and others. It is natural and often informative to allow other people control over an aspect of our lives. Many people seek jobs that afford them the opportunity to fulfill a basic need in a socially acceptable manner, and success at many jobs actually requires people to be forceful and capable of exerting their will over others. In these positions, people with a high need for power will outperform those with a low need for power.

Like Maslow's needs theory, McClelland's theory suggests that people vary in the degree to which their motive for behavior is determined by any one or a combination of these needs. McClelland's work fits well with Herzberg's view of achievement as a motivator and with Maslow's concept of higher-order needs satisfaction as a source of motivation. In addition, McClelland's research moves beyond basic or lower-level needs as explanations for behavior. Maslow, Herzberg, and McClelland all recognize the importance of achievement and social relations as motivational factors. But only McClelland moves one step beyond by adding another dimension—the need for power. As we will see, the need for power can be an important explanation for human behavior.

Managerial Application of Need Theories

The need theories we have reviewed in this chapter point to the conclusion that sources of individual motivation can be both internal and external. McClelland's achievement and affiliation needs, Maslow's esteem and self-actualization needs, Alderfer's growth needs, and Herzberg's intrinsic motivators—responsibility, personal growth, and the work itself—are consistent with the belief that motivation and worker commitment come from basic intrinsic needs. Reflections of these intrinsic needs are pride of workmanship and the joy of work. Maslow's physiological and safety needs, Herzberg's pay and working conditions, and McClelland's recognition that needs are acquired or learned reflect the external nature of certain needs.

With an increasingly better educated workforce, organizations are placing more emphasis on understanding how higher-order intrinsic individual needs can be satisfied at work. However, managers often underestimate employees' need for achievement. A climate of achievement in the workplace can be cultivated in several ways. First, work that is challenging and gives the employee a sense of responsibility is motivational. Second, managers can identify and recognize contributions of individual employees rather than simply attributing a firm's success to managers. Need theories of motivation often help managers better understand the motives that drive workers to expend effort in the completion of tasks at work.

PROCESS THEORIES OF MOTIVATION

Process theories describe cognitive processes and decisions that help predict subsequent behavior. These theories include equity and expectancy. Whereas need theories view motivation as subconscious and instinctive, process theories view motivation in relation to workers' explicit thought processes (cognitions) and conscious decisions to select and pursue a specific alternative (choice). According to process theory, then, a worker is likely to consider a variety of methods, weighing each method based on how attractive its expected outcomes might be, before engaging in an activity. The two major process theories are expectancy theory and equity theory.

Expectancy Theory

Victor H. Vroom developed an expectancy theory of motivation sometimes referred to as *VIE (valence, instrumentality, expectancy) theory*. In a nutshell, expectancy theory describes

EXHIBIT 10.4
Expectancy Theory

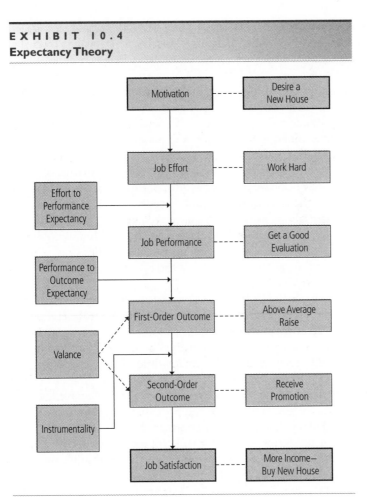

the process people use to evaluate (1) the likelihood that their effort or expenditure will yield the desired outcome and (2) how much they want the outcome. In this theory, motivation is based on three factors that determine the degree of effort to put forth (Exhibit 10.4).[10]

The first factor in VIE theory is **expectancy**—the individual's subjective assessment that an effort will lead to job performance, and job performance leads to a first-order outcome. The **effort to performance expectancy** is the subjective assessment that a person can complete the job. This is the "can do" (perceived capability) component of an employee's approach to work. The **performance to outcome expectancy** is the probability that hard work will be rewarded. Expectancy is a probability assessment rated between 0 (certain not to produce results) and 1.0 (certain to produce results).

Valence, the second factor in VIE theory, refers to the value of the outcome to the individual (i.e., the rewards). Valence represents the outcome's desirability to the individual. Desirable rewards encourage effort; undesirable rewards discourage effort. A valence can range from negative to positive depending on whether the individual believes the outcome is personally undesirable or desirable.

The third factor is the **instrumentality** of successful task performance in leading to a second-order outcome or a desired reward. If a first-order outcome is successful completion of your job or working at an above-average level of performance, a second-order outcome might be a raise or a promotion. So the instrumentality of a task is the employee's assessment of how instrumental or likely it is that successful task performance will be rewarded with a raise. Thus instrumentality is a measure of the association between performance and rewards.

The valence of the potential reward, the instrumentality of the performance linked to the reward, and the expectancy of achieving the reward determine the level of effort. Then the values are multiplied to produce a force to perform for each effort. Presumably the actual level of effort will be determined by the highest VIE score.

Determining the VIE score can be complicated. For example, the levels of possible effort are often infinite rather than discrete; in other words, it's not simply a matter of effort versus no effort. An employee may not have an accurate idea of expectancy—she may not know if her efforts will produce the level of performance needed to earn a reward. The employee may also be uncertain about how performance will be rewarded. If so, the instrumentality for each level of effort cannot be determined. But for limited, discrete choices of effort (e.g., attend or not attend) and known instrumentalities (e.g., a score of 95 on an exam will guarantee the student an A grade), the calculations are simple and the research is generally supportive of expectancy theory.[11]

It's difficult to visualize expectancy theory, because it mainly involves an individual cognitive assessment of "if I do this—I will get that." Nonetheless, here are several points that can help you remember VIE theory (you may want to look again at Exhibit 10.4). Remember that *outcomes* are the consequences of individual behavior. What this means is that we have a choice to spend our time at work in many different ways, and some of them are more likely to lead to the outcomes we want most. *Valence* is an index of the values of competing outcomes. The outcome we choose has the highest value. Next, determine the effort-to-performance expectancy. This is the probability that an individual's effort will lead to the outcome. Finally, determine the performance-to-outcome expectancy. As the example in Exhibit 10.4 illustrates, if I perform, I will receive an above-average raise that will lead to a promotion. The increased income from the raise and promotion will boost my income enough so that I can afford a new house.

Here are some guidelines we can infer from the insights offered by expectancy theory:

- *Ask what outcomes workers desire.* Workers often prefer rewards that differ from management's assumptions. For example, for some workers in dual-career families, healthcare benefits may be irrelevant if the spouse's employer already provides them. Also, workers may prefer to get time off for child and elderly parent care rather than receive bonuses, promotions, and job transfers to new locations.

- *Break down effort-to-performance barriers.* Providing workers with tools, information, and an effective production support system will help translate effort into performance.

- *Clarify and communicate instrumentalities.* Workers who know that performance will lead to rewards are more likely to work hard. For those rewards that are controlled by management (e.g., bonuses and promotions), management must let workers know the performance level required to achieve these rewards.

- *Develop meaningful self-administered rewards.* Intrinsic rewards have a perfect instrumentality correlation (−1.0 or 1.0) and require no management action to award them. For example, developing pride of workmanship builds a self-motivated worker.

Expectancy theory provides a general guide to the factors that determine the amount of effort a worker puts forth. Expectancy theory also helps explain how a worker's goals influence his efforts. The utility of VIE theory for managers lies in its suggestion of the complex thought process that individuals use in the process of becoming motivated.

Equity Theory

J. Stacy Adams' **equity theory** concerns the worker's perception of how she is being treated. In particular, equity theory is based on the *assessment process* a worker uses to evaluate the fairness or justice of organizational outcomes and the *adjustment process* used to maintain perceptions of fairness. The concepts of fairness and equilibrium (internal balance) are central to equity theory. The basic idea in equity theory is that an employee first considers his outcomes (rewards) and then his inputs (effort). Next the employee compares his personal reward-to-effort ratio to the same ratio of a referent. The referent is usually another employee doing basically the same work, some standard ratio based on a fair day's work, or another employee at approximately the same level in an organization.[12]

This ratio of a comparison person's outcome (rewards, recognition, pay) to inputs (time, effort, actual work performed) is called a **reference ratio** (Exhibit 10.5). If the employee believes that his outcomes-to-inputs ratio is lower than the reference ratio, he can (1) reduce his effort or (2) seek higher rewards to bring his outcomes-to-inputs ratio in line with the reference ratio. Conversely, if the employee's ratio is higher than the reference ratio, she can increase her effort or reduce her rewards. If Georgia feels that she's overrewarded for her work, she might feel guilty. To reduce this tension, she could work harder or find more work to do. Her actions would reflect the need to adjust her internal state of fairness. Likewise, John, an under-rewarded worker, is off balance in the opposite direction. He too would seek an equity adjustment. If no pay increase appeared to be forthcoming, equity theory suggests that in order to create an equitable outcome, John would decrease his effort again.

EXHIBIT 10.5
Equity Theory

Adams' Equity Model

$$\frac{\textbf{Outcomes}_{own}}{\textbf{Inputs}_{own}} \quad EQUALS \quad \frac{\textbf{Outcomes}_{others}}{\textbf{Inputs}_{others}}$$

where:

Outcomes$_{own}$	= Worker's perception of own outcomes.
Inputs$_{own}$	= Worker's perception of own inputs.
Outcomes$_{others}$	= Worker's perception of another worker's outcomes.
Inputs$_{others}$	= Worker's perception of another worker's input.

Restoration of Equity

You Feel Under-Rewarded	You Feel Over-Rewarded
1. Ask for raise.	1. Try to get raise for other workers.
2. Lower inputs.	2. Raise inputs.
3. Rationalize why you get less than others.	3. Rationalize why you get more than others.
4. Change your comparison worker.	4. Change your comparison worker.

Source: Adapted from Ramon Aldag and T. Stearns. *Management*, 2nd ed. (Cincinnati, OH: South-Western, 1991), 422–423.

Note that a worker's inputs and outcomes need not be in exact balance to one another, as long as the reference ratio imbalance matches the worker's ratio. That is, a worker may feel that she is working very hard, but may not feel unfairly treated as long as her comparison workers are also working very hard. Many workers are willing to work hard as long as the burden is shared. Equity theory helps to account for workers' feelings of mistreatment by highly paid managers.

ENVIRONMENTAL THEORIES OF MOTIVATION

Environmental theories of motivation describe how we acquire knowledge that we later use. In this section we discuss two major environmental theories—reinforcement and social learning. Reinforcement theory states that we learn to express behavior that is rewarded and to avoid behavior that is punished. Hence, our behavior is influenced by its consequences, and we learn by the environment acting *directly* on us. Social learning theory informs us that we can also learn *indirectly* by observing the success or failures of others. When we observe the successful behavior of others, we attempt the same behavior in the hope of getting similar results. Likewise, when we observe unsuccessful behavior in another that results in a negative outcome, we avoid using the behavior that produced the negative outcome.

Reinforcement Theory

Reinforcement theories describe motivation largely in relation to external factors, and they suggest the conditions under which behavior is likely to be repeated. In reinforcement theory, the interpretation of motivation is different from content and process theories of motivation. Both process and content theories consider motivation a function of either internal needs or internal cognition. On the other hand, **operant conditioning** (also called **reinforcement theory**) characterizes motivation as largely determined by external factors. People's experience with past situations dictates or guides their future behavior.

Noted psychologist B. F. Skinner stated that behavior is a function of its consequences.[13] Behaviors that have positive consequences are likely to be repeated, and those that have negative consequences are likely to be avoided in the future. According to reinforcement theory, workers are motivated by the consequences of their work behavior. In the process of experiencing rewards at work, workers often see a link between their own actions (i.e., their behaviors) and the reward (i.e., the consequences of their behavior). For example, a manager rewards workers at a plant that has reduced the number of accidents in the plant by holding a company-paid picnic for workers and their families.

The basis or method of distributing rewards or disincentives—and the nature of the rewards and disincentives themselves—profoundly influences behavior. Rewards may be made on a contingent or noncontingent basis. **Contingent rewards** are distributed based on a specific, preceding behavior. For example, a sales clerk may receive a free weekend trip for having the highest sales in her department for the preceding quarter. **Noncontingent rewards** are not linked to any specific behavior. For example, a paid holiday may be available to all staff regardless of their level of performance. A newly hired worker and a worker with twenty years of experience with the company receive the same reward.

Reinforcement theory deals with two types of behavior: desirable—which we want to increase, and undesirable—which we want to decrease. In the next section we will describe how reinforcement works in different situations.

Increasing the Behavior.   **Reinforcement** is the process of using contingent rewards to increase future occurrences of a specific behavior. Reinforcement can take either of two forms—positive or negative. **Positive reinforcement** occurs when a positive consequence (reward) is applied to a desired behavior. Positive reinforcement increases the frequency of the particular behavior that it follows. *Positive* refers to the nature of the consequence; *reinforcement* refers to the strengthened likelihood of the subsequent behavior. For example, for each bag of fruit she picks, a fruit picker receives $2. **Negative reinforcement** occurs when an unpleasant consequence is withdrawn after the desired behavior occurs. For example, a manager stops criticizing an employee when he *achieves the daily production quota*. Both positive and negative reinforcement increase the likelihood that a desired behavior will occur.

Decreasing the Behavior.   To decrease a current behavior, reinforcement theories suggest using either punishment or extinction. **Punishment** is the process of administering an undesirable consequence for an undesirable behavior. Although punishment holds many negative connotations for many people, it is a naturally occurring phenomenon in the learning process.[14] For example, a child who falls off a bicycle learns quickly to maintain balance. The famous **hot stove rule** suggests that being burned by a hot stove represents punishment at the most general level and in its most vivid form.[15] The hot stove rule suggests that nature is a good teacher; through it, we learn that punishment should be swift, intense, impersonal, and consistent, and it should provide an alternative.[16] Reduced to its basic components, punishment provides the recipient with useful information. As with all reinforcement, the objective is to associate the behavior with its consequence.

Although the term *punishment* is often objectionable, the concept is widely applicable to work settings. Punishment naturally occurs in all work settings. A worker drops a box on his big toe and breaks the toe. In the future, he'll either exercise greater care or risk more physical injury. Although few would disagree with the informational content in this example, it still doesn't fit our concept of punishment. We think of punishment as being yelled at or being passed over for promotion due to poor performance. But regardless of the form punishment takes, it is still the same process of applying an unpleasant consequence contingent upon the occurrence of an undesired behavior.

According to reinforcement theory, the other way of decreasing undesired behavior is through **extinction** (the process of non-reinforcement of a behavior). Or, more simply put, if the behavior is unrewarded, its occurrence will diminish over time. For example, an employee who tells off-color jokes at meetings could be rewarded for the behavior with laughter. By not laughing at the jokes (i.e., removing the reward), meeting attendees could eliminate the joke telling in the future.

Exhibit 10.6 illustrates the use of various reinforcement contingencies in increasing and decreasing desired and undesired behaviors.

To be effective, positive reinforcement, negative reinforcement, punishment, and extinction must be applied on a contingent basis. That is, the consequence of the behavior must be known by the worker prior to the expression of the behavior. Without this contingency, the behavior's consequence may actually reinforce a variety of behaviors, not all of them desirable. It's frequently necessary to use trial and error to determine if a consequence (i.e., possibly a reward) truly reinforces a target behavior.

The nature of the reward also helps to determine the efficacy of the reinforcement. Not all rewards produce a reinforcing effect. Some workers prefer some rewards that other workers may want to avoid. For example, one worker may want to work overtime hours to make extra income, whereas another worker may not want the additional income,

EXHIBIT 10.6
Contingencies of Reinforcement

	Contingencies	
	Applied	Withdrawn
Increase Desired Behavior	Positive Reinforcement • Reward Applied	Negative Reinforcement • Negative Consequence Withdrawn
Decrease Undesirable Behavior	Punishment • Negative Consequence Applied	Extinction • Reward Withdrawn

given the work required. Thus "rewarding" overtime hours only to productive workers may punish rather than reinforce productivity.[17] For a reward to qualify as a reinforcer, the reward must increase the frequency of the worker's behavior. Managers use rewards in hopes of motivating employees and influencing them to perform better.

Managerial Applications of Reinforcement.   Several factors can influence the effectiveness of reinforcement. These principles help to ensure conditions of optimum reinforcement.

- *Immediate reinforcement.* Reinforcement should coincide as closely as is practical with the completion of the target behavior.

- *Reinforcement size.* The larger the reinforcement delivered after the occurrence of a target behavior, the greater effect the reinforcement will have on the frequency of the behavior in the future.

- *Relative reinforcement deprivation.* The more a person is deprived of the reinforcement, the greater the effect the reinforcement will have on the future occurrence of the target behavior.[18]

Social Learning Theory

Albert Bandura is the chief architect of **social learning theory.**[19] Discontent with the explanations offered by Skinner and others regarding human motivation, Bandura proposed that motivated behavior was a function of observing the success of other people and then doing what worked for them. He held that rather than being merely a function of environmental conditioning, learning was influenced by an individual's cognitive assessment of what behaviors were previously rewarded in the environment.

Exhibit 10.7 describes the social learning process. Step one is *attention,* during which another person is observed while successfully performing a behavior. Step two is *retention* of the behavioral response to memory. The observer remembers not only the specifics of the behavior but also its content. Step three is *reproduction* of the behavior exactly as

EXHIBIT 10.7
Bandura's Social Learning Theory

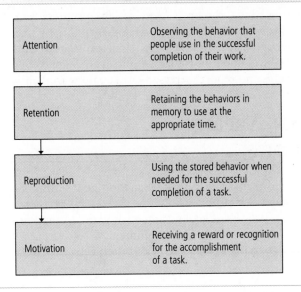

Attention	Observing the behavior that people use in the successful completion of their work.
Retention	Retaining the behaviors in memory to use at the appropriate time.
Reproduction	Using the stored behavior when needed for the successful completion of a task.
Motivation	Receiving a reward or recognition for the accomplishment of a task.

Source: Adapted from Albert Bandura. *Social Learning Theory* (Upper Saddle River, NJ: Prentice Hall, 1977).

it was committed to memory in the appropriate context or situation. Step four is *motivation* for the successful performance of the behavior. At this stage, the individual often administers a self-reward or is granted an external reward or recognition.

Social learning theory has many applications at work. Managers can use concepts of social learning theory to illustrate the behaviors they desire in all workers. For example, if punctuality is deemed important, managers might arrive early to work each day, signaling the importance of preparing for the day before the 8 o'clock shift begins. Similarly, the manager who pays brief visits to workers' cubicles or offices to discuss the daily schedule before a new shift starts shows through his actions that he arrives early to plan, and so should they.

We learn our work partly by watching others. In daily practice, workers observe the desired behaviors modeled by managers or successful colleagues. The modeled behaviors are those that management wants the workers to exhibit. For example, a manager always smiles and is polite and courteous to customers, or the quality work of a successful employee always seems to get noticed and rewarded by management.

In summary, then, both operant conditioning (reinforcement) and social learning theory are important explanations of human motivation. By understanding and using operant conditioning, a manager can create a work environment that automatically rewards certain behaviors (e.g., hard work) and discourages other behaviors (e.g., carelessness). Social learning theory broadens the context of learning to include the observation of other people's experiences in our own learning. In the following example, social learning theory is used to create a behavior, model the behavior, provide a context for workers to reproduce the behavior, and ultimately reward the workers for successfully reproducing the desired behavior.

At a large metropolitan hospital, the head nurse makes it clear to her department nurses that each of them should set goals for achieving daily, weekly, and monthly tasks. The head nurse follows suit; she always carries a daily planner and offers a planner to any nurse who wants one. At weekly meetings, the head nurse reviews progress from her planned activities and reports on her own degree of goal attainment. One by one, her nurses ask for planners; soon they begin exhibiting behavior similar to that of the head nurse. Over the course of a year, the head nurse finds that her nurses are 50 percent more productive, 20 percent more efficient, and report increased satisfaction with their work.

GOAL SETTING: AN APPLIED MOTIVATION THEORY

One of the most widely researched theories of human behavior is goal-setting theory. Simply put, **goal-setting theory** states that people who set goals outperform those who don't set goals.[20] The organizational process of goal setting deals with (1) aligning personal and organizational goals and (2) rewarding goal attainment. Goal-setting principles are evident in such popular programs as management by objective (MBO) and self-management.

Advantages of Goal Setting

Goals help workers to translate general intentions into a specific action. **Goals,** which we introduced in Chapter 5, are targeted levels of performance set before doing the work. Goal-setting research emphasizes the role of conscious intentions in work.[21] That is, people with goals perform at higher levels than people without goals. Goals can help to:

- Direct attention and action
- Mobilize effort
- Create persistent behavior over time
- Lead to strategies for goal attainment[22]

Attributes of Effective Goals

In general, employees need to feel that working to achieve the goal is in their own best interest, not just the manager's interest. Employees also need support for their efforts, including time, tools, information, and other resources needed to do the job. Finally, employees must feel confident that their work will be rewarded.

Goal-setting theory defines **goal acceptance** as a psychological embracing of the goal as the worker's own aspiration; **goal commitment** is a behavioral follow-through, meaning persistent work effort to achieve the goal. Five goal attributes, which we discuss next, enhance the potential for goal acceptance and enduring goal commitment.[23]

Goal Specificity.   Specific goals are more effective than ambiguous (such as "do your best") goals. Statements of specific goals include four elements: action verb, outcome, deadline, and cost.[24] The verb (e.g., *increase, complete, reduce*) establishes the action to be followed. The outcome is expressed as a single measurable result (e.g., quarterly sales of $250,000; a completed report; increased hiring of minority job applicants). The deadline establishes the time (e.g., hour, day, or shift) when the goal should be achieved. The cost identifies the resources to be consumed in reaching the goal.

Goal Difficulty.   Difficult but attainable goals lead to higher performance than easy goals. A difficult but attainable goal is typically established based on relevant data, knowledge, and skills. If an employee is new and her skills are untested, she and her manager might use historical data from similar cases to assign a goal. Managers often establish an operational definition of a goal's ease or difficulty by looking at the worker's or team's prior performance record. In some cases, new tasks require employees to set a difficult goal without benefit of a historical baseline. For example, in designing the first personal digital assistant (PDA), Apple had no historical records to use as a baseline. Determining a challenging goal for completing the design required original, creative thinking.

Goal Feedback.   Feedback can occur at three levels: (1) in setting the goal ("What should I aim for?"), (2) in ongoing feedback after the goal is set and work commences ("How am I doing?"), and (3) in evaluating the final result ("How did I do?").

In establishing an appropriate goal, the worker and manager need to exchange information on their aspirations, skills, schedules, and other work priorities. Ongoing feedback keeps the worker focused. Finally, a manager's feedback when a goal is met ("You met the goal under difficult circumstances. Great job!") maintains the worker's faith in the goal-setting process.

Participating in Goal Setting.   Employees need to be involved in and have control over setting their own goals. Allowing workers to be involved in the goal-setting process encourages a higher degree of commitment to meeting those goals. Early research in goal setting emphasized assigned goals over worker participation.[25] But more recent research suggests that active employee participation in setting goals can be more effective. Employees can be involved in the goal-setting process to a greater or lesser extent, depending on their experience and skill. For inexperienced employees, management helps clarify task expectations by assigning goals based on relevant data and knowledge. These clarified task expectations are called *assigned goals.* For more experienced employees, the manager and the employee exchange information and jointly establish goals. This process produces *interactive or negotiated goals.* Finally, well-trained veteran workers can set their own goals with little or no input from the manager, resulting in *self-set goals.*

Competition.   Sometimes a worker's or work group's goal is defined in relation to exceeding the performance of another worker or work group. This form of competition within the firm can increase the goal's specificity and difficulty. Finding a relevant competitive standard can be the most productive way to facilitate performance initiated by goals.

However, competition also has its disadvantages. When one team's performance depends upon the performance of another team, cooperation rather than competition is necessary.

POSITIVE ASSUMPTIONS ABOUT EMPLOYEES' WORK ETHIC

As Douglas McGregor noted some thirty years ago, worker behavior is often a product of managerial assumptions, attitudes, and behavior toward the worker. Treat a worker with respect and dignity, and you engender trust and cooperation. If managers treat workers like dumb, replaceable machines, they should not be surprised when the workers unplug their "work brains" at shift's end—regardless of the circumstances or the cost to the organization. This phenomenon is known as the **Pygmalion effect** (or self-fulfilling prophecy), whereby increasing a manager's expectations of subordinates' performance actually improves performance.[26]

In comparing the Big Three U.S. auto producers (GM, Ford, and Chrysler) to the Japanese transplants (e.g., Diamond-Star Illinois and NUMMI in California) on the number of work rules contained in each contract, we find some interesting facts. Work rules limit worker autonomy and discretion. Both autonomy and discretion can be important ways of involving workers in improving quality. We find the Big Three are far more rule-bound and oriented toward Theory X management. With fewer rules and limits on employee autonomy, the transplants from Japan follow the Theory Y approach more closely. Organizational goals can best be attained by involving all members of the organization; this is achieved only when management actively encourages greater worker participation in decision making.

A participative management frames its core question about how to motivate employees something like this: How do we enable workers to feel a natural sense of pride in their work and to be self-motivated? This approach to motivation is based on the assumption that employees inherently want to do a good job. In this view, management sees employees as assets, not liabilities. Negative assumptions about employees' desire to do a good job ("if you don't watch them every minute, they're sure to slack off") are seen as counterproductive. These negative assumptions can lead to a system in which employees are motivated by fear.

Conclusion
Motivation

In this chapter we have traced the development of a theoretic basis for work motivation. Content, process, and environmental theories of motivation are useful in understanding worker behavior. To be effective in the long run, however, managers must do more than memorize theory. With an understanding of motivation theory, managers can more easily draw the linkage between organizational goals and individual needs. By asking the simple question, "What does this worker want from the job?" managers can use applied motivational concepts such as goal setting to meet both individual needs and organizational goals.

Motivating employees is a challenge to managers. Workers are often members of teams, empowered to make decisions that were once the domain of managers. In this environment the manager's role is not an "enforcer," but rather a "coach" who gives workers the freedom to express themselves. In fact, at many companies a new breed of manager is reshaping the way workers are motivated. As mentioned, such managers coach rather than command, prod rather than push, and empower rather than order.[27]

Worker participation in decisions made in an organization can have a positive impact on their motivation. In the workplace of tomorrow, workers will not only be given interesting tasks, but increasingly participate in decisions about how to perform them. This approach results in high intrinsic motivation; it inspires people to do high-quality work because it satisfies their need to feel good about the work for which they are responsible. In an organizational context, need satisfaction is sometimes monetary, but most often it deals with achievement. Organizations allow people to express themselves by offering the opportunity to fulfill of a wide range of human needs.

SUGGESTED READINGS

Conger, Jay A. "The Necessary Art of Persuasion." *Harvard Business Review,* May–June 1998.

Kerr, Steven. *Ultimate Rewards: What Really Motivates People to Achieve?* Cambridge, MA: Harvard University Press, 1997.

Maccoby, Michael. *Why Work?—Motivating the New Workforce.* Alexandria, VA: Miles River Press, 1995.

ENDNOTES

1. E. L. Thorndike. *Animal Intelligence,* (New York: Macmillan, 1911), 244.

2. Craig Pinder, *Work Motivation in Organizational Behavior* (Upper Saddle River, NJ: Prentice-Hall, 1998), 11.

3. Douglas McGregor, *The Human Side of Enterprise* (New York: McGraw-Hill, 1960), 33–58.

4. Lyman W. Porter and Edward Lawler, *Managerial Attitudes and Performance* (Burr Ridge, IL: Irwin, 1968), 17.

5. Abraham H. Maslow, *Motivation and Personality* (New York: Harper & Row, 1954).

6. Clayton Alderfer, *Existence, Relatedness, and Growth: Human Needs in Organizational Settings* (New York: Free Press, 1972).

7. Frederick Herzberg, Bernard Mausner, and Barbara Bloch Snyderman, *The Motivation to Work* (New York: Wiley, 1959).

8. See Robert J. House and Lawrence A. Wigdor, "Herzberg's Dual-Factor Theory of Job Satisfaction and Motivation: A Review of the Empirical Evidence and a Criticism," *Personnel Psychology* 20 (Winter 1967): 369–389. Also see Joseph Schneider and Edwin A. Locke, "A Critique of Herzberg's Classification System and a Suggested Revision," *Organizational Behavior and Human Performance* 6 (1971): 441–458.

9. David C. McClelland, *The Achieving Society* (Princeton, NJ: Van Nostrand, 1963).

10. Victor H. Vroom, *Work and Motivation* (New York: Wiley, 1964).

11. Hugh J. Arnold, "A Test of the Multiplicative Hypothesis of Expectancy—Valence Theories of Work Motivation," *Academy of Management Journal* (March 1981): 128–141.

12. J. Stacy Adams, "Inequity in Social Exchange," in *Advances in Experimental Social Psychology,* vol. 2, ed. L. Berkowitz (New York: Academic Press, 1965).

13. B. F. Skinner, *Contingencies of Reinforcement: A Theoretical Analysis* (New York: Appleton-Century-Crofts, 1969).

14. Albert Bandura, *Principles of Behavior Modification* (New York: Holt, Rinehart and Winston, 1969).

15. G. Strauss and L. Sayles, *Personnel: The Human Problems of Management* (Englewood Cliffs, NJ: Prentice Hall, 1967).

16. R. D. Arvey and J. M. Ivancevich, "Punishment in Organizations: A Review, Propositions, and Research Suggestions," *Academy of Management Review* 5 (1980): 123–132.

17. M. E. Schnake and M. P. Dumler, "Some Unconventional Thoughts on Punishment: Reward as Punishment and Punishment as Reward," *Journal of Social Behavior and Personality* 3 (1989): 89–107.

18. Ibid.

19. Albert Bandura, *Social Learning Theory* (Englewood Cliffs, NJ: Prentice-Hall, 1977).

20. Edwin A. Locke and Gary P. Latham, *A Theory of Goal Setting and Task Performance* (Englewood Cliffs, NJ: Prentice Hall, 1990).

21. E. A. Locke and G. P. Latham, *Goal Setting: A Motivational Technique That Works* (Englewood Cliffs, NJ: Prentice-Hall, 1984).

22. E. A. Locke, K. M. Shaw, L. M. Saari, and G. P. Latham, "Goal Setting and Task Performance: 1969–1980," *Psychological Bulletin* 90 (1981): 125–152.

23. J. R. Hollenbeck and H. J. Klein, "Goal Commitment and the Goal-Setting Process: Problems, Prospects, and Proposals for Future Research," *Journal of Applied Psychology* 72 (1987): 212–220; J. R. Hollenbeck, J. R. Williams, and H. R. Klein, "An Empirical Examination of the Antecedents of Commitment to Difficult Goals," *Journal of Applied Psychology* 74 (1989): 18–23.

24. J. M. Ivancevich and M. T. Matteson, *Organizational Behavior and Management* (Burr Ridge, IL: BPI/Irwin, 1990), 164–166.

25. G. P. Latham and G. A. Yukl, "A Review of Research on the Application of Goal Setting in Organizations," *Academy of Management Journal* 18 (1975): 824–845.

26. Helen Rheem, "Effective Leadership: The Pygmalion Effect," *Harvard Business Review,* May–June 1995, p. 146.

27. Geoffrey Brewer, "The New Managers," *Incentive,* March 1995, pp. 30–35.

Chapter

Eleven

Leadership

It seems safe to say that, without someone taking charge (a leader), very little planning of purposeful action, mobilizing of resources, and motivating of organizational members would be accomplished. Make no mistake—leadership is a prime component of effective organizations; yet regrettably, leadership is often elusive. Some people believe that leadership training can enhance leadership skills in virtually anyone; still others believe that leadership is a trait or a personality dimension, that is, some people have it and others do not. What is leadership? What behaviors do leaders exhibit? What skills are necessary to become an effective leader? How does a leader differ from a manager? To better understand the concept of leadership, we address all of these questions—and possibly a few more—in this chapter. We look at related topics such as followers, the context of leaders, and power and leadership. Then we delve into the major theories of leadership, to which we devote most of our energies. An amazing array of research challenges managers to think about how they lead along a variety of insightful dimensions. We also look at possible substitutes for leadership and the role that emotional intelligence has in effecting successful leadership. Last, we analyze the concept of self-leadership, which is increasingly viewed as indispensable to organizational and personal advancement.

WHAT IS LEADERSHIP?

We begin by answering the question, "What is leadership?" Most scholars agree that leadership is creating a vision of the future for an organization, but leadership is also about the relationship between the *leader* and *followers,* and the *situation* in which the leadership occurs. First and foremost, leadership creates a plausible vision of the future for employees and others. The vision must be general enough to allow for change, yet specific enough to guide daily activities. Leadership further defines vision in relation to future goal attainment. For a vision to become reality, everyone in an organization must believe it and act in ways that will make the vision a reality. Just like pouring a foundation for a building signifies the beginning of a new structure, the periodic attainment of goals marks progress toward reaching a vision. Effective leadership focuses human effort and physical resources on the attainment of goals. All organizational stakeholders are influenced in one manner or another by leadership. Another aspect of leadership is the art of motivating and persuading others to follow a course of action (a plan). The leader oversees the development of strategies to achieve this end. An effective leader matches environmental opportunities with an organization's core competencies as well as with the skills of its employees. Ultimately, successful leaders build organizations that meet the needs of multiple stakeholders.

Our understanding of effective leadership has evolved and matured considerably over the years. As a historical picture of leadership, some people may think of World War II Army General George Patton barking commands from a tank turret as the troops surround him, eagerly awaiting orders. Today's generation will recall from Operation Iraqi Freedom the leadership of four-star Army General Tommy Franks briefing the media at a news conference from headquarters in Qatar regarding troop activities. From the business world, a vivid example of leadership occurred when Carly Fiorina of Hewlett-Packard forged a merger with computer giant Compaq, creating a powerful new corporation for the future. All of these leaders had a vision of the future, mobilized their resources, and motivated people to join them in their quest.

But as society, people, and situations change, the actions of leaders must also change. Gone are the days of blind obedience to autocratic leaders; contemporary leaders rely on greater employee participation and self-leadership. Our review in this chapter describes the journey from autocratic to more participative and democratic styles of leadership. In the end, the goal of effective leadership is the efficient production of a high-quality product or service, creating value for the customer and a financial return for stockholders or owners.

Traditional models of leadership have been tested, and many doubts have been raised about their capacity to produce a competitive workforce for the twenty-first century. The trend in leadership styles is toward more participative leadership and away from the dogmatic, authoritative approaches of yesteryear. Because leaders have always been expected to be able to both manage and anticipate change, most models of leadership require the effective leader to have a vision. A **vision** is a clear sense of an organization's future. Without vision, leaders have nowhere to lead workers. Without an understanding of the global demands of the market, leaders are not likely to be successful. With this in mind we will begin with a brief and clear definition of leadership. **Leadership** is defined as the process of influencing other people to attain organizational goals.[1] Further, understanding leadership involves three components—the leader, the subordinate (follower), and the situation.[2] The interaction among the three determines the form of the leadership style as well as the relationship between the leader and each subordinate.

Role of the Leader

Are leaders and managers different? Noted Harvard psychologist Abraham Zaleznick thinks so.[3] He believes managers focus on demands and constraints of the moment, rather than on more far-reaching matters. Unlike leaders, managers must deal with internal daily production concerns. Often managers seem more concerned with "getting things done" than with "getting the right things done." At the worst, managing is reduced to little more than people processing and product massaging. In the process, managers sometimes show little concern for the customer or the product's final use. This preoccupation with what Zaleznick calls *process* orientation leads to mediocrity. For the manager, the goal becomes preserving the status quo.

Zaleznick believes that, unlike managers, leaders are often bored with routine; or, as Tom Peters[4] puts it, they "thrive on chaos" and seek innovative and novel solutions. Rather than being preoccupied with process, the leader is concerned with substance. *Substance* is the true purpose of the work. For example, if quality is paramount, then the leader must focus energy on creating quality. For a leader, substance is everything. The manager asks: "What is the best way to consistently maintain quality and meet production targets?" The leader asks an entirely different question: "For a particular product, what is quality—and how will the definition change in the future?" The difference between managers and leaders is based upon what they do. Managers deal with the pressures of the moment; they are concerned with the process surrounding the work flow. The leader is concerned with providing meaning or purpose in work for employees as well as with creating meaning in the product for customers.

Lee Iacocca's transformation of Chrysler is an example of how a leader can create vision and meaning for both workers and customers. Through Iacocca's leadership, Chrysler workers believed that they were part of the solution to problems facing the auto industry. They were creating the new Chrysler. Iacocca's leadership fostered two innovations that formed the organizational nucleus of the new Chrysler: the K-Car and the Minivan. The K-body design, or simply the K-Car as it was known at the time, was a revolutionary concept. The K-Car was a single platform design with one standard power train over which different body styles were mated, forming a standard base (low cost) with multibody fabrication that offered the consumer functionality (2 door, 4 door, station wagon). The minivan is a transportation icon today, but it wasn't always so. The minivan was an innovative replacement for the gas-guzzling V8 station wagon. Iacocca believed that a family-sized vehicle that offered versatility and fuel efficiency was needed by consumers. He was right! Remember, at the time (early 1980s) there was no minivan—Iacocca and Chrysler created the concept and brought it to market. During this process, Iacocca had to persuade the government, stockholders, and employees that his vision for Chrysler would benefit all members of the Chrysler family and possibly even society in the long run. What followed is history—sales of the industry's first minivan went through the roof, and Iacocca brought his company back from the brink of bankruptcy. Certainly, the automaker's customers believe that in its minivan, Chrysler created a new alternative to the gas-guzzling station wagon that fit the needs of the family and the environment. Iacocca's strategic vision of new products, new markets, and new ways of creating quality and value for the consumer became a reality. Workers produced a better, higher-quality product—not just because of technology, but because they believed they could. As noted, the results were dramatically increased customer demand and profitability.

Leadership is both an individual property and a process. As an individual property, leadership is a combination of personal attributes and abilities such as vision, energy, and knowledge. As a process, leadership is the individual's ability to create a shared vision of the future and direct individual efforts at work toward the vision. Creating a shared vision requires the leader to set goals, motivate employees, and establish a supportive and productive culture in the organization. Indeed, it's often difficult to separate the individual from the process. This is because the leadership process is an extension of the leader's personality and ideas. Collectively then, individual leadership properties and the leadership process influence employee behavior.

Followers

At a superficial level the concept of a follower sounds somewhat simplistic. Leadership occurs when someone is willing to defer to a leader's influence. To gain this acquiescence, effective leaders instill trust and confidence in their subordinates or followers. Good followers support the leader by recognizing their own role in the process of being led or guided toward goal attainment. Organizations can develop more effective followers by creating organizational systems that encourage desirable follower behaviors. Effective followers are not passive; they don't wait to be told where to go and what to do. As author Robert Kelley notes, effective followers are not only active and technically competent, but they understand their role in the organization. Further, they know their value to the organization and how to use their knowledge to attain organizational goals. Here are some other qualities of effective followers:[5]

- Capable of self-management
- Committed to the organization's purpose, principles, and goals
- Willing to increase their competence and skills and apply them to organizational outcomes
- Courageous, honest, and credible

What can organizations do to develop better followers? Kelly offers this advice:

- Redefine the role of the leader and the follower.
- Hone effective followership skills.
- Use the performance evaluation process and feedback to shape behavior.
- Use the organization structure to encourage effective followership.

The Situation

The **situation** is the context in which leadership occurs. Often, it is the situation that determines how successful a leader can be in influencing and persuading subordinates. When the leader is not in a good position to influence an employee, the employee may not be very responsive to influence attempts. For example, tough economic times may mean no raises or promotions. This situation limits the leader's ability to use financial rewards as a source of employee motivation. In other situations, leaders may be very effective with little or no direct intervention. Such is the case in self-leadership contexts, or in situations that encourage greater job involvement through worker autonomy. Autonomy allows the worker greater decision-making latitude. However, worker autonomy is not without limits. For example, a retail clerk may be given greater decision-making autonomy to appease a disgruntled customer. The clerk can offer the customer one of three options: an exchange, refund purchase price, or offer them a new product–no other options are possible. Also, the manager knows what the decision-making options are prior to granting the increase in autonomy, thus limiting the sales clerk's range of autonomy. The leadership substitute facilitates leadership without active intervention by the leader. The net result is a situation where leadership occurs easily and naturally as a consequence of the work context.

Power and Leadership

Influencing the behavior of others is at the core of leadership. To accomplish this, leaders use their **power**, which is, simply, the ability to get people to do something they otherwise wouldn't do.[6] Managers usually have several sources of power at their disposal.

EXHIBIT 11.1
Why Do Employees Respond to Different Types of Power?

Type of Power	Leader Action	Why an Employee Responds
Reward	Provides money or psychological rewards	Seeks a material reward or a feeling of job satisfaction
Coercive	Threatens or forces	Avoids physical force or discipline
Expert	Has knowledge of the situation or task	Believes that another person knows more than they
Referent	Uses personal attractiveness to gain support	Has emotional attachment to the leader's beliefs
Personal	Uses unique combination of expert and referent power	Complies due to being influenced by leader's personal behavior

The following list summarizes the various sources of power within organizations.[7] For examples of how leaders use each type of power, and why employees respond to different types of power, see Exhibit 11.1.

- **Reward power** is the manager's ability to allocate organizational resources in exchange for cooperation. This is probably the most widely used form of power. Rewards controlled by managers include pay raises, promotions, bonuses, and recognition.

- **Coercive power,** sometimes called *punishment power,* is the opposite of reward power. Coercive power is the manager's ability to apply penalties when an employee fails to cooperate. For example, an employee who exhibits inappropriate behavior or violates company policy might be given a below-average performance evaluation or even be passed over for promotion. But punishment power can generate fear and distrust among employees. These negative aspects of punishment must far outweigh the benefits before punishment can be successfully used to alter an employee's behavior.

- **Expert power** is based on an individual's technical or expert knowledge about a particular area. Expertise may be in the form of experience, information, or advanced education. Special knowledge allows an individual to persuade others to do as she wishes. The advertising executive who has developed many successful campaigns is sought after for advice and so has expert power.

- **Referent power** arises from an individual's personal characteristics that are esteemed by others. Referent power stimulates imitation and loyalty. Thus people we admire have referent power. When someone we admire asks us to do something, we are more inclined to do it than if someone we don't admire makes the request. We also emulate the admired person's behavior in the hope that by doing so, we will be as successful as he or she is.

- **Personal power** consists of both expert and referent power, or a combination of both. A sense of personal power comes from the belief that we can reach our goals in our own way; a sense of personal power is communicated by developing authority, accessibility, assertiveness, a positive image, and solid communications skills.[8]

Authority

Whereas power is a personal quality, **authority** is granted by membership in the organization and is generally related to one's position or job. For example, by virtue of their position, managers have the decision-making authority to buy office furniture. Thus anyone in their position can make the decision (i.e., has the authority) to buy office furniture.

However, only a powerful manager can buy ugly furniture without much opposition from employees. A less-powerful manager might not be able to make the same decision without meeting considerable opposition.

THEORIES OF LEADERSHIP

Leadership is one of the most studied aspects of management. A tremendous variety of research, terms, and values underlie leadership definitions, theories, and findings. Three widely accepted historical models have evolved through the twentieth century. Trait theory, the first attempt to systematically describe effective leaders, focuses on a **trait** such as a physical or personality attribute of the leader. Studies of trait theory led to the behavioral model. Behavioral models focus on (1) the work itself and (2) worker attitudes. Behavioral models, in turn, led to contingency models of leadership. **Contingency leadership models** state that the leader's behavioral style must be contingent on the situation if the leader is to be effective. Contingency models emerged as two different approaches: (1) fit the leader to the situation, and (2) fit the leader's behavior to the situation. Subsequent leadership theorists have sought alternative explanations for effective leadership, including visionary leadership and substitutes for leadership.

Trait Theory of Leadership

Today we tend to notice effective leaders—Bill Gates at Microsoft, Peg Whitman at eBay, Larry Ellison of Oracle, the late Anita Roddick at The Body Shop—and ask what personal characteristics make them effective. This question is at the root of the **trait theory of leadership**, which identifies effective leaders based on certain physical and psychological attributes (e.g., intelligence, height, articulateness). Trait-based leadership approaches focus on traits of those who emerged or assumed power as the leader and on traits of those leaders believed to be effective. For example, Edwin Ghiselli found that among other traits, leader initiative, self-assurance, decisiveness, and maturity are important for leader success.[9] Exhibit 11.2 is a summary of some other common leadership traits.

Trait theory was an early attempt to find those elusive qualities of the individual that are necessary for effective leadership. Researchers identified individual traits such as personality, skills, and physical characteristics. These early studies focused on the idea that effective leadership was a naturally occurring phenomenon among people. The question was, if certain traits could be identified in individuals, then could organizations more efficiently select people with high leadership potential? In response to the often conflicting research results and to lack of clear support for trait theory, psychologist Ralph Stogdill[10]

E X H I B I T   1 1 . 2
Some Common Leadership Traits

Capacity	Intelligence, alertness, originality, and judgment
Achievement	Knowledge, accomplishments, and scholarship
Responsibility	Dependability, initiative, persistence, and aggressiveness
Participation	Activity, sociability, cooperation, and adaptability
Status	Popularity, and social status

Source: Adapted from Bernard Bass, *Stogdill's Handbook of Leadership,* revised and expanded ed. (New York: Free Press, 1981), 66.

reviewed the findings of trait theory research from 1904 to 1947. He concluded that something other than traits worked to determine leader effectiveness. Traits did not appear to transfer well from one situation to another. In other words, a leader might be successful in one situation but not in another. So finding traits didn't seem to be the answer. As a result of the work of Stogdill and other leadership researchers the focus of leadership effectiveness shifted toward understanding situational requirements rather than a quest for universal traits. However, it is still a widely held belief that effective leaders share certain common traits but that these traits alone do not explain why they were effective.

Trait theory constitutes an important yet incomplete approach to leadership. Although supporters of trait theory were unsuccessful in explaining leader effectiveness, it is important to recognize that individual qualities are still important. The lesson from trait theory is that such qualities are not the exclusive source of leader effectiveness; rather, individual characteristics, the situation, and leader behaviors are all contributors. Clearly, not all effective leaders are tall—nor are they all exceptionally smart. Further, serious cultural differences exist; attributes seen as positive in some cultures are seen as negative in others. For example, American leadership practices have tended to endorse direct, forceful leaders. But not all successful leaders are dominating, extroverted, or self-confident. The trait approach is a simple—perhaps too simple—method of trying to identify or predict effective leadership. Yet, at the same time, it presents an appealing potential explanation for the effectiveness of people like Sam Walton and Lee Iacocca.

A disadvantage of trait theory is that it generally ignores the workers. Lists of traits also fail to give weight to the relative importance of the many possible traits. For example, is decisiveness more important than intelligence? In addition, due to their focus on small groups of leaders, many trait studies had limited ability to generalize, especially across cultures and countries. Most of all, trait theory studies were inconsistent in their findings and in their value to management. Trait theory does suggest that some value can be found in giving attention to both the task and the workers. The deficiency of trait theory in explaining significant variance in leadership effectiveness has led to the behavioral models of leadership. The Management Highlight on page 210 presents a contemporary perspective on gender differences of leaders.

Behavioral Theory of Leadership

As research shifted away from the idea that leaders are endowed with certain characteristics, it moved toward the notion that different leaders have or could develop different leadership styles. This approach, known as the behavioral style, defines leader effectiveness based on *leader behaviors*—what the leader does, rather than which traits the leader has. Researchers have identified specific behavioral styles, which we examine next.

Task-Oriented and Relationship-Oriented Styles.   In the **behavioral style model,** effective leaders focus not only on the work, but on workers' attitudes and expectations. A **task-oriented behavioral style** consists of behaviors such as setting goals, giving directions, supervising worker performance, and applauding good work. Since Frederick W. Taylor (the father of scientific management), regular attention has been paid to the leader's role as a task-driven manager. But as we learned from the human relations movement, focusing attention on task alone was insufficient (see Appendix A for a discussion of the Human Relations Movement). Workers not only needed specific direction but they also had personal and social needs that managers needed to consider if they hoped to attain optimal performance from the worker. The behavioral approach with its emphasis on leader behaviors focused on the task as well as a concern for people; thus there evolved a **relationship-oriented behavioral style.** It consists of behaviors such as showing empathy for worker

---

MANAGEMENT HIGHLIGHT
Do Men and Women Have Different Leadership Traits?

Though the subject of men's and women's leadership traits has been debated a great deal, and with mixed opinions, author Judy Rosener has identified certain leadership style differences. She has found that through socialization, men and women are taught differently. Thus, while both men and women make good—and bad—leaders, it is important to understand the different leadership styles they use. The most effective leader will combine the positive traits of both men and women and use them appropriately.

Characteristics Attributed to Men.

- *Lead by command and control.* This works best in the military, but has drawbacks when managing across gender lines.

- *Encourage rewards for services rendered.* This is the traditional reward system, much like the old barter system. Creating more flexibility in what an organization rewards is very important in helping a diverse group of workers to find success.

- *Rely on positional power.* Because males have held many of the power positions, it is not surprising that they derive power from their position.

- *Follow a hierarchical structure.* Historically, leaders have relied on lines of authority in getting the job done. As TQM has gained popularity, the end result is a flatter organization, and it may become more difficult to follow a hierarchical structure.

- *Action orientation.* Aggressive, take-charge managers have succeeded in the past, and they will succeed in the future, though an overly aggressive stance turns workers off.

- *Think analytically.* Leaders with this trait have a great track record, especially when combined with intuitive thinking.

Characteristics Attributed to Women.

- *Share power and information.* Power, to some extent, stems from position and information, and can be used to influence others. Women are skilled at maintaining power through relationships, and are more willing to share power than men.

- *Enhance self-worth of others.* Female leaders tend to build their coworkers' esteem. This trait builds employee commitment and is essential in managing a diverse group.

- *Encourage participation.* This is a powerful and important characteristic of a leader. Employees feel motivated when they know they are part of the organization and that their opinions count.

- *Get others excited about their work.* Female leaders place great emphasis on process as well as product; they want to enjoy the journey. This trait is useful because it helps employees find intrinsic value in their work.

Source: Adapted from Judy B. Rosener, "The Valued Ways Men and Women Lead," *Human Resources,* June 1991, p. 149; Judy B. Rosener, "Ways Women Lead," *Harvard Business Review,* November–December 1990, pp. 119–125; and Lee Gardenswartz and Anita Rowe, *Managing Diversity* (Burr Ridge, IL: Business One Irwin, 1993), 356–361.

---

needs and feelings, being supportive of group needs, establishing trusting relationships with workers, and allowing workers to participate in work-related decisions.

Job-Centered and Employee-Centered Leader Behaviors. Studies conducted at the University of Michigan focused on job-centered and employee-centered leader behaviors. These two categories of leader behaviors represent directions that are either task oriented or people oriented. At first an employee-centered leader was found to be effective, but the original study did not separate cause and effect. Did an employee-centered leader produce good work, or did good work produce an employee-centered leader? More careful subsequent research found that whereas employee-centered leaders did create more positive worker attitudes, job-centered leaders achieved higher worker productivity.[11]

Initiating Structure and Consideration.   The Ohio State studies, conducted at the university beginning about fifty years ago, identified **initiating structure** and **consideration** as task- and relationship-oriented behavioral styles, respectively.[12] Leaders emphasizing initiating structure usually follow a behavioral pattern whereby they insist that workers follow rigid work methods, insist on being informed of worker behavior, push workers for greater efforts, and make detailed decisions for the workers concerning what work is to be done, and how. Leaders emphasizing consideration appreciate a job well done, stress high morale, treat workers as their equals, and are friendly and approachable. Subsequent studies generally found that leaders who score high on both behaviors are more effective than leaders scoring low on these behavioral styles.

Even when exhibiting a constant, well-trained, and focused set of task- or relationship-oriented behaviors, leaders were not found to be consistently effective. Some workers did not respond well to task-oriented leaders. At times, people orientation helped task performance; at other times, it detracted from task performance. Dissatisfaction with the ability of behavioral style theories to explain effective leadership led researchers to the third phase in traditional leadership approaches, namely, contingency or situation-based leadership effectiveness models (we discuss those theories shortly).

At Wal-Mart, managers employ a combination of relationship-oriented management with task skills and modern technology. Visiting senior managers ask employees, "Is there anything we can do for you?" Simultaneously, they track task performance via a computer terminal that provides sales figures by store and department; measures labor hours and inventory losses; and compares these numbers with data for previous time periods, other stores or sales districts, and the national standards for Wal-Mart.[13]

Leadership Grid.   Basing their early work on the leadership research conducted at the University of Michigan and Ohio State University, Robert R. Blake and Jane S. Mouton developed what was originally called the Managerial Grid® and in later editions of their work was retitled the Leadership Grid® as a vehicle for leader behavior assessment and development.[14] In a series of questionnaires and structured seminars, Blake and Mouton used the grid to assess leadership orientation. The Managerial Grid incorporates both task orientation (concern for results) and people orientation (concern for people) into a two-dimensional matrix grid (Exhibit 11.3). *Concern for people* and *concern for results* are each arrayed along a nine-point continuum. A leadership style with a high concern for people and low concern for results would be represented by cell (1, 9)—Country Club—suggesting an emphasis on relationship building and the needs of people.

In the reverse situation, a leadership style with high degree of concern for results and low concern for people would be located at cell (9, 1)—Authority-Compliance—suggesting a strong concern for task completion and very little concern for the worker. In the midrange position is the leader who is moderate on both dimensions, represented by the cell (5, 5)—Middle of the Road or Balanced—suggesting a balance between task accomplishment and demonstrating concern for the worker. A leader rated at the top on both dimensions would be in cell (9, 9)—Team Management—suggesting a leader with common stakes, commitment, mutual trust, and respect. This technique demonstrates that rather than indicating distinct or different leader behaviors, the results and people orientations are usually more or less present in all managers. Leaders must be able to demonstrate concern for both people and results.

Further, Blake and Mouton believe that Team Management—cell (9, 9)—representing high people orientation and high task orientation, is the preferred leadership style. The rationale for their belief is that a leader must not only support the worker, but structure the work setting toward task achievement. At the opposite end of the matrix is

EXHIBIT 11.3
The Leadership Grid®

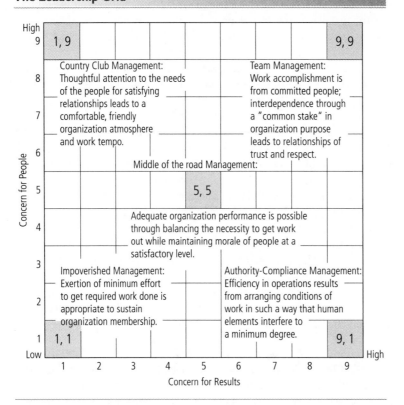

Source: The Leadership Grid® (formerly the Managerial Grid by Robert R. Blake and Jane S. Mouton) from R. R. Blake and A. A. McCanse, *Leadership Dilemmas—Grid Solutions* (Houston: Gulf Publishing, 1991), 29, Copyright © 1991 by Scientific Methods, Inc. Reproduced by permission of the owners.

Impoverished Management—cell (1, 1). This cell represents the leader with low task orientation and low people orientation; clearly, an undesirable situation and untenable in the long run.

Finally, through a series of seminars, leaders are guided more toward the (9, 9) orientation. A positive feature of the Leadership Grid is its recognition that both types of leader behaviors are important, and that people bring different orientations or predispositions to the management process. Later work by Blake and McCanse has broadened the Managerial Grid to include understanding leader motivation. A negative feature of this approach is the assumption that leader behaviors can be readily changed through seminar participation. As we will see, management scholars don't commonly make this assumption.

Situational Theories of Leadership

In response to the lack of success in trait theory and behavioral theory, researchers turned to the situation as a determinant of effective leadership. According to **situational theories of leadership**, the appropriate leader behavior is the one best fitting the constraints of a specific situation. Further, leader effectiveness is contingent on displaying behavior appropriate to the situation's demands. In this context, situational leadership theories (1) identify important leadership situations and (2) suggest various leadership behaviors that increase worker satisfaction and productivity.

Two contrasting approaches to leadership situational effectiveness have emerged. One fits the leader to the situation (i.e., assign a manager to the situation that matches his fixed leadership style); the other fits the leader's behavior to the situation (i.e., expect a manager to change her behavior in response to the situation). The first approach assumes a leader's behavioral style is relatively fixed or not easily changed; thus, the best course is to find the situations in which particular leaders are most effective and avoid those in which they are least effective. Is this always possible? Probably not. But the idea has merit. If we can find the situations in which a manager's dominant leadership style is most effective, both leader and follower are best served. An example of this approach to situational leadership is Fiedler's LPC theory (discussed in the next section).

In the second approach to leadership situational effectiveness, it is assumed that both the leader's decisions and the work situation are relatively fluid and subject to change. This perspective removes the assumption of a rigid leadership style that nothing can change. It views managers as adaptive and able to respond effectively to different people and different situations. An example of this approach is the Hersey-Blanchard situational leadership theory, which we explain later in this section.

Both approaches to situational leadership hold merit and have research support. But the second, fitting the decision to the situation, appears to offer a more realistic view of human nature. Leaders face people with different personalities, abilities, and motivations. To assume that a leader would treat them all alike is simplistic at best.

Fiedler's LPC Theory.   In the mid-1970s, Fred Fiedler developed one of the first situational theories of leadership.[15] **Least preferred coworker (LPC) theory** describes effective leadership as a behavioral predisposition of the leader matched with a favorable situation. This theory asserts that the leader's behavioral style must first be measured and determined. Next, says Fiedler, a situation has to be found or created that is conducive to the leader's fixed style. Thus, LPC theory fits the characteristics of the individual with the requirements of the situation.

Determining Leadership Style.   Fiedler believes that the leader's personality determines how they are likely to respond to their workers. Based on previous behavioral research, Fiedler states that people have a primary orientation (or leadership style) that emphasizes task completion or concern for people. He also notes that a person's primary orientation is fixed and thus not likely to change over time. A task-oriented leader is consistently more concerned with getting the work done. A relationship-oriented leader is consistently more concerned with workers' feelings and understanding the impact of personal problems on work performance.

Measuring Leadership Style.   Fiedler measures leadership style in reference to how the leader treats their least preferred coworker. Fiedler developed a series of questions that form the LPC (Least Preferred Coworker) scale to measure the leader's attitude about their least preferred coworker. The LPC scale measures the leader's behavioral style relative to task orientation and people orientation. One way to think about the LPC score is that it represents an enduring personality characteristic of the leader. With that in mind, the LPC score should identify a consistent behavioral style for each individual leader. With this measure, a leader who identifies his LPC in terms critical of the worker's task initiative and accomplishment is described as task oriented. In other words, the leader's relationship with the workers is focused on the task, not the person. On the other hand, if the leader identifies his LPC in relatively positive terms (that is, prefers not to work with this person but finds little to criticize), he is described as people oriented.

Situational Characteristics.   In his work, Fiedler identified the following three **situational characteristics:**

- *Leader-member relations* represent the follower's trust and confidence in the leader. To be effective, a leader must be able to influence the follower and elicit cooperation. High trust and confidence makes for high leader-member relations. Conversely, low trust and a lack of confidence create a situation described as low leader-member relations.

- *Task structure* is the degree to which a task is well defined and clearly understood. A high degree of task structure represents a situation with a well-defined, easily understood job. In a situation with low task structure, the job is ill-defined and the specific steps for task completion unclear.

- *Position power* is the power available to the leader to reward or punish the follower. Leaders with high position power can and do reward their followers for successes, and they discipline inappropriate behavior. Leaders with low position power lack the power to gain compliance through reward and punishment; such leaders find it difficult to gain compliance from their followers.

Fiedler combines these three characteristics into eight cells, describing various situations that leaders are likely to confront in an organization (Exhibit 11.4). The situations range from being relatively favorable to the leader to unfavorable. For each situation, Fiedler also identifies recommended leadership styles. In Exhibit 11.4, we can see that the manager experiences a high degree of control in cells I–III, a moderate degree of control in cells IV–VII, and a low degree of control in cell VIII.

EXHIBIT 11.4
Fiedler's LPC Theory of Leadership

	HIGH LEADER CONTROL			MODERATE LEADER CONTROL			LOW LEADER CONTROL	
	I	II	III	IV	V	VI	VII	VIII
Leader-Member Relations	Good	Good	Good	Good	Poor	Poor	Poor	Poor
Task Structure	High	High	Low	Low	High	High	Low	Low
Position Power	Strong	Weak	Strong	Weak	Strong	Weak	Strong	Weak
Recommended Leadership Style	Task-Oriented			Relationship-oriented				Task-Oriented
Very Favorable to Leaders				⎯⎯⎯⎯⎯⎯⎯⎯⎯⎯⟶				**Very Unfavorable to Leaders**

Adapted from: Fred E. Fiedler, "The Effects of Leadership Training and Experience: A Contingency Model Interpretation," *Administrative Science Quarterly,* 17, 1972, 455; Fred E. Fiedler, "How to Engineer the Job to Fit the Manager," *Harvard Business Review,* September-October 1965.

In the following situations, Fiedler recommends the task-oriented leadership style:

- Difficult work situations, where the leader has poor relationships with workers, little power over workers, and an unstructured task (Exhibit 11.4, cell VIII).

- Relatively undemanding work situations, where the leader has good relationships with workers, high power over workers, and a clearly structured task (Exhibit 11.4, cells I–III).

In contrast, Fiedler says the relationship-oriented leadership style works best in moderately difficult situations (neither easy nor difficult) (Exhibit 11.4, cells IV–VII).

Criticisms of LPC Theory. LPC theory has its critics. Despite being developed more than thirty years ago, the theory has limited research support. In fact, some studies have been quite critical of LPC theory—especially regarding Fiedler's strong belief that leaders have a fixed style that doesn't change in going from one situation or person to another.[16] In many organizations today, Fiedler's fixed leadership style seems at odds with the requirements for success. Successful leadership requires flexibility and adaptability—not inflexible, autocratic responses. In addition, some note, the measurement of leadership style using the concept of a least preferred coworker as a referent is an indirect and sometimes unreliable approach.

Although this relatively unique method of assessing a leader's style has been questioned, Fiedler's own research shows an improvement over noncontingent approaches to leadership. He describes different situations in which the leader will have the most power and influence with subordinates, thus giving the leader greater control over the outcome of the work. Fiedler's contingency-based LPC theory is still considered an important explanation of situational constraints on leader behavior.

Fiedler's Cognitive Resources Theory. Fiedler's recent work has focused on stress and leadership effectiveness. Leaders rely on their cognitive resources, developed through education, experience, and personality, to make decisions. Therefore, Fiedler says, intelligent leaders are more likely to be effective than less intelligent leaders. Fiedler and Garcia pondered the question, "Is an effective leader an intelligent leader or an experienced leader?" In other words, what resources do effective leaders rely on to make decisions? What Fiedler and Garcia found was that the degree of stress confronting the manager influences leader effectiveness.[17] In stressful situations, the leader tended to focus on the source of the stress instead of the situation, thereby leading to ineffective performance. Fiedler found that in high-stress situations effective leaders tended to rely on their previous experience with a similar situation. In low-stress situations, effective leaders relied more on their intelligence to resolve the issue.

Fielder and Garcia have heightened our awareness about consequences of stress on leader effectiveness. The general message these authors send is that in high-stress situations, leaders should rely on their experience; in low-stress situations, they should rely on their intelligence. Fiedler and Garcia believe that in stressful leadership situations, rather than trying to invent a new program, leaders perform better when they use a program that worked well in a similar situation. However, in less stressful situations leaders have time to evaluate the situation; then they perform better by using intelligence to resolve the situation.

Hersey-Blanchard Situational Leadership® Theory. Ken Blanchard and Paul Hersey believe that leaders can and should adjust their behavior to suit the decision-making situations they confront in the workplace. For leaders, the most important of these situations is dealing with people in their formal leadership capacity. **Hersey-Blanchard**

Situational Leadership Theory® uses the traditional dimensions of concern for production (task behavior) and concern for the worker (relationship behavior).

Exhibit 11.5 presents the theory in graphic form. In the topmost chart, **task behavior** (guidance) is the amount of task-specific direction a worker needs; **relationship behavior** (supportive behavior) is the amount of emotional support needed to complete

EXHIBIT 11.5
Hersey-Blanchard Situational Leadership® Theory

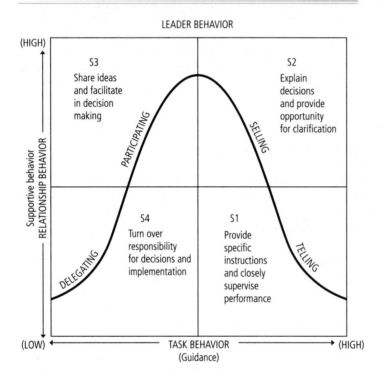

Source: P. Hersey, K. Blanchard, and D. E. Johnson, *Management of Organizational Behavior: Leading Human Resources,* 8th ed. (Upper Saddle River, NJ: Prentice Hall, 2001), 182. Copyright © Copyrighted material. Adapted/reprinted with permission of the Center for Leadership Studies, Escondido, CA 92025. All Rights Reserved.

a task. The leader's allocation of guidance to supportive behavior depends on the level of **follower readiness** (willingness, confidence, ability), as shown in the bottom chart.

In making a situational assessment, the leader also considers group performance in relation to decision making and dispute resolution. Based on follower readiness and group interaction, four leadership styles are recommended—telling, selling, participating, and delegating. Each style affects the degree of leader directedness. As we can see in Exhibit 11.5, follower readiness levels R1 and R2 require greater leader direction than do R3 and R4, which allow greater follower participation in decision making and less leader direction. Follower readiness also determines the degree to which the leader shares decision-making authority. The higher the readiness, the more willing the leader is to allow greater follower autonomy in decision making. This makes sense because the leader wants predictable outcomes. A good leader is not likely to let a follower make decisions until he or she is ready to make good decisions. The theory describes a mutually beneficial model of leadership. Ready followers, capable of independent action, require less leader intervention; less ready followers need greater guidance and more leader intervention.

On the positive side, Situational Leadership® theory suggests there is no one preferred leadership style. The best leadership style is the one that best matches the situation. Leadership style depends on the readiness of the follower for independent action. While the Hersey-Blanchard theory builds on early work and offers additional considerations, it too has its critics.[18] The theory has been criticized for its methods as well as substance. In other words, the model may not depict reality or be as consistent with earlier work (i.e., the Managerial Grid®) as the authors suggest.

Path-Goal Theory of Leadership

Robert House and Terrence Mitchell's **path-goal leadership theory** is based on the expectancy theory of motivation. The role of the leader is twofold: (1) clarify for the follower the path by which an individual can achieve personal goals (salary increases and promotions) and organizational outcomes (increased productivity and profitability); and (2) increase rewards that are valued by the follower. In a sense, the leader facilitates the organizational learning process. To do this, the leader engages in behaviors that help followers better understand how their actions are linked to organizational rewards. An effective leader helps followers engage in behaviors that lead to the rewards followers value. In essence, the leader motivates followers toward outcomes valued by the individual and the organization.

Path-goal theory identifies four types of leader behaviors:

- **Directive behavior.** The leader makes clear task expectations by setting goals, structuring work flow, and providing advice and comments through regular performance feedback. This leader behavior is similar to the traditional leader behavior known as initiating structure.

- **Supportive behavior.** The leader demonstrates concern for the follower and, when problems occur, is ready and willing to offer advice or just listen. Supportive behavior is the same as the traditional leader behavior known as consideration.

- **Participative behavior.** The participative leader actively seeks ideas and information from workers. Participative behavior implies that followers actually participate in making decisions that affect them. For participative style to be effective, workers must perceive that their participation is meaningful and will be used by management.

- **Achievement behavior.** Achievement leadership translates into setting expectations and task goals at a high level. This involves making the job challenging but not impossible to accomplish.

These four behaviors form a repertoire of meaningful actions that a leader might exhibit under different work situations. The theory also suggests that leaders have the ability to increase rewards that are valued by the follower. Leaders are effective to the extent that they can motivate their followers, influence their ability to perform, and increase their job satisfaction. The model specifies that a follower's attitudes and behaviors are influenced by two factors: leader behaviors and situational factors. Followers' attitudes and behaviors include their level of job satisfaction and their ability to perform their task. Situational factors (sometimes referred to as environmental factors) include task requirements, the work group, and the formal authority structure. Personal characteristics of the follower include locus of control and perceived ability.

Path-goal theory prescribes which leader behaviors are likely to be effective with different situational constraints. Leaders are expected to change their behavior toward the follower when situational changes occur. From the workers' perspective, the leader behaviors must be seen as facilitating or enabling workers to accomplish both immediate task goals and their own personal goals.

The theory suggests, for example, that the following matches between leader behaviors and situations result in effective leadership:

- Directive behavior is suggested for situations that require more task structuring, monitoring, and feedback. Directive behavior may be particularly appropriate for a new employee with limited job experience.

- Supportive behavior might be suitable in a situation where workers know the job well, are experiencing delays or "client conflict," and just need to know that they're doing the right thing.

- Participative behavior is appropriate for workers who know their jobs well enough to make meaningful contributions to decisions that affect themselves and their department.

- Achievement behavior is suitable in situations where high performance is in the best interest of both the employee and the organization. A sales department that compensates employees on a commission basis would provide an opportunity for achievement-oriented leader behavior. Here achievement-oriented leader behavior sets high sales expectations that, when met, yield the sales department greater financial rewards. Achievement-oriented leadership works best when the followers have a high need for achievement.

In summary, path-goal leadership theory views the leader as the vital link between the organization and the individual. Leaders need to motivate workers to understand how their work efforts are tied to valued salary increases, promotions, praise, recognition, and respect. Exhibit 11.6 presents the path-goal theory.

Leader-Member Exchange Theory

Leader-member exchange theory is based on the concept of an exchange that occurs between the leader and followers.[19] Although many leadership theories describe leadership behavior as universal across people, the facts speak otherwise. In fact, few leaders are really that egalitarian. More likely is the situation where the leader shares demographics, attitudes, hobbies, interests in sports, and other social interests with some followers (or subordinates) and not others. It isn't unusual for a leader and a follower to become friends. Most of us have found ourselves associating with leaders outside work. While we may be friends with our boss today, in the future we might have a different boss with whom

EXHIBIT 11.6
Path-Goal Theory

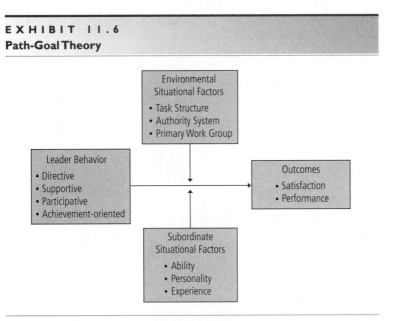

Adapted from: R. J. House and T. R. Mitchell, "Path-Goal Theory of Leadership," *Journal of Contemporary Business,* Autumn 1974, 81–97; R. J. House, "A Path-Goal Theory of Leader Effectiveness," *Administrative Science Quarterly,* September 1971, 321–338.

we don't care to associate outside of work. Likewise, leaders form strong bonds with some followers and not with others. Leader-member exchange theory is an attempt to understand leadership from the perspective of the relationships existing between the leader and each follower.

Leader-member exchange theory (LMX), sometimes called the vertical dyad linkage model,[20] explains effective leadership in relation to the role-making process that occurs between the leader and followers. Leaders develop different relationships with each subordinate. These relationships are based on a variety of factors including compatibility, attitudes, and interests. In the process of negotiating a relationship with each subordinate, the leader enters into exchanges with each subordinate. A **low-exchange relationship** is based on rules and procedures. As long as the subordinate complies with the rules, the subordinate receives benefits from the leader. A **high-exchange relationship** involves the allocation by the leader of more discretionary rewards such as support, travel, new computer, and so on in exchange for compliance from the subordinate. The leader's intent is to build commitment and encourage task accomplishment. However, codependence between the leader and the follower can develop. This results in greater resource allocations by the leader in exchange for compliance and task performance by the follower.

From a practical standpoint, leaders often find themselves working with a small number of people—not their whole department. In many cases, group formation is often at the discretion of the leader. LMX theory suggests that *in-group* members are more likely to be included in important decision making groups than are *out-group* members. Over time, in-group and out-group membership becomes entrenched. When this situation occurs, the result is that in-group members are more informed and better respected in the unit, department or organization than are out-group members. Too often out-group members, holding the same job with the same leader, are in the unenviable position of not being highly regarded by the leader, and may be denied information and interesting group assignments.

Leader-member exchange theory describes both of the preceding situations as common. Over time, the leader forms a so-called in-group based on friendship, respect, and admiration for some of the followers. Other followers who hold less respected relationships with the leader are relegated to the out-group. The in-group shares a special relationship with the leader that provides security, information, and privilege. The out-group includes people the leader believes are unmotivated and lacking in commitment and loyalty. Leader-member exchange is an attribution theory that helps us better understand leader behavior and the differential treatment of followers.

SUBSTITUTES FOR LEADERSHIP

In many work situations, traditional approaches to leadership are ineffective or sometimes just not possible. Authors Steven Kerr and John Jermier believe that situational characteristics can reduce the need for traditional leadership.[21] They identify three situational attributes that include characteristics of the subordinate, the task, and the organization. These characteristics can act as either neutralizers or substitutes for leadership.

In certain situations, leader behavior can be neutralized by an organizational characteristic. A **neutralizer** is any situation that prevents the leader from acting in a specified way. For example, a union contract may require that all union members in the organization receive the same raise, regardless of job performance. This situation neutralizes the leader's ability not only to reward or reinforce positive behavior but also to sanction negative behavior. In this illustration, the union contract prohibits the leader from rewarding top performers at a higher rate than low performers. The leader loses the ability to influence worker behavior.

In other situations, **substitutes for leadership** replace the need for traditional leadership. New employees often require more direct, task-oriented leader behaviors. But training and education can reduce the need for task-oriented leader behaviors; so in effect, training and education serve as substitutes for leadership. Exhibit 11.7 gives examples of substitutes for leadership.

EXHIBIT 11.7
Substitutes for Leadership

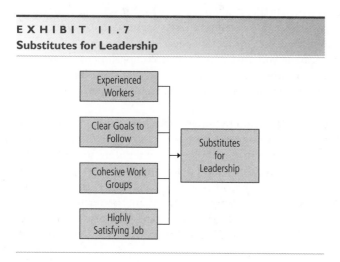

TRANSFORMATIONAL AND TRANSACTIONAL LEADERSHIP

Early in the chapter, we considered the differences between leaders and managers. We also discussed trait theory—an early theory suggesting that leaders have certain characteristics that can be identified or may be developed for those deficient in the trait. For many years, trait theory took a back seat to behavioral and situational explanations of leadership; today most management scholars use the terms *managing* and *leading* to refer to two different processes.

Several theorists use the term **transformational leadership** to describe an inspirational form of leader behavior based on modifying followers' beliefs, values, and ultimately their behavior. Bernard Bass refers to this process as leadership that creates "performance beyond expectations."[22] For example, Lee Iacocca transformed Chrysler not just by changing products, but by changing the attitudes of both workers and customers. Similarly, Larry Quadracci's inspirational leadership transformed a small Midwestern printer, Quad Graphics, into a highly profitable national corporation. Home Depot, after three years of sagging stock prices, has hired back one of its founders, Pat Farrah. A self-proclaimed "radical," Farrah was given much of the credit for the retailer's initial success; since his return, Home Depot stock shot up 28,000 percent since the company went public in 1981.[23] While the stock price slipped in the late 1980s, and early 1990s, since Pat Farrah's return in 1995 the stock price has soared. Pat Farrah is a tough boss and relentless worker, but people are energized by his charismatic leadership style.

In contrast, **transactional leadership** is more closely related to both behavioral and situational leader behaviors. Transactional leaders appeal to their followers' rational exchange motive. Workers exchange labor for wages. Leaders help clarify the path from effort to reward. For the worker, it's a form of self-interested exchange—do this, and you get a reward. For the leader, it's a process of keeping workers riveted to organizational goals.

Both transactional and transformational leadership are valid approaches to leadership. Transformational leadership helps us to realize that leaders who transform organizations are unique and individually different. As you will recall, early trait theorists were unsuccessful in identifying physical attributes and personality types needed for effective leadership. But transformational leadership research holds the promise that individual qualities are a critical element in transforming an organization. Successful companies often have bold, dominant leaders who guide, inspire, and create a vision of the future. Larry Ellison of Oracle, Steve Jobs in the early years of Apple Computer, and Jack Welch of GE are examples of leaders who made a difference in the performance of their organizations.

Do leadership traits exist? Sure they do. But can we teach people these traits and expect them to go out and transform organizations? Certainly not. It is foolish, however, to assume that some people are genetically endowed with leadership traits whereas other people lack them. Finding that elusive leader within requires more than having a requisite set of traits. Nor should we assume that leaders just magically appear as the circumstances require. On the contrary, leadership is personal and situational, requiring an investment in education, skill building, experience, and—undoubtedly—some luck.

EMOTIONAL INTELLIGENCE

Recent work by Daniel Goleman[24] suggests that **emotional intelligence** plays a key role in leader success. According to Goleman, emotional intelligence allows people to more

EXHIBIT 11.8
Emotional Intelligence

Components	Definition	Behaviors
Self-Awareness	The ability to recognize and understand your moods, emotions, and drives, as well as their effects on others	Self-confidence Realistic self-assessment Self-deprecating sense of humor
Self-Regulation	The ability to control or redirect disruptive impulses or moods The propensity to suspend judgment to think before acting	Trustworthiness Integrity Comfort with ambiguity Openness to change
Motivation	A passion to work for reasons that go beyond money or status A propensity to pursue goals with energy and persistence	Strong drive to achieve Optimism Organizational commitment
Empathy	Ability to understand the emotional makeup of other people Skill in treating people according to their emotional reactions	Expertise in building and retaining talent Service to clients and customers
Social Skill	Proficiency in managing relationships and building networks Ability to find common ground and build rapport	Effectiveness in leading change Persuasiveness Expertise in building and leading teams

Adapted from: P. Salovey and J. Mayer (1990). "Emotional intelligence." *Imagination, Cognition, and Personality* no. 3, 185–211; D. Goleman (1995). *Emotional intelligence* (New York: Bantam); D. Goleman, "Leadership that gets results," *Harvard Business Review,* March–April 2000, 79–90.

effectively manage themselves and their relationships with others. Contemporary organizations are more complex and diverse, and they employ a highly educated workforce that enjoys instant access to a variety of information. Leaders have to deal not only with a new workforce, but a more complicated business environment. The Enron and Arthur Andersen debacles exemplify the complexity of the business environment and the problems leaders face in seeking financial success. Leadership is a balance, tempering the leader's vision for the future with the expectations of corporate constituents. To do so, leaders need to understand themselves and how other people react to them.

Effective leadership requires more than intelligence and experience; it also requires emotional intelligence. Emotional intelligence consists of self-awareness, self-regulation, motivation, empathy, and social skill.[25] Exhibit 11.8 defines the components of emotional intelligence and provides some example behaviors.

SELF-LEADERSHIP

Two societal trends will greatly affect future leadership approaches. First, a highly educated workforce in a democratic society will seek greater decision-making participation and other forms of power sharing. Second, a highly competitive world economy has led to the necessity for increased cost-cutting measures. For instance, U.S. firms have historically used more middle managers than their foreign competitors. To be more competitive, U.S. firms have permanently reduced their white collar workforce. Both trends make a shift toward greater worker control more likely in the future.

Shifting societal trends call for new leadership strategies. For effective leadership in the future, two things must occur. First, leaders must engage in behaviors that actively encourage workers to gain control over their work destiny. Empowering workers means sharing power, which takes a confident, secure leader as well as willing, able workers. Second, workers need to develop the requisite self-control strategies such as self-management and self-leadership. New leadership approaches to managing increasingly competitive markets will, of necessity, increase worker participation in the decision-making process. As noted earlier, this means more democratic rather than authoritarian leaders.

A pioneer in leadership, Lincoln Electric in Cleveland, Ohio, has earned a reputation for product quality. Lincoln's leadership system assumes workers are self-motivated and capable of self-management. Workers can rearrange tasks, and any improvement in quality of output earns the worker more money, so both the employee and the company benefit. Teamwork and reliability are rewarded; some employees are doubling their base pay with incentive compensation. Each manager is responsible for about 100 employees, who are graded on their ability to work without a supervisor.[26]

Self-leadership is a management philosophy that encompasses a systematic set of behavioral and cognitive strategies leading to improved performance and effectiveness.[27] This philosophy encourages individual employees to develop their own work priorities that are consistent with organizational goals. What happens to the manager in the self-leadership process? Interestingly, rather than abdicating control, the manager must actively encourage the development of self-leadership capabilities in subordinates.

Developing self-leadership may not be as easy as it sounds. Many people believe that workers would jump at the chance for more control, but some actually resent it. Why would this be? Mainly, it's from fear of the unknown. For decades, workers have been encouraged to complete their work according to procedures and standards designed by their managers or specialists. With the self-leadership approach, workers are asked to assume new responsibilities. Often, workers believe they are untrained or unable to accomplish this new role successfully. One way to increase worker self-control is to use empowerment to overcome worker resistance or fear. **Empowerment** is the process of providing workers with skills, tools, information, and—above all—authority and responsibility for their work. Worker empowerment gives workers direct control over many aspects of their work. Self-leadership transfers control of directing individual work behavior from the manager to the worker. Leadership becomes an internal process. Real empowerment involves the worker's commitment to **self-management,** which is the use of work strategies that help to control daily activities in order to achieve organizational goals.

The manager's role in the self-leadership organization is to encourage workers to develop self-control skills. By self-control, we mean the workers' ability to control their own work destiny in both the short and long term. Self-leadership deemphasizes external forms of control. The primary vehicle leaders use to encourage self-leadership is **role modeling,** a process by which leaders exhibit behaviors that they expect other employees to follow. For example, leaders need to set goals for themselves in ways that their employees can observe. Although the idea of role modeling seems simple, in reality it seldom happens. For role modeling to be successful, it must be apparent to the worker that the manager is demonstrating a work behavior she would like the employee to emulate. Further, the worker needs to see some connection between adopting the behavior and achieving positive outcomes. Research also suggests that workers are most likely to emulate the behavior of successful managers.[28]

Behavioral Self-Management

Behavioral self-management refers to a set of strategies that help people gain greater control over their lives; common strategies include self-set goals, self-observation, self-rewards, self-cueing, and self-designed jobs.

- With **self-set goals**, the initiative for setting the goal and the level of the goal itself comes from the worker, not the manager. Self-set goals are consistent with the firm's overall goals and are based on the worker's commitment to the firm's goals. Self-set goals free the manager from traditional supervisory duty and empower workers with a greater sense of personal control. This autonomous approach to goal setting is recommended as a matter of ethics, not just effectiveness.[29]

- **Self-observation** is a process in which a worker monitors his own behavior and notes actions, events, or outcomes. The self-leadership philosophy assumes that workers can monitor their own behavior. Self-observation includes keeping performance records. For example, a package delivery worker might keep a notebook recording the time of each delivery. Self-observation increases worker empowerment and autonomy.

- **Self-rewards** (also called *self-administered rewards*) recognize our own accomplishments. A worker monitors, evaluates, and applies a reward or disincentive at the completion of a task. Self-rewards enable the individual to personally recognize that a performance milestone has been surpassed. An example of self-reward is giving yourself break time only after completing a major portion of the assigned task. Another type of self-reward is recognizing the naturally rewarding aspect of the work itself—for example, reminding yourself that it feels good to do your best or that it is intrinsically rewarding to clear your desk of pending cases each day. Although these ideas have a simplistic edge, they get back to basics and are powerful motivators. The worker decides the measure and worth of an activity rather than adhering to a universal definition. Self-administered rewards add meaning and purpose to work. In essence, the worker knows what she is supposed to do; she does it, and then pats herself on the back or rewards herself with a break.

- When a mechanic lays out the necessary tools before commencing work, he is practicing **self-cueing**—the process of planning or making arrangements for an activity prior to its performance. This practice helps to prevent defects from occurring during the execution stage. One type of self-cueing, *behavioral rehearsal,* involves practicing an activity under simulated or controlled conditions. For example, the night before a meeting with a customer, a sales team might conduct a role play in which some members of the sales team play the role of the customers and ask appropriate questions, giving the sales team a chance to rehearse their answers.

- **Self-designed jobs** allow workers to propose and design work-process changes, rather than simply imposing external constraints on them. This can result in a personal sense of competence, self-control, and purpose. At the Federal Express facility in Memphis, Tennessee, in response to the problem of late-arriving and mislabeled packages, management implemented a system called *minisort.* But the minisort process was inefficient and unpopular among workers. One worker observed, "If you got on someone's nerves, they sent you to minisort." So a team of 12 workers was appointed to solve the problem. The team cut minisort staff from 150 to 80 workers (saving $30,000), clarified minisort tasks, and implemented prevention measures that cut the number of packages sent to minisort in the first place from 10,000 down to 4,000 per night. In four months the number of late packages dropped from 4,300 to 432. The team's work actually caused a decrease in its members' own wages, yet as one worker said, "For management to listen to me, that's important."[30]

Cognitive Self-Management

Not all self-management strategies are observable and measurable. Using **cognitive self-management** principles, the individual worker creates mental images and thought patterns that are consistent with the firm's goals. Two basic cognitive self-management strategies are opportunity building and positive self-talk.

The process of seeking out and/or developing new possibilities for success is referred to as **opportunity building.** An oft-told marketing story involves two shoe salespeople who are sent to sell shoes in a foreign country. The negative thinker reports to the firm's headquarters, "Opportunities nonexistent. Nobody here wears shoes." The positive thinker says, "Opportunities unlimited. Nobody here wears shoes." Thus, depending on how we perceive and define a problem, an obstacle may be converted to an opportunity.

Positive self-talk is the process of creating mental imagery that reinforces a worker's sense of self-esteem and enhances effectiveness. For example, a customer service agent, upon dealing with an angry customer, reminds herself that she has been successful in calming and satisfying angry customers in the past by listening for important words or phrases used by the customer. By maintaining her self-confidence, the agent is using positive self-talk to help her manage a difficult situation.

Developing a Self-Leadership Culture

The process of developing an effective self-leadership culture begins with a commitment from the top levels of management. Three keys to establishing a self-leadership culture are sharing information, training, and reinforcement.

- *Sharing information.* Self-managed workers need a great deal of information. Many traditional management secrets must become part of their information base. Workers need information concerning costs and profits if they are to set goals and commit to certain actions. When they're informed, workers become more willing to accept responsibility for their actions. In addition, open communication sends a message to employees that they are respected and trusted.[31]

- *Training.* Training in the use of self-management strategies might focus on improving communication skills, team building, or developing the various self-management strategies discussed in this chapter. Training helps to reinforce managerial policy statements at all levels of an organization. Managers may feel threatened by the idea of a self-managed workforce, so in addition to training, they also need assurance that they will continue to have an important role in organizational success.

- *Reinforcement.* In addition to sharing information and conducting training programs, the administration of performance rewards can help to reinforce the use of self-management behaviors. For instance, a "team player" or "star performer" award might be issued to an employee who demonstrates outstanding self-leadership ability.

LEADERSHIP CHALLENGES

Critical global issues confront the economy and firms as we face the twenty-first century.[32] The most effective managers will be those who understand leadership as a broad, empowering tool, and who have a special capability to develop self-managed leadership in others.

Effective leadership in the future will most likely mean leading others to lead themselves. Workers will have to develop self-management skills; those who do so are better able to control the pace and flow of their work. To facilitate this process, effective leadership in the future must also encourage employees to develop self-leadership skills. Here is a summary of some challenges future leaders will face:

- Increasing global competition
- Emphasis on speed, service, and information
- Lean and flexible work demands for more value-added labor and reduced indirect labor costs
- Need to employ untrained, unskilled, and disenfranchised employees
- Fewer low-skilled jobs available as more low-skilled workers enter the market
- Increasing gaps, particularly (1) between elite, skilled employees with lifetime employment and a working underclass with limited skills and few employment options; and (2) between knowledge-intensive, highly educated employees and labor-intensive, unskilled employees
- Employee demands for greater participation; shift to teams, skill-based pay, and cooperation with the firm
- Further expansion of information technologies; flatter, decentralized organizations with greater employee need for self-management

Empowering workers through self-leadership is a good start, but it may not be enough when an organization's competitive position has eroded. Visionary transformational leadership may be required to resuscitate a poorly performing organization. Take the reign of IBM CEO Louis Gertsner Jr., who faced tremendous challenges from the beginning. The once mighty IBM had lost market share and was unable to change the organization to match the needs of the future. For IBM to regain competitive ground in the computer industry, Gertsner had to communicate a new vision of IBM to employees, customers, and competitors. Gertsner transformed the firm's image, changing not only how IBM thought about itself but also how consumers viewed IBM. In the 1950s, the transformational leadership of Thomas Watson Jr. was the cornerstone of IBM's success for the next three decades. Gertsner called on the creativity of the IBM spirit and reconstituted the Big Blue of yesteryear. Through his leadership, he rebuilt the ailing giant and crafted a new vision for IBM in the future.

Conclusion
Leadership

Effective leadership requires an employee-oriented viewpoint—putting people first. By placing the interests of employees above their own, leaders gain loyalty, respect, and motivated workers. Effective leaders listen to subordinates, acquiring the necessary information to make sound decisions. As we noted early in the chapter, leaders and managers are different. Effective leaders encourage employees to develop supportive work relationships with others; communicate their personal values and organizational commitment; and articulate a vision of what the organization can be in the future. Moreover, effective leaders move the organization in new directions, by rejecting the status quo, communicating and explaining decisions, favoring risk and change, and generating a feeling of value and importance in work.[33] In the workplace of the future, effective leaders will be employee centered, customer focused, and respected for their ability to develop employees to their full potential.

The mix of skills needed to be an effective leader is changing. Effective leaders need *technical skills*—including specialized knowledge, analytical ability, and the ability to use tools and techniques of the discipline. They also need *conceptual skills*—the ability to see the enterprise as a whole and recognize how the various parts of the organization interact. Finally, leaders need *human skills*—the ability to work effectively as a group member to build cooperative effort.[34] But additionally, management scholars suggest that future leaders need three new skills. They will need the personal skill to *manage ambiguous situations*, the organizational skills to *manage and understand complex systems*, and the leadership skill to *direct the work of groups* as well as individuals.[35] Leaders will continue to make use of these skills, with greater emphasis on human skills such as communication and team building. Effective leaders will be those who can successfully navigate their way through the conflicting organizational goals and changes demanded in the marketplace.

SUGGESTED READINGS

McGill, Michael, and John Slocum. "A Little Leadership Please." *Organizational Dynamics* 26 (Winter 1998) 26: 39–49.

Teerlink, Rich. "Harley's Leadership U-Turn." *Harvard Business Review*, July–August 2000, pp. 3–7.

Goleman, David, Richard Boyatzis, and Annie McKee. "Primal Leadership: The Hidden Driver of Great Performance." *Harvard Business Review*, December 2001, pp. 42–51.

ENDNOTES

1. R. Tannenbaum, I. R. Weschler, and F. Massarik, *Leadership and Organization* (New York: McGraw-Hill, 1961), 24.

2. R. Tannenbaum and Warren H. Schmidt, "How to Choose a Leadership Pattern," *Harvard Business Review*, May–June 1973 (Classic reprint originally published in HBR in 1958).

3. Abraham Zaleznick, "Leaders and Managers: Are They Different?" *Harvard Business Review*, 1977, pp. 31–42; "Real Work," *Harvard Business Review*, 1989, pp. 52–64; and *The Managerial Mystique* (New York: Harper & Row, 1989), 1–42.

4. Tom Peters, *Thriving on Chaos* (New York: Knopf, 1987), 561.

5. Robert E. Kelley, "In Praise of Followers," *Harvard Business Review*, November–December 1988, pp. 3–8.

6. Robert Dahl, "The Concept of Power," *Behavioral Science* 2 (1957): 201–215.

7. John R. P. French Jr. and Bertram Raven, "The Bases of Social Power," in *Studies in Social Power*, ed. Dorwin Cartright (Ann Arbor: University of Michigan Press, 1959), 150–167.

8. Patricia Haddock, "Communicating Personal Power," *Supervision*, July 1995, p. 20.

9. Edwin E. Ghiselli, "Managerial Talent," *American Psychologist* 71 (October 1963): 631–641.

10. Ralph M. Stogdill, "Personal Factors Associated with Leadership," *Journal of Applied Psychology* (January 1948): 35–71.

11. Rensis Likert, *New Patterns of Management* (New York: McGraw-Hill, 1961).

12. Edwin A. Fleishman and James G. Hunt, eds., *Current Developments in the Study of Leadership* (Carbondale, IL: Southern Illinois Press, 1973), 1–37.

13. Bill Saporito, "A Week aboard the Wal-Mart Express," *Fortune,* August 24, 1992, p. 79.

14. R. R. Blake and Jane S. Mouton, *The Managerial Grid* (Houston: Gulf Publishing, 1964); R. R. Blake and A. A. McCanse, "The Leadership Grid®," in *Leadership Dilemmas—Grid Solutions* (Houston: Gulf Publishing Company), 29, Copyright © 1991 by Scientific Methods, Inc.

15. Fred E. Fiedler and Martin M. Chemers, *Leadership and Effective Management* (Glenview, IL: Scott Foresman, 1974).

16. Victor Vroom, "Leadership," in *Handbook of Organizational Psychology,* ed. Marvin Dunnette (Chicago: Rand McNally College Publishing, 1976), 1316.

17. F. E. Fiedler and J. E. Garcia, *New Approaches to Leadership, Cognitive Resources and Organizational Performance* (New York: Wiley, 1987).

18. R. K. Hambleton and R. Gumpert, "The Validity of Hersey-Blanchard's Theory of Leader Effectiveness," *Group and Organization Studies* 7, no. 2 (1982): 225–242. Also see C. L. Graeff, "The Situational Leadership Theory: A Critical Review." *Academy of Management Review* 8 (1983): 285–296.

19. George Graen, "Role-Making Processes in Organizations," in *Handbook of Organizational Psychology,* ed. Marvin Dunnette (Chicago: Rand McNally College Publishing, 1976).

20. Chester Schriesheim, C. A. Castro, and C. C. Coliser, "Leader-Member Exchange Research: A Comprehensive Review of Theory, Measurement, and Analytic Procedures," *Leadership Quarterly* 10 (1999): 63–113; also see George Graen and Mary Uhl-Bien, "Relationship-Based Approach to Leadership: Development of Leader-Member Exchange (LMX) Theory over the Past 25 Years: Applying a Multilevel Multi-Domain Approach," *Leadership Quarterly* 6 (1995): 219–247.

21. Steven Kerr and John M. Jermier, "Substitutes for Leadership: Their Meaning and Measurement," *Organizational Behavior and Human Performance,* December 1978, pp. 375–403.

22. Bernard M. Bass, *Leadership: Performance Beyond Expectations* (New York: Free Press, 1985), 43; and Bernard M. Bass, "Leadership: Good, Better, Best," *Organizational Dynamics* (1985) Winter, vol. 13: 26–40.

23. J. M. Burns, *Leadership* (New York: Harper & Row, 1978), 1–52; Bernard M. Bass, *Leadership: Performance Beyond Expectations* (New York: Free Press, 1985), 43; and Bernard M. Bass, "Leadership: Good, Better, Best," *Organizational Dynamics* (1985) Winter, vol. 13: 26–40.

24. Daniel Goleman, "Leadership That Gets Results," *Harvard Business Review,* March–April 2000, pp. 80–90.

25. Daniel Goleman, "What Makes a Leader?" *Harvard Business Review,* November–December 1998, pp. 93–102.

26. W. Baldwin, "This Is the Answer," *Forbes,* July 5, 1982, p. 52.

27. Charles C. Manz and Henry P. Sims Jr., *Superleadership* (New York: Berkeley, 1990), xviii.

28. Howard Weiss, "Subordinate Imitation of Supervisor Behavior: The Role of Modeling in Organizational Socialization," *Organizational Behavior and Human Performance* 19 (1977): 89–105.

29. M. Sashkin, "Participative Management Is an Ethical Imperative," *Organizational Dynamics* 12 (1984): 5–22.

30. Martha T. Moore, "Sorting Out a Mess," *USA Today,* April 10, 1992, p. 5B.

31. Rich Teerlink, "Harley's Leadership U-Turn," *Harvard Business Review,* July–August 2000, pp. 4–7.

32. See M. Porter, "Why Nations Triumph," *Fortune,* March 12, 1990, pp. 94–98. Also see J. Dreyfuss, "Get Ready for the New Work Force," *Fortune,* April 23, 1990, pp. 165, 168, 172, 176, 180–181.

33. F. A. Manske Jr., *Secrets of Effective Leadership* (Memphis, TN: Leadership Education and Development, Inc., 1987).

34. Robert L. Katz, "Skills of an Effective Administration," *Harvard Business Review,* September–October, 1974, pp. 23–35.

35. Management Update, "Three Skills for Today's Leaders," *Harvard Business Review,* 1999, pp. 3–4.

Chapter
Twelve

Interpersonal and Organizational Communication

The view that communication is critical to organizational excellence dates back at least to 1938, when Chester Barnard wrote his famous book, *The Functions of the Executive*.[1] In it, Barnard described one of the major responsibilities of executives as developing and maintaining a system of communication. It is a fact of workaday life that managers and employees alike must solve increasingly complex problems. And, increasingly, researchers and practitioners are examining the role that effective communication has in propelling individuals to overcome barriers, work through problems, and achieve goals. Do you believe that employee retention and productivity can be improved simply by communicating more forthrightly and more frequently to workers about how their pay and salary increases are determined?[2] In fact, research does support the proposition that constructive conversations of this type drive up performance.

As you'll see in this chapter, communication is an important part of the leadership function; and leading, as we have stressed earlier, is a core function of management. Managers cannot be effective as leaders if they cannot communicate well. Successful leaders have vision; they set direction and mobilize resources.[3] Whereas leaders don't necessarily create budgets, they have a clear picture of what they want the organization to be and communicate that vision just as clearly to other members of the organization. This chapter's topic is interpersonal and organizational communication. First, we discuss the nature and scope of communication. Then, we examine various types of interpersonal and organizational communication. Finally, we look at barriers to organizational communication and strategies for facilitating communication.

COMMUNICATION

The term *communication* is a common one. Most of us have used it in one way or another to describe our interactions with others. Historical figures are often compared by their ability to communicate. TV, radio, and newspapers are referred to as communication media (the plural of *medium*); the telephone and computer are called communication devices. Unfortunately, communication is often taken for granted, though in fact it is a complex activity. Failure to understand this complexity often leads to problems with communication.

Communication is defined as the exchange of information between a sender (source) and a receiver (audience). If meaning is not shared, communication has not taken place. A production worker stopped her machine to fix it because it was making defective products. The foreman came by and ordered: "Run it," so she turned the machine back on. When asked to explain her behavior, the worker replied, "He ordered me to make defectives."[4] The foreman surely didn't mean to order the worker to make defective products, but that's the message that was communicated.

The Communication Process

Communication can be described as a process in which a message is encoded and transmitted through some medium to a receiver who decodes the message and then transmits some sort of response back to the sender. It is through the communication process that the sharing of a common meaning takes place. As Exhibit 12.1 shows, communication begins

EXHIBIT 12.1
The Communication Process

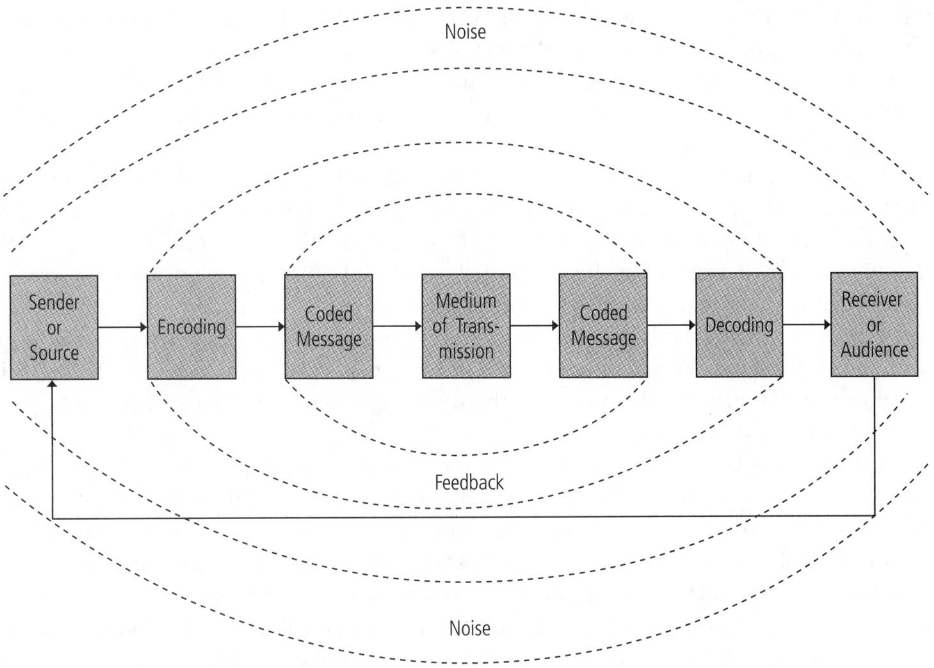

with a **sender**—a person, group, or organization that has a message to share with another person or group of persons.

In organizations, executives, managers, workers, departments, and even the organization itself can be the source of a message. Executives must communicate not only with the board of directors and top-level managers, but with groups and individuals outside the organization such as stockholders, regulators, and customers. Managers must communicate with managers in other departments, superiors, subordinates, customers, and suppliers. Workers must communicate with superiors, customers, and each other. Clearly, we could go on and on. The point is that every organization member is a source with a message to communicate to internal and external parties.

A **message** is an idea or experience that a sender wants to communicate. Messages can be communicated both verbally and nonverbally. For instance, a manager may want to communicate a process to a worker. This can be done in many ways: by explaining the process, illustrating it, or providing a written explanation. The critical issue is that the message is presented in such a way that the manager conveys the intended meaning.

To convey meaning, the sender must **encode** the message by converting it into groups of symbols that represent ideas or concepts. Encoding translates ideas or concepts into the coded message that will be communicated. We use symbols (languages, words, or gestures) to encode ideas into messages that others can understand. When encoding a message, the sender must use symbols that are familiar to the intended receiver. A person with a message to communicate should know the audience and present the message in language that the audience can grasp. A computer company developing a sales presentation targeted at a nontechnical audience should ensure that its presentation is written and delivered using words and graphics familiar to that audience. In referring to concepts, the sender should use the same symbols that the receiver uses to refer to those concepts, and should avoid using symbols that can have more than one meaning.

To relay the message, the sender must select and use a **medium of transmission** (a means of carrying an encoded message from the source to the receiver). Ink on paper, vibrations of air produced by vocal cords, and electronically produced airwaves such as radio and TV signals are examples of transmission media. If a sender relays a message through an inappropriate medium of transmission, the message may not reach the right receivers. Organizations use memos, meetings, reward systems, policy statements, production schedules, and many other mediums to communicate with members. Some may not always be appropriate.

Decoding is the process by which the receiver interprets the symbols (coded message) sent by the source by converting them into concepts and ideas. Seldom does the receiver decode exactly the same meaning that a sender encoded. When the receiver interprets the message differently from what the sender intended, the cause may be **noise** (interference that affects any or all stages of the communication process). Noise has many sources, such as competing messages, misinterpretation, radio static, faulty printing, or use of ambiguous or unfamiliar symbols. Yelling at a subordinate may result in noise, even though the manager uses familiar words to convey the message. Noise may be present at any point in the communication process.

Feedback is the receiver's response to the sender's message. During feedback, the receiver becomes the source of a message that is directed back to the original sender, who then becomes a receiver. Thus communication can be viewed as a circular process, as Exhibit 12.1 shows. But feedback may not take place immediately. For instance, a consumer products manufacturer may advertise the benefits of a product (the message), but the consumer may not actually purchase the product (feedback) until some time after receiving the source's message. In organizations, effective feedback must be two-way, engaging, responsive, and directed toward a desired outcome.[5] Goals can best be achieved when people in organizations communicate with each other and work cooperatively. It is often nonmanagers who are closest to production problems, suppliers, and customers. If they do not have the capacity to provide feedback, managers will miss out on valuable information.

The communication process has a **channel capacity**, a limit on the volume of information that it can handle effectively. Channel capacity is determined by the least efficient component of the communication process. With verbal communications, there is a limit to how fast a source can speak and how much a receiver can decode. If a manager transmits more than one message, the communication process may not be totally effective. The audience (receivers) may not be able to decode all the messages at the same time, especially if they are inconsistent. For instance, suppose a manager at a branch bank says to all the new tellers that customers are important; but he also tells them to close their windows early, so they can balance their windows and get out of the bank on time. The result is longer lines at closing times, and the new tellers don't get the message that customers are important.

Selecting a Communication Medium

Media selection is a critical aspect of effective communication. A **communication medium** is a conduit or channel through which data and meaning are conveyed.[6] Communication media include oral, written, and nonverbal communication. The Management Highlight below provides examples of communication media. Managers must determine which media to use in sending and in receiving information. Suppose, for instance, a sales manager wants to communicate a new compensation plan to the selling force. How should the new plan be communicated? What media should be used? Would letters, memos, oral presentations, telephone calls, or some other medium work best? The answers to these questions will likely affect the success of the new compensation program.

One factor that has been stressed in choosing media is the **media richness** (media's capacity to convey data).[7] One medium may be richer than another; that is, one medium may have a greater capacity to carry data than another. **Data-carrying capacity** refers to the degree to which a medium can effectively and efficiently convey data. Thus the best medium can be determined by its richness or effectiveness. Research has shown that managers rely most on media richness when making media selection choices.[8]

Several criteria are used to evaluate a medium's richness: the medium's capacity for timely feedback; its capacity for multiple uses, such as audio and visual; the extent to which the message can be personalized; and the variety of language, such as natural and body language, that can be used.[9] Face-to-face is the richest medium because feedback is the

---

MANAGEMENT HIGHLIGHT
Alternative Communication Media

Oral	Written	Nonverbal
Face-to-face	Letters	Touch
Telephone	Computer printouts	Eye contact
Speeches	Electronic mail	Body language
Video conferencing	Memos	Time
Intercom	Bulletin boards	Space

fastest, both audio and visual cues can be used, the message is personal, and a variety of languages can be used. Conversely, formal numeric media such as computer printouts are the least rich because feedback is very slow and data-carrying capacity is limited to visual information.

Suppose a firm's sales manager decides that the most effective way to inform the selling force about the new compensation plan is through face-to-face communication. The meaning of the spoken word; the rate, pitch, and force of the verbal message; and facial expressions can all combine to give a single, powerful message. Each salesperson will have the opportunity to see the manager, hear the message, interpret it, and give and receive feedback. This seems to be the best way to ensure the new plan's success. Unfortunately, the firm has thousands of salespeople in several countries throughout the world. Face-to-face communication is simply not possible.

In addition to richness, several other factors must be considered in selecting a communication medium. First, cost must be weighed against the medium's speed of transmission and its overall effectiveness. A telephone call, for instance, may be the fastest and most effective medium when speed is critical in communication, even though a letter would be much less expensive. Some messages have a greater impact when delivered in person. Communicating a promotion personally, or both in person and by letter, may convey the maximum impact. Second, the purpose of the communication influences the media choice. To communicate technical or quantitative information, a written report may be most effective. Third, the extent to which interaction is necessary should be considered when selecting a medium. A performance review could be in writing, but a face-to-face meeting would allow for questions, feedback, and understanding. Finally, the receiver's capabilities also influence which medium is selected. A receiver who tends to forget oral communication may need written reminders, providing documentation for the future.

In summary, media choice depends on the situation's requirements. Some situations may call for oral communication, some for written, and others for a combination. Always select a communication medium that most effectively conveys the intended message to the target audience.

The Role of Communication in Organizations

Throughout this book we have discussed several functions of management, including planning, organizing, and leading. Controlling will be discussed in the next part of the book. Management is largely a profession that functions through the vehicle of communicating with people—most good managers are good communicators. Indeed, managers need technical, analytical, and conceptual skills to perform their functions and develop a culture that is conducive to quality. But communication is an essential part of all other management functions and processes. Put another way, "The job of the manager is, ultimately, communication, regardless of how varied or specialized the activity of the moment might be."[10]

Many managers stress open communication as a means of improving organizational effectiveness and quality. The goal of constantly improving quality can be achieved only if it supersedes differences, jealousies, competition between individuals and departments, and turf battles. Silence has been attributed to failed products, broken processes, and poor career decisions; indeed, breaking the silence can lead to a flow of ideas from all levels of the organization.[11] But open communication requires more than simply maintaining open offices. It also involves managers' accessibility to workers, day-to-day interaction with employees, and breaking down barriers and resistance to change. If an organization decides to implement teams, communication is essential. Resistance to the change should be expected. Here communication helps people deal with change, work through it, and adapt to the new way of doing things, whether it be teams or some other change. In short, communication pervades every aspect of the organization—every individual, team, or department, and each external relationship with customers, suppliers, and competitors. The organization cannot achieve its goals without open, two-way communication.

INTERPERSONAL COMMUNICATION

Individuals spend a great deal of time in organizations interacting with each other. **Interpersonal communication** is communication between two people, usually face-to-face.[12] Other communication media such as the telephone or e-mail also can be used to communicate interpersonally; e-mail is preferred to telephone by 80 percent of business professionals responding to a survey.[13] Through interpersonal communication we develop and maintain human relationships—the basic social units of any organization. Thus interpersonal communication is the fundamental building block of organizational communication.

Oral Communication

Oral communication takes place when the spoken word is used to transmit a message. Conversations can take place in person, via telephone, or through some other mechanism that allows individuals to speak to one another. Oral communication enables prompt, two-way interaction between parties. Many meetings and conferences that involve people from different locations, even different parts of the world, are conducted using TV hookups so participants can interact personally. Perhaps the major benefit of this type of communication is that ideas can be interchanged and prompt feedback can be provided. Questions can be addressed, positions and issues debated, and a plan for action or resolution established. Oral communication that takes place in person also allows the use of gestures, facial expressions, and other emotions such as tone of voice.

Oral communication, because of its immediacy, can result in poor communication. If, for instance, a person becomes angry, noise enters the communication process. Messages that are not clearly encoded may also fail to communicate the intended idea. A hurried manager may give an oral instruction or initiative without thinking about the outcome. (Recall what happened when the foreman instructed the factory worker to turn the machine on.) While feedback is immediate, it may also be without thought, reducing the quality of the communication. Individuals often feel the need to respond immediately in a face-to-face meeting, when in fact they should take some time to prepare a well-thought-out response.

Written Communication

Transmitting a message through the written word is called **written communication**. This type of communication can help eliminate the problem we just discussed. Written messages allow a manager to think about the message, reread it several times, and perhaps get others to review the message before it's transmitted. The receiver can take time to read the message carefully and accurately. Written messages are also more permanent than oral, providing a record of the communication. Whether it's a long report or a short memo, written communication can be referred to in the future as needed. Managers often find it necessary to document their decisions for legal reasons.

Despite the advantages of written communication, managers generally prefer to communicate orally. Written communication takes more time to prepare and does not allow interaction or immediate feedback. Managers rely on two-way communication to resolve problems quickly. It takes much longer to get ideas on paper, to distribute them to others, and to receive written responses; a telephone call or meeting is quicker. Written communication, by its formal nature, may also discourage open communication. E-mail, a form of written communication, is timelier and allows quick response, perhaps explaining its popularity.

Nonverbal Communication

All intentional or unintentional messages that are neither written nor spoken are referred to as **nonverbal communication**. Examples include vocal cues, body movements, facial expressions, personal appearance, and distance or space. A certain look or glance, seating arrangements at a meeting, or a sudden change in voice tone can communicate a strong message. Nonverbal messages can be powerful, depending on the situation. For instance, a salesperson's ability to actively listen and detect the other party's nonverbal communication cues often determines whether the relationship is successful.[14]

The difficulty with nonverbal communication is that in order to accurately decode a message, the receiver must know the specific background or frame of reference of its source. Suppose that on her first day of work, a new employee witnesses her boss screaming at a coworker. She's shocked, and asks the coworker if this happens often. He explains that the boss is a great guy and a great manager, will do anything for you, but happens to yell all the time. Now she has a different perspective. On the other hand, imagine the effect when a manager who is known to be cool and calm—and rarely changes expressions—suddenly glares at someone in a meeting.

Managers must recognize that nonverbal communication can occur unintentionally. After being on the job for about three months, a computer programmer comes to the conclusion that his supervisor doesn't like him. He is so concerned that he decides to look for another job; but he decides to talk to his supervisor before quitting. He tells the supervisor, "Obviously I did something to upset you." The manager looks at him without emotion, tells the programmer he's doing a great job and can expect a nice raise at his six-month review, and offers no other explanation. The point? Managers have to understand the potential of nonverbal communication and realize that they may be unintentionally sending the wrong message.

Nonverbal communication is important to multinational corporations (MNCs) operating in a foreign country. People in different countries and cultures have different sets of nonverbal symbols and meanings. Nonverbal cues such as touch, body language, and personal distance are used differently across cultures. Managers encounter difficulty in interpreting nonverbal communication while working in foreign countries. Likewise, they are uncertain what nonverbal messages they may be transmitting. A business deal in Japan can fall through if a foreign executive refuses a cup of green tea while visiting a Japanese firm.[15] Representatives working in a foreign country should receive adequate training in that country's nonverbal customs.

Empathic Listening

For some time now, you have been reading this book that we have written. Reading and writing are both forms of interpersonal communication, but they are not the only ones. Speaking and listening are other forms. We all have a lot of experience speaking, but perhaps listening is the one form of communication that we have the least experience with.

In his best-selling book *The 7 Habits of Highly Effective People,* Stephen Covey suggests that the key to effective listening is to seek first to understand, and then to be understood.[16] Covey describes **empathic listening** as listening with the intent to understand. This is not easy—it requires looking at an issue from another person's point of view. It requires listening not only with your ears, but with your eyes and your heart as well. Successful management starts with empathic listening.[17]

Distractions such as interruptions, telephone calls, and unfinished work are a major barrier to effective listening. Creating an environment free of such distractions will improve listening. Many listeners also take detours during a communication. For instance, if someone mentions a word that brings out certain emotions, we become distracted and tune out the message. Many receivers also begin to mentally debate a point, thinking ahead and planning a response. When you do this, you're likely to miss the message.

It is not easy to listen, but we can all start by taking time to listen. Relax, try to close out other distractions, and give both your mental and physical attention to the other person. Help the other person relax by assuming a nonthreatening listening posture, maintaining eye contact and a warm facial expression. This demonstrates that you, the listener, are interested in what is being said.

Communication can also be improved by giving and requesting constructive feedback. If people say what they think others want to hear, feedback is of limited value. Honest feedback can be used to determine if the listener understood the intended message. Effective listeners focus on the message's meaning, postpone judgments until the communication is complete, actively respond to the speaker, and avoid focusing on emotionally charged words.

Effective, empathic listening takes time and practice. Listening with empathy puts you on the same level with another person. It's difficult to listen when you don't understand the other person. Effective listening is not a passive exercise; it is an active skill that requires full participation. Good listeners take notes, ask questions, and are totally attentive to what is being said. Although listening may not come naturally to all of us, with practice we can become better listeners and reap the benefits of effective communication.

ORGANIZATIONAL COMMUNICATION

We noted earlier that individuals and groups must communicate effectively for organizations to be successful. In this section we examine formal and informal channels of organizational communication and their impact on the communication process. It is the manager's job to ensure that effective, efficient channels are available to facilitate communication. Exhibit 12.2 illustrates the forms of organizational communication, both formal and informal. Managers must understand these forms; they must also be aware of the barriers to organizational communication and know how to remove them.

Formal Channels of Communication

Formal channels of communication are the official paths prescribed by management. These formal channels generally follow the organization's chain of command. Information can be communicated downward, upward, or horizontally; and it can be oral, written, or nonverbal.

Downward Communication.   Information flows down the organizational hierarchy from managers and supervisors to subordinates through **downward communication.** As Exhibit 12.2 shows, this communication follows the formal lines of authority prescribed

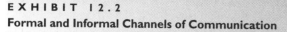

EXHIBIT 12.2
Formal and Informal Channels of Communication

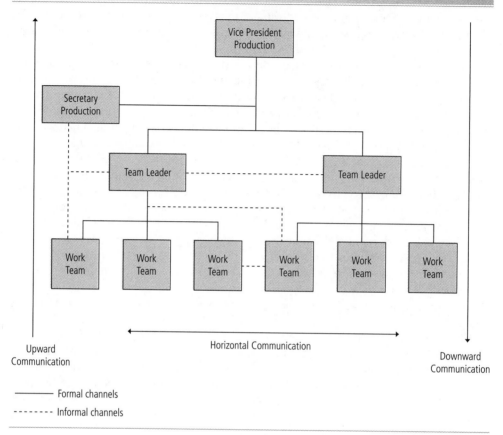

by the chain of command. Downward communication generally involves job instructions, manuals, policy statements, memos, motivational appeals, and other forms of formal instruction or feedback. Downward communication has been associated with job performance and job satisfaction.[18] Downward communication is not always adequate, because workers need more information than just job instructions. They also need to know, for instance, what other members of the organization are doing. Nevertheless downward communication is important because lack of communication from superiors can leave workers misinformed, feeling disconnected, and less satisfied with their jobs.

One problem managers face is deciding which, and how much, information to communicate to subordinates. Too much information, especially if it is irrelevant, is eventually ignored. Every Friday some salespeople find dozens of reports and summaries in their mailboxes—many of them useless—and begin to ignore the material. Unfortunately, some of it may be valuable. Managers who wish to empower workers must provide quality information that can enable workers to improve. This may also require communicating information that was once considered only for managers, such as financial and performance data.

Upward Communication.   Information that flows up the organization from subordinates to supervisors and managers is called **upward communication.** This type of communication is necessary for managers to evaluate the effectiveness of downward communication. It also enables workers to feel they are a meaningful part of the organization. Many types of messages are communicated upward, including suggestions for improvements, feelings about the job or the organization, problems or grievances, requests, and responses to downward communication. Many workers face a dilemma concerning what they should communicate to superiors. In any event, upward communication should be encouraged, because it helps to drive fear out of the organization. A factory worker must not be afraid to tell the supervisor that the machine is making defective products.

Obviously, information is not effective unless it is accurate. Upward communication is often distorted in one way or another to make it more acceptable to managers. Workers may be reluctant to report problems if they think managers will blame them. Managers should create an environment in which workers feel comfortable reporting good news and bad. Empowered workers are more likely to report accurate information than less powerful or fearful employees. Managers can demonstrate that upward communication is valued by replying or acting promptly and positively.

Horizontal Communication.   Messages flow between persons at the same level of the organization through **horizontal communication.** This includes staff meetings, face-to-face interactions, and sharing of information through memos and reports. Horizontal communication is needed to coordinate the activities of diverse but independent units or departments. For instance, the manager of marketing and sales needs to communicate with the manager of production to avoid under- or overstocking a product.

Traditionally, horizontal communication took place more among managers than nonmanagers. But as organizations have begun to utilize work teams and quality circles, workers from different units or departments are often called together to work on a project or problem. Many organizations are placing increasing emphasis on horizontal communication. In their book *Re-inventing the Corporation,* John Naisbitt and Patricia Aburdene observe, "The top-down authoritarian management style is yielding to a networking style of management, where people learn from one another horizontally, where everyone is a resource for everyone else, and where each person gets support and assistance from many different directions."[19] Horizontal communication between subsidiaries of the same multinational corporation can be a problem, especially when subsidiaries are located in countries where different languages are spoken. Research suggests that corporate training should focus on the broad spectrum of international communication rather than on increasing the knowledge of any one language.[20]

Informal Channels of Communication

Informal channels of communication are outside of the official chain of command established by management (see Exhibit 12.2). One informal channel of communication is the grapevine. The **grapevine** cuts across formal channels of communication and carries a variety of facts, opinions, rumors, and other information. All organizations, large or small, have grapevines; it is futile for managers to try to eliminate this informal channel. Conversely, communications must be managed effectively, so that the grapevine is not the main source of information. When properly nurtured, the grapevine can help managers get a feel for the morale of organizations, understand the anxieties of the workforce, and evaluate the effectiveness of formal communication efforts.[21]

While grapevines don't always have negative consequences, they are frequently troublesome to managers. A middle manager once learned she was being considered for an impending transfer when she received a telephone call from a real estate agent in another part of the country. She eventually discovered that the real estate agent's contact at corporate headquarters had learned about the transfer and passed it on to the realtor. Unfortunately, the woman's supervisor had not yet told her about the transfer. The grapevine can also be the source of harmful rumors and gossip; it is especially dangerous when managers manipulate it to communicate with employees instead of using normal, open communication channels. Managers can control the grapevine to some extent by communicating accurate, timely information, by maintaining and cultivating open channels of communication in all directions, and by moving quickly to dispel rumors and correct inaccurate information.

Despite its limitations, the grapevine offers an abundance of operating data, generates corporate memory, and can communicate important insights with speed and economy. As organizations move toward the new paradigm of flat, borderless, and globally dispersed network organizations, informal communication—more than ever before—provides an important source of needed information.

BARRIERS TO ORGANIZATIONAL COMMUNICATION

Communication isn't always effective. Breakdowns occur for many reasons. Some can simply be attributed to poor habits—lack of preparation or vague directions. Barriers such as these can be overcome without too much difficulty if the communicator is willing to work at it. Other barriers can be much more difficult to overcome. In this section we examine common barriers to organizational communication.

Personal Characteristics

One major barrier to organizational communication is the personal makeup of the parties involved. People have attitudes about work-related matters, conditions in the world, their personal life, and communication in general. Some individuals have defensive attitudes and interpret messages as an order or threat. Some people simply have incompatible personalities. Others feel inferior or threatened, become defensive in an attempt to cover up their feelings, and respond aggressively. Constantly being on the offensive is an obstacle to communication.

Another problem involves the parties' credibility. **Source credibility** refers to the receiver's confidence and trust in the source of a message. If the receiver has little or no faith in the source, it will be difficult for the two parties to communicate. For example, a recent study reported that when auditors thought a client's reputation was not squeaky clean, they were less likely to believe the client, and in turn collected more audit evidence than usual.[22] Individuals lose credibility when they pass along inaccurate information or fail to follow through with directives or initiatives. New leaders are often greeted with a sense of excitement and hope by other members of the organization. But if they make promises they don't keep—pay raises, new offices, lower taxes, and so on—they lose their credibility and their ability to communicate effectively.

Several other personal characteristics can inhibit communication. Some individuals tend to be disorganized, which carries over to their communication efforts. Poor listening habits on the part of the receiver are also a communication barrier. Some people, rather than listening, are thinking ahead to how they will respond and thus do not receive the message. Receivers may also have certain predispositions and tune out the communicator because the message is not consistent with their beliefs. Finally, individuals may be biased due to age, gender, looks, or some other factor, and these biases inhibit the communication process. Such biases are especially alarming as the workforce becomes more diverse.

Frame of Reference

As individuals, we all have different backgrounds and have had many different experiences that shape the meanings we assign to words. There is a great deal of difference between your or my saying, "I'm starved," as we head to a restaurant, and a child who hasn't eaten in ten days uttering the same words. We have a different *frame of reference,* so we may have difficulty achieving common understanding. When a parent tells a child, "I never had so many toys when I was a kid," the child may find it difficult to understand because the parent and the child have different frames of reference. Likewise, if a supervisor and a subordinate or two coworkers have different backgrounds and experiences, organizational communication may suffer.

A related problem in communication concerns people blocking out information they aren't comfortable with. **Selective perception** occurs when people screen out information that is not consistent with their beliefs or background. When people receive information that conflicts with what they believe, they tend to ignore it or distort it to make it conform to their beliefs. Managers, for instance, generally analyze problems based on their frame of reference. In other words, a sales manager analyzes a problem from the sales point of view, whereas an environmentalist analyzes problems based on a different set of beliefs.

Conflicting frames of reference and selective perception can hamper organizational communication in various ways. As individuals move up the organizational hierarchy, for instance, they may develop different frames of reference. A salesperson, who is concerned with closing the deal, may attach different meanings to words from those of a sales manager, who must be concerned with cost control and other management issues. Likewise, an individual in the production department may have a different frame of reference from a marketing staffer. This can reduce the effectiveness of upward, downward, or horizontal communication.

One challenge faced by organizations implementing teams is breaking down barriers between individuals and departments. Because traditional organizations are structured to encourage competition among individuals, units, departments, or divisions, these entities develop their own frames of reference. This makes it difficult for people to communicate and work together toward the same goal. In the worst scenario, individuals care only about their own job and their own department's performance. A worker is rewarded for reaching a production quota; quality control and customer satisfaction are somebody else's problem. Under these circumstances, effective communication is difficult, and the organization's overall performance is likely to suffer.

Resistance to Change

All organizations go through change, whether it be a new sales program, new leadership, or new owners. Change is a constant in today's organizations. Yet no matter how innocuous or even beneficial change may be, we all have a human tendency to resist it. Change triggers rational and irrational emotional reactions because it involves uncertainty. People resist change for several reasons: they fear the loss of something they value; they mistrust management; they view the change differently from those initiating it; or they have low tolerance for change.[23] Whatever the reason, resistance to change is a significant barrier to communication. When firms change the way employees do their jobs—by reengineering business processes or implementing new systems—they must be prepared to deal with resistance to change.[24]

The CEO at a major bank felt that change was needed due to the branch managers' lack of interest in doing anything other than making loans and performing administrative duties; the managers had little interest in other management issues confronting the bank. The CEO decided to schedule monthly meetings with all bank officers, including branch managers, to discuss broad issues like the bank's overall goals, personnel policy, productivity, strategies, and compensation programs. At the meetings, the managers expressed few ideas on how they could assume more managerial responsibility. The CEO increased the number of meetings, then asked for individual reports to obtain each manager's input on how to deal with management problems and issues. The results of this approach were even more disappointing. The reports demonstrated a clear lack of communication between the CEO and the branch managers. In this case, the branch managers' resistance to change proved to be a significant barrier to the CEO's objective of prompting managers to take on more responsibility.

FACILITATING ORGANIZATIONAL COMMUNICATION

Although some barriers to communication cannot be completely removed, organizational communication can be facilitated in several ways. By understanding the barriers and striving to be better communicators, individuals can improve the communication process. In some cases this may be relatively simple, perhaps accomplished just by breaking a few bad habits. In other cases, improving communication can be a lengthy, ongoing, demanding process.

Developing Communication Skills

Perhaps the best way to facilitate communication is to develop the skills needed to be a better communicator. Both managers and nonmanagers need to develop communication skills. Managers must improve their ability to understand workers and to be understood. With more individual responsibility, workers must also be able to communicate effectively. Individuals can acquire these skills through managerial training programs in communication.

We have already discussed the importance of *listening* in effective communication. A good communicator listens with *empathy*. By understanding the feelings of others, the communicator can anticipate how a message will be decoded. And by encouraging *feedback,* the communicator can determine whether the message was properly decoded. The use of *simple language* can also facilitate communication. Complex language and the use of confusing or misleading terms introduces noise into the communication process. Good communicators also *question* others, asking for ideas and suggestions, thus encouraging participation. They *initiate* new ideas and calls for action, and *evaluate* ideas of others, offering insightful summaries.

Minimizing Resistance to Change

As we said, many workers resist change, which is a major barrier to communication. By minimizing resistance to change, managers can help facilitate the communication process. Otherwise change will be poorly implemented, resulting in no change at all or a very short-term, superficial change. In some instances, because of the resulting miscommunication and lack of trust, organizations are worse off after the change effort fails.

Managers have several methods to minimize resistance to change.[25] One way is to deal with change before it occurs, through education and communication. Preparing people for change helps cut down on resistance. Also, by having those who are affected by the change participate in it, managers can increase these people's commitment to the change. Being supportive when change is being implemented is critical. Managers can show their support by being understanding, being a good listener, and going to bat for subordinates on important issues. Reducing resistance to change can also be accomplished through negotiation and agreement. Regardless of which method is used, managers responsible for implementing change must overcome resistance to change in order to facilitate effective communication and a successful change effort. An organization is more likely to adapt to change if it has many means of two-way communication that reach all levels and that all employees can understand.

Communicating with a Diverse Workforce

Managers increasingly face the prospect of communicating with a diverse workforce, which makes communicating more difficult. To facilitate communication in such an environment, managers must be aware of diversity and understand its value. Differences in gender, race, culture, and the like can influence how people interpret (decode) messages. A good communicator should not only be aware of an individual's background and experiences, but anticipate the meaning that person will attach to different messages.

The globalization of the world's economy has placed increased emphasis on cross-cultural communication. Whenever two parties have different cultural backgrounds, communication breakdowns may result. People often tend to communicate based on their own background or culture. Thus, when communicating with someone from another culture, they are more likely to send a message that is not intended or to misinterpret a message they are receiving. Effective listening skills are especially important for individuals involved in cross-cultural communication.

Communicating with an increasingly diverse workforce is critical to an organization's viability. This isn't a question of civil rights or affirmative action, which are something different. It concerns the demands a diverse workforce places on the communication skills of managers and coworkers. It requires not only the skills in listening, empathy, feedback, and language already discussed but also skills in understanding other cultures, as well as the ability to overcome hidden biases and stereotypes about other people.

Conducting Communication Audits

The communication audit is a useful tool for managers to use in understanding and improving organizational communication. A **communication audit** is a systematic method of collecting and evaluating information about an organization's communication efforts. The purposes of a communication audit are to:

- Provide information about communication behavior in the organization

- Provide a means for diagnosing discontent or revealing problems in communication

- Provide a clear picture of current communication patterns and determine those aspects that may be most affected by change

- Provide a before-and-after picture of organizational communication in relation to change

Benefits of communication audits are described in the Management Highlight on page 244.

MANAGEMENT HIGHLIGHT
Benefits of Communication Audits

Improved productivity

Positive impact on programs

Reduced communication costs

More efficient use of time

Verification of facts

Better use of communication/information technology

Improved morale

A more vibrant organizational culture

Discovery of hidden information resources

Communication changes

Sources: C. W. Downs, *Communication Audits* (Glenview, IL: Scott, Foresman, 1988); G. M. Goldhaber and D. P. Rogers, *Auditing Organizational Communication Systems. The ICA Communication Audit* (Dubuque, IA: Kendall/Hunt, 1979); and S. Hamilton, *A Communication Audit Handbook: Helping Organizations Communicate* (New York: Longman, 1987).

There are no black-and-white guidelines for conducting a communication audit. Information can be collected from managers and workers via surveys, interviews, observing operations, and reviews of formal and informal reports and procedures used in communicating. Organizations use many different formats when conducting a communication audit.

As firms in the next decade struggle with such issues as global competition, downsizing, reorganization, and so on, communication in organizations is taking on increased significance. Effective communication characterizes successful organizations, whereas poor communication leads to such problems as lower quality and productivity, anger, and mistrust. Through effective communication, individuals can solve complex problems and achieve organizational goals.

Conclusion
—Interpersonal and Organizational Communication—

Communication is critical to the success of organizations. Successful communication requires shared meaning between the sender of a message and the receiver. Managers function by communicating with others through both formal and informal channels. Barriers to communication include personal characteristics of the parties involved, conflicting frames of reference and selective perception, and reactions triggered by change.

SUGGESTED READINGS

Clarke, Boyd, and Ron Crossland. *The Leader's Voice: How Communication Can Inspire Action and Get Results.* New York: SelectBooks, 2002.

Dunning, Stephen. *The Springboard: How Storytelling Ignites Actions in Knowledge-Era Organizations.* Woburn, MA: Butterworth-Heinemann, 2000.

Keller Johnson, Lauren. "Does E-Mail Escalate Conflict?" *Sloan Management Review,* Fall 2002, pp. 14–15.

Lepsinger, Richard, and Anntoinette D. Lucia. *The Art and Science of 360 Degree Feedback.* San Francisco: Jossey-Bass, 1997.

Perlow, Leslie, and Stephanie Williams. "Is Silence Killing Your Company?" *Harvard Business Review*, May 2003, pp. 52–58.

Wenger, Etienne, Richard McDermott, and William M. Snyder. *Cultivating Communities of Practice.* Boston: Harvard Business School Press, 2002.

ENDNOTES

1. Chester Barnard, *The Functions of the Executive* (Cambridge, MA: Harvard University Press, 1938).

2. Lin Grensing-Pophal, "Communication Pays Off," *HR Magazine,* May 2003, pp. 76–82.

3. Frank M. Corrado, *Getting the Word Out* (Burr Ridge, IL: Business One Irwin, 1993), 10.

4. W. Edwards Deming, *Out of the Crisis* (Cambridge, MA: Center for Advanced Engineering Study, Massachusetts Institute of Technology, 1986), 78.

5. Lawrence R. Birkner and Ruth K. Birkner, "Communication Feedback: Putting It All Together," *Occupational Hazards,* August 2001, pp. 9–10.

6. Stephen R. Axley, "Managerial and Organizational Communication in Terms of the Conduit Metaphor," *Academy of Management Review* (July 1984): 428–437.

7. Sim B. Sitkin, Kathleen M. Sutcliffe, and John R. Barrios-Choplin, "A Dual-Capacity Model of Communication Choice in Organizations," *Human Communications Research,* June 1993, pp. 563–598.

8. Patricia J. Carlson and Gordon B. Davis, "An Investigation of Media Selection among Directors and Managers: From 'Self' to 'Other' Orientation," *MIS Quarterly* (September 1998): 335–362.

9. Richard Daft, Robert H. Lengel, and Linda Klebe Trevino, "Message Equivocality, Media Selection, and Manager Performance: Implications for Information Systems," *MIS Quarterly* 1 (1987): 353–364.

10. Richard K. Allen, *Organizational Management through Communication* (New York: Harper & Row, 1977), 2.

11. Leslie Perlow and Stephanie Williams, "Is Silence Killing Your Company?" *Harvard Business Review,* May 2003, pp. 52–58.

12. Gary L. Kreps, *Organizational Communication* (New York: Longman, 1986), 53–54.

13. Charles Whaley, "Phone Calls Are Futile," *Computing Canada,* May 23, 2003, p. 13.

14. Al Auger, "Speak Not . . . Sell a Lot," *Advisor Today,* March 2003, p. 76.

15. Ted Holden and Suzanne Woolley, "The Delicate Art of Doing Business in Japan," *Business Week,* October 2, 1989, p. 120.

16. Stephen R. Covey, *The 7 Habits of Highly Effective People* (New York: Fireside, 1990), 237.

17. Wayne K. Tandy, "Non-Tech Talk: Leadership and Management," *ITE Journal* (May 2000): 20–21.

18. Jose R. Goris, Bobby C. Vaught, and John D. Pettit Jr., "Effects of Communication Direction on Job Performance and Satisfaction: A Moderated Regression Analysis," *Journal of Business Communication* (October 2000): 348–368.

19. John Naisbitt and Patricia Aburdene, *Re-inventing the Corporation* (New York: Warner Books, 1985), 62.

20. Mirjaliisa Charles and Rebecca Marschan-Piekkari, "Language Training for Enhanced Horizontal Communication: A Challenge for MNCs," *Business Communication Quarterly* (June 2002): 9–29.

21. Lorenzo Sierra, "Tell It to the Grapevine," *Communication World,* June–July 2002, pp. 28–48.

22. Philip R. Beaulieu, "Reputation Does Matter," *Journal of Accountancy* (January 2002): 87.

23. John P. Kotter and Leonard A. Schlessinger, "Choosing Strategies for Change," *Harvard Business Review,* March–April 1979, pp. 106–116.

24. Marianne Kolbasuk McGee, "Political Skills Required," *Information Week,* April 23, 2003, pp. 62–64.

25. Kotter and Schlessinger, "Choosing Strategies for Change," p. 112.

Controlling

part five

Chapter
Thirteen

Control Systems

Control is a fundamental management responsibility, closely linked with the planning and organizing processes. It also has an important impact on motivation and team behavior. Control is both a process (e.g., working to keep things on schedule and according to plan) and an outcome (e.g., the product has met standards). In traditional terms, the controlling function includes all activities that a manager undertakes in attempting to ensure that actual results conform to planned results. For instance, control systems implemented at El Paso Field Services Company's Thompsonville, Texas, gas plant enabled the plant operator to reduce unexpected upsets caused by tower flooding using a flooding prevention strategy, which included online estimation of liquid rates and automatic exchanges balancing to limit liquid production and feed rates.[1] In some contexts, the controlling function of management is a very technical thing indeed.

But like many management terms, control has different meanings to different people, and manifests in different ways, depending on a host of variables. Not surprisingly, an individual's concept of control often reflects a personal perspective. Statisticians may think of control in relation to numbers (variances, means, errors, control limits); engineers, in relation to specifications, monitoring, and feedback; and managers, in relation to directing the activities, attitudes, and performance of subordinates.

In order to achieve results, some characteristics of all organizations must be controlled: key among them are production and operations, financial resources, human resources, and organizational change and development. In this chapter we examine the various elements of the control process, the types of control, and quality control systems.

ELEMENTS OF THE CONTROL PROCESS

Control is a process used (1) to evaluate actual performance, (2) to compare actual performance to goals, and then (3) to take corrective action to reduce discrepancies between performance and goals.[2] Quality statistician Walter Shewhart elaborated these three elements within the control process under the concepts of specification, production, and inspection[3] (see Exhibit 13.1).

- **Specification** is the statement of the intended outcome. Control requires the specification of a standard. A standard is an operationally defined measure used as a basis for comparison. Specification fully describes the preferred condition, which may take the form of a goal, standard, or other carefully determined quantitative statement of conditions.

- **Production** means making the product or delivering the service. Shewhart defines this element as the work required to achieve objectives. It's important to note that this element of the control process applies as much to service as to manufacturing.

- **Inspection** is a judgment concerning whether the production meets the specifications. Inspection determines whether corrective actions need to be taken.

Clear specification of a performance standard requires an **operational definition.** An operational definition converts a concept into measurable, objective units.[4] For example, the concept of *weight* can be operationally defined in terms of grams, pounds, or another standard measure. These measures are not subject to personal interpretation. In contrast, the concept of *heavy* can be interpreted differently by different people. For some, six ounces is heavy; for others, six pounds is heavy. An operational definition should bring uniform agreement to the meaning of a concept.

The process of setting performance standards must begin with a strategy, conveyed in terms of operationally defined measures. Operational measures underlie the control process.

EXHIBIT 13.1
Steps in the Control Process

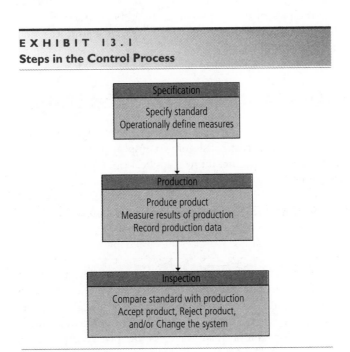

Not only do they control operations through finished-product or after-service inspections; they also enable workers to evaluate processes as they are occurring.

Production and operations are controlled by performance standards. Appendix B provides a discussion of production and operations. Standards determine the activity or outcome to be measured. Control of production and operations requires measurement to identify deviation from standards. Through measurement and assessment, workers can find possible improvements within the product or process and indicate where to initiate change. The act of measuring errors or defects often has an immediate, direct effect on reducing them.

It is important to point out that control applies to all types of organizations, not just manufacturing. Businesses that provide a service must also be concerned with controlling their operations and the quality of their work. Service organizations control performance principally through employee training. Small and large firms alike have recognized the importance of giving employees the knowledge and information they need to serve customers. Home Depot, the hardware and home repair discounter, has made an art of empowering employees to exceed each customer's expectations. Home Depot doesn't conduct extensive marketing surveys, but relies on its associates, who are trained to ask customers what they want and expect.

Inspection in traditionally managed companies typically occurs at the end of production or upon the provision of a service. Quality management discourages this type of inspection. In fact, of quality pioneer W. Edwards Deming's 14 points, the third states, "Cease dependence on mass inspection." As Deming put it, "Routine 100 percent inspection to improve quality is equivalent to planning for defects, acknowledgment that the process has not the capability required for the specifications."[5] Quality-based firms use statistical sampling techniques concurrent with the production process to ensure that most products or service encounters exceed performance specifications.

When statistical sampling indicates a deviation from specifications, corrective action may be necessary. People undertaking corrective actions must know that they're responsible, and they must have the authority to effect change. Job descriptions that have specific, operationally defined performance objectives are necessary to control performance. Responsibilities that fall between the jobs of two individuals should be avoided. For the control function to be most effective, operationally defined objectives, clear authority, and accurate information are requisite.

TYPES OF CONTROL

Management has numerous control methods at its disposal. Each has strengths and limitations. Managers must decide what type of control system to employ in different situations. Some control techniques have very specific, limited application. Nonetheless, all control techniques must be economical, accurate, and understandable.

The techniques managers use to control production and operations can be classified under three main types: preliminary control, concurrent control, and feedback control.

Preliminary Control

Preliminary control focuses on preventing deviations in the quality and quantity of resources used in an organization. For example, human resources must meet the job requirements as defined by the organization; employees must have the physical and intellectual capabilities to perform assigned tasks. Materials used in production must meet acceptable levels of quality and must be available at the proper time and place. Capital must be on hand to ensure an adequate supply of plants and equipment. Financial resources must be available in the right amounts and at the right times.

Preliminary control procedures include all managerial efforts to increase the probability that actual results compare favorably with planned results. From this perspective, policies are an important means of implementing preliminary control, because policies are guidelines for future actions. It's important to distinguish between *setting* policies and *implementing* them.[6] Setting policy is included in the planning function, whereas implementing policy is part of the control function.[7] Similarly, job descriptions are aspects of the control function because they predetermine the activity of the jobholder.[8] At the same time, however, we must distinguish between defining and staffing the task structure. Defining jobs is part of the organizing function; staffing them is part of the controlling function.

Management needs to be concerned with preliminary control of processes in four areas: human resources, materials, capital, and financial resources.

Human Resources.   The organizing function defines the job requirements and predetermines the skill requirements of jobholders. These requirements vary in degree of specificity, depending on the nature of the task. Preliminary control of human resources is achieved through the selection and placement of managerial and nonmanagerial personnel. Exhibit 13.2 shows the steps involved before a person actually begins to work at a firm. Each step along the way, including placement, is a preliminary control step during which the potential worker's skills, abilities, and attitudes are assessed for his or her qualifications for a given position.

EXHIBIT 13.2
Preliminary Control of Human Resources

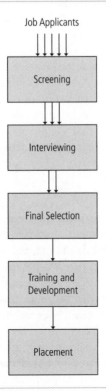

Job Applicants

Screening

Interviewing

Final Selection

Training and Development

Placement

Candidates for positions must be recruited from inside or outside the firm, and the most promising applicants must be selected based on matching skills and personal characteristics to the job requirements. The successful candidate must be trained in methods and procedures appropriate for the job. Most organizations have elaborate procedures for providing training on a continual basis.

Appropriate attention to preliminary control of human resources ensures that the organization will have a match between its needs and individual skills, abilities, and attitudes. With increasing emphasis on information and knowledge as the primary focus of global business, the search, selection, and placement of people is an increasingly vital function. Where human resource professionals had been relegated to staff support in the past (typically, under the rubric *personnel*), many firms today have line positions for human resources. This significant shift reflects the growing awareness that competitive advantage can be gained through proper screening and development of people. In their human resource planning, managers should distinguish between procedures designed to obtain qualified subordinate managers (staffing) and those designed to obtain qualified nonmanagers and operatives (selection and placement). Although basic procedures and objectives are essentially the same, the distinction is important because managerial competence is a fundamental determinant of the organization's success.

Materials.   The raw materials that are converted into a finished product must conform to quality standards *before* they are used in the production process. At the same time, a sufficient inventory or delivery system must be maintained to ensure a continuous inflow of raw materials so the manufacturer can meet customer demand.

Numerous methods that use statistical sampling to control the quality of materials have been devised. These methods typically involve inspection of samples rather than an entire lot. Thus statistical methods are less costly; but there's a risk of accepting defective material if the sample is nonrandom or, by chance, contains none of the defective items.

We do not provide a complete discussion of statistical sampling procedures in this text. However, the essence of the procedures can be described. As an example, suppose management establishes a standard that it will accept no more than a 3 percent defect rate from a supplier. The incoming material would be inspected by selecting random samples and calculating the percentage of defective items in the sample. Based on this sample, managers must make a decision to accept or reject the entire order, or to take another sample. This method is not perfect. Based on the sampling technique, managers could reject an entire lot even though the overall defect rate is less than 3 percent, or they may accept a lot even though the defect rate is greater than 3 percent. The control system used is based on balancing the relative costs of these two types of potential errors.[9] We'll say more about the role of statistics in control later in this chapter.

Capital.   The acquisition of capital reflects the need to replace existing equipment or to expand the firm's productive capacity. Managers of this process are often faced with complicating factors such as financial risk and uncertainty about potential outcomes.[10] Capital acquisitions are controlled by establishing criteria of potential profitability that must be met before the proposal is authorized. Such acquisitions ordinarily are included in the **capital budget,** an intermediate and long-run planning document that details the alternative sources and uses of funds. When connected with strategic planning, capital budgeting has been found to improve financial performance.[11] Several major imperatives are driving managers to wager money on capital budgets: customer service, quality, productivity, and capacity expansion. Managerial decisions that involve the commitment of present funds in exchange for future funds are termed **investment decisions.** The methods that serve to screen investment proposals are based on economic analysis. The following are several widely used capital control methods. Each involves formulating a standard that must be met to accept the prospective capital acquisition.

Payback Method.   Payback is the simplest method of capital control, and it is widely used. One study of Swedish corporations found the payback method was the most used method of capital control in all industries.[12] The **payback method** calculates the number of years needed for the proposed capital acquisition to repay its original cost out of future cash earnings. For example, a manager is considering implementing new information technology that would reduce labor costs by $20,000 per year for each of the four years of the new technology's expected life. The cost of the technology is $40,000. If we use the 36 percent marginal tax rate on corporations with taxable income over $10 million, the additional after-tax cash inflow from which the machine's cost must be paid is calculated as follows:

Additional cash inflow before taxes		
(labor cost savings)		$20,000
Less: Additional taxes		
Additional income	$20,000	
Depreciation ($40,000/4)	$10,000	
Additional taxable income	$10,000	
Tax rate	0.36	
Additional tax payment		$3,600
Additional cash inflow after taxes		$16,400

The payback period can be calculated as follows:

$$\frac{\$40,000}{\$16,400} = 2.44 \text{ years}$$

The proposed new information technology would repay its original cost in about two and one-half years; if the predetermined standard requires a payback of three years or less, the information technology would be an appropriate investment.

The payback method suffers many limitations as a standard for evaluating capital resources. It doesn't produce a measurement of profitability. More important, it doesn't take into account the time value of money; that is, it doesn't recognize that a dollar today is worth more than a dollar at a future date. Other capital control methods do include these important considerations. The primary reason for using the payback method is that in situations where the technology changes rapidly and new products become obsolete quickly, corporations should look for investment opportunities that pay back within a short period of time.

Rate of Return on Investment.   One alternative measure of profitability, consistent with methods ordinarily employed in accounting, is the simple **rate of return on investment.** Using the preceding example, the calculation would be as follows:

Additional gross income	$20,000
Less: Depreciation ($40,000/4)	$10,000
Taxes	$3,600
Total additional expenses	$13,600
Additional net income after taxes	$6,400

The rate of return is the ratio of additional net income to the original cost:

$$\frac{\$6,400}{\$40,000} = 16\%$$

The calculated rate of return would then be compared to some standard of minimum acceptability, and the decision to accept or reject would depend on that comparison. In this case, if the standard rate of return were 10 percent, the purchase of the information technology would be a good investment. The measurement of the simple rate of return has the advantage of being easily understood. It has the disadvantage of not including the time value of money. The discounted rate of return method overcomes this deficiency.

Discounted Rate of Return. The **discounted rate of return** is a measurement of profitability that takes into account the time value of money. It is similar to the payback method, only cash inflows and outflows are considered. The method is widely used because it is considered the correct method for calculating the rate of return. Based on the preceding example,

$$\$40,000 = \frac{\$16,400}{(1+r)} + \frac{\$16,400}{(1+r)2} + \frac{\$16,400}{(1+r)3} + \frac{\$16,400}{(1+r)4}$$

where $r = 23\%$

The discounted rate of return (r) is 23 percent, which is interpreted to mean that a $40,000 investment repaying $16,400 in cash at the end of each of four years has a return of 23 percent.

The rationale of the method can be understood by thinking of the $16,400 inflows as cash payments received by the firm. In exchange for each of these four payments of $16,400, the firm must pay $40,000. The rate of return—23 percent—is the factor equating cash inflows and present cash outflow. This rate of return can be compared to a company minimum standard to determine its acceptability.

Financial Resources. Adequate financial resources must be available to ensure payment of obligations arising from current operations. Materials must be purchased, wages paid, and interest charges and due dates met. The principal means of controlling the availability and cost of financial resources is budgeting—particularly cash flows and working capital budgets.

These budgets anticipate the ebb and flow of business activity when materials are purchased, finished goods are produced and inventoried, goods are sold, and cash is received.[13] This operating cycle results in a problem of timing the availability of cash to meet obligations. When inventories of finished goods increase, the supply of cash decreases as materials, labor, and other expenses are incurred and paid. As inventory is depleted through sales, cash increases. Preliminary control of cash requires that cash be available during the period of inventory buildup and be used wisely during periods of abundance. This requires the careful consideration of alternative sources of short-term financing during inventory buildup, and alternative short-run investment opportunities during periods of inventory depletion.

Managers use certain ratios to control financial resources. For example, the control standard may be stated in the current ratio (the ratio of current assets to current liabilities), and a minimum and a maximum set. The minimum ratio could be set at 2:1 and the maximum at 3:1, which would recognize the cost of both too little and too much investment in liquid assets. The control would involve corrective action taken when the actual current ratio deviates from the standard. Other financial ratios contributing to control of financial resources include the acid-test ratio, inventory turnover, and average collection period. These ratios are discussed in greater detail in the section on feedback control methods.

Concurrent Control

Concurrent control involves monitoring ongoing operations to ensure that objectives are pursued. The standards guiding ongoing activity are derived from job descriptions and from policies resulting from the planning function. Concurrent control is implemented primarily by the supervisory activities of managers. Through personal, on-the-spot observation, managers determine whether the work of others is proceeding in the manner defined by policies and procedures. Delegation of authority provides managers with the power to use financial and nonfinancial incentives to effect concurrent control.

Concurrent control consists primarily of actions of supervisors who direct the work of their subordinates. **Direction** refers to the acts of managers when they (1) instruct subordinates in proper methods and procedures and (2) oversee subordinates' work to ensure that it's done properly.

Direction follows the formal chain of command, since the responsibility of each superior is to interpret for subordinates the orders received from higher levels. The relative importance of direction depends almost entirely on the nature of the tasks performed by subordinates. The supervisor of an assembly line that produces a component part requiring relatively simple manual operations may seldom engage in direction. On the other hand, the manager of a new product research unit must devote considerable time to direction. Because research work is inherently more complex and varied than manual work, it requires more interpretation and instruction.

Directing is the primary function of the first-line supervisor, but at some point every manager in an organization engages in directing employees. The direction given should be within the stated organizational mission, goals, and objectives. As a manager's responsibilities grow, the relative time spent directing subordinates diminishes as other functions become more important.

The scope and content of directing vary according to the nature of the work being supervised. In addition, several other factors determine differences in the form of direction. For example, since direction is basically a process of personal communications, the amount and clarity of information are important factors. Subordinates must receive sufficient information to carry out the task, and they must understand the information they receive. On the other hand, too much information and detail can be distracting.

The tests of effective direction are similar to the tests of effective communication. To be effective, a directive must be reasonable, understandable, appropriately worded, and consistent with the organization's overall goals. Whether these criteria are met isn't the manager's decision. Rather, it's the subordinate who decides. Many managers have assumed that their directives were straightforward and to the point, only to discover that their subordinates failed to understand or to accept them as legitimate.

Feedback Control

Feedback control methods focus on end results. Corrective action is directed at improving either the resource acquisition process or the actual operation. This type of control derives its name from its use of results to guide future actions. A simple illustration of feedback control is a thermostat, which automatically regulates the temperature of a room. Since the thermostat maintains the preset temperature by constantly monitoring the actual temperature, future results (activation of heating or cooling units at time x) are directly and continually determined by feedback (room temperature at time $x - 1$). Room temperature at time x then feeds back to control the heating and cooling units at time $x + 1$, and so on.

In the following two subsections, we outline feedback control methods widely used in business: financial statement analysis and standard cost analysis.

Financial Statement Analysis.   A firm's accounting system is a principal source of information managers can use to evaluate historical results. Periodically, the manager receives a set of financial statements that usually includes a **balance sheet** and **income statement.** These financial statements summarize and classify the effects of transactions in assets, liabilities, equity, revenues, and expenses—the principal components of a firm's financial structure. The balance sheet describes an organization's financial condition at a specified point in time. The income statement is a summary of an organization's financial performance over a given time period.

A detailed analysis of the financial statement's information enables management to determine the adequacy of the firm's earning power and its ability to meet current and long-term obligations. Managers must have measures of and standards for profitability, liquidity, and solvency. Whether a manager prefers the rate of return on sales, on owner's equity, on total assets, or a combination of all three, it's important to establish a meaningful norm—one that's appropriate to the particular firm, given its industry and stage of growth. An inadequate rate of return negatively affects the firm's ability to attract funds for expansion, particularly if a downward trend over time is evident.

The measures of **liquidity** reflect the firm's ability to meet current obligations as they become due. The widest known and most often used measure is the **current ratio** (the ratio of current assets to current liabilities). The standard of acceptability depends on the particular firm's operating characteristics. Bases for comparison are available from trade associations that publish industry averages. A tougher test of liquidity is the **acid-test ratio,** which relates only cash and near-cash items (current assets excluding inventories and prepaid expenses) to current liabilities.

The relationship between current assets and current liabilities is an important one. Equally important is the composition of current assets. Two measures that indicate composition and rely on information found in both the balance sheet and income statement are the accounts receivable turnover and the inventory turnover. The **accounts receivable turnover** is the ratio of credit sales to average accounts receivable. The higher the turnover, the more rapid the conversion of accounts receivable to cash. A low turnover would indicate a time lag in the collection of receivables, which in turn could strain the firm's ability to meet its own obligations. Appropriate corrective action might be tightening of credit standards or a more vigorous effort to collect outstanding accounts. The **inventory turnover** also facilitates the analysis of appropriate balances in current assets. It's calculated as the ratio of cost of goods sold to average inventory. A high ratio could indicate a dangerously low inventory balance in relation to sales, with the possibility of missed sales or a production slowdown. Conversely, a low ratio might indicate an overinvestment in inventory to the exclusion of other, more profitable assets. Whatever the case, the appropriate ratio must be established by the manager, based on the firm's experience within its industry and market.

Another financial measure is **solvency,** the ability of the firm to meet its long-term obligations—its fixed commitments. The solvency measure reflects the claims of creditors and owners on the firm's assets. An appropriate balance must be maintained—a balance that protects the interest of the owner yet doesn't ignore the advantages of long-term debt as a source of funds. A commonly used measure of solvency is the ratio of net income before interest and taxes to interest expense. This indicates the margin of safety; ordinarily, a high ratio is preferred. However, a very high ratio combined with a low debt-to-equity ratio could indicate that management hasn't taken advantage of debt as a source of funds. The appropriate balance between debt and equity depends on many factors. But as a general rule, the proportion of debt should vary directly with the stability of the firm's earnings.

Firms also use *debt ratios* to assess the amount of financing being provided by creditors. Two popular debt ratios are the debt/equity ratio and the debt/asset ratio. The **debt/equity ratio** is a measure of the amount of assets financed by debt compared to that amount financed by profits retained by the firm and investments (stocks and other securities). The **debt/asset ratio** is an expression of the relationship of the firm's total debts to its total assets.

Standard Cost Analysis.   Standard cost accounting systems are considered a major contribution of the scientific management era. A **standard cost system** provides information that enables management to compare actual costs with predetermined (standard) costs. Management can then take appropriate corrective action or assign to others the authority to take action. The first use of standard costing was to control manufacturing costs. In recent years, standard costing has also been applied to selling, general, and administrative expenses. Here we discuss standard manufacturing costs.

The three elements of manufacturing costs are direct labor, direct materials, and overhead. For each of these, an estimate must be made of cost per unit of output. For example, the direct labor cost per unit of output consists of the standard usage of labor and the standard price of labor. The standard usage derives from time studies that fix the expected output per labor hour; the standard price of labor is fixed by the salary schedule appropriate for the kind of work necessary to produce the output. A similar determination is made for direct materials. Thus, the standard labor and standard materials costs might be as follows:

Standard labor usage per unit:	2 hours
Standard wage rate per hour:	$5.00
Standard labor cost (2 × $5.00):	$10.00
Standard material usage per hour:	6 pounds
Standard material price per pound:	$.30
Standard material cost (6 × $.30):	$1.80

The accounting system enables the manager to compare incurred costs and standard costs. Today, cost accounting practices are undergoing significant changes to keep pace with the rapidly evolving manufacturing environment. **Activity-based accounting,** a new system of cost accounting based on activity, has been advocated by many academicians and practitioners. Its underlying principle is that activities consume resources and products consume activities. The labor costs of supporting departments can be traced to activities by assessing the portion of each person's time spent on each activity, which can then allow for restatement of departmental cost in activities and their associated costs. Activity costs then are traced to the product based on the amount of activity volume each product consumes. The overall impact is more accurate product cost information.

QUALITY CONTROL TECHNIQUES

The total quality movement has brought with it a set of tools and techniques for controlling organizational processes. Three approaches in particular— statistical process control, total quality control, and total quality management—are in wide use in a broad spectrum of industries. These approaches are all similar in their focus on exceeding customer expectations as a central value. Another central value is a focus on the system (in contrast to the traditional focus on the worker) as the source of most production or service errors or defects.

Statistical Process Control

The approach of statistical process control has long played an important role in business and industry. **Statistical process control (SPC)** is based on two assumptions: (1) nature is imperfect and (2) variability exists everywhere in systems. Therefore, probability and statistics play a major role in understanding and controlling complex systems. Charts, diagrams, and graphs are conceptual tools managers can use to summarize statistical data, measure and understand variation, assess risk, and make decisions. The Management Highlight below summarizes the seven tools of quality control. **Statistics** is defined as "that branch of applied mathematics which describes and analyzes empirical observations for the purpose of predicting certain events as a basis for decision making in the face of uncertainty."[14]

Statistics come in two varieties: descriptive and inferential. **Descriptive statistics are a computed measure of some property of a set of data, making possible a statement about its meaning.** An example of a descriptive statistic is the average (mean) time it takes to answer the telephone in the customer service department. Other descriptive statistics include the mode (the most common data point) and the median (the point at which 50 percent of the other points lie above, and 50 percent below). Mean, median, and mode are also often referred to as measures of central tendency.

MANAGEMENT HIGHLIGHT
Seven Tools of Quality Control

Flowcharts provide a visual description of the steps in a process or work activity. The sequence of events that makes up the process is shown. Generally, flowcharts begin with inputs, show what takes place to transform these inputs, and end with outputs. Flowcharts are especially helpful in visualizing and understanding how things are currently being done, and how they can be done differently to improve the process.

Run charts are used to plot measurements taken over specific time intervals such as a day, week, or month. Usually the quantity measure is plotted on the vertical axis, and time is on the horizontal axis. The run charts can be used to determine how something is changing over time, and whether problems are taking place at certain periods of time.

Control charts show the result of statistical process control measures for a sample, batch, or some other unit. Such charts can be used to study variation in a process and to analyze the variation over time. A specified level of variation may be acceptable, but deviation beyond this level is unacceptable.

Fishbone diagrams, also called cause-and-effect diagrams, look like a fishbone. The problem, such as a defect, is defined as the effect. Events that contribute to the problem are called causes. The effect is the "head" of the fishbone, while the causes are the "bones" growing out of the spine. The fishbone chart can be used to see how different causes occur and lead to a problem. Once the causes are identified, corrective measures can be implemented.

Pareto charts are used to display the number of problems or defects in a product over time. Fairly simple to construct, Pareto charts display the results as bars of varying lengths. The basic premise of the Pareto chart is that only a few causes account for most problems.

Histograms, also called **bar charts**, show the frequency of each particular measurement in a group of measurements. This information is useful in analyzing the variability in a process.

Scatter diagrams show the relationship between two characteristics or events, such as the relationship between diameter and strength for samples of wires. By measuring these two variables and plotting the results, quality control managers can observe how one variable changes as the other changes.

Inferential statistics are computations done on a set of data, or among several sets of data, that are designed to facilitate prediction of future events, or to guide decisions and actions. An example of an inferential statistic might be the correlation of (a) the average time the customer service department takes to answer the telephone with (b) customer attitudes about the organization. It might be found that faster average response time is correlated with increased customer satisfaction. In that case, this statistic would be a catalyst to action centered on reducing telephone response time.

Because variation exists in any process, no two products or service encounters are exactly alike. The control of quality is largely the control of variation. The job of statistical process control is to limit this variation within an acceptable range. For example, statistical process control is used to control the variation in the weight of packages of biscuits; underweight packages result in customer dissatisfaction, while overweight packages reduce profits.[15] So how do we determine what is acceptable variation?

There are two types of variation in any system—random and nonrandom. Random variation is often referred to as the "normal" variation of a system. Random variation potentially affects all components of a process. Nonrandom variation is not considered to be part of the normal cause processes of a system. This type of variation leads to unpredictable outcomes, something management wants to eliminate.

Random and nonrandom variation are explained in turn by two different types of causes: common and special. **Common cause variation** is just the random variation in a system and, typically, it can't be completely eliminated. Managers should work to minimize the range of common cause variation as part of their continuous improvement process. **Range** refers to the extreme upper and lower measures of a variable. But, given the assumption that the perfect system isn't likely to be achieved, managers need to be aware that some common cause variation is likely to remain.

Special cause variation, on the other hand, is due to some *external* influence upon a system. This could be anything from drug abuse by workers to earthquakes. Managers want to eliminate special cause variations to the extent possible. In our examples, this would be done by screening workers and offering drug abuse counseling, or by locating in areas not prone to earthquakes. A **stable system** is one that has eliminated special cause variation and is subject only to the unavoidable (yet reducible) common cause variation.

For example, consider a firm that wants to establish quality control over one of its key suppliers. One critical measure may be the percentage of orders that are delayed each week. To develop a baseline, the company may randomly sample 100 orders each week from this supplier for, say, 20 weeks to develop a mean percentage of orders that are delayed. With these data, it's possible using well-tested statistical methods to establish upper and lower control limits. The range of values within these limits would be the range of expected variation due to common causes. If the mean percentage of delays during the 20-week baseline period is .06 and the upper and lower control limits are .11 and .01, respectively, then any subsequent weeks where the percentage of delays is between these values is probably due to common cause variation (e.g., traffic conditions, worker absences, misplaced orders).

However, if for several weeks the manager notices that the percentage of delays is above .11 (or below .01), a special cause may be operating and action may need to be taken. Some possible special causes are (1) the supplier was bought out and is under new management, and (2) a trucker strike is delaying deliveries. Managers use statistical measures to know when key processes are affected by special cause variation and need immediate attention.

The practice of quality management in any type of organization—whether it's service, manufacturing, retail, nonprofit, or something else—can benefit from applying statistical methods to organizational processes or customer expectations. Although statistical techniques are common to most quality management environments, each manager must decide how best to apply these techniques to his or her own organization. What's common across organization types is the fundamental purpose of quality control—to minimize variation.

Total Quality Control

In traditional production management (see Appendix B), quality control consisted of assigning the last person on the assembly line the responsibility of ensuring that the product worked. Today, quality control begins at the beginning; that is, quality control is maintained from the design process through manufacturing, sale, and use of the product. The sum of all these efforts is called total quality control. The principles of total quality control can be applied equally well to either products or services. Customers will always seek products and services of consistently high quality. To understand how total quality control can transform an organization, consider that each worker within a company can be viewed as providing a product or service for some other individual, and that the product or service can be evaluated using the tools of total quality control (see Management Highlight on page 258).[16]

Armand Feigenbaum is often credited with coining the term **total quality control (TQC)**.[17] TQC represents a more comprehensive form of quality control than SPC, although it recommends using statistics to improve quality. According to Feigenbaum,

> Total quality control is an effective system for integrating the quality-development, quality-maintenance, and quality-improvement efforts of the various groups in an organization so as to enable marketing, engineering, production, and service to perform at the most economical levels which allow for full customer satisfaction.[18]

The fundamental purpose of TQC is to manufacture products or deliver services that meet the level of quality demanded by customers. TQC's emphasis is on customer satisfaction. Feigenbaum identifies several TQC benchmarks: quality is what the customer says it is; quality is a way of managing; quality and innovation are mutually dependent; quality requires continuous improvement; and quality is implemented with a total system connected with customers and suppliers.[19]

According to Feigenbaum, there's no such thing as a permanent quality level. Demands and expectations for quality are constantly changing. A distinction of good management is personal leadership in mobilizing the knowledge, skill, and positive attitudes of everyone in the organization to recognize that what they do to make quality better helps to make everything in the organization better. Quality is also essential for successful innovation, for two reasons. The first reason is the rapid speed of new product development. The second is that when a product design is likely to be manufactured globally, where international suppliers must be involved in every stage of development and production, the entire process must be clearly structured.[20]

In a quality-based system, control is a conscious, positive, preventive stance created in the system. TQC begins with planning—planning that's aimed at preventing quality problems. Here are some concerns addressed by quality planning:

- Establishing quality guidelines.
- Building quality into the design.
- Procurement quality.

- In-process and finished product quality.

- Inspection and test planning.

- Control of nonconforming material.

- Handling and following up on customer complaints.

- Education and training for quality.[21]

Total Quality Management

Total quality management (TQM), the generic name given to the Deming approach to quality-based management, is heavily oriented toward treating the *system* as the primary source of error or defects in manufacturing or service work. Although quality management uses a myriad of statistical techniques to control processes, there are also some fundamental lessons for control from a human psychology perspective. Deming stresses in his 14 points such things as "pride of workmanship," "self-improvement," and "drive out fear" (see the Management Highlight on page 262). These are all elements of the "softer" side of management (the nonquantitative side), but they are equally important to master. Managers who use only SPC are likely to ignore the need for pride in workmanship that most workers share. Thus, the *total* in TQM requires managers to be familiar with a wide range of facts about the workplace, both those that can be described mathematically and those that can't.

Let's examine just a few of the important elements of TQM, including the worker's role and the manager's role in a TQM environment.

The Worker's Role in TQM. Workers play an important role in implementing TQM programs. Deming provides an example of successful worker quality control in the production of stockings. Managers with the stocking company first recognized a problem in production costs when they faced a situation where costs were soon to exceed revenues. Management hired a statistician to help them diagnose their problem. The statistician recommended that the company send 20 supervisors to a 10-week training course to learn techniques for charting the number of defective stockings. When the supervisors returned, they were asked to apply some of the principles they had learned.

In all but two cases, defects fell within statistically established control limits with a mean defect rate of 4.8 percent per production worker (called "loopers" in the stocking business). Next, individual loopers were charted. Management found (1) an excellent looper whose skills were passed on to others by training them, (2) a looper who improved markedly with eyeglasses, and (3) a looper whose performance changed dramatically after charting. One of the loopers remarked, "This is the first time that anybody ever told me that care mattered." Within seven months, the mean number of defects dropped to 0.8 percent. Instead of 11,500 stockings rejected each week, only 2,000 were rejected.[22]

A quality-based system of control must be built on worker trust and pride of workmanship, which provides a basis for worker self-control.[23] In this quality-based view, control must be seen as an internal, individual process before it can result in an external process. Control becomes an internal quality guide practiced by all employees rather than an external set of rules applied by managers. Juran defines self-control as "A means of knowing what the goals are . . . a means of knowing what the actual performance is . . . a means for changing the performance in the event that performance does not conform to goals and standards."[24]

Although workers play an important role in implementing a TQM approach, management has the responsibility of leadership. In most organizations, workers below the

MANAGEMENT HIGHLIGHT
Deming's 14 Points of Total Quality Management

1. *Create constancy of purpose for improvement of product and service.* Deming suggests a radical new definition of a company's role. Rather than to make money, it's to stay in business and provide jobs through innovation, research, constant improvement, and maintenance.

2. *Adopt the new philosophy.* Americans are too tolerant of poor workmanship and sullen service. We need a new religion in which mistakes and negativism are unacceptable.

3. *Cease dependence on mass inspection.* American firms typically inspect a product as it comes off the assembly line or at major stages along the way; defective products are either thrown out or reworked. Both practices are unnecessarily expensive. In effect, a company is paying workers to make defects and then to correct them. Quality comes not from inspection, but from improvement of the process. With instruction, workers can be enlisted in this improvement.

4. *End the practice of awarding business on price tag alone.* Purchasing departments customarily award business to the lowest-priced vendor. Frequently, this leads to low-quality supplies. Instead, buyers should seek the best quality in a long-term relationship with a single supplier for any one item.

5. *Improve constantly the system of production and service.* Improvement isn't a one-time effort. Management is obligated to continually look for ways to reduce waste and improve quality.

6. *Institute training.* Too often, workers have learned their job from another worker who was never trained properly. They're forced to follow unintelligible instructions. They can't do their jobs well because no one tells them how to do so.

7. *Institute leadership.* The supervisor's job isn't to tell people what to do or to punish them, but to lead. Leading consists of (1) helping people do a better job and (2) learning by objective methods which workers need individual help.

8. *Drive out fear.* Many employees are afraid to ask questions or to take a position, even when they don't understand what their job is or what's right or wrong. They will continue to do things the wrong way or not do them at all. Economic losses from fear are appalling. To ensure better quality and productivity, people must feel secure.

9. *Break down barriers between staff areas.* Often a company's departments or units are competing with each other or have goals that conflict. They don't work as a team so they can solve or foresee problems. Worse, one department's goals may cause trouble for another.

10. *Eliminate slogans, exhortations, and targets for the workforce.* These never helped anybody do a good job. Let workers formulate their own slogans.

11. *Eliminate numerical quotas.* Quotas take into account only numbers, not quality of methods. They're usually a guarantee of inefficiency and high cost. To hold their jobs, people meet quotas at any cost, without regard for damage to their company.

12. *Remove barriers to pride of workmanship.* People are eager to do a good job and distressed when they can't. Too often, misguided supervisors, faulty equipment, and defective materials stand in way of good performance. These barriers must be removed.

13. *Institute a vigorous program of education and retraining.* Both management and the workforce must be educated in new methods, including teamwork and statistical techniques.

14. *Take action to accomplish the transformation.* A special top management team with a plan of action is needed to carry out the quality mission. Workers can't do it on their own, nor can managers. A critical mass of people in the company must understand the 14 points.

Sources: W. Edwards Deming, *Out of the Crisis,* 2nd ed. (Cambridge, MA: MIT Center for Advanced Engineering Study, 1986); Lloyd Dobyns and Clare Crawford-Mason, *Quality or Else* (Boston: Houghton Mifflin, 1991); and Marshall Sashkin and Kenneth J. Kiser, *Total Quality Management* (Seabrook, MD: Ducochon Press, 1991).

managerial level are unlikely to lead a revolution in organizational philosophy. It's up to management to steer the ship. Managers must create the vision for the organization. This is no different in a TQM environment or a scientific management environment. What's different is the behavior of managers.

Management's Role in TQM.   Quality-based management believes control of work processes is effected first by the work force, then by automation, then by managers, and finally by upper managers. Upper management is responsible for creating the system; workers are trained to maintain control. Thus a quality-based approach locates control at the lowest levels of the firm—the workers on the line who provide the service.[25]

The traditional managerial control function has focused on supervision during the production process. Supervision has been widely practiced as a traditional method of keeping an eye on workers—looking for mistakes. Some managers have even resorted to using information technologies to eavesdrop on employees. This type of practice has debilitating effects on performance and is ethically questionable. In some cases, the corporate trend toward downsizing and rightsizing has led workers lower down in the corporate hierarchy to tell bosses only what they think they want to hear, even resorting to lying. Extreme pressure to perform can lead to improper behavior.

The responsibility for quality control ultimately rests with management; however, managers must also promote worker self-management. To further employee self-management, managers must develop worker participation programs and policies. With knowledge of the company's costs and goals, workers can practice control with minimal supervision. Management's job is to ensure that workers have the knowledge, the tools, and the power to prevent problems from arising. Managers must also encourage employee suggestions and cost consciousness by recognizing and implementing worker quality improvement decisions. And, if there are problems, management should give workers the first opportunity to solve them.

Managers need patience to transform their organizations using the principles and tools of TQM. Workers are not always readily willing to embrace new practices. Managers are responsible for creating an atmosphere filled with enthusiasm for change and improvement.[26] Most workers want responsibility and control over their work. Most will understand and accept a new approach to their work if management demonstrates commitment to improving the system. That means workers need to be trained in the tools and techniques of TQM, SPC, and TQC. They need to be empowered to control their work processes. And they need to be encouraged constantly to develop pride in their work and their organization. These elements of quality are the least quantifiable, but no less important.

Conclusion
Control Systems

Control is an important responsibility of managers. The three elements of the control process are specification, production, and inspection. The techniques managers use to control production and operations include preliminary control, concurrent control, and feedback control. The total quality movement has given rise to three additional approaches for controlling organizational processes: statistical process control, total quality control, and total quality management.

SUGGESTED READINGS

Cokins, Gary. *Activity-Based Cost Management: An Executive's Guide.* New York: Wiley, 2001.

Cole, Robert E. "Learning from the Quality Movement: What Did and Didn't Happen and Why?" *California Management Review* (Fall 1998): 43–73.

Crosby, Philip B. *Quality Is Free: The Art of Making Quality Certain.* Mentor Books, 1992.

Deming, W. Edwards. *Out of the Crisis.* Cambridge, MA: MIT Press, 2000.

George, Michael L. *Lean Six Sigma: Combining Six-Sigma Quality with Lean Production.* New York: McGraw-Hill, 2002.

ENDNOTES

1. "Low-Maintenance Control Systems Improve NGL Recovery at Texas Gas Plant," *Oil and Gas Journal,* May 19, 2003, pp. 56–63.

2. Joseph M. Juran, *Juran on Leadership for Quality: An Executive Handbook* (New York: Free Press, 1989), 145.

3. Walter A. Shewhart, *Statistical Method from the Viewpoint of Quality Control* (Washington, D.C.: Graduate School, U.S. Dept. of Agriculture, 1939), 1.

4. W. Edwards Deming, *Out of the Crisis* (Cambridge, MA: Center for Advanced Engineering Study, Massachusetts Institute of Technology, 1986), Chapter 9, esp. pp. 276–277.

5. Deming, *Out of the Crisis,* p. 28.

6. Peter Lorange and Declan Murphy, "Considerations in Implementing Strategic Control," *Journal of Business Strategy* (Spring 1984): 27–35.

7. George Schreyogg and Horst Stenman, "Strategic Control: A New Perspective," *Academy of Management Review* (January 1987): 91–103.

8. Luis R. Gomez Mejia, Henry Tosi, and Timothy Hinkin, "Managerial Control, Performance, and Executive Compensation," *Academy of Management Journal* (March 1987): 51–70.

9. Joel G. Siegel and Matthew S. Rubin, "Corporate Planning and Control through Variance Analysis," *Managerial Planning,* September–October, 1984, pp. 33–36.

10. Michael R. Walls, "Integration Business Strategy and Capital Allocution: An Application of Multi-Objective Decision Making," *Engineering Economist* (Spring 1995): 247–266.

11. Jane Beckett-Camarata, "An Examination of the Relationship between the Municipal Strategic Plan and the Capital Budget and Its Effect on Financial Performance," *Journal of Public Budgeting, Accounting, and Financial Management* (Spring 2003): 23–40.

12. "Capital Budgeting Methods among Sweden's Largest Groups of Companies," *International Journal of Production Economics* (April 11, 2003): 51–69.

13. Frank Collins, Paul Munter, and Don W. Finn, "The Budgeting Games People Play," *Accounting Review,* January 1987, pp. 29–49.

14. Gabriel A. Pall, *Quality Process Management* (Englewood Cliffs, NJ: Prentice-Hall, 1987), 94.

15. Susanta Kumar Gauri, "Statistical Process Control Procedures for Controlling the Weight of Packets of Biscuits," *Total Quality Management and Business Excellence* (July 2003): 525–535.

16. Thomas Pyzdek, *What Every Manager Should Know about Quality* (New York: Marcel Dekker, 1991), 3.

17. A. V. Feigenbaum, *Total Quality Control* (New York: McGraw-Hill, 1991); Mary Walton, *The Deming Management Method* (New York: Perigree, 1986), 122–130; and Kaoru Ishikawa, *What Is Total Quality Control?* (Englewood Cliffs, NJ: Prentice Hall, 1985), 90–94.

18. Feigenbaum, *Total Quality Control,* p. 5.

19. Feigenbaum, p. 828.

20. Feigenbaum, pp. 828–833.

21. Pyzdek, *What Every Manager Should Know about Quality,* pp. 3–4.

22. Deming, *Out of the Crisis,* pp. 380–387.

23. Juran, *Juran on Leadership for Quality,* chap. 5.

24. Juran, pp. 147–148.

25. Juran, pp. 148–150.

26. Richard A. Roberts, "You Want to Improve? First You Must Change," *SuperVision,* May 2003, pp. 8–10.

Chapter Fourteen

Managing Services

Most organizations today are aware that the service they offer to their customers is a significant source of competitive advantage. Even manufacturing companies, whose primary activity is the production of a tangible good, must be concerned with the way they interact with customers of the firm. Customer satisfaction measurement and management has the overall objective of satisfying—perhaps even delighting—customers, and exceeding customer expectations is now widely recognized as an effective route to strategic, market-driven organizational behavior.[1] Consequently, the ability to manage the service side of an enterprise should never be undersold. The cost of failing to meet customers' expectations of service quality is colossally high no matter how you measure it—whether in terms of lost customers, bad publicity, or responses needed to rectify customer complaints and win back once-loyal customers. An interesting case that cuts across many of the topics we will examine in this chapter is the evolving dilemma of the Recording Industry Association of America (RIAA) which, in September 2003, took the unprecedented step of suing 261 of its own customers for downloading music from the Internet. It remains to be seen if these lawsuits will backfire.

In this chapter we examine how services are managed, starting with a discussion on the nature and importance of services. We then examine characteristics that distinguish services from other goods. After presenting a scheme for classifying services, we look at quality and productivity in service organizations and issues related to developing and managing services. Finally, we discuss developing a performance culture.

THE NATURE AND IMPORTANCE OF SERVICES

A **good** is a tangible product that consumers can physically possess. A **service** is an intangible product that involves human or mechanical effort.[2] Another way to think about a service is that it's instantaneously perishable; the transaction and consumption occur at the same time. In contrast, a product can be stored and used at some time after the transaction between buyer and seller. Most workers in the United States today are employed in some type of service organization. Some of America's largest service firms can be found in the telecommunications and entertainment industries.

Few products can be classified as a pure good or pure service; most products contain both tangible and intangible elements. When you order your favorite meal in a restaurant, you're purchasing a tangible product. Yet we often compare and evaluate restaurants on their quality of service. This is an important point. Any business, whether it's primarily involved in manufacturing or mining, or any other process, typically also provides services to a customer. Many businesses that had traditionally conceived of themselves as manufacturers are building competitive advantage around customer service. For example, according to William Toller, CEO of Witco Chemical Company, satisfying the customer is no longer the ultimate business virtue. He says companies must go beyond satisfaction and create customer loyalty. To create loyalty among Witco customers, Toller says his company looks for those things that customers perceive as adding value to their relationship with the company. This allows Witco to focus on the critical few issues that affect the company's performance for both customers and profitability.[3]

Exhibit 14.1 illustrates the concept of tangibility on a continuum ranging from pure goods to pure services. Salt or some other staple good is an example of a pure good. A consultant is an example of a pure service. Products falling in the middle have a mix of both tangible and intangible elements. Though most products are neither a pure good nor a pure service, one element usually predominates, and this is the basis for classifying a product as a good or service. Air travel is considered a service because it is generally intangible. Pilots, jets, and airports, however, are tangible. As we will show later, these tangible elements are important in managing services.

Services are an important part of the American economy. Service industries account for well over 50 percent of the U.S. gross domestic product (GDP).[4] In 2002, growth in GDP was led by the services-producing sector, which increased by 2.8 percent; growth in the goods-producing sector increased 1.3 percent.[5] The U.S. Bureau of Labor Statistics forecasts that nearly all new jobs created in the United States will be in service-producing industries.[6] Several service industries—including insurance and retailing—face intense

EXHIBIT 14.1
A Continuum of Product Tangibility

Goods							Services
			Fast Food	Air Travel	Health Care	Financial Services	Consulting
Salt	VCR	Car					

Tangible Dominant ← → Intangible Dominant

competition, some from foreign firms. Nonetheless, service jobs are expected to grow faster than jobs in other sectors of the economy.

CHARACTERISTICS OF SERVICES

We must recognize several important characteristics of services. These characteristics affect the manner in which services are produced and managed. Production and management of cars, for instance, is somewhat different from production and management of financial services. This is because financial and other services are distinguished by four characteristics: intangibility, inseparability of production and consumption, perishability, and heterogeneity. Later in the chapter we will examine how these characteristics influence the management of services.

Intangibility

The major feature distinguishing services from other products is that they cannot be physically possessed. **Intangibility** is the quality of not being able to be assessed by the senses of sight, taste, touch, smell, or hearing. Intangibility is especially important because the other three unique characteristics of services are derived from this trait. Think of some services we have discussed or some you have purchased lately. Can you touch or feel them? Usually not. Services such as haircuts, banking, medical exams, and the like cannot be physically possessed like a tangible good.

Because services are intangible, they are difficult for customers to evaluate. If you have a physical exam, the best outcome is a clean bill of health. But how do you know you had a thorough physical? A physical exam cannot be evaluated in the same manner as a tangible product. A consumer can test drive a car, kick the tires, and form an opinion.

Although it is hard to evaluate a service, it is not impossible. Before selecting a physician, you could visit her office, look at the facilities, talk to nurses and doctors, and observe the clinic's atmosphere. These are *tangible cues* used to evaluate an intangible service. Many services have a tangible element, just as goods have an intangible element. Airlines have pilots and planes, banks have tellers and facilities, and clinics have doctors and nurses. Research has shown that tangible cues can be used to maximize the effectiveness of a website for service firms.[7] Management of these tangible elements is critical to the success of services.

Inseparability of Production and Consumption

Services are also characterized by **inseparability** of production and consumption, meaning they are produced and consumed at the same time. Goods can be carefully designed, produced, and consumed at a later date. This is not the case for services. Inseparability has two important implications. First, the *service provider* plays a critical role in delivery of services and may in fact be the service. Service providers play a critical role in services in that customers will often associate the service provider with the service. Insurance agents, bank tellers, hair stylists, flight attendants, and many other occupations represent the entire business to a customer. Many service organizations have implemented extensive training programs to ensure that these key employees have the skills needed to deal with customers. For example, Canadian Airlines International's "Service Quality" program was also the means for carrying out one of the largest employee training projects in North American business history. Employees were provided with quality skills training and brought together in teams to change the systems and processes with which they work.[8]

A second implication is that because production and consumption occur simultaneously, the *customer* also has an important role in service delivery.[9] Most services cannot be performed unless the customer is present or directly involved in the production process. The customer must be present to get a haircut, fly on a plane, or see a movie. In some cases the customer actually shares part of the responsibility for delivering services. Most gas buyers pump their own gas, bank customers operate automatic teller machines (ATMs), and some restaurant customers even cook their own meals. Similarly, a sightseer who interacts with local residents is involved in the production and consumption of a city's tourism services. Likewise, a patient must tell a doctor the symptoms of an illness before treatment can be prescribed.

Because customers are so involved in service transactions, these critical service encounters are an excellent opportunity for businesses to gain feedback on their performance. A **critical service encounter** is one in which customers are likely to be forming opinions about the overall quality of the business. Front-line service employees most often manage these critical service encounters and are an important source of information about customers. Customer knowledge obtained by contact employees can be used to improve service in two ways: by facilitating the interaction with customers, and by guiding the firm's decision making. Employees who have frequent contact with customers often have a better understanding of customer needs and problems than others in the firm. Research has shown that open communication between managers and customer service employees improves customer service quality.[10] Research has also shown that the warmth of communication style from the service provider to the customer can affect customer perception of service quality. Results from eighty-three participants in a simulated bank interview experiment indicated that the warmth of the service personnel contributed to a high-quality service rating and increased the participants' future confidence of dealing with the bank.[11]

Because customers often play an active role in producing services, the service customer also must have the ability, skill, training, and motivation needed to engage in the production process. The service encounter can't be completed unless customers have the skills needed to participate in the transaction. This makes management of services even more complex. A TV is poor quality because it's made that way; a bank may be poor quality because the customer never learned how to use the ATM card.

Perishability

Perishability results from the inseparability of production and consumption; it means that unused service capacity can't be stored and used at a later date. As we noted in Chapter 13, manufacturing firms use inventory control methods to resolve this problem. Service organizations can't handle this problem in the same way. If a movie theater is half empty for the matinee, seats can't be stored for the crowded evening show. Services must be produced and consumed simultaneously; any unused capacity is wasted.

Many service organizations have tried to deal with this problem through pricing. Airlines offer deep discounts, knowing that unused capacity can't be recovered. Movie theaters drop prices for the matinee. In some cases the bulk of a firm's service activities must be performed at one time. Accounting firms are busiest in the weeks before April 15 when taxes are due. Heating repair firms can't handle all the calls they get on the first cold day of fall. Because services cannot be stored, such fluctuations in demand are a challenge to managers. In part, the explosion in the temporary help industry in the United States over the past few years is a response to fluctuating demand for services. For only a portion of the year, many businesses need to hire people who have strong customer service skills. Temporary agencies are able to provide well-trained people who help companies meet their peak demand challenges. Using temporary help allows managers to avoid laying off people, or having employees idle during non-peak periods.

Heterogeneity

Robots are fairly consistent in their performance, but services are often performed by humans—and people are not always consistent. **Heterogeneity** refers to the inconsistency or variation in human performance. Two different service providers can be inconsistent in their performance, as can a single provider from one service encounter to another. For example, you may have a favorite hair stylist whom you feel performs better than anyone else. But on a given day, even your favorite stylist may be inconsistent, for one reason or another, and do a below-par job. Services are simply more difficult to standardize than tangible goods.

Service quality in the hotel and restaurant industry contains elements that are tangible and intangible. Hotels frequently have standardized procedures regarding reservations, front-desk procedures, and check-out. For a restaurant, intangible and standardized components include the amount of time a customer must wait before being seated, when dirty dishes are cleared, and when the check is presented. As with tangible and standardized output, restaurants may have strict specifications about these activities. At the least, a firm that has established specifications that are closely aligned with its customers' desires has a competitive advantage over organizations that haven't accurately identified customers' wishes.[12]

CLASSIFYING SERVICES

It is important to develop a classification scheme for services. Not only do such schemes help managers understand customer needs, but they also provide insights into the management of services.[13] For instance, a categorization scheme for services answers questions like these:

- Does the customer have to be present to initiate or terminate the service transaction?
- Does the customer have to be present for the service to be delivered?
- Does the customer participate in the service transaction?
- Is the customer or target of the service changed in some way after the service transaction is completed?
- Is there a high degree of labor intensiveness?
- How much skill is required of the service provider?

Answers to such questions help managers enhance service quality. Consider taking a car to an auto repair shop. If customers have to drop off the car to initiate the service, their satisfaction with the service will be determined, to some extent, by interactions with the personnel, success in explaining their problem, and getting satisfactory results. On the other hand, using an ATM card requires little contact with the bank. The ATM must work and the transaction must be satisfactory, but how the money gets into the machine—the process—is of little interest to customers.

Services are classified according to the type of market or customer (consumer or organizational) they serve. This distinction is important because the buying decision process differs between organizations and consumers. Consumers purchase (and consume) services to satisfy personal needs and wants. Organizational services are used (1) to produce other goods and services or (2) in an organization's ongoing operation. For example, both consumers and organizations need insurance, accounting services, and perhaps lawn care. But the nature of these needs is usually quite different between the two groups. An accountant may help consumers prepare their income tax returns, whereas an organization must maintain a complex set of records for tax purposes. See the Management Highlight below for a classification of services and some examples of each type of service.

Services are also classified by degree of labor intensiveness. Many services—including repairs, education, and hair styling—depend heavily on the knowledge and skills of service providers. Other services, such as telecommunications, gyms, and public transportation, rely more on equipment. Labor-intensive (people-based) services are generally more heterogeneous than are equipment-based services. Consumers tend to view providers of people-based services as the service itself. As we said earlier, flight attendants represent an airline to many people. Consequently, service providers must pay special attention to the selection, training, motivation, and control of employees. Labor-intensive services are especially difficult to standardize.

Managers of labor-intensive services must be on guard for *employee burnout*. Customer service representatives are particularly susceptible to burnout because they are often required to deliver high levels of service quality while caught in the stressful position of perceiving that their organization cannot or will not meet a customer's demand. Service representatives typically work long hours, lack autonomy, bear responsibility without authority, have insufficient resources and guidelines to handle problems, face demanding quotas, and often endure manager apathy. The results of a survey offer clear evidence of burnout's consequences for customer service representatives. The higher the level of burnout, the lower the employee's job satisfaction and organizational commitment. Burnout reduces the employee's energy and leads to reduced efforts at work. Managers should view burnout as a result of stressful work environment. They can alleviate the problem by creating a work culture that supports, recognizes, and rewards customer service representatives.[14]

The third way to classify services is by degree of customer contact. Healthcare, hotels, real estate agencies, and restaurants are examples of high-contact services. With high-contact

---

MANAGEMENT HIGHLIGHT
Classification of Services

Categories	Examples
Type of market	
Consumer	Life insurance, car repairs
Organizational	Lawn care, management consulting
Degree of labor intensiveness	
Labor based	Repairs, executive recruiting
Equipment based	Public transportation, air travel
Degree of customer contact	
High contact	Hotels, healthcare
Low contact	Dry cleaning, motion pictures
Skill of the service provider	
Professional	Legal counsel, accounting services
Nonprofessional	Taxi, janitorial
Goal of the service provider	
Profit	Financial services, overnight delivery
Nonprofit	Government, education

services, actions are generally directed toward individuals. The consumer must be present during production; in fact, the consumer must often go to the production facility. The service facility's physical appearance may be a major factor in the consumer's overall evaluation of a high-contact service. With low-contact services (such as repairs, dry cleaning, and mail services) customers generally do not need to be present during service delivery. (For example, consumers do not wait at a dry cleaner while their clothes are being laundered.) As a result, physical appearance is not as important for low-contact facilities.

A fourth way to classify services is by the service provider's level of skill. Professional services tend to be more complex and more highly regulated than nonprofessional services. In the case of a doctor's physical exam to diagnose a medical problem, consumers often don't know what the actual service or its cost will be until the service is completed, because the final product is situation specific. Also, doctors and surgeons are regulated by laws and by professional associations. Even less-skilled service providers, such as airline pilots, undergo extensive training and retraining, and they must comply with a host of regulations and policies. However, clerks in the concession stands of movie theaters need lower skill levels to carry out their jobs.

Finally, services can be classified according to the service provider's goal: profit or nonprofit. There are several differences between profit and nonprofit services. The objectives of nonprofit organizations are not stated in financial terms, and the benefits of nonprofit services are not measured by profit or return on investment. In addition, nonprofit organizations usually have two audiences: clients and donors. A public school system is targeted to families with school-age children but also relies on the general public for support through taxes. Many nonprofit services, such as legal aid, are targeted to low-income segments.

QUALITY AND PRODUCTIVITY IN SERVICE ORGANIZATIONS

Two major challenges facing service organizations are to improve quality and productivity. Service-quality improvement centers on the quality theme of exceeding customer expectations. Service providers are taught to listen to customers, and to go beyond their expressed needs to deliver service that also meets tacit or implicit needs. For example, the best service organizations help customers determine what they want by giving them options and examples of what will help them achieve their objectives. Good clothing stores don't just have racks of clothing and fitting rooms; they also have helpful employees who can assist the customer in designing a wardrobe.

Service productivity is also a major issue for managers. It goes far beyond merely asking employees to work harder. Service productivity improvements most often come from designing a better system, one that takes advantage of both the skills of the people in the organization and available technology. Delta Air Lines has designed a new service system to help reduce the cost gap with discount airlines. The system makes use of automated kiosks to enable customers to bypass long check-in lines and check their baggage. Delta is the first airline to put all these services—ticketing, baggage checking, and boarding—together as a comprehensive system.[15] The best companies know that real productivity gains come from challenged, empowered, excited, rewarded teams of people. Yet, not all companies are rushing ahead to manage their businesses this way. Two reasons teams have not caught on are that teams aren't easy to manage, and results are not measurable or tangible.[16] We'll discuss these issues more fully in the next section.

Service Quality

Only the customer can judge the quality of services. Thus **service quality** is the conformance of the service to customer specifications and expectations.[17] To a medical clinic's administrators, service quality is often viewed as physicians' credentials; consumers, however, are more concerned with waiting time and interactions with doctors and staff members than with where doctors obtained their degrees. We are moving into a time when service organizations do not merely produce, they perform; and customer value is the focus of competitive advantage. Service organizations must first determine what benefits customers expect to receive and then develop service products that meet those expectations. Performing the wrong functions well for customers isn't service quality. Only by consistently meeting customer expectations can an organization deliver service quality.

True service quality rarely goes unnoticed. But providing service quality is easier said than done. Evidence of poor service is increasing; planes are late, restaurants provide slow or inefficient service, sales clerks are rude. Such occurrences have led humorists to call poor service a growth industry.

To improve the quality of its services, a service provider must first understand how consumers judge service quality. Intangibility makes service quality hard to evaluate. Because the service itself is intangible, consumers generally make quality judgments based on *how* the service is performed. As the extent to which the service is tangible increases (see Exhibit 14.1), consumers' expectations of service quality also increase.[18] Several studies have reported that reliability is the most important determinant of service quality.[19] Building a zero-defects culture is as important in service industries as it is in manufacturing. But doing it right the first time is more difficult for services because of (1) the inseparability of production and consumption and (2) heterogeneity.

Increasing numbers of service-quality measurement instruments are now available for customer service managers. One instrument that managers have applied to a number of service settings, including higher education, is called SERVQUAL.[20] **SERVQUAL** is a survey instrument designed to measure expectations and evaluations of service quality by consumers. The survey provides feedback on two to three dozen specific areas of service. Each area is categorized into five determinant factors, and a score is created for each determinant. The determinant scores are averaged to generate an overall service-quality score.[21]

Some industries have developed their own measurement instrument that allows managers to compare their service rating with others in the industry. For example, dining consumers determine which restaurants meet their quality and value standards using an instrument known as **DINESERV.** Restaurateurs who fail to measure up will soon see declining customer counts as guests switch to competing restaurants. The DINESERV tool is a reliable, relatively simple tool for determining how consumers view a restaurant's quality. The twenty-nine-item questionnaire comprises service-quality standards that fall into five categories: (1) assurance, (2) empathy, (3) reliability, (4) responsiveness, and (5) tangibles. By administering the DINESERV questionnaire to guests, a restaurant manager can get a reading on how customers view the restaurant's quality, identify where problems are, and determine how to solve them. DINESERV also gives managers a quantified measure of what consumers expect in a restaurant.[22]

One danger of measurement instruments used to assess service quality is that they can become ends in themselves. Customer satisfaction managers have a tendency to become more concerned with simply measuring customer satisfaction than actually using the resulting information to improve service quality.[23] Quality-based managers use customer feedback on service quality to improve operations on a continuous basis. The Management Highlight on page 274 presents criteria for judging the quality of services.

MANAGEMENT HIGHLIGHT
Criteria for Judging Service Quality

Criteria	Examples
Reliability: Consistency in performance and dependability	Accuracy in billing Keeping records correctly Performing the service at the designated time
Tangibles: Physical evidence of the service	Physical facilities Appearance of personnel Tools or equipment used to provide the service
Responsiveness: Employees' willingness or readiness to provide service	Mailing a transaction slip immediately Calling the customer back quickly Giving prompt service (e.g., setting up appointments quickly)
Assurance: Employee's knowledge and ability to convey trust and confidence	Knowledge and skill of contact personnel Company name or reputation Personal characteristics of contact personnel
Empathy: Caring and individualized attention to customer	Learning customers' specific requirements Providing specialized individual attention Consideration for the customer

Source: Leonard L. Berry and A. Parasuraman, *Marketing Services; Competing through Quality* (New York: Free Press, 1991), 16; A. Parasuraman, Valerie A. Zeithami, and Leonard L. Berry, "A Conceptual Model of Service Quality and Its Implications for Future Research," *Journal of Marketing,* Fall 1985, p. 47; and A. Parasuraman, Valerie A. Zeithaml, and Leonard L. Berry, "SERVQUAL: A Multiple-Item Scale for Measuring Consumer Perceptions of Service Quality," *Journal of Retailing,* Spring 1988, p. 23.

Service quality is difficult to improve. In some cases companies simply do not recognize that service-quality problems exist. Many dissatisfied customers never complain to the company. For example, airline passengers may not complain to airline companies about the food. Service quality is also difficult to manage. One airline employee may interact with hundreds of customers every day. Managers can't possibly observe each of these encounters and evaluate the quality of services, especially if unhappy customers do not complain. Nonetheless, studies have shown that customers tell twice as many people about bad service experiences as they do about good ones.[24] Customers left unhappy, whether they complain or not, may destroy a service organization.

Service quality is not an accident. It definitely can be nurtured and improved through total organizational commitment. First, managers must take quality seriously. Without commitment to quality at the highest levels of the organization, lower-level employees cannot be expected to follow suit. Next, all employees must be committed to quality. Organizations must develop specific service guidelines that are communicated to employees and enforced by management. Finally, high-quality service must be recognized and rewarded.

In any service organization the front-line workers—bank tellers, flight attendants, receptionists—are the most critical resource. Part of what a service firm sells is its employees.[25] A rude flight attendant is a rude airline; an incompetent receptionist is an incompetent doctor's office. Unfortunately, these front-line employees are often the organization's least-trained and lowest-paid members. Before it can improve service quality, a firm must realize that its employees are the critical link to the service customer.

Service Productivity

According to Peter Drucker, a manager's single greatest challenge is to raise knowledge and service workers' productivity.[26] This involves getting the most out of people. Like manufacturing productivity, **service productivity** is the output per person per hour.

Productivity improves in services when the volume or value of output increases relative to the volume or value of inputs. This can be accomplished by working employees harder, recruiting and training more productive workers, reducing worker turnover, buying more efficient equipment, automating the tasks performed by service employees, eliminating bottlenecks in the production and delivery of services that lead to downtime, and standardizing the process and the services output.[27]

Productivity in the service sector has shown little growth in recent years. Because it is nearly twice as large as the manufacturing sector, the low productivity growth in services pulls down the national average. Nonetheless, capital spending in services has increased steadily for several years. Some economists suggest that service productivity is understated because no data are available for services that employ about 70 percent of the people in service jobs.

The major way to improve service productivity is to invest in people. Frederick W. Taylor used the term *working smarter* to describe a means for increasing productivity without working harder or longer. Working smarter is critical in service jobs. Productivity can be increased by defining the service task and eliminating unnecessary work. Since services are often human performances, or at the very least involve humans, service workers must be trained and retrained; continuous learning must be part of productivity improvements.

The **critical success factors** approach to boosting productivity of service workers directs managers to determine those things that must go right in order to succeed in achieving goals and objectives. The method itself has three stages: (1) list goals and objectives; (2) identify the critical success factors necessary to achieve the goals and objectives; and (3) suggest ways in which the critical success factors are to be measured. Generalized notions of productivity make little sense in a service environment. For example, whereas the number of pages typed is easy to see and count as output, the relationship that a secretary creates between the manager and the outside world is an outcome that's difficult to measure. The context-specific nature of productivity requires an understanding of how a knowledge worker achieves goals and objectives. Once the nature of productivity is understood, measuring it becomes a much simpler task.

Some organizations, because of increased competition and a stagnant economy, have attempted to increase productivity by doing more with less. This involves trimming the number of workers and increasing the remaining employees' efficiency through training and labor-saving technology. New technology provides the tools corporations need, not only to automate existing processes and leverage resources but also to redefine what work gets done and how it gets done. For example, in managing the accounts receivable process, only large firms may be able to justify the cost of in-house, technology-based productivity enhancements. An alternative is to outsource all or part of a firm's operations to computer services firms, commercial finance companies, and banks. The best path to implementing an effective automated solution varies, but a broad range of technology applications can deliver new levels of productivity and customer service.

Under the pressure of international competition, businesses are intent on improving productivity and service in the realization that they have entered the high-performance era. In some ways, offices are like manufacturing plants. White-collar productivity can be measured and improved. Waste can be eliminated. A reliable method of work organization, with service standards for every activity and a favorable work environment, must be established. There has to be a willingness by management to change the organization, to train employees to manage the system, and to encourage them to think and act like owner-managers. Research by the National Center on the Educational Quality of the Workforce has shown that an educational increase of 10 percent among workers in the service sector increases productivity by an average of 11 percent.[28]

Developing a Performance Culture

Obviously performance is important for all businesses, but performance is especially important for service businesses. Service businesses do not *produce,* they *perform;* they don't sell things, they sell performances. And these performances are often labor intensive, meaning the service is a human performance. The human performance is the actual product that customers buy. If human effort is unresponsive and incompetent, so is the product. Most of the complaints that come into Toyota or IBM are aimed at products; most of the complaints that come into Delta or Citicorp are aimed at people.

Service productivity and efficiency, as we already noted, can be increased by investing in people. One such investment is developing a performance culture. An organization has a **performance culture** when everyone can do his or her best work. A major advantage of having a performance culture is increased employee commitment.[29] Managers are responsible for developing a culture in which service employees have the training, knowledge, and freedom to meet customers' needs. Many organizations make the claim that they are "customer driven," but as we will soon see, it takes much more than rhetoric or good intentions to develop a performance culture.

The Components of Peak Performance

Suppose a customer named Josh walks into a post office, asks to buy ten rolls of stamps, and counts out $370. But, after looking in his stamp drawer, the employee says he can sell Josh only sheets, not rolls. Josh explains that sheets will cause a great deal of unnecessary work for his assistant and that rolls are exactly what he needs and wants. The employee replies that if he sells Josh ten rolls, he will have none left in his drawer. "That's great," Josh responds. "You're having a good day. You've sold out."

The employee then explains to Josh that it's a post office policy that he can't sell all of his rolls, because then he won't have any for other customers later in his shift. Josh notes that a recurring fantasy of every businessperson he knows is to sell out. Josh then suggests to the employee that he buy four rolls, and then come back later (perhaps in disguise) and buy three more, and so on.[30]

We can learn several important lessons from this story. First, customer satisfaction is not the organization's objective. Second, a company policy is stopping the employee from doing his job. Third, the customer is being penalized by a policy he knew nothing about until he engaged in the transaction.

Here's another scenario to consider. On the first hot day of May, Maria, a woman with a 1993 model car, finds that the car's air conditioner is broken. Even though the car is over ten years old, it has been driven only 35,000 miles, has never had a single problem, and would cost over $20,000 to replace. So, deciding to get the car repaired, Maria takes it to the dealership where she bought it. There, the dealer agrees that the car is in great shape and is worth repairing, gives Maria a ride to work, and promises the car for later that day.

The air conditioner problem is diagnosed as a faulty o-ring that caused the freon to leak out. Though the part was inexpensive, the labor bill is over $200. The car is ready as promised, and the air conditioner works like a charm—for two days. Unfortunately, the mechanic missed the real problem, a more serious one with the condenser. When Maria returns to the dealership, the man working at the counter offers to put the amount already paid toward replacing the condenser, but Maria doesn't want to invest another $400 in the car even though it's in good shape. The employee asks her, "What would you like us to do?" She replies, "Refund my money." She leaves with a check five minutes later.

There is something to be learned from this scenario also. First, the service department at this dealership is customer oriented. Second, service quality is delivering what you promise when you promise it. And third, even though some problems cannot be prevented, organizations can recover from them. Recovery training should be employed to teach service workers how to make decisions on their own and to help them develop an awareness of customers' concerns.[31] Without the authority, the ability, and a sense of the customer's feelings, the service employee wouldn't have refunded the money.

The first episode illustrates an organization that lacks the culture to enable employees to perform at their best. The second episode illustrates a peak performance. The postal worker was operating at a minimum, the worker at the service garage at a maximum. Interestingly, both workers chose to do what they did. But in one case the worker voted in favor of the customer—probably because leaders of that organization had established a performance culture.

The foundation of all peak performances and the development of a performance culture is **discretionary effort**, the difference between the minimum amount of effort a worker must expend to keep from being penalized (acceptable performance) and the maximum amount a person can bring to a job.[32] Discretionary effort is that effort over which workers have the most control and over which managers have the least control. As Exhibit 14.2 shows, jobs highest in discretionary effort are customer contact jobs and knowledge jobs. As we move from the manufacturing sector to the service sector, the discretionary content of jobs increases. Assembly-line workers don't bring much discretionary effort to their jobs because machines dictate workers' output. Teachers or consultants, on the other hand, bring a great deal of discretion to their jobs.

Peak performance (the highest level of performance a worker can achieve) is the sum of acceptable performance and discretionary effort.[33] Returning to our two episodes, workers become or fail to become peak performers when their work requires discretionary effort, the "choose-to-do" part of their job and not the "have-to-do" part of their job—acceptable performance. Thus discretionary effort is the common denominator of

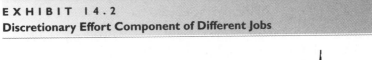

EXHIBIT 14.2
Discretionary Effort Component of Different Jobs

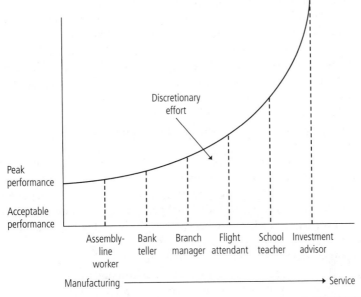

peak performance, and it is the critical element for managers who wish to develop a high-performance culture in their organizations.

Achieving Peak Performance

Naturally firms want to encourage peak performance. But this is quite difficult because discretionary effort—the key to achieving peak performance—is not easily controlled by managers. Some service workers are satisfied with acceptable performance, which their customers come to accept. But the reality of today's highly competitive global economy is that acceptable performance is not acceptable. There may be little difference between products offered by various banks, such as checking accounts, auto loans, and savings accounts. But one bank may provide better service than another. When services are the same, a firm wins or loses with performance. The challenge facing managers is to unleash workers' discretionary effort. Additional discretionary effort can be gained by giving employees responsibilities for results, focusing on employees' strengths, celebrating successes, and building better communication.[34]

Empowering employees to make decisions and take action without management's approval increases the likelihood that discretionary effort will be exercised. Employees who fear the consequences of making a mistake or who, because of policies, cannot make a decision on their own are less likely to exercise discretion. The postal worker couldn't sell the stamps in rolls because of a policy, and either didn't care about the customer or (more likely) was afraid to break the policy. Service managers have begun to empower workers and encourage them to exercise discretion, realizing this has a positive impact on service quality and customer satisfaction. But empowerment alone does not ensure that a performance culture is created.[35] Managers must be committed to developing a responsive organizational structure that encourages performance, and employees must be motivated and committed to the organization's goals. This means taking extra care in hiring workers and paying close attention to matters of personality and psychology (matching the right worker with the right job). It also means giving employees adequate authority, giving them more training, and linking at least part of their pay with customer satisfaction.

Management Commitment.   In Chapter 6 we said that an appropriate organizational structure reinforces and rewards behaviors that accomplish the organization's goals. It is management's job to articulate these goals and develop a structure that facilitates achieving them. If managers aren't committed to customers, workers are likely to behave in the same way. Thus managers must identify performances that enhance the organization's efficiency and effectiveness. In many service organizations managers and workers alike spend an inordinate amount of their time, energy, and resources performing activities that aren't critical. Managers must identify those activities that are most critical and focus the organization's attention on being the best in the world at these activities. To do this, managers must train employees well, provide them with the tools and resources needed to do their job, and then let them do it.[36]

Managers should also tie rewards directly to performance that enhances the work's efficiency and effectiveness. Recognition should be given to individuals who perform beyond the acceptable level. Employees should be encouraged to participate with management in defining goals and standards against which individual performance can be judged. In short, if there is no incentive to perform above acceptable levels, individuals likely perform at minimums rather than maximums. Managers must be fully committed to a performance culture; their every action must clearly demonstrate this commitment to subordinates. The worst thing a manager can do is talk performance culture but take actions that convey a much different message to workers. Achieving competitive success through people involves fundamentally altering how one thinks about the workforce and the employment relationship. It means achieving success by working with people, not by replacing them or limiting the scope of their activities. It entails seeing the workforce as a source of strategic advantage, not just as a cost to be minimized or avoided. Firms that take this different perspective are often able to successfully outmaneuver and outperform their rivals.[37]

Employee Commitment. Services clearly differ greatly from goods. In many instances the service is a human performance. Unfortunately the front-line worker is often the lowest-paid and least-trained member of the organization. With new technologies in banking—automatic teller machines, direct deposit of paychecks, direct withdrawal of bills and other payments—we rarely have to go into a bank. This has led some bankers to conclude that service encounters with the bank are becoming less important, when the opposite is actually true. With all this technology, a customer personally visits a bank only when he or she has a special problem or need. Service contact personnel at the bank now take on increased significance as machines complete the more routine tasks. The same can be said for many other services.

Organizations can encourage employee commitment by investing in service workers. Most performance cultures are characterized by a high degree of training. Workers are trained not only to perform their job, but also to solve problems, deal with irate customers, and deal with other members of the organization. Knowledge is important—knowledge of how one job fits into the overall scheme of the organization, knowledge of other jobs, knowledge of the organization's goals, and knowledge of the customers. The conditions under which quality service can be provided must also be present. When a service worker needs operational support or advice to help a customer, the support must be readily available. Without training, knowledge, and support, a worker cannot be truly empowered. Unfortunately, some managers believe empowerment merely means telling workers that they are free to make decisions. To make the right decisions, however, employees also need training and knowledge.

Conclusion
Managing Services

Services have become a vital part of today's economy. Because services are intangible, and often involve human effort, they present some unique problems to managers. By understanding these unique aspects of services, managers should be in a better position to manage service employees.

SUGGESTED READINGS

Berry, Leonard. *On Great Service: A Framework for Action.* New York: Simon & Schuster, 1995.

———. *Discovering the Soul of Service: The Nine Drivers of Sustainable Business Success.* New York: Simon & Schuster, 1999.

Chase, Richard B., and Sriram Dasu. "Want to Perfect Your Company's Service? Use Behavioral Science," *Harvard Business Review,* June 2001, pp. 79–84.

Heskett, James L., W. Earl Sasser Jr., and Leonard A. Schlesinger. *The Service Profit Chain.* New York: Simon & Schuster, 1997.

Shaw, Colin, and John Ivens. *Building Great Customer Experiences.* New York: Palgrave MacMillan, 2002.

Zeithaml, Valarie. *Delivering Quality Service.* New York: Simon & Schuster, 1990.

ENDNOTES

1. Paula M. Saunders, Robert F. Scherer, and Herbert E. Brown, "Delighting Customers by Managing Expectations for Service Quality: An Example from the Optical Industry," *Journal of Applied Business Research* (Spring 1995): 101–109.

2. Steven J. Skinner, *Marketing* (Boston: Houghton Mifflin, 1994), 348.

3. Joan O. Fredericks and James M. Salter, "Beyond Customer Satisfaction," *Management Review,* May 1995, pp. 29–32.

4. *Statistical Abstracts of the United States,* 2002, p. 419.

5. Robert E. Yuskavage and Erich H. Strassner, "Gross Domestic Product by Industry for 2002," *Survey of Current Business,* May 2003, pp. 7–15.

6. Martha Farnsworth Riche, "America's New Workers," *American Demographics,* February 1988, pp. 34–41.

7. Stephen K. Koernig, "E-scapes: The Electronic Physical Environment and Service Tangibility," *Psychology and Marketing,* February 2003, pp. 151–167.

8. Rob Muller, "Training for Change," *Canadian Business Review,* Spring 1995, pp. 16–19.

9. Peter K. Mills and James H. Morris, "Clients as 'Partial' Employees of Service Organizations: Role Development in Client Participation," *Academy of Management Journal* (December 1986): 726–735.

10. Sandy Jap, "The Employee's Viewpoint of Critical Service Encounters," *Stores,* January 1995, pp. RR4–RR6.

11. Choy L. Wong and Dean Tjosvold, "Goal Interdependence and Quality Marketing Services," *Psychology & Marketing,* May 1995, pp. 189–205.

12. Carol A. Reeves and David A. Bednar, "Quality as Symphony," *Cornell Hotel & Restaurant Administration Quarterly,* June 1995, pp. 72–79.

13. Christopher H. Lovelock, "Classifying Services to Gain Strategic Marketing Insights," *Journal of Marketing* (Summer 1983): 9–20.

14. Jagdip Singh, Jerry R. Goolsby, and Gary K. Rhoads, "Employee Burnout and Its Implications for Customer Service Representatives," *Stores,* April 1995, pp. RR8–RR9.

15. Charles Haddad, "Delta's Flight to Self-Service," *Business Week,* July 7, 2003, pp. 92–93.

16. John Hagerman, "Teams and Measurable Results," *CMA Magazine,* March 1995, p. 6.

17. Leonard L. Berry, David R. Bennett, and Carter W. Brown, *Service Quality: A Profit Strategy for Financial Institutions* (Burr Ridge, IL: Dow Jones-Irwin, 1989), 26.

18. Charlene Pleger Bebko, "Service Intangibility and Its Impact on Consumer Expectations of Service Quality," *Journal of Services Marketing,* no. 1 (2000): 9–26.

19. Leonard L. Berry and A. Parasuraman, *Marketing Services* (New York: Free Press, 1991), 15–16.

20. Elizabeth Anderson, "High Tech v. High Touch: A Case Study of TQM Implementation in Higher Education," *Managing Service Quality*, 1995, pp. 48–56.

21. John Chidchester, "Tailoring Your Survey," *Credit Union Management*, April 1995, pp. 30–31.

22. Pete Stevens, Bonnie Knutson, and Mark Patton, "DINESERV: A Tool for Measuring Service Quality in Restaurants," *Cornell Hotel & Restaurant Administration Quarterly*, April 1995, pp. 56–60.

23. Scott M. Broetzmann et al., "Customer Satisfaction: Lip Service or Management Tool?" *Managing Service Quality*, 1995, pp. 13–18.

24. Patricia Sellers, "How to Handle Customers' Gripes," *Fortune*, October 24, 1988, pp. 88–100.

25. A. Parasuraman, "Customer Oriented Corporate Cultures Are Crucial to Services Marketing Success," *Journal of Services Marketing* (Summer 1987): 39–46.

26. Peter F. Drucker, "The New Productivity Challenge," *Harvard Business Review*, November–December 1991, pp. 70–79.

27. Curtis R. McClaughlin and Sydney Coffey, "Measuring 'Productivity' in Services," in *Managing Services*, ed. Christopher H. Lovelock (Englewood Cliffs, NJ: Prentice Hall, 1992), 395–396.

28. Regina Eisman, "Higher Education, Higher Output," *Incentive*, July 1995, p. 15.

29. Jeff Rosenthal and Mary Ann Masarech, "High-Performance Cultures: How Values Can Drive Business Results," *Journal of Organizational Excellence* (Spring 2003): 3–18.

30. James H. Donnelly Jr. and Steven J. Skinner, *The New Banker* (Burr Ridge, IL: Dow Jones-Irwin, 1989), 33–34.

31. Christopher W. L. Hart, James L. Heskett, and W. Earl Sasser Jr., "The Profitable Art of Service Recovery," *Harvard Business Review*, July–August 1990, pp. 148–156.

32. Donnelly and Skinner, *The New Banker*, pp. 21–24.

33. Donnelly and Skinner, pp. 21–26.

34. Ed Emde, "Voluntary Efforts," *Executive Excellence*, January 1999, p. 10.

35. Scott W. Kelley, "Discretion and the Service Employee," *Journal of Retailing* (Spring 1993): 104–126.

36. Bill Catlette and Richard Hadden, "Increasing Employee Performance," *Security Management*, May 2003, pp. 26–30.

37. Jeffrey Pfeffer, Toru Hatano, and Timo Santalainen, "Producing Sustainable Competitive Advantage Through the Effective Management of People," *Academy of Management Executive*, February 1995, pp. 55–72.

Chapter
Fifteen

Managing Organizational Change

Change is inevitable, as you know, but it can be evolutionary or revolutionary. *Evolutionary change* occurs gradually, sometimes almost without notice. Behavioral change, such as an increased tolerance for the differences among us, is an outgrowth of evolutionary societal changes. *Revolutionary change* is abrupt; it happens—and the change is forever. Technological advances, such as the introduction of a new chemical compound or the release of a new microprocessing device, make existing products quickly obsolete. Managers, who must navigate the changing domain determining whether they face evolution or revolution, have a twofold obligation to meet daily operational demands as well as adapt to changing future circumstances. To some in our contemporary world, change appears to be occurring at an unprecedented and accelerating rate. Perhaps what makes these managers believe this era is uniquely challenging is that much of modern organizational change is driven by external forces beyond their control, such as market competition or technology. In the 1950s and 1960s, large American firms had few competitors and there was little pressure for organizational change. Social, demographic, and economic changes of the past few decades have altered the competitive landscape. Today the economic picture is far different than it was even a few years ago. Global competition, which gives consumers more choices, is a major driver of organizational change. In fact, truly global competition is a phenomenon that has become reality only slowly, over the past 20 years or so. But the perception doesn't always measure up to that reality.

In this chapter you'll learn about four targets of change and how to overcome resistance to change. We'll take a look at a model for managing change in organizations, the role of change agents, and the strategy of change.

The global nature of competition requires that managers think of ways to change their organization continuously in order to gain competitive advantage. Today's managers must anticipate the future and then change their organization in the present to prepare for that future. But it is not just their company that they must consider; managers must speculate about the future of the industry as well as its future economic circumstances.

During the past decade, managers have led the following organizational changes:

- *Internet access and local computer networks*—increasing worker productivity and connecting company to suppliers.

- *E-commerce*—using the Internet to market products or services.

- *Flexible work systems*—job sharing, telecommuting, and other innovative approaches.

- *Empowerment*—sharing power with more organizational stakeholders. Management has given the worker more power in the workplace, including involvement in decision making, planning, and customer satisfaction.

- *Restructuring and downsizing*—restructuring has decreased costs mainly by reducing the number of workers required to run the organization. Many organizations have downsized to become leaner, with less middle management and fewer layers in the corporate hierarchy.

- *Quality*—implementing strategies to increase product quality. Such tangible outcomes as high reliability, fewer defects, and better fit and finish are today's management mantras.

CHANGE TARGETS

At the most general level of distinction, change has four targets. *Organization-wide change* targets, such as restructuring or TQM, have an impact on the entire organization. *Group change* targets several people working collectively on a common goal. For example, using new group decision-making software to enhance group performance requires a change in how the group functions and group members interact. *Intergroup change* targets the nature of the interaction between groups. Introducing Groupware software into the organization requires different groups to change their behavior and attitudes. *Individual change* targets the person, or in this case, the employee. Safety training required by the Occupational Safety and Health Administration (OSHA) is an example of change targeted at the individual and possibly attempting to change both attitudes and behavior.

We can summarize these changes taking place in American business and industry as follows: (1) global competition; (2) restructuring; (3) technological advances; and (4) digital technology, including the Internet and e-commerce. These changes will pressure managers to make a wide variety of adjustments if they want their companies to remain competitive in the twenty-first century. New companies will come into being, and old ones that don't change their strategies will die. This is an era of instant communication and fast-changing technologies. It's an era in which customers demand quality and value; it's also an era of employee empowerment and changing global relationships and structures. Traditional ways of doing business are gone, along with comfortable relationships. It's hard to let go of systems and habits that have developed over a lifetime; but for companies to achieve and maintain success, they must continuously reinvent themselves.[1]

Over the past decade, many companies have tried to remake themselves into better competitors. Their efforts are carried on under many banners: total quality management, reengineering, rightsizing, restructuring, and cultural change. In almost every case, the goal has been the same—to cope with a new, more challenging market by changing the way business is conducted. A few of these change programs have been very successful. A few have been utter failures. Most fall somewhere in between, though with a distinct tilt toward the failure end of the scale. The lessons learned from these failures will be relevant to more and more organizations as the business environment becomes increasingly competitive. One lesson companies have taken away is that change involves numerous phases that, together, usually take a long time to complete. A second lesson is that critical mistakes in the management of any of the phases can have a devastating impact on the success of the change effort.[2]

In the following sections, we discuss some forces of change. We present frameworks and models that can serve not only as blueprints for ordering managerial thinking about change but also as guidelines for first diagnosing and then managing change. In a later section, we'll discuss various intervention methods in relation to change.

CHANGE FORCES

Today's organizational domain includes unpredictable and uncontrollable domestic and international forces. New developments in mergers and acquisitions, regulation, privatization, downsizing, union–management collaboration, high-involvement participation, plant closings, reengineering, managing culturally diverse workers, and environmental protection occupy managers' time. These and many other forces from outside and inside the organization demand attention.

Organizations around the world have been experiencing increasingly rapid change for much of the second half of the twentieth century. With the globalization of markets, worldwide telecommunications, and increasingly rapid and efficient travel over the past decade, the need for organizations to continuously reinvent themselves is greater than ever. The average U.S. business lasts only about forty years. Complex and rapid changes in the world's economic and social climates heighten the threat of survival. Organizations that learn to search creatively for the future can transform themselves when they confront the chaos of a constantly changing competitive environment.[3]

Strategies for Change

All change strategies have one common purpose—adaptation. The success of a change strategy rests on its ability to be adapted to changing circumstances in a timely manner; otherwise, an organization risks becoming noncompetitive and ultimately going out of business. Change strategies help the organization adapt to changing circumstances while creating greater value for organizational stakeholders. Exhibit 15.1 shows three common change strategies.

EXHIBIT 15.1
Common Organizational Strategies

Strategy	Purpose
Restructuring	Efficiency—eliminate organizational layers and people to reduce costs.
Reengineering	Efficiency—better service through the redesign of organizational processes.
Continuous Improvement	Increase quality or service—ongoing assessment of product or service, including customer satisfaction.

- **Restructuring** is a revolutionary change that focuses on redesign of the organization's structure. In most cases it means "de-layering," or eliminating units or departments. It can also mean the consolidation of functions. The purpose of restructuring is to create value by both increasing performance and reducing costs.

- **Reengineering** is a revolutionary change that focuses on an organization's processes. As part of a larger system, a **process** is a series of activities or tasks that require external inputs in the creation of outputs. For example, purchasing, manufacturing, and sales represent three common organizational processes. The purpose of reengineering is to create value by redesigning efficient organizational processes that meet customer needs.[4]

- **Continuous improvement** is the evolutionary process of reexamining organizational practices. Continuous improvement processes identify key organizational performance indicators at all levels of the organization. Next, they periodically compare an actual organization transaction against standards. The goal is to compare actual performance against a standard and make needed adjustments to better serve the customer.[5]

These three organizational change strategies are common, but they don't guarantee success. Their success depends largely on top management support, employee commitment, and the organization's ability to make tough decisions. Change strategies can be effective only to the degree that their leader has a good understanding of the industry and its future direction.

Internal Forces

Internal change forces are pressures that come from within the organization. Internal sources for change can be a need for cost reduction, negative morale or poor employee attitudes, and the overall organization design (structure).

Cost Reduction.   Sometimes the internal pressure is the cost of producing a microchip or car. For example, unit cost increases; therefore, pricing the product at a reasonable amount to make a sale is a force that may signal a need for change. If the product costs too much to produce, it can't be priced competitively.

Employee Attitude.   Poor worker morale over some inequity in the reward system could be an internal pressure point that a manager becomes aware of and must address. Although attitudes may be difficult to observe directly, increased grievance rates, absenteeism, or turnover may suggest poor or decreasing morale. Identifying internally driven forces for change is sometimes difficult. Is poor morale caused by the culture, the structure, or the manager; or, does the worker bring this attitude to work? It's a difficult question to answer.

Organization Design.   A common problem that calls for an assessment of the current organization design is a mismatch between a new strategy and an old structure. For example, suppose that as part of a new strategy, a CEO mandates a 20 percent cost reduction, including staff, for all departments. As a result, some departments can be absorbed into other departments and still others might be outright eliminated as part of the implementation plan. The outcome is a mismatch between the new strategy and the old structure. Remember, the old structure was in support of the old strategy—not the new strategy. For optimal performance, the new strategy needs a new structure.

Regardless of changes in an organization's environment, mission, or structure, employee satisfaction and quality of work life remain significant concerns for most organizational change and development efforts. Although morale and motivation are not often the impetus for such change programs, they are almost always tied inextricably to the problems that have manifested themselves. One of a manager's most effective tools for understanding and diagnosing the issues involved is the organizational survey. Surveys can be conducted by using questionnaires or through interviews. They help managers stay in touch with the forces of change that are at work among employees. By staying in touch with these forces, managers can anticipate changes and turn them to positive outcomes.[6]

External Forces

External change forces are pressures that originate outside the organization; they can be a signal that change is needed. External sources for change can be governmental actions, competitive forces, and social forces.

Governmental Forces. In 1991 an executive order of the governor created the California Environmental Protection Agency (EPA). The agency's mission was to restore, protect, and enhance the environment in order to ensure public health, environmental quality, and economic vitality. In the process of fulfilling its mission, the California EPA created laws that required organizations to alter their way of conducting business. For example, automobile emissions laws mandated lower amounts of emissions. Automobile manufacturers failing to meet the environmental requirements would be unable to sell any vehicles in the state of California—and California accounts for 30 percent of all domestic vehicle sales. Manufacturers had to comply or risk substantial losses.

On a more positive note, sometimes a government mandate has mixed blessings. Take the example of the use of oxygenators to meet environmental requirements. Typically, gasoline refiners use MTBE (a hydrocarbon oxygenator) to meet emission standards. However, MTBE is toxic and has a negative impact on the environment. Ethanol, a form of alcohol, is an environmentally friendly substitute for MTBE. California and other states have given ethanol producers an economic boost by eliminating MTBE use in their states. As a result, MTBE sales have dropped but ethanol sales have increased. This is an unintended benefit for ethanol producers and good news for the environment. Ethanol can be used as an additive to increase octane ratings in gasoline and also results in lower emissions at the same time. However, it is more expensive than MTBE. As a result, the change in California law will ultimately create more demand for ethanol, resulting in production efficiencies, and lowering the price in the long run.

Competitive Forces. Competitors force change by introducing new products, new supplier relationships (business-to-business software connections), new uses of technology, or new legal strategies. Change forced by competitors requires action. The success of General Motors in the diesel engine market is one example of competitive change. GM's successful Duramax™ diesel engine is quiet, produces no smoke and less odor, and has greater fuel efficiency than similar diesel engines produced by Ford and DaimlerChrysler. In response, Ford and DaimlerChrysler had to develop similar attributes in their diesel engines or risk a significant loss of market share in the diesel truck market.

Social Forces. Concern with equity and fairness is a hallmark of American life. Our emphasis on cultural diversity today is a powerful external force that often causes organizations to change their practices. Sometimes cost prohibitions make organizations less than enthusiastic about change, but the law encourages and often mandates a timeline for change. Integrating and utilizing the talents of a more diverse workforce, and effectively rewarding this culturally diverse workforce, will require changes in attitude, interpersonal interaction, and perception. Changes in managers' cultural awareness are also needed.

RESISTANCE TO CHANGE

Any change, no matter how clearly beneficial to employees and the organization as a whole, will meet with and often be sabotaged by resistance. Management scholar Paul Lawrence noted many years ago that resistance to change is more often a social or human problem than a technical one.[7] The failure of many recent large-scale efforts at corporate change can be traced directly to employee resistance. Total quality management (TQM) is an example. Evidence shows that many firms that have attempted to apply TQM in their organization have gained little competitive advantage. Similarly, many reengineering efforts have also fallen short of expectations.[8] A major reason for these disappointing results is employee resistance to change. The following are some reasons that people resist change.

Self-Interest

Some employees resist change because they have a personal interest in the way things are currently done. They know how to successfully complete the work as it is defined today; they are comfortable with their boss and peers, but threatened by change. For most of us, our interactions at work are based on our technical knowledge and expertise. Think about how threatening the introduction of desktop computing and e-mail was to people whose expertise was based on old methods and ideas, such as microfiche and fax machines. Many employees felt unable to learn new technology and resisted efforts to learn new ways. When such changes take place, people often fear a loss of social position that can accompany decreasing expertise. They know that fewer people will seek them out as a source of knowledge and expertise in the future.

Habit

For many employees, the routine of working the same way day after day has a certain appeal. Life is a pattern of getting up, going to work, coming home, and going to bed. People become accustomed to sameness; they get in the habit of doing tasks a certain way. Changes in personnel, work flow, structure, or technology threaten the continuation of a pattern or set of habits.

Fear

Change introduces uncertainty and a degree of fear. People fear having to learn a new way or trying to become accustomed to a new leader—and possibly failing. Employees are sometimes given an opportunity to relocate and take a different, better-paying job in the firm. But such changes are considered risky, and they introduce the possibility of failing.

Peer Pressure

Peers often apply pressure to resist change. For example, peers may resist the introduction of automation because they assume, sometimes correctly, that fewer workers will be needed to perform the job. These peers can create pressure on their colleagues, who might otherwise emotionally and personally support automation and its potential to improve productivity.

Bureaucratic Inertia

Large government institutions, educational institutions, and business organizations have a built-in resistance to change because of the traditional rules, policies, and procedures. The refrain is: "This is how we've done things for years." Why change? The Big Three auto manufacturers had a degree of bureaucratically built-in resistance to the smaller Japanese cars that arrived in the 1970s. These smaller, more gas-efficient cars caught the attention of American consumers—especially after the gas shortages of 1973. But the Big Three simply didn't respond in a timely or aggressive fashion. All three were steeped in traditional thinking about small cars—especially Japanese autos.

Inflexible rules, policies, and procedures preclude the use of adaptive changes in any organization. Bureaucracy, red tape, and traditionally built-in ways of conducting business are difficult to overcome. Often managers know they're in a bureaucratic maze, but find it difficult to wrestle through the barriers, delays, and stonewalling that can become common.

REDUCING RESISTANCE TO CHANGE

Before an organization can implement changes, its leaders must not only overcome or reduce resistance but also encourage and build support for those changes. There are no simple, always-perfect prescriptions for reducing resistance, but the following six options may prove useful.

Education and Communication

When lack of information is the problem, managers will find it especially helpful to explain in meetings, through memos, or in reports why change is needed. Open communication helps people prepare for the change. Paving the way, showing the logic, and keeping everyone informed lowers resistance. This option is usually time-consuming. The emphasis of a communications plan should be proactive rather than reactive. All messages should be consistent and repeated through various channels such as videos, memos, newsletters, e-mail, and regular meetings.

Participation and Involvement

Bringing together those to be affected to help design and implement the change likely will increase their commitment. Empowering employees, paying attention to customers, and customizing the change program to company culture all contribute to successful implementation. Behavioral change is essential to long-term success. Change means different attitudes, behaviors, and often a new way of thinking about the familiar. It may mean embracing technology.

Facilitation and Support

When implementing change, it's important for managers to be supportive. They must provide training opportunities and help to facilitate the change by showing concern for subordinates, being good listeners, and going to bat for their employees on important issues. Behaviors exhibited by leaders and managers can influence employees' attitudes and perceptions about their work and their organization. Research conducted during a change effort in the marketing and sales division of an international pharmaceutical firm showed that different types of behaviors for managers and senior managers were significantly related to employee attitudes and perceptions.[9] Managers need to behave in ways that show commitment to the change as well as support for employees while they are learning to deal with the change.

Negotiation and Agreement

Resistance can be reduced through negotiation. Discussion and analysis can help managers identify points of negotiation and agreement. Negotiated agreement involves giving something to another party to reduce resistance. For example, convincing a person to move to a less desirable work location may require paying them a bonus or increasing their monthly salary. Once this negotiation agreement is reached, others may expect the manager to grant similar concessions in the future.

Manipulation and Co-optation

Manipulation involves the use of deception to convince others that a change is in their best interests. Holding back information, playing one person against another, and providing one-sided information are examples of manipulation. **Co-opting** an individual involves giving the person critical of the change a major role in the design or implementation of the change. For example, during the federal government bailout of Chrysler Motors, Chrysler appointed then president of the UAW Douglas Fraser to Chrysler's board of directors. The union had demanded a wage increase, or a strike would follow. However, once Fraser was a member of the board, he had a new understanding of the situation. Chrysler turned an adversary into a member of a decision-making body, thus co-opting Fraser. In the end, the strike was averted by using the strategy of co-optation.[10]

Coercion

In using coercion, managers engage in threatening behavior. They threaten employees with job loss, reduced promotion opportunities, poor job assignments, and loss of privileges. The coercion is intended to reduce a person's resistance to the management-initiated change. Coercive behavior can be risky because it can generate bad feelings and hostility.[11]

Companies that are successful in implementing change report much greater employee commitment to initiatives, smaller productivity fluctuations during implementation, and significantly shorter implementation timelines. Managers who want to overcome resistance to change must collect data to identify the relative strength of each factor that is causing the resistance as well as how it varies by stakeholder group.[12]

A MODEL FOR MANAGING CHANGE IN ORGANIZATIONS

Change is, obviously, a process that occurs over time. Managers must recognize that change is needed and then initiate the process. For example, suppose a firm's CEO recognizes that the competition has reduced the price of its product, resulting in increased sales and market share for price cutters. To ensure that his organization has the ability to

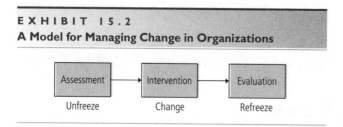

EXHIBIT 15.2
A Model for Managing Change in Organizations

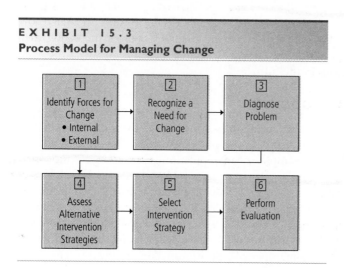

EXHIBIT 15.3
Process Model for Managing Change

better control future pricing, the CEO wants to reduce overall costs to gain pricing flexibility. His solution is to begin an organization-wide restructuring. While the impetus for restructuring was external, the organization will have many internal changes in the form of processes, structures, and people to ultimately reach the CEO's goal of reducing system-wide costs.

Noted psychologist Kurt Lewin developed an elegant and concise model of change. He believed that change occurs in three stages: unfreezing, changing, and refreezing. The first stage in the process of change is **unfreezing** or readying people for the change. The second stage involves the **intervention** or actual change. The final stage is **refreezing** or implementing the change. The model illustrated in Exhibit 15.2 is based on Kurt Lewin's general concept of change as well as other factors that influence change. Exhibit 15.3 illustrates a more detailed process model for managing change, which emphasizes six distinct stages that managers must consider when making decisions.

Stage 1 Identify Forces for Change

The forces that drive a change can be internal or external. For example, an internal force (employees) generates concerns about compensation. But it may be an external force (the market) that stimulates the change in compensation practices due to the organization's inability to hire sufficient employees to conduct business. Thus the impetus for change can come either from an internal force, an external force, or a combination of the two forces.

Stage 2 Recognize a Need for Change

Managers must recognize that change is needed, or that the present state is inadequate. Recognition is easy if the magnitude of the problems (such as market-share losses, more equal employment opportunity discrimination suits, rising turnover, or declining profit margins) is significant. Unfortunately, the indicators that change is needed aren't always dramatic. A loss here and there, a complaining group of customers, a disgruntled technician, or a lost contract isn't always a sign that change is necessary.

Some companies have adopted a new technique for helping managers recognize the need for change. The technique is known as the sense-and-respond (SR) model. The SR model involves sensing change earlier and responding to it faster. According to Steve Haeckel of the IBM Advanced Business Institute, the SR model requires managers to be very good at conceptual thinking.[13] That means managers must be able to think broadly and to entertain two or more (possibly contradictory) ideas about issues at once. The SR model requires managers to build an organizational context that delegates operational decision making and the design of adaptive systems to the people or teams accountable for producing results (unfreezing begins). The model encourages all employees to be alert to changes in the environment and to act on those changes to improve the company's competitive position.[14]

Stage 3 Diagnose the Problem

Diagnosis is an analytical process that generates valuable information to determine the exact nature of a problem or the need for change. While direct observation is quite common, diagnosis can be conducted using a variety of techniques.

Force Field Analysis. **Force field analysis** is a popular diagnosis strategy developed by Kurt Lewin. This technique is a means of diagnosing situations and analyzing the various change strategies that can be used in a particular situation.

Gap Analysis. **Gap analysis** identifies the difference between the current state of the organization and the desired state of the organization. Once the gap is identified, then force field analysis becomes a useful tool. Before undertaking any change strategy, it's useful for managers to determine what they have working in their favor (driving forces) and what forces are working against them (restraining forces).

- **Driving forces** are those forces affecting a situation that are pushing in a particular direction; they tend to initiate a change and keep it going. In relation to improving productivity in an organization, examples of driving forces are words of praise from a manager, effective reward systems, and a high level of employee involvement in decision making.

- **Restraining forces** are those forces that act to restrain or decrease driving forces. Low morale, anger, or inadequate work tools are examples of restraining forces. **Equilibrium** is the point at which the sum of the driving forces equals the sum of the restraining forces.

To understand these concepts, imagine that you manage a fast-food restaurant. If you decide to initiate a significant change in the restaurant, some driving forces might be customer demand, competition, cost pressures, government regulations, and franchise policies. Restraining forces might include lack of resources, low employee morale, low employee skill level, employee resistance to change, or lack of knowledge.

In utilizing force field analysis for developing a change strategy, managers can use these guidelines:

- *When driving forces far outweigh the restraining forces* in power and frequency in a change situation, managers interested in driving for change can often push on and overpower the restraining forces.

- *When restraining forces are much stronger than the driving forces*, managers interested in driving for change have several choices: (1) They can give up the change effort, realizing that it will be too difficult to implement; or (2) they can pursue the change effort, but concentrate on maintaining the driving forces in the situation while attempting, one by one, to change each of the restraining forces into driving forces— or somehow to immobilize each of the restraining forces so that they are no longer factors in the situation. The second choice is possible, but very time-consuming.

- *When driving forces and restraining forces are fairly equal* in a change situation, managers probably will have to begin pushing the driving forces, while at the same time attempting to convert or immobilize some or all of the restraining forces.

Stage 4 Assess Alternative Intervention Strategies

In stage 4, managers must assess several different intervention methods, and choose one of them. We'll discuss several intervention methods later in the chapter, including survey feedback, team building, empowerment, and foresight-led change.

Stage 5 Select Intervention Strategy and Implementation

After evaluating the pros and cons of various change techniques, the manager should select one or some combination of alternatives and then implement it. This is the change phase of the model in Exhibit 15.2. Implementation often isn't given enough consideration in attempts to bring about lasting change. At this point refreezing begins.

Stage 6 Perform Evaluation and Begin the Process Again

Managers want to learn whether changes have occurred, and if so, what has been accomplished. Is the profit margin improved? Has morale improved? Have customers returned to our brand? It's hard to measure change over time, because many uncontrollable changes often influence the original change effort. In the middle of a structural change, a new government regulation may have been passed that directly affects employees in the units undergoing change. Suppose the regulation means that employees must now file additional government paperwork. But employees have continually complained about paperwork, and with the new regulation, now there's even more of it. Did the structural change cause the lower morale that currently exists, or was it the new regulation? It would be hard to say what lies behind the lower morale.

Measurement

Measuring skills, attitudes, and values before, during, and after change is often difficult. But measurement is necessary for evaluating the effectiveness of a change. When a complete measurement is not possible or cost effective, general reactions to the change can be assessed. Example reactions to a change might include (1) global reaction—did you like the change program? (2) learning—what was learned? (3) and outcomes—is quality of output higher, lower, or about the same?

Based on years of research and attempts to measure changes in reaction, learning, behavior, and outcomes, some general guidelines are useful:

- *Measurements should be conducted over a period of time*. Soon after change has occurred, participants may be generally excited and interested because they're being asked for responses. Conducting measurement over a period of time will identify lag effects, extinction effects, and long-term results.

- *Compare groups that have undergone change with those that have not undergone change*. Comparisons are a form of internal benchmarking—how does a unit that was changed compare on outcomes or behavior with a unit that wasn't changed?

- *Avoid exclusive reliance on quantitative measures* such as cost, profit, units produced, or defective units. What do participants say? How do participants look? What do participants do without being asked? These types of qualitative measures provide insight into effects of change.

Guidelines like these can be applied to both small and major changes. Unfortunately, too many organizations bypass evaluation because it is difficult. But since change is a continual process, starting over requires feedback. If done properly, the evaluation step can provide feedback to the next cycle of change; that is, the model output becomes an internally based force for change.

TYPES OF CHANGE AGENTS

A **change agent** is an individual or team of individuals whose responsibility is to practice the stages suggested in Exhibit 15.3. Typically an outsider (consultant) or someone from inside the organization heads up the change effort. Whether an outsider, insider, or combination change agent leader is best hasn't been determined and may depend on the situation. But four types of change agents have been identified: outside pressure (OP), people-change-technology (PCT), analysis for the top (AFT), and organizational development (OD).[15]

Outside Pressure

The **outside pressure (OP) change agent** is an individual or group that isn't regularly employed by the firm, but still applies pressure on the firm to change. For example, in many parts of the world we have witnessed a shift from a manufacturing-based economy toward a predominantly service-based economy driven by digital technology, knowledge or intellectual capital, and information. In the mass production era, people made their career choice at about the time they graduated from high school and then stuck with it. Today, organizations know that to survive into the next century, they must obtain high performance from their workers. As a result, organizations are continually eliminating nonproductive functions and constantly reassessing, reshuffling, and retraining staff. Intelligent career and life planning in the knowledge-service era necessitates ongoing assessment, decision making, problem solving, and creating opportunities. Because of societal changes, organizations must change the career paths they create for people.

People-Change-Technology

The **people-change-technology** (PCT) change agent attempts to bring about change via various behaviorally oriented techniques. To be successful in the long term, most change programs must involve more than superficial, isolated behavioral changes. What's called for is a system-wide approach involving changes in a company's fundamental operations, beliefs, and values. Resistance to change can also be reduced if employees understand how the changes will increase organizational effectiveness and ultimately lead to greater job security and more meaningful work.[16]

Analysis for the Top

Analysis for the Top (AFT) agents offer advice on how best to change technology and structure to increase overall organizational effectiveness. Reengineering, restructuring, and technology change are methods used by AFT agents.

Organizational Development

Organizational development (OD) focuses on longer-term change that affects the firm's culture. OD change programs and specific interventions are often headed up by outside consultants. They help plan and implement the change, occasionally help evaluate changes, and assist the manager in becoming involved with all aspects of the change process.

Which change agent(s) should be used to introduce a total quality management program or a program on quality of work life? To some extent the answer rests with the issue of involvement. How much involvement of the change agent is needed to start, sustain, and evaluate the change program? In general, the greater the outside pressure, the less need there is for direct management involvement in creating change. In fact, some managers have even successfully invented the pretext of outside pressure to encourage change within their organization.

INTERVENTION METHODS

As we mentioned earlier in discussing Kurt Lewin's model of change, **intervention** is used to describe a method, technique, or means of change that improves an individual, group, organization, or all of these entities. An intervention can respond to forces for change, or it can create forces that give employees the impetus to accept change more readily. Types of interventions include individual, group, intergroup, and organizational change.

The type of intervention selected depends on the diagnosis, cost, time available, organization culture, management's confidence in the anticipated results, and depth preferred. **Depth of intervention** is defined as the degree of change that an intervention is intended to bring about.[17] A shallow intervention seeks mainly to provide information that's helpful to make improvements. A manager coaching a subordinate is an example of shallow intervention. A deep intervention is intended to bring about psychological and behavioral changes that are reflected in improved job performance. Sensitivity training is an example of deep intervention. With deep intervention, caution and the use of qualified experts should be top requirements.

Moderate-depth interventions such as team building are intended to alter attitudes and perceptions. Different perspectives are presented and analyzed with the result being better understanding, greater tolerance of other viewpoints, and modification of negative stereotypes.

In this text, we discuss only three intervention methods. However, many more methods are available for use in stimulating changes in people, structure, and technology. Again, as is often the case, no single method is perfect or even effective in every situation or case.

Survey Feedback

Survey feedback is an organizationally focused, shallow intervention method. It's shallow because it doesn't attempt to directly effect psychological or behavioral changes. This method is typically conducted in four stages.[18] First is the planning stage, during which a change agent works with top management to design the questions to be used in a survey. Next, data are collected from a sample or an entire unit population (department, division, organization). Data may be collected using a survey questionnaire, interviews, historical records, or some combination of data collection techniques. In the third stage, the change agent categorizes, summarizes, and interprets information collected during the survey and prepares reports. Finally, in the fourth stage, employees are given feedback, meetings are held to discuss the findings, and action plans for overcoming identified problems are developed and implemented.

Survey feedback is a popular intervention method. It's efficient and participatory, and it provides much job-relevant information. Top management's endorsement and involvement are needed to help the survey feedback approach achieve its goals.

Team Building

Teamwork is quickly becoming an essential component of most organizations today. An effective team communicates well, cooperates, stimulates its members, and provides recognition and rewards. **Team building** is a moderate-depth intervention that attempts to improve diagnosis, communication, cooperation, and the performance of members and the overall team. Be careful not to confuse team building with the widespread use of teams in most organizations. *Team building* is the term used to refer to helping work groups perform at a higher level. It isn't focused on solving workplace problems through teams, but rather in making a team out of a work group.

Team-building interventions often work toward establishing specific goals and priorities, analyzing a group's work methods, examining the group's communication and decision-making processes, and examining interpersonal relationships within the group. With these group functions in place, it's easier for the group to explicitly recognize each group member's contributions (both positive and negative).[19]

The process by which these aims are achieved begins with *diagnostic* meetings. Often lasting an entire day, the meetings enable all team members to share with other members their perceptions of problems. If the team is large enough, subgroups engage in discussion and report their ideas to the total group. These sessions are designed to allow expression of all members' views and to make these views public. In this context, diagnosis emphasizes the value of open confrontation of issues and problems that previously were discussed in secrecy.

Identifying problems and concurring on their priority are two important initial steps in team building. But a *plan of action* must also be agreed on. The plan should call on each group member, individually or as part of a subgroup, to act specifically to alleviate one or more problems. If, for example, an executive committee agrees that one problem is a lack of understanding of and commitment to goals, a subgroup can be appointed to recommend goals to the total group at a subsequent meeting. Other team members can work on different problems. For example, if problems are found in the relationships between members, a subgroup can initiate a process for examining each member's role.

Team building is also effective when new organizational units, project teams, or task forces are being created. Typically such groups have certain characteristics that need to be altered if the groups are to perform effectively—for example:

- Ambiguity about roles and relationships
- Members having a fairly clear understanding of short-term goals
- Group members having technical competence that puts them on the team
- Members often paying more attention to the team's tasks than to the relationships among team members

In the last case, the new group will focus initially on task problems but ignore the interpersonal relationship issues. By the time relationship problems begin to surface, the group can't deal with them, and performance begins to deteriorate.

To combat these characteristic tendencies, a new group should schedule team-building meetings during the first weeks of its life. Meetings should be held away from the work site; one- or two-day sessions often suffice. The format of such meetings varies, but essentially their purpose is to enable the group to work through its timetable as well as each member's role in reaching group objectives. An important outcome of such meetings is to establish an understanding of each member's contribution to the team and of the reward for that contribution. Although reports on team building indicate mixed results, the evidence suggests that group processes improve through team-building efforts.[20]

Empowerment

Empowerment is an important part of changing an organization; it is achieved through encouraging greater participation by managers and workers. As noted earlier, empowerment is a process that increases people's involvement in their work (design, flow, interactions, decision making). Empowerment isn't limited to individual actions; in fact, the growth of teamwork in organizations often leads to the opportunity for greater group decision-making autonomy or group empowerment. To the degree that the preceding occur, empowerment can be a high depth intervention.

Empowerment involves far more than giving employees greater decision-making ability. At its most practical level, empowerment is recognizing and releasing into the organization the power that people already have in their wealth of useful knowledge and internal motivation. Research indicates three simple keys to successful employee empowerment:

1. Open and candid sharing of information on business performance with all employees.

2. More structure (rather than less) as teams and employee groups move into self-management.

3. Replacing the organizational hierarchy with teams.[21]

However, not all companies are rushing ahead to manage their business through the use of employee teams. Two commonly agreed upon reasons that teams have not caught on at some companies are (1) teams are not easy to manage, and (2) team performance is not easily measurable.

Ultimately, for a manager to achieve competitive success through people involves fundamentally altering how he or she thinks about the workforce and the employment relationship. It means achieving success by working with people, not by replacing them or limiting the scope of their activities. It entails seeing the workforce as a source of strategic advantage, not just as a cost to be minimized or avoided. Firms that take this different perspective are often able to successfully outmaneuver and outperform their rivals.[22]

Over the long term, workers are motivated by a sense of achievement, recognition, enjoyment of the job, promotion opportunities, responsibility, and the chance for personal growth. Worker motivation and performance are tied directly to the style of management that's applied and to the principles of positive or negative reinforcement.

THE STRATEGY OF CHANGE: FORESIGHT-LED CHANGE

In their book, *Competing for the Future,* Gary Hamel and C. K. Prahalad argue that most organizations don't spend enough time thinking about the future of their industry and their business. In fact, they state that organizations typically fall under the "40/30/20 rule." This rule reflects their finding that about 40 percent of senior executive time is spent looking outward (i.e., outside the business). Of the time spent looking outward, only 30 percent is spent peering three or more years into the future. And of that time spent looking into the future, only about 20 percent is spent attempting to build a collective view of the future. Thus, on average, senior management spends less than 3 percent of its energy ($40\% \times 30\% \times 20\% = 2.4\%$) building an organizational perspective of the future.[23]

To compete effectively for the future, organizations must develop what Hamel and Prahalad call **industry foresight-led.** According to them, "industry foresight-led is based on deep insights into the trends in technology, demographics, regulation, and lifestyles that can be harnessed to rewrite industry rules and create new competitive space."[24] The authors distinguish this term from the more commonly used *vision,* which they dislike because it connotes unreality and intangibility.

Foresight-led change involves looking into the future, determining what the future is projected to be, and then using that insight to change an organization in the present. **Stretch target** is another term for describing this "pull" approach to change (as in pulling an organization into the future).

Stretch targets reflect a major shift in the thinking of top management. Executives are recognizing that incremental goals, however worthy, invite managers and workers to perform the same comfortable processes a little better every year. Unfortunately, the all too frequent result is average performance. Stretch targets require big leaps of progress on such measures as inventory turns, product development time, and manufacturing cycles. Imposing such imperatives can force companies to reinvent the way they conceive, make, and distribute products. Exhibit 15.4 provides guidelines on setting stretch targets.

For CEO John Snow of CSX, the $9.5-billion-a-year railroad and shipping company, stretch targets were a natural extension of his business approach. In 1991, CSX's return on capital hovered well below its capital charge—in the 10 percent range. Snow's bold goal was to make sure CSX would earn the full cost of capital by 1993 and thereafter. As Snow predicted, the stretch target he established forced managers to look hard at the railroad's core problem—that the company's fleet of locomotives and railcars sat loafing much of the time at loading docks and seaport terminals. Raising the company's return on capital would mean working the massive fleet far harder than had ever been attempted.

Having set the target, Snow then got out of the way. The strategy proved to be a winner. Since 1991, while handling a surge in business, CSX has eliminated from its rolling stock 20,000 of its 125,000 cars—enough to form a train stretching from Chicago to Detroit. That caused capital expenditures for supporting the fleet to shrink from $825 million a year to $625 million. CSX is now earning its full cost of capital.[25]

For most of the twentieth century, organizations orchestrated change management based on what has been called the **strategy-structure-systems doctrine.** The doctrine

---

EXHIBIT 15.4
Guidelines for Stretch Targets

Stretch targets should:

✓ Establish measurable stretch targets

✓ Give teams autonomy and power

✓ Modify work structures to support change

✓ Develop culture of support and encouragement

Adapted from: Kenneth R. Thompson, W. Hochwarter, and Nicholas J. Mathys. "Stretch Targets: What Makes Them Effective?" *Academy of Management Executive* 11, 3 (1997): 54.

took hold as organizations increased in size and complexity, leading senior managers to delegate most of the operating decisions to division-level managers. Senior managers then recast their own jobs as defining strategy, developing structure, and managing the systems required to link and control the company's parts.

This approach to management has been successful for more than fifty years. It has enabled central managers to maintain contact with increasingly far-flung operations. But, while senior managers saw these increasingly sophisticated systems as necessary links to operations, those at the operational level felt them to be burdens that too often called them to heel.

Today, top-level managers at some of the most successful organizations are creating organizational change through people, information, and technology. Management's challenge is to use technology to create useful information that engages the unique knowledge, skills, and abilities of every individual in the organization. Managers are developing a management philosophy based on a more personalized approach that encourages diverse viewpoints and empowers employees to contribute their own ideas.

As managers pay more attention to organizational culture, they need to have some insight into how it can be shaped and managed. In the next section, we'll explore some ways that managers can shape and manage organizational culture.

RESHAPING CULTURE AND STRUCTURE

The intervention methods available to managers for implementing change are impressive. But their impact is often limited by two aspects of organizations: culture and structure. Interventions can be attempted at either a shallow or deep level, but ultimately, culture and structure significantly influence the changes that occur.

Cultural Reshaping

An organization's culture is rooted in its nation's cultures. Because organizational culture consists of rules, rituals, and procedures, creating an ideology that helps direct employees' everyday experience and customs, it influences how change is received and coped with in relation to outcomes. History informs us that as U.S. firms expanded overseas, the national cultures of host nations, a diverse workforce, and new competitors helped shape the firms' internal cultures. Changing the internal organizational culture of a domestic or international firm is extremely difficult, perhaps impossible. Reshaping, altering, or modifying long-standing rules, procedures, rituals, and ideology is a better way to present change objectives.

Here are five keys to creating cultural change:

- Provide a clear vision and decisive leadership.
- Change the old guard.
- Tackle many problems at the same time.
- Change how the company's employees are judged and rewarded.
- Have full backing from the board, along with full accountability.

Employees are socialized into a firm's culture through a wide variety of practices. Shared meals, rituals, dress codes, and group membership result in socialization. By encouraging extensive interaction among employees, organizations help them become more attuned to the culture.

To reshape cultures to fit employees' mood and thinking, managers have moved toward a reward system that focuses on individual and group contributions to productivity rather than seniority, loyalty, and friendships. To counter the potentially negative consequences of individually based merit pay rewards, an increasing number of firms are using company-wide or group-based profit-sharing and bonus plans.

Changes in society and in perceptions among employees have pointed out some significant inequities in distribution of rewards, opportunities to learn new skills, and power within organizations. The widely publicized golden parachutes that in many cases over-rewarded senior managers involved in mergers and acquisitions, and the large paychecks managers receive, have alienated many employees, lowering their productivity and commitment. If done effectively, encouraging and practicing more equity within the culture can result in positive attitudes and feelings being transmitted through the employees' system of socialization.

Where cultural features support past ineffective or failed strategies, they can constrain change. Generating change involves (1) understanding the powerful force of culture, (2) aligning culture with positive ethical and equitable values, and (3) devising sound reward, education, and socialization systems. In a growing number of firms, managers realize that reshaping culture requires reshaping organizational structures.

Structural Reshaping

Structural reshaping requires an understanding of power, authority, and personal interactions in organizational settings. The organization blueprint is the organization chart. Unfortunately, charts present a firm's structure as fixed and rigid. This, of course, isn't how most real interactions occur. Firms must use a dynamic approach to structure, so that they can respond to changing conditions. Viewing the structure as temporary, fluid, and flexible is more compatible with today's world than establishing a set structure and using it for a long time.

As changes become more intense and rapid, and as competition becomes more innovative, managers must be more responsive and astute at modifying their structures. The technological change and environmental forces are ever present as new ideas are turned into innovative products. Competition in technology has become fierce; it revolves largely around such features as product quality, production costs, and the ability to deliver products in a timely manner. As examples we find robotics used to create better products, Just In Time (JIT) inventory management systems that lower production costs, and database-supported supply chain management used to create, build, and deliver better products that meet consumers needs and maximize organizational profits.

To derive the highest quality, managers must stimulate line employees' cooperation, problem-solving ability, and commitment. This means more employee involvement in decision making. Using teams, such as quality circles, is a structural change made by organizations in responding to the need for higher quality. Generating a bottom-up flow of ideas is easier with a decentralized structure.

The disintegration of large, tightly centralized bureaucratic structures continues. Large organizations still exist, but with reshaped structures. Such reshaping in structures proves that progressive managers are eliminating layers of administrators, decentralizing decision making, encouraging employee involvement, and improving communication. These processes are easy to state but often difficult to implement due to outdated cultural norms, policies, rituals, and ideology. The productivity loss due to fixed, rigid, and culturally bound structures is incalculable. We can safely assume that these structures are costly in terms of lost efficiency, customers, and global competitiveness.

INFLUENCE OF THE FOUNDER—OR TOP MANAGEMENT SEALS THE DEAL

The power to make change happen is often largely vested in management and most notably in the founder of the company. It is the founder's vision and values that create mental images of the future in the minds of employees. The founder's energy and enthusiasm often engage employees to produce greater effort and higher levels of task performance.[26] Everyone recognizes the role played by the late Dave Thomas, founder of Wendy's International, in creating and shaping the future of Wendy's. But not everyone knows that above all, Thomas believed in clear, clean communication to all organizational stakeholders.[27] Improved communications, initiated by the leader, must be a top priority. Merely informing workers that change is coming is not enough to guarantee success. Communication must be a two-way process. Participation creates more information about the impact of a change. However, along with empowering employees, managers must maintain some controls to keep the change process on target.

The chief executive officer (CEO) communicates a commitment to support a total change in the way everything is done in the organization. The CEO must commit to establishing a companywide communication program that involves managers and workers. The communication must include the following:

- Communicate specific actions required to implement the change.
- Distinguish what is important from what is merely desirable.
- Develop action plans for achieving concrete timely results.
- Assert that CEO involvement symbolizes the importance of a change.
- Identify the benefits of the implemented change to the organization.

Management must be prepared for resistance to change that affects any normal pattern or set of procedures. Because change often represents a change in culture, it may take several years to become effective and ingrained. Even though managers can initiate change, it must be practiced by everyone in the organization. The Management Highlight on page 301 offers some guidelines for managing organizational change.

Institutionalizing a change and achieving consistency between goals and performance measures is one of the most important tasks of upper management. Once a goal has been achieved, then the company can shift its focus to the next priority. This building-block approach has produced concrete results for some companies, and many others are now adopting it. For example, not only did CEO Carly Fiorina create a mega-giant with the Hewlett-Packard/Compaq merger, but she also needed to create a cultural change that emphasized efficiency. The new HP has fifty percent of the consumer PC market, however, that may not be enough for financial success unless economy-of-scale efficiencies help reduce costs.

Achieving significant change in the workplace is a long-term challenge for managers of any type of organization. One of the most difficult obstacles to overcome is giving up too early in the implementation process. For those companies that persevere, it has been worth the struggle.

CHANGE AND CONFLICT MANAGEMENT

Although an organization's managers and employees may recognize that change is inevitable, new ideas and old ways are often on a collision course. Change means greater uncertainty; it generates conflict among organizational members, who often have different

---

MANAGEMENT HIGHLIGHT
Managing Organizational Change

At one time or another, all organizations are confronted with the reality that a major change in the way business is conducted is necessary. To successfully achieve needed change, it is helpful to have a plan. Here, we offer a general set of guidelines for the process of change, ideas about how to reduce resistance to change, and an example based on a change toward greater quality.

Process for Creating the Change	Process for Reducing Resistance to Change	Example: Creating a Change toward Greater Quality
Step 1: Establish a sense of immediacy.	Step 1: Facilitation and support.	Step 1: Create performance standards.
Step 2: Create a leadership team.	Step 2: Manipulation and co-optation.	Step 2: Develop visible quality for product or service.
Step 3: Create and communicate a vision.	Step 3: Education and communication.	Step 3: Build in reliability and consistency.
Step 4: Encourage involvement.	Step 4: Participation and involvement.	Step 4: Create durability.
Step 5: Set short-term goals as guides to behavior.	Step 5: Negotiation and agreement.	Step 5: Emphasize the value or uniqueness of the product or service.
Step 6: Change the institution's strategies, structures, and processes.	Step 6: Explicit and implicit coercion.	Step 6: Build a reputation for quality.

Source: Adapted from John P. Kotter and Leonard A. Schlesinger, "Choosing Strategies for Change," *Harvard Business Review,* March–April 1979; John P. Kotter, "Leading Change: Why Transformation Efforts Fail," *Harvard Business Review,* March–April 1995, pp. 59–67; David A. Garvin, "Competing on the Eight Dimensions of Quality," *Harvard Business Review,* November–December 1987, pp. 101–109; and Ronald F. Ricardo, "Overcoming Resistance to Change," *National Productivity Review,* Spring 1995, pp. 5–12.

strategies for managing change. As we discussed earlier in the book, uncertainty decreases our ability to understand and effectively manage the future. The uncertainty inherent in change is no different. Whether conflict occurs inside or outside of an organization, the people, groups, and organizations it affects will seek strategies that maximize their outcomes in the aftermath of the change.

Conflict is a struggle between competing ideas and/or values. Author L. R. Pondy developed a five-stage model of conflict.[28] *Latent conflict* represents the underlying source of the conflict. For example, the sales department is rewarded for volume or the amount of units its employees sell. As a source of latent conflict, the production department might be more concerned with a steady flow of product that is easy to produce. *Perceived conflict* describes the situation where both departments become aware of the basic differences between their departments. *Felt conflict* occurs when one of the parties to the conflict takes some action that disadvantages the other party. For example, an e-mail is circulated in which the writer makes it clear that production and sales are at odds with one another. *Manifest conflict* is the actual or open conflict between the parties. It could take the form of verbal attacks or more subtle political actions to further a position. Finally, the *conflict aftermath* describes the long-term consequences of the conflict to the parties as well as other members of the organization. It often takes years to smooth over bitter disagreements and organizational actions.

How do organizations go about managing conflict? Exhibit 15.5 offers a rational yet strategic approach to understanding a conflict participant's level of involvement in the conflict; it also offers strategies to maximize the participant's outcomes in the aftermath of the conflict.

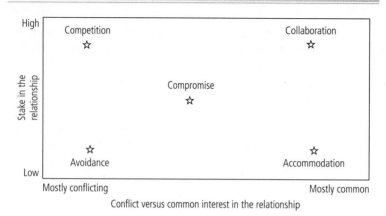

EXHIBIT 15.5
Managing Conflict Resolution

Source: Adapted from Thomas Ruble and Kenneth Thomas, "Support for a Two-Dimensional Model of Conflict Behavior," *Organizational Behavior and Human Performance* 16 (1976): 145.

As Exhibit 15.5 shows, these five strategies depend on two factors: (1) your stake in the relationship and (2) whether your interest in the relationship is common or conflicting. The strategies and situations in which they are appropriate are described below.

- **Avoidance** Low stake in the relationship and conflicting interests. You have little to gain by becoming involved in the conflict.

- **Collaboration** High stake in the relationship and mostly common interests. It is in your interest to develop an ally and work together for your collective good.

- **Compromise** Middle-ground position with no strong position on either dimension, yet a willingness to see the conflict resolved to the mutual benefit.

- **Accommodation** Low stake in the relationship and mostly common interests. A low stake means that you can afford to yield to the needs of the other party to preserve the common interests that bind you together.

- **Competition** High stake in the relationship and mostly conflicting interests. Direct conflict requires a defensive strategy to protect your interests.

Conflict is never as clear or concise as examples make it out to be. However, managers who are armed with a model to help understand the nature of the conflict, as well as a set of strategies to choose from, have much going in their favor.

Conclusion
Managing Organizational Change

We began this chapter by saying that "change is inevitable." We can now update that statement by adding that organizational change is inevitable. It is important for a manager to be willing and open to change—and, in fact, to seek it out. By reading the environment correctly and embracing change, a manager will maintain currency in her discipline and be an asset to her employer. However, no manager is an island. The organization must encourage and reward risk taking in the form of successful organizational change. A wise admonition is that it is foolish to change for the sake of change. More to the point, pursuing change because other organizations are changing will be ineffective. Strategic change or change that is driven by plans, values, and vision will most likely endure and be rewarded in the marketplace.

SUGGESTED READINGS

Abrahamson, Eric. "Change without Pain." *Harvard Business Review*, July–August 2000, pp. 75–79.

Hirschhorn, Larry. "Campaign for Change." *Harvard Business Review*, July–August 2002, pp. 2–7.

Sugarman, Barry. "A Learning-Based Approach to Organizational Change: Some Results and Guidelines." *Organizational Dynamics* 30 (2002): 62–76.

ENDNOTES

1. Howard Isenberg, "The Second Industrial Revolution: The Impact of the Information Explosion," *Industrial Engineering*, March 1995, p. 15.

2. John P. Kotter, "Leading Change: Why Transformation Efforts Fail," *Harvard Business Review*, March–April 1995, pp. 59–67.

3. Tom Broersma, "In Search of the Future," *Training & Development*, January 1995, pp. 38–43.

4. Michael Hammer and James Champy, *Reengineering the Corporation* (New York: Harper Collins, 1993), 35; and Frank Ostroff, *The Horizontal Organization* (New York: Oxford University Press, 1999).

5. D. Keith Denton, "Creating a System for Continuous Improvement," *Business Horizons*, January–February 1995, pp. 16–21.

6. Allan H. Church, Anne Margiloff, and Celeste Coruzi, "Using Surveys for Change: An Applied Example in a Pharmaceuticals Organization," *Leadership & Organizational Development Journal* 16, no. 4 (1995): 3–11.

7. Paul Lawrence, "How to Overcome Resistance to Change," *Harvard Business Review*, May–June 1954; reprinted in *HBR* (January–February 1969), pp. 1–10.

8. Barry K. Spiker and Eric Lesser, "We Have Met the Enemy . . . ," *Journal of Business Strategy* (March–April 1995): 17–21.

9. Allan H. Church, "Managerial Behavior and Work Group Climate as Predictors of Employee Outcomes," *Human Resource Development Quarterly*, Summer 1995, pp. 173–205.

10. Biography of Douglas Fraser; available online at www.frasercenter.wayne.edu/about/fraser.asp (accessed 10 April 2003).

11. Perry Pascarella, "Resistance to Change: It Can Be a Plus," *Industry Week*, July 27, 1987, p. 45 ff.

12. Ronald F. Recardo, "Overcoming Resistance to Change," *National Productivity Review,* Spring 1995, pp. 5–12.

13. Robert M. Randall, "The Sense-and-Respond Model," *Planning Review,* May–June 1995, pp. 43–44.

14. Stephan H. Haeckel, "Adaptive Enterprise Design: The Sense-and-Respond Model," *Planning Review,* May–June 1995, pp. 6–13.

15. Noel Tichy, "How Different Types of Change Agents Diagnose Organizations," *Human Relations,* December 1975, pp. 771–779.

16. Judith A. Neal et al., "From Incremental Change to Retrofit: Creating High-Performance Work Systems," *Academy of Management Executive,* February 1995, pp. 42–54.

17. Roger Harrison, "Choosing the Depth of Organizational Intervention," *Journal of Applied Behavioral Science* xx (1970): 181–202.

18. Wendell L. French and Cecil H. Bell Jr., *Organizational Development: Behavioral Science Interventions for Organizational Improvement* (Englewood Cliffs, NJ: Prentice-Hall, 1990), 170.

19. Cynthia Reedy Johnson in "An Outline for Team Building," *Training,* January 1986, p. 48; Richard L. Hughes, William E. Rosebach, and William H. Glover, "Team Development in an Intact, Ongoing Work Group," *Group and Organizational Studies,* June 1983, pp. 161–181.

20. Kenneth P. deMeuse and S. Jay Liebowitz, "An Empirical Analysis of Team-Building Research," *Group and Organizational Studies,* September 1981, pp. 357–378.

21. W. Alan Randolph, "Navigating the Journey to Empowerment," *Organizational Dynamics,* Spring 1995, pp. 19–32.

22. Jeffrey Pfeffer, Toru Hatano, and Timo Santalainen, "Producing Sustainable Competitive Advantage through the Effective Management of People," *Academy of Management Executive,* February 1995, pp. 55–72.

23. Gary Hamel and C. K. Prahalad, *Competing for the Future* (Boston: Harvard Business School Press, 1994), p. 4.

24. Hamel and Prahalad, 76.

25. Shawn Tully, "Why to Go for Stretch Targets," *Fortune,* November 14, 1994, pp. 145–155.

26. Edgar Schein, "The Role of the Founder in Creating Organizational Culture," *Organizational Dynamics,* 1983, pp. 13–28.

27. "Wendy's to Cite Thomas in the New Dave's Way Ads," *Nation's Restaurant News,* June 3, 2002, p. 3.

28. L. R. Pondy, "Organizational Conflict: Concepts and Models," *Administrative Science Quarterly* 2 (1967): 296–320.

Appendix A

HISTORY OF MANAGEMENT

Management: Its Beginning

The systematic recording and reporting of managerial practice is primarily a twentieth-century phenomenon, yet magnificent feats of management practice and application can be found from almost every period of our history. The construction of the great pyramid of Cheops in 4000 B.C., a massive undertaking by any measure, was planned, organized, led, and controlled with no modern technology to move heavy stones great distances, no laws about the length of the workday, and no safety procedures.

Although the trials and tribulations of management today may not seem as dramatic as those that we imagine the Egyptians faced thousands of years ago, management still offers plenty of excitement and challenges. By common assent we date the beginning of the modern era of management to the Industrial Revolution, particularly as exhibited in the United Kingdom in the mid-1700s. In brief, the Industrial Revolution shifted manufacturing to a factory setting from a household setting. One of the first to recognize the significance of human resources was Robert Owen (1771–1858), a Scottish factory owner who refused to use child labor—a common practice of his era. Owen emphasized good working conditions, cooperation, and tolerance for differences in worker capabilities. Andrew Ure (1778–1857), another early manager who recognized the importance of human resources, provided workers with tea at breaks, medical treatment, and sickness payments. Owen and Ure, who considered workers to be more than mindless cogs, were definitely on to something. Slowly, what was meant by *management* began to change. Workers, if treated well, could perform excellently.

Management: Its Modern Manifestations

Modern societies depend on human resources within organizations to provide the goods and services customers seek. These organizations, large and small, are headed by one or more individuals designated "managers." Even the sole proprietor of a business is a manager. It's the cadre of managers and the workers who have, since the Industrial Revolution, created organizations of all sizes that enhance the standard of living and quality of life in societies around the world.

Managers are the people who allocate society's resources to various (often competing) ends. Managers have the authority and responsibility to build safe or unsafe products, seek war or peace, build or destroy cities, and clean up or pollute the environment. Managers establish the conditions under which we're provided jobs, incomes, lifestyles, products, services, protection, health care, and knowledge. It would be difficult to find anyone in a developed or developing nation who is neither a manager nor affected by a manager's decisions.

Two Unique Contributors.   The list of twentieth-century management scholars, consultants, and practitioners who have made lasting contributions to how management is and will be practiced in the twenty-first century is endless. In this appendix we introduce a few contributors, however, so that readers can better understand many of the management practices that are covered in this book. Both Peter Drucker and W. Edwards Deming made unique contributions to modern management, and they are discussed next.

Peter Drucker (1909–2005).   Born in 1909 in Austria, Peter Drucker was educated as a lawyer and worked as a journalist in Germany. He's now an educator, consultant, and philosopher whose work emphasizes the importance of managers in organizational societies. Drucker believes that managers must always make economic performance the top priority. His central issue is how best to manage a business so that it is successful over time.

Drucker has argued that profits aren't the major objective of business:

> There is only one valid definition of business purpose: to create a customer.... What the business thinks it produces is not of first importance—especially not to the future of the business and to its success. What the customer thinks he is buying, what he considers "value" is decisive—it determines what a business is, what it produces, and whether it will prosper.[1]

Drucker considers the present era of management to be a period of transformation; thus the modern organization must be organized for constant changes. He proposes that to stay abreast of changes, management must engage in three practices. The first is continuing improvement of everything the organization does (the process the Japanese refer to as **kaizen**). Continuous improvement in services, product design, and product use has to become part of daily organizational life. Second, every organization must learn to exploit its knowledge. Taking the knowledge and developing one product after another from the same invention is one of the most successful practices of Japanese business. Finally, every firm must innovate. Every organization can accomplish these practices only by acquiring the most essential resource—qualified, knowledgeable people.[2]

In today's organizations individuals who weren't trained as managers often find themselves in managerial positions. Many people presently training to be teachers, engineers, accountants, musicians, salespersons, artists, physicians, or lawyers will one day earn their livings as managers. They'll manage schools, accounting firms, symphonies, sales organizations, museums, hospitals, and government agencies. The United States and other countries are organizational societies that rely on managers to manage work, operations, and people to efficiently accomplish goals. Because the growth in the number and size of organizations is relatively new in history, the study of management is also relatively new.

W. Edwards Deming (1900–1993).   W. Edwards Deming was born in 1900 in Sioux City, Iowa. He received a Ph.D. in mathematical physics and worked for the U.S. Census Bureau during and after World War II.[3] In 1950, Deming went to Japan to help conduct a population census and lectured to Japanese business managers on statistical quality control. The Japanese were impressed with Deming and listened carefully to his views about quality. Deming stressed that quality is whatever the customer needs and wants. Deming was extremely critical of American management and its failure to properly address quality. He claimed that managers were responsible for 94 percent of quality problems.

Deming proposed fourteen points of total quality management that reveal an emphasis on learning, worker involvement, leadership, and continuous improvement. Deming stated: "People are born with intrinsic motivation. . . . People are born with a need for relationships with other people and with a need to be loved and esteemed by others. . . . One is born with a natural inclination to learn and to be innovative. One inherits a right to enjoy his work."[4] The three key ingredients of these fourteen points, according to Deming, are continual improvement, constancy of purpose, and profound knowledge.

The Classical Management Approach

A critical problem facing managers at the turn of the twentieth century was how to increase workforce efficiency and productivity. The effort to resolve these issues marked the beginning of the study of modern management. It was eventually labeled the **classical approach**, as is usually the case with the beginning effort of every field of study.

We believe that the classical approach to management can be best understood by examining it from two perspectives. One perspective, **scientific management,** concentrated on lower-level managers dealing with everyday problems of the workforce. The other perspective, **classical organization theory,** concentrated on top-level managers dealing with the everyday problems of managing the entire organization. For management students, the contributions of the classical approach are critical. These insights, in fact, constitute the core of the discipline of management and the process of management and comprise a major part of this book. Let's briefly examine each perspective.

Scientific Management.   At the turn of the twentieth century, business was expanding and creating new products and new markets, but labor was in short supply. Two solutions were available: (1) substitute capital for labor or (2) use labor more efficiently. Scientific management concentrated on the second solution.

ignored the human element

Frederick Winslow Taylor (1856–1915).   Frederick W. Taylor, called the Father of Scientific Management, was an engineer by training. He joined Midvale Steel Works in Pennsylvania as a laborer and rose through the ranks to become a chief engineer.[5] Taylor believed that management's primary objective should be to secure the maximum prosperity for the employer, coupled with the maximum prosperity of each employee. The mutual interdependence of management and workers was a common message he expressed.

Taylor's view of "science" insisted upon the systematic observation and measurement of worker activities. He was driven by the notion of applying science to answer questions about efficiency, cooperation, and motivation. Taylor believed that inefficient rules of thumb used by management inevitably lead to inefficiency, low productivity, and low-quality work. He recommended developing a science of management, the scientific selection and development of human resources, and personal cooperation between management and workers. Taylor believed that conflict among employees would obstruct productivity and so should be eliminated.

Taylor advocated maximum specialization of labor. He believed each person should become a specialist and master of specific tasks. Also, he assumed that increased efficiency would result from specialization. Taylor was unhappy with anything short of the one best way. He searched, through the use of scientific methods, for the one best way to manage. This often included the design of custom tools to increase worker productivity.

Taylor tried to find a way to combine the interests of both management and labor to avoid the necessity for sweatshop management. He believed that the key to harmony was seeking to discover the one best way to do a job, determine the optimum work pace, train people to do the job properly, and reward successful performance by using an incentive pay system. Taylor believed that cooperation would replace conflict if workers and managers knew what was expected and saw the positive benefits of achieving mutual expectations.[6]

To the modern student of management, Taylor's ideas may not appear to be insightful. Given the times in which he developed them, however, his ideas were lasting contributions to how work is done at the shop-floor level. He urged managers to take a more systematic approach in performing their job of coordination. His experiments with stopwatches and work methods stimulated many others at that time to undertake similar studies.[7]

Interestingly, if we evaluated scientific management on the basis of its impact on management practice at the time of its development, it would receive a low grade. Although some firms adopted scientific management, the methods of Taylor and his followers were largely ignored. One cause of the seeming failure was that Taylor and other scientific management supporters did not fully understand the psychological and sociological aspects of work. For example, scientific management made the implicit assumption that people are motivated to work primarily by money. In the late nineteenth century, this was undoubtedly a valid assumption. To assume this today, however, is far too simplistic.

Frank Gilbreth (1868–1924) and Lillian Gilbreth (1878–1972). The Gilbreths were essentially "efficiency experts." Their main contribution was time and motion studies of work processes. They analyzed each step in a repetitive work task and developed methods and procedures for performing the task more efficiently. The efficient Gilbreths' had twelve children, managing their home life according to their penchant for minimizing waste in the form of time, material, and human potential. Hollywood chronicled their lives and times in the movie "Cheaper by the Dozen."

Classical Organization Theory. Another body of ideas was developed at the same time as scientific management. These ideas focused on the problems faced by top managers of large organizations. Since this branch of the classical approach focused on the management of organizations (while scientific management focused on the management of work), it was labeled *classical organization theory.* Its two major purposes were (1) to develop basic principles that could guide the design, creation, and maintenance of large organizations and (2) to identify the basic functions of managing organizations.

Engineers constitute many of the prime contributors to scientific management; numerous practicing executives were the major contributors to classical organization theory. We'll now take a look at the contributions of one such engineer.

Henri Fayol (1841–1925). A French mining engineer by training, Henri Fayol eventually became a managing director of a French mining and metallurgical combine, Commentary-Fourchamboult-Decazeville. Besides many articles on administration, his most famous writing was the book *General and Industrial Management,* translated by Constance Storrs and first issued in 1949.[8] Fayol divided an organization's activities into six categories:

- Technical (production, manufacturing)
- Commercial (buying, selling)
- Financial
- Security (protecting property and persons)
- Accounting
- Managerial (planning, organizing, commanding, coordinating, and controlling)

Many of Fayol's ideas are as true today are they were in the early twentieth century. These six categories (often under contemporary names or titles) are essential and present in all organizations even today.

Fayol's Principles of Management. Fayol proposed fourteen principles to guide the thinking of managers in resolving problems (see Exhibit A.1). He never recommended total obedience to the principles, but suggested that a manager's "experience and sense of proportion" should guide the degree of application of any principle in a particular situation.

EXHIBIT A.1
Fayol's Fourteen Principles of Management

Fayol's Principle	Description	Fayol's Principle	Description
1. Division of Work	Specialization of task.	8. Centralization	Decision making rests with management.
2. Authority	Right to give orders.	9. Scalar Chain	Formal chain of command.
3. Discipline	Obedience to supervisor.	10. Order	Work is conducted in a clean, orderly environment.
4. Unity of Command	Employee reports to one supervisor.		
5. Unity of Direction	Individual effort focused on organizational goals.	11. Equity	Reward in contribution to performance.
6. Subordination of Individual Interest	Personal interests set aside for the good of the organization.	12. Stability and Tenure	Stable employment.
		13. Initiative	Self-starting responsibility.
7. Remuneration	Fair pay.	14. Esprit de Corps	Harmonious culture.

As with scientific management, the reader should keep in mind the time in which Fayol developed his principles and his intent. He was probably the first major thinker to address problems of managing large-scale business organizations, which were a relatively new phenomenon in his time.

Functions of Management. Fayol was perhaps the first to discuss management as a process with specific functions that all managers must perform. He proposed four management functions.

- *Planning.* Fayol believed that managers should (a) make the best possible forecast of events that could affect the organization and (b) draw up an operating plan to guide future decisions.

- *Organizing.* Fayol believed that managers must determine the appropriate combination of machines, material, and humans necessary to accomplish the task.

- *Commanding.* In Fayol's scheme, commanding involved directing the subordinates' activities. He believed that managers should set a good example and have direct, two-way communication with subordinates. Finally, managers must continually evaluate both the organizational structure and their subordinates; they should not hesitate to change the structure if they consider it faulty, nor to fire incompetent subordinates.

- *Controlling.* Controlling ensures that actual activities are consistent with planned activities. Fayol did not expand on this idea except to state that everything should be "subject to control."

Max Weber (1864–1920). Max Weber, who was born in Germany, studied law and then entered an academic career at Berlin University. He studied and reported on the theory of authority structures in organizations. He made a distinction between power (the ability to force people to obey) and authority (where orders are voluntarily obeyed by those receiving them). In an authority system, those in the subordinate role (workers) see the issuing of directives by those in the authority role (managers) as legitimate.

The first mode of exercising authority is based on the qualities of the leader. Weber used the Greek term *charisma* to mean any quality of an individual's personality that sets him or her apart from ordinary people. A second mode of exercising authority is through precedent and usage. Managers in such an interpretation have authority by virtue of the status and the position they've achieved or inherited.

Weber believed that the "bureaucratic" organization is the dominant institution in society because it's the most efficient. Precision, speed, unambiguity, continuity, unity, and strict subordination are results of bureaucratic arrangements. As used by Weber,[9] **bureaucracy** refers to a management approach based on formal organizational structure with set rules and regulations that rely on specialization of labor, an authority hierarchy, and rigid promotion and selection criteria.

Contributions and Limitations of the Classical Approach.   The greatest contribution of the classical approach was that it identified management as an important element of organized society. Management has, if anything, increased in importance in today's more global and competitive world. Advocates of the classical approach believe that management—like law, medicine, and other occupations—should be practiced according to principles that managers can learn. It's these principles that global managers must now learn in order to compete with the West.

The identification of management functions such as planning, organizing, commanding, and controlling provided the basis for training new managers. How management functions are presented often differs, depending upon who's presenting them. But any listing of management functions acknowledges that managers are concerned with *what* the organization is doing, *how* it's to be done, and *whether* it was done.

Contributions of the classical approach, however, go beyond the important work of identifying the field of management and its process and functions. Many management techniques used today (for example, time and motion analysis, work simplification, incentive wage systems, production scheduling, personnel testing, and budgeting) are derived from the classical approach.

One major criticism of the classical approach is that most of its insights are too simplistic for today's complex organizations in a constantly changing world. Critics argue that scientific management and classical organization theory are more appropriate for the past, when most organizations operated in stable, predictable environments. The changing environment, shifting expectations of workers, increasing competition, growing diversity of the workforce, rising government regulations, and changing public responsibility and ethical expectations of society today are all characteristics of contemporary organizations that were never contemplated by classical management theorists.

The Behavioral Approach

The behavioral approach to management developed partly because practicing managers found that the ideas of the classical approach didn't lead to total efficiency and workplace harmony. Managers still encountered problems because subordinates didn't always behave as they were supposed to. Thus, interest grew in helping managers become more efficient.

The behavioral approach to management has two branches. The *human relations approach* became popular in the 1940s and 1950s. The *behavioral science approach* became popular in the 1950s and still receives a great deal of attention today.

The Human Relations Approach.   The **human relations approach** focuses on individuals working in group settings. Managers and workers are studied in relation to what occurs within the group. Elton Mayo is considered the father of the human relations movement.

Elton Mayo (1880–1949).　An Australian, Elton Mayo, has been called the founder of both the human relations and the industrial sociology movements. The research work that he directed at Harvard University showed the importance of the group in affecting individual behavior at work.

Mayo's initial research in textile mills was on reorganizing the work schedule to include more rest pauses for workers to use in completing their jobs. The major effects of adding rest pauses were to reduce turnover. Mayo and his team acquired a new application for rest pauses and took their experience to the Hawthorne Works of the Western Electric Company (more fully explained later in this section).

Mayo's writings and thinking led to a more complete realization and understanding of the human factor in work situations. Central to this was the discovery of the informal group as an outlet and source of motivation for workers. His work also led to an emphasis on the importance of an adequate upward-flowing communication system.

A prominent contributor to human relations theory was Hugo Munsterberg (1863–1916), a German psychologist and philosopher. He published a book that linked scientific management and human behavior. Mary Parker Follett (1868–1933), another contributor to the human relations approach, laid the foundation for studies in group dynamics, conflict management, and political processes in organizations.

Followers of this approach believe that to develop good human relations, managers must know not only why their workers behave as they do, but what psychological and social factors influence them. Students of human relations bring to management's attention the important role individuals play in determining an organization's success or failure. They try to show how the process and functions of management are affected by differences in individual behavior and the influence of groups in the workplace. Thus, while scientific management concentrates on the job's *physical* environment, the human relations approach concentrates on the *social* environment.

Human relations experts believe that management should recognize employees' needs for recognition and social acceptance. They suggest that since groups provide members with feelings of acceptance and dignity, management should look upon the work group as a positive force that could be utilized productively. Therefore, managers should be trained in people skills as well as technical skills.

The Behavioral Science Approach and the Hawthorne Studies.

Other individuals who were university trained in the social sciences such as psychology, sociology, and cultural anthropology began to study people at work. They had advanced training in applying the scientific approach to the study of human behavior. These individuals have become known as *behavioral* scientists, and their approach is considered to be distinct from the human relations approach.

Individuals using the **behavioral science approach** believe that workers are much more complex than the "economic man" described in the classical approach or the "social man" described in the human relations approach. The behavioral science approach concentrates more on the nature of work itself and the degree to which it can fulfill the human need to use skills and abilities. Behavioral scientists believe that an individual is motivated to work for many reasons in addition to making money and forming social relationships.

As mentioned previously, the **Hawthorne Studies** (1927–1932, in a Western Electric Plant) are the most famous in management literature.[10] The company (which manufactured equipment for the telephone company) was known for its concern for its employees' welfare. It had maintained high standards in wages and hours. The study's original aim was to determine the relationship between intensity of illumination and two groups of workers' efficiency, measured in output. The intensity of light under which one group worked was varied, but was held constant for the other group.

Before Mayo and his Harvard research team arrived, another research group had completed the initial illumination studies. Mayo and his team were presented with the findings that when illumination increased, productivity increased. However, when illumination decreased, productivity increased. It appeared that workers reacted more to the presence and expectations of the researchers rather than to the actual increase or decrease in illumination. Scholars refer to this phenomenon as the **Hawthorne effect.**[11]

The Harvard researchers also set up an experiment involving the relay assembly test room at the Hawthorne plant. Six women were selected to work on assembling telephone relays in the test room. The women were studied over a long period of time, during which the researchers altered their working conditions (e.g., method of payment, length of rest periods). The researchers introduced twelve different changes, and determined that in each experimental period, output was higher than in the preceding one.

The researchers concluded that changes and improvement in output were less affected by any of the twelve changes in work conditions that were introduced than by the attitudes of the six work team individuals. The cohesiveness and friendships among the team members were found to be significant. The group developed leadership and a common purpose—to increase the output rate.

The Hawthorne Studies pointed out that workers are motivated by more than economic factors. Workers' attitudes are affected by their feelings about each other and by having a common purpose. Today this is a commonsense thought; but it wasn't generally believed when the research was being done (from 1927–1932).[12] The Hawthorne Studies were conducted before the era of collective bargaining and safety regulations, when workdays averaged 10 to 12 hours and twelve-year-olds worked alongside adults.

Contributions and Limitations of the Behavioral Approach.   For the student of management, the behavioral approach has contributed a wealth of important ideas and research results on the people-managing aspect of management. The basic rationale is that because managers must get work done through others, management is really applied behavioral science; that is, a manager must motivate, lead, and understand interpersonal relations.

The efficiency emphasis of the classical management approach was supplemented with a focus on people and their needs, emotions, and thoughts. The work of the behavioral management approach resulted in organizations being considered as social systems with both formal and informal patterns of authority and communications. Workers, their skills, and their involvement in groups and motivation were proposed to be at the core of any success that management achieves.

The basic assumption that managers must know how to deal with people appears valid, but management is more than applied behavioral science. For the behavioral approach to be useful to managers, it must make them better practitioners of the process of management. It must help them in problem situations. In many cases this objective has not been achieved, due to the tendency of some behavioral scientists to use technical terms when introducing their research findings to practicing managers. Also, in some situations, one behavioral scientist (a psychologist) may have a different suggestion from another (a sociologist) for the same management problem. Human behavior is complex, and it is studied from differing viewpoints. This complicates the problem for a manager who is trying to use insights from the behavioral sciences.

The Decision Sciences Approach

The **decision sciences approach** to management is, in one sense, a modern version of the early emphasis on the "management of work" by those interested in scientific management. Its key feature is the use of decision making, information systems, mathematics, and statistics to aid in resolving production and operations problems. Thus, the approach focuses on solving technical rather than human behavior problems.

Origins of the Decision Sciences Approach.   The decision sciences approach has formally existed for only about 50 years. It originated during the early part of World War II, when England was confronted with some complex military problems that had never been faced before, such as antisubmarine warfare strategy. In an effort to solve these problems, the English formed teams of scientists, mathematicians, and physicists. The units, named *operations research teams,* proved to be extremely valuable in winning the war. When the war was over, American firms began to use the approach.

Herbert Simon (1916–2001).   Herbert Simon, a distinguished American political and social scientist, influenced the thinking and practice of decision- and information-science-based management.[14] He viewed management as equivalent to decision making, and his major interest has been how decisions are made and how they might be made more effectively.

Simon describes three stages of decision making:

1. Finding occasions requiring a decision (intelligence)
2. Inventing, developing, and analyzing possible courses of action (design)
3. Selecting a course of action (choice)

In Simon's thinking, all managerial action is decision making. Economists' traditional theory is that decisions are made on the basis of rationality. However, in the real world, there are limits to rationality—such as the emotions of the decision maker. In place of the "economically rational" decision maker, Simon proposes a "satisficing" decision maker. That is, decisions are made that are satisfactory or "good enough." Instead of searching for a decision to maximize profits, managers can seek an adequate profit.

Simon views decisions on a continuum ranging from programmed, or routinely occurring, to nonprogrammed, or nonroutine and unstructured. Because many decisions are toward the nonprogrammed end of the continuum, techniques such as mathematical analysis, operations research, and computer simulation have gained prominence. These techniques were first used for programmed decisions. However, with the use of computers and mathematics, more and more elements of judgment can now be incorporated into the decision-making process. As computer technology becomes more advanced, more complex decisions will become programmed.

Contributions and Limitations of the Decision Sciences Approach.   Today the most important contributions of the decision and information sciences management approach are in the areas of production management and operations management and information systems. **Production management** focuses on manufacturing technology and the flow of material in a manufacturing plant. Here, management science has contributed techniques that help solve production scheduling problems, product and service quality improvement problems, budgeting problems, and maintenance of optimal inventory levels.

Operations management is similar to production management except that it focuses on a wide class of problems and includes organizations such as hospitals, banks, government, and the military, which have operations problems but don't manufacture tangible products. For such organizations, management science has contributed techniques to solve such problems as budgeting, planning for workforce development programs, and aircraft scheduling.

Information systems involve the use of computers in helping managers to make better decisions and to increase an organization's efficiency. The computer now permits managers to gather and accurately process large volumes of data, produce reports in a timely manner, make projections about the future, communicate with geographically separate parts of the organization, and apply quantitative techniques to improve the enterprise's efficiency and performance.

Information is a chief ingredient used by managers. It is data evaluated or processed for a particular use. Information is disseminated up, down, and across an enterprise's units. Large volumes of information are now commonly stored in databases (centralized collections of data and/or information for a particular subject). Organizations of all sizes now depend on the flow of information and the availability of databases to make more informed and timely decisions. Planning, organizing, commanding, and controlling decisions have been enhanced through the availability of information systems.

We noted in our discussion of the behavioral approach that management is more than applied behavioral science. At this point, we should stress that decision and information sciences are no substitute for management. Decision science techniques are especially useful to the manager performing the management process. If there's a flaw in decision science, it's that too little emphasis has been placed on people and how they can use the tools and techniques available. What good is information provided by a computer if it's not interpretable, relevant, or specific? What good is a new statistical quality control chart if the worker can't interpret its meaning or even produce the chart? What good is the mathematically oriented inventory model if the data entered are inaccurate? Workers, customers, and managers using decision science techniques and approaches need to be viewed as users, interpreters, and benefactors. Their needs, reactions, and understanding must be weighed in deciding on an appropriate decision science technique to use.

The Systems Management Approach   *OK for strategic*

A system consists of four components: input, processing, output, and feedback. Systems can be closed to environmental influence, such as a clock, or open to influences from the environment, as in the case of an organization with an online Internet ordering system. Exhibit A.2 illustrates an open systems model.

The **systems approach to management** is essentially a way of thinking about organizations and management problems. A **system** is a collection of parts that operate interdependently to achieve common goals.[15] The whole of the system is considered to be greater than the sum of its parts—known as the synergistic effect. Minnesota Mining and Manufacturing Co. (3M) is more than a research and development, marketing, and production unit. The success of 3M is a result of a system of interrelated units that work in concert to produce new and better products.

but not for tactical

EXHIBIT A.2
Open Systems Model

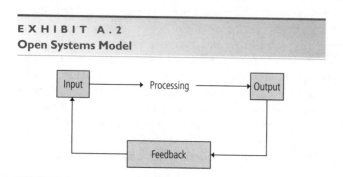

From the systems perspective, management involves managing and solving problems in each part of the organization, but doing so with the understanding that actions taken in one part of the organization affect other parts of the organization. For example, implementing a solution to a problem in a firm's production department will likely affect other aspects of the company such as marketing, finance, and personnel. Each part is tightly linked to other organizational parts; no single part of an organization exists and operates in isolation from the others. Thus, in solving problems, managers must view the organization as a dynamic whole and try to anticipate their decision's unintended as well as intended impacts.

Chester Barnard (1886–1961).   Chester Barnard bridged the behavioral school and the decision-making school. However, his contributions also included the description of the organization as a behavioral system. Barnard's ideas reflect a new understanding of leadership, motivation, and communication. In fact, Herbert Simon's famous classic text *Administrative Behavior* developed many groundbreaking ideas from Barnard's earlier work the *Functions of the Executive*. At the time of his contributions to the management literature Chester Barnard was president of New Jersey Bell Telephone and a systems advocate. He viewed an organization as an aggregation of units that interact. He introduced the concept of the "system of coordination." Barnard was the first major theorist after the Hawthorne Studies to emphasize the importance and variability of individuals in the work setting.

Barnard believed that an essential element of organizations is people's willingness to contribute their individual efforts to the cooperative system. The need for cooperation and interdependence is clearly presented in Barnard's classic management book, *The Functions of the Executive,* in the following:

> A cooperative system is a complex of physical, biological, personal, and social components which are in a specific systematic relationship by reason of the cooperation of two or more persons for at least one definite end.[16]

Open Systems.   According to the systems approach, the elements of an organization are interconnected. The approach also views the organization as linked to its environment. Organizational effectiveness, even survival, depends on the organization's interaction with its environment. A battery-powered digital watch would be considered a relatively closed system. The installation of the battery is the only outside intervention. Once in place, the watch operates with no input from the external environment.[17]

To further your understanding of these ideas, let's consider Hewlett-Packard (HP) as an example of a computer manufacturer interacting with their environment. As a computer manufacturer, HP operates in an **open system** that actively interacts with its environment. Active interaction means that HP both obtains resources from and provides resources to its environment. For example, in order to function, HP must obtain *inputs* from the environment. The company needs motivated, skilled employees who can design and manufacture innovative, high-quality personal and business computers. HP obtains this resource from the environment—specifically, from the graduating classes of universities nationwide, from competitors, and from other organizations.

Financial resources (money) are needed to build manufacturing facilities, to fund R&D efforts, and to meet any number of other expenses. HP obtains the funds from the environment—from banks, other lending institutions, and people who buy shares of HP's stock. Raw materials (e.g., computer parts) are obtained from outside suppliers in the environment. Information about the latest computer product technology and about the latest products developed by HP competitors is also needed. This information substantially influences the design and manufacture of HP's computers. Information is obtained from the environment—from research journals, computer conferences, and other external contacts.

These inputs are used, coordinated, and managed in a *transformation* process that produces *output*—in this case, personal and business computers. However, the company's task isn't complete. HP provides this resource (output) to the environment by delivering its computers to retail outlets for sale to customers. Does the company survive? Only if the customer reacts to HP's computers and decides to purchase the product. The customer's decision to buy or look elsewhere (for an IBM, Apple, or Dell computer) provides HP with *feedback*.

If the feedback is positive (customers buy HP), the environment provides a critical input to HP—cash that the company uses to obtain other inputs from the environment such as top-quality employees, materials, and knowledge. Negative feedback (no sales) presents HP with a serious problem. Regardless, HP must closely monitor feedback and act upon it (e.g., changing a failing product's design or features based on customer responses). As an open system in a dynamic environment, HP can't afford to ignore the environment. Neglecting the environment (e.g., technological innovations, competitors' moves) will, over time, render the company non-competitive.

Contributions and Limitations of the Systems Management Approach. Importantly, most organizations today operate as open systems to survive and utilize a systems perspective of management. Managers must think broadly about a problem and avoid concentrating only on desired results, because these results will affect other problems and parts of the organization as well as the environment beyond the organization. The age-old confrontation between the production objective of low manufacturing costs (achieved by making one product in one color and style) and the marketing objective of a broad product line (requiring high production costs) is a good example. It's not possible to achieve both objectives at the same time. In this situation, a compromise is necessary for the overall system to achieve its objective. And in seeking a compromise, the organization must always be mindful of the environment (e.g., will customers accept the product's price or design?). The objectives of a firm's individual parts must be compromised for the objective of the entire firm.

Using the systems approach in the preceding example, individual managers must adopt a broad perspective. With a systems perspective, managers can more easily achieve coordination between the objectives of the organization's various parts and the objectives of the organization as a whole.[18]

Critics consider the systems approach to be abstract and not very practical. Talking about inputs, transformations, and outputs isn't how everyday managers discuss problems, make decisions, and face reality. The HP manager must think, respond, and observe. He or she doesn't consider how transformation will occur, or what the production unit will think about the decision made to go head-to-head with the competition and reduce personal computer prices. The systems concept is good for classroom analysis, but being in the middle of daily decision-making precludes the luxury of deep systems-like analysis and thinking.

The Contingency Management Approach

The systems approach to management advocates that managers recognize that organizations are systems comprised of interdependent parts and that a change in one part affects other parts. This insight is important. Beyond this, however, managers need to see how the parts fit together. The **contingency management approach** can help you better understand their interdependence.

> The contingency view of organizations and their management suggests that the organization is a system composed of subsystems and delineated by identifiable boundaries from its environmental suprasystem. The contingency view seeks to understand the interrelationships within and among subsystems, as well as between the organization and its environment, and to define patterns of relationships or configurations of variables. It emphasizes the multivariate nature of organizations and attempts to understand how organizations operate under varying conditions and in specific circumstances. Contingency views are ultimately directed toward suggesting organizational designs and managerial systems most appropriate for specific situations.[19]

Universal versus Situational Theories. *template* In the early years of management theory, some individuals, like Frederick W. Taylor, advocated the "universal" view of management effectiveness. *Universal theorists* argued that there indeed exists a one best way to perform different management functions. In their view, the task of management theorists is to identify these superior management prescriptions by developing and then testing theory via research.

However, other management theorists, called *situational theorists,* disagreed. They asserted that no one best approach to management exists, because each situation is too different. No one principle or prescription is supremely applicable across totally unique situations. In fact, situational theorists said, very few principles and concepts are useful across situations. Because each managerial situation is unique, a manager must approach each situation with few if any guidelines to follow. Management effectiveness first requires that a manager evaluate each situation from scratch before deciding which action to take.

The contingency approach attempts to bridge the extreme points on this continuum of views. Like the situational theorists, contingency theorists don't subscribe to any one best approach to management. In their view, the situations that managers face do differ and thus prohibit any one best prescription. Ray Kroc, founder of the fast-food giant McDonald's, used contingency thinking in always searching for innovations to stay ahead of competition.

The Impact of Technology, Structure, and Environment: A Contingency *Probability varied* **Approach.** In a historical context and in the tradition of organization theory, technology, structure, and environment are important contingency variables. **Technology** is best defined as the conversion process used in organizations to transform raw materials into a complete product. Examples of three different conversion processes might be small-batch job shops, mass production, and continuous production such as in a refinery. Early theorists speculated that both structure and technology influenced the long-term success of an organization. *System composed of parts where each play on each other*

Joan Woodward (1916–1971). Research exploring the relationship between organizational structure and production technology was popularized through the work of industrial sociologist Joan Woodward. Her work encouraged managers to avoid seriously considering the "one best way" claims being made by consultants and other managers. Many were proposing such solutions to decisions regarding organizational structure; that is, they claimed that a particular structure should be used because it is the "one best way." Woodward's research and writing challenged such views.[13]

While working as a professor of industrial sociology in London, Woodward—from 1953 to 1957—led the South-East Essex research team studying manufacturing firms. She investigated characteristics such as span of control (number of workers reporting to a manager), number of levels of authority, amount of written communications, and clarity of job definitions. She found significant differences across firms.

Woodward's research work and additional case studies showed that a firm's technology plays a significant role in its structure. She, unlike Frederick W. Taylor, found that there is no best way to manage or structure an organization. She warned against accepting principles of management as universally applicable.

Woodward's work pioneered an improved understanding of how empirical research can be used to change an organization's structure. She elevated empirical work to a level where managers could derive value from the results. Woodward also illustrated how comparisons of a large number of firms could be designed so that generalizations could be made to other organizations.

Another important contingency variable—the **environment**—was offered by Paul Lawrence and Jay Lorsch at about the same time as Woodward's research as a potential influence on organizational success.[20] Their rationale for its inclusion is that a high demand environment presents an entirely different competitive situation for an organization than does a low demand environment. Thus, the environment presents a unique contingency factor that can contribute to organizational success or failure.

Identifying and Evaluating Contingency Variables.   Contingency theorists stop short of asserting that all managerial situations are totally unique. Rather, they argue that situations are often similar to the extent that some principles of management can be effectively applied. However, the appropriate principles must be identified. This is done by first identifying the relevant *contingency variables* in the situation and then by evaluating those variables.[21]

Contemporary Influences on the Evolution of Management

Frederick W. Taylor, Herbert Simon, Henri Fayol, and other pioneers of twentieth-century management thinking and practice are historical sources of inspiration that management students read about. These pioneers set the course for reporting about, understanding, and studying management and workers. In addition to these historical giants, there are a number of contemporary philosophers and advocates of management practices. For their contributions to the shaping of management practices, these modern-day thinkers may eventually stand beside the early pioneers.

Tom Peters: Sources of Excellence.   Management consultant Tom Peters was a principal in the consulting firm of McKinsey & Company when his first book, *In Search of Excellence,* co-authored with Robert Waterman, became a runaway best-seller. Peters has since written several best-selling texts advocating a customer-oriented systems approach to organizational effectiveness. Today he travels around the world giving advice and inspirational talks about managing. His advice focuses on some basic ideas from *In Search of Excellence,* including the nine aspects of excellently run companies:

1. *Managing ambiguity and paradox.* Chaos is the rule of businesses, not the exception. The business climate is always uncertain and always ambiguous. The rational, numerical approach doesn't always work because we live in irrational times.

2. *A bias for action.* Do it, try it, fix it. The point is to try something, without fear of failure. Sochiro Honda, founder of Honda, said that only one out of a hundred of his ideas worked. Fortunately for him, he kept trying after his ninety-ninth failure.

3. *Close to the customer.* Excellent companies have an almost uncanny feel for what their customers want. This is because they're a customer of their own product and they closely listen to their customers.

4. *Autonomy and entrepreneurship.* Decision-making autonomy and the entrepreneurial spirit are essential ingredients for excellence. Great companies allow and encourage autonomy and within-company entrepreneurship.

5. *Productivity through people.* Not surprisingly, people act in accordance with their treatment. Treat them as being untrustworthy, and they will be. Treat them as business partners, and they will be. Excellent companies have taken the leap of faith required to trust their employees to do the right thing right.

6. *Hands-on, value-driven.* Practice management by walking around. Constantly ask the value added of every process and procedure.

7. *Stick to the knitting.* Stay close to your organization's basic industry. The skills or culture involved in a different industry may be a shock that's fatal to the organization.

8. *Simple form, lean staff.* Organizations with few layers of management unencumbered by a bloated headquarters characterize the excellent companies.

9. *Loose-tight properties.* Tight control is maintained while at the same time allowing staff far more flexibility than is the norm.

Peters believes that he designed a modest, close-to-the-customer plan in *In Search of Excellence.* In another of his books, *Liberation Management*,[22] Peters states that being close to the customer isn't really enough. Management must remove structural impediments to being close to the customer. Liberating the organization from rigid rules, hierarchies, stilted policies, and stifling demands are steps in the direction of developing what Peters calls a "symbiosis" with both domestic and foreign customers.

Peters's contribution isn't found in his methods of study, the ability to replicate his conclusions, or attempts to conform to practices he recommends. In fact, researchers have determined that the excellent firms identified by Peters and Waterman, may not have applied the principles called for by the authors.[23] Peters's contribution is that he has stimulated managers, researchers, and theorists to think more seriously about organizations, the tasks of managers and workers, and ways to improve management practices. He and his coauthors literally put management on the front burner. Prior to the publication of *In Search of Excellence,* few people paid much attention to management practices, managerial dilemmas, or managerial excellence.

William Ouchi: Theory Z.   Given the success of many Japanese organizations in the 1980s and early 1990s, many researchers and management practitioners have been motivated to analyze the factors behind these successes. One set of recommendations for American managers was introduced by UCLA management professor William Ouchi in 1981.[24] He introduced what was called **Theory Z,** or the combining of American and Japanese management practices, which Ouchi based on studies conducted in U.S. and Japanese organizations. Exhibit A.3 compares American and Japanese organizations to a modified version Ouchi calls Theory Z.

Ouchi visualized a Theory Z organization as having a distinct American flavor (e.g., individual responsibility) and a unique Japanese emphasis (e.g., collective decision making). The Theory Z approach doesn't work in every situation, but it encourages managers to consider combining philosophy, methods, and tools to create a more effective organization.

EXHIBIT A.3
Comparison of Ouchi's Theory Z Typology to U.S. and Japanese Organizations

Type A American Organization	Type J Japanese Organization	Type Z Modified American Organization
Short-term employment	Lifetime employment	Long-term employment
Individual decision making	Collective decision making	Collective decision making
Individual responsibility	Collective responsibility	Individual responsibility
Rapid promotion	Slow promotion	Slow promotion
Explicit control	Implicit control mechanism	Implicit informal control, with explicit, formalized measurement
Specialized career paths	Nonspecialized career paths	Moderately specialized career paths
Segmented concern for the employees	Holistic concern for the employee	Holistic concern, including the family

Michael Porter: Competitive Advantage.   Michael Porter, a Harvard Business School professor of industrial organization and a consultant, was one of the first contemporary scholars to apply traditional economic thinking to management problems.[25] Porter explains corporate strategy in relation to a competitive marketplace. He identifies four generic strategies: (1) cost leadership, (2) differentiation, (3) cost focus, and (4) focused differentiation. **Competitive advantage** can be gained through lower cost or differentiation—the ability to provide unique and superior value to customers in terms of product quality, special features, or after-sale service.

Competitive scope refers to the breadth of a firm's target within its industry. A firm must choose the range of product variables it will produce, the way to distribute its products, the geographic area it will serve, and the array of industries in which it will compete.

The **cost leadership** strategy involves keeping costs and prices lower than those of competitors. Korean shipyards produce ships at lower costs and lower prices than their main competitors, Japanese firms. **Differentiation** is a strategy that attempts to improve a firm's competitive position by developing unique products. Nike's Air Jordan™ shoes are unique because of their high-technology "air" construction; Coca-Cola has a unique taste and can be bought anyplace in the world; and Benneton sweaters have unique color and patterns.

A **cost focus** emphasizes gaining competitive advantage through cost control in a narrow market area. Atlantic Richfield (ARCO) adopted this strategy in the early 1980s when it decided to service customers west of the Rocky Mountains. The fast-growing western states were close to the company's resource base, Alaska; ARCO was thus able to cut distribution and transportation costs. The result was a lower price of gas and paying attention to a narrower western states market area.

A **focused differentiation** strategy involves providing a competitive and unique product and/or service to a narrow market area. Fiesta Food Mart has adopted a focused differentiation strategy in the border state of Texas. The store provides a unique array of foods for the different ethnic groups. The food products aren't found in the natural food chains, nor in the stores of other competitors. Fiesta's customers find the normal array of goods; but immigrants from Vietnam, El Salvador, Mexico, Peru, and Brazil also find familiar ethnic foods.

Porter's approach is insightful and provocative. He is unique in concluding that the best analytical focus for explaining economic performance is neither the individual firm nor macroeconomic forces. Porter proposes that the explanation about performance is found in studying why nations succeed in particular industries. A handful of nations dominate any one industry. Also, competitors tend to be tightly bunched in a geographic area within a nation (e.g., Silicon Valley in California).

Peter Senge: Learning Organization. The leading champion of the learning organization is Peter Senge.[26] Senge argues that for organizations to be successful, they need to learn and adapt. According to Senge, learning occurs through adapting to changes in the environment. For example, children exploring their world adapt their attitudes and behaviors to what works. In the same way, organizations learn by adapting to their successes. Senge calls this **adaptive learning.** The next stage in becoming a learning organization is generative learning. **Generative learning** involves developing a new understanding of the organization. "Generative learning requires seeing the systems that control events."[27]

Senge believes that an organization's problems are largely built into complex systems that need to change before events will change. For example, an Internet order entry system that allows customers to order out-of-stock products without informing them of a delivery delay is a problem. The firm's customer service department will eventually receive complaints, and ultimately customers will buy from competitors, resulting in lost sales and market share. When viewed as a system, a problem in one part of the organization has the potential to affect other parts of the organization.

Senge suggests that we build a learning organization by teaching discrete new skills. These skills include developing personal mastery or competence, developing mental models, creating a shared vision, participating in team learning, and finally engaging in systems thinking. The leader's role in the learning organization is to be a teacher, designer, and visionary who encourages the development of these skills in employees.

ENDNOTES

1. Peter F. Drucker, *The Practice of Management* (New York: Harper & Row, 1954), 37.

2. Peter F. Drucker, *Post-Capitalist Society* (New York: HarperCollins, 1993), 72.

3. Bruce Brocka and M. Suzanne Brocka, *Quality Management* (Burr Ridge, IL: Business One Irwin, 1992), 64–71.

4. W. Edwards Deming, *Out of the Crisis,* 2nd ed. (Cambridge, MA: MIT Center for Advanced Engineering Study, 1986).

5. A comprehensive analysis of Taylor is found in Charles D. Wrege and Ronald G. Greenwood, *Frederick W. Taylor: The Father of Scientific Management* (Burr Ridge, IL: Business One Irwin, 1991), 131.

6. Lyndall Urwick, *The Golden Book of Management* (London: Newman Neame, 1956), 72–79.

7. Frederick W. Taylor, *Principles of Scientific Management* (New York: Harper & Row, 1911), 36–37. Also see Claude S. George Jr., *The History of Management Thought* (Englewood Cliffs, NJ: Prentice-Hall, 1968); and Edwin A. Locke, "The Ideas of Frederick W. Taylor: An Evaluation," *Academy of Management Review* (January 1982): 14–24.

8. Henri Fayol, *General and Industrial Management* (London: Pitman and Sons, 1949).

9. Max Weber, *The Theory of Social and Economic Organization* (New York: Free Press, 1947).

10. Fritz J. Roethisberger and William J. Dickson, *Management and the Worker* (Cambridge, MA: Harvard University Press, 1931), 24.

11. Mayo, E. *The Human Problems of an Industrial Civilization* (New York: MacMillan, 1933), Ch. 3.

12. Stephen R. G. Jones, "Worker Interdependence and Output: The Hawthorne Studies Reevaluated," *American Sociological Review,* April 1990, pp. 176–190.

13. Joan Woodward, *Industrial Organization: Theory and Practice* (London: Oxford University Press, 1965).

14. Herbert Simon, *Administrative Behavior* (New York: Free Press, 1945); and James March and Herbert Simon, *Organizations* (New York: Wiley, 1958).

15. Ludwig von Bertalanffy, "The History and Status of General Systems Theory," *Academy of Management Journal* (December 1972): 411.

16. Chester I. Barnard, *The Functions of the Executive* (Cambridge, MA: Harvard University Press, 1938), 65.

17. L. von Bertalanffy, "The History and Status of General Systems Theory," *Academy of Management Journal* 15 (1972): 407–426.

18. Steven Cavaleri and Krzysztof Obloj, *Management Systems: A Global Perspective* (Belmont, CA: Wadsworth, 1993), 6–10; Fremont E. Kast and James E. Rosenzweig, "General Systems Theory: Applications in Organizations and Management," *Academy of Management Journal* (December 1972): 447–465; and Daniel Katz and Robert L. Kahn, *The Social Psychology of Organizations* (New York: Wiley, 1966), 47.

19. Kast and Rosenzweig, "General Systems Theory: Applications in Organizations and Management," *Academy of Management Journal* (December 1972): 447–465.

20. Paul R. Lawrence and Jay Lorsch. Organizations and Environment, Homewood, II: Richard D. Irwin, 1967.

21. See Fred Luthans, "The Contingency Theory of Management: A Path Out of the Jungle," *Business Horizons* (June 1973): 63–72; and Harold Koontz, "The Management Theory Jungle Revisited," *Academy of Management Review* (April 1980): 175–188.

22. Thomas Peters, *Liberation Management* (New York: Knopf, 1992).

23. Michael A. Hitt and R. Duane Ireland, "Peters and Waterman Revisited: The Unending Quest for Excellence," *Academy of Management Executive* 1, no. 2 (1987): 91–98.

24. William G. Ouchi, *Theory Z: How American Business Can Meet the Japanese Challenge* (Reading, MA: Addison-Wesley, 1981).

25. Michael E. Porter, *The Competitive Advantage of Nations* (New York: Free Press, 1990), 101.

26. Peter M. Senge, *The Fifth Discipline: The Art and Practice of the Learning Organization* (New York: Doubleday, 1991).

27. Peter Senge, "The Leader's New Work: Building the Learning Organization," *Sloan Management Review,* Fall 1990, p. 7.

Appendix B

MANAGING PRODUCTION AND OPERATIONS

Defining Production, Manufacturing, and Operations

Production is the total process by which a company produces finished goods or services. This process might involve the work, ideas, and plans of the design engineers as well as the production manager, plant manager, plant superintendent, and their crews plus any other department actually involved with bringing forth the product. Production isn't limited to the manufacture of goods; it applies to both the service and manufacturing sectors of the economy. For example, a company might produce shampoo and conditioner for hair, which are manufactured goods; another company might operate a chain of hair salons, which produce a service. The word *production* can also be used to name the total amount of product brought forth, as in the statement "Total production increased by 20 percent in 1990."

Manufacturing refers only to the physical process of producing goods; services are not manufactured. The word *manufacturing* comes from the ancient Latin words *manu* (meaning "hand") and *factor* ("create" or "make")—in other words, handmade. In ancient Rome, distinguishing between machine-made and handmade was not an issue; all goods were handmade. If someone sang for the Romans, it was a service; if someone crafted a brand new jar for storing olive oil, it was a manufactured good, something created by the work of hands.

Operations are the functions needed to keep the company producing and delivering. They're literally any function or series of functions enacted to carry out a strategic plan. In a firm such as Ford Motors, operations usually include purchasing, materials management, production, inventory and quality control, maintenance and manufacturing engineering, and plant management. The importance of operations cannot be overstated if firms—and nations—are to be successful. The tasks involved in producing and delivering a product or service are the value-added elements that build individual, corporate, social, and national wealth.

Role of the Production and Operations Manager

Production and operations managers are responsible for producing the goods that business needs to sell. There are many kinds of production and operation systems, just as there are many kinds of products—goods and services—wanted by people in the marketplace. Production and operations vary in size from a single person in a very small company—like family-owned baker, L'Madiellenes—to thousands of employees in a huge multinational corporation such as Procter & Gamble.

The production goals of every business are focused on producing products—and on producing the best, the fastest, and at the least cost. Thus the production and operations manager must produce with effectiveness and efficiency while maintaining quality control. To do this, these managers oversee a number of company operations. Typical functions include planning site selection and layout; managing materials purchasing and inventory; scheduling; and managing quality control.

Planning Site Location and Layout. When a company starts up or opens a new branch, the production and operations manager is heavily involved in planning the site location and layout. Company officers, engineers, and heads of departments add their ideas and lists of requirements.

Site Selection. A site may be bought or leased with or without a building already in place. If the site is to be leased, all managers involved should make their plans and submit their needs to a commercial or industrial real estate broker. The broker then submits a list of properties available in the area within the price range required. Sites may come with a "build to suit" lease, or they may be a turnkey location whose building and interior facilities are already completed.

The type of business dictates the kind of facility. Service sector businesses often require small office facilities in heavy-traffic areas convenient to customers or to the electronic communications and other services the business itself requires. Heavy industry, on the other hand, requires vast space near ship operations as well as transportation to market. A production and operations manager's plan for site location considers most if not all of the following factors:

- Economies of cost or other economic advantages for land, buildings, or units
- Taxes, insurance, and other costs
- Proximity to related industries and suppliers, warehouses, and/or service operations
- Availability of an appropriate labor force, considering such factors as quality and cost
- Availability of economical transportation for materials and supplies as well as for finished goods
- Proximity to market for goods
- Air and water conditions
- Proximity to plentiful, economical energy services
- Climate and environment that's in line with the industry's needs and amenable to employees' lifestyle
- Ample space for current and future needs of firm
- Proximity to such employee needs as housing, schools, mass transportation, religious facilities, day care, shopping, and recreational facilities
- Community receptiveness

Some site choices may be based on the overriding advantages of one factor—such as availability of labor or market, or low cost of land. In recent years, for example, many American companies have chosen to locate in Mexico and China due to the low costs of facilities, land, and labor. Clothing manufacturers have settled in Korea and Taiwan because of abundant cheap labor. Another increasingly popular production site is eastern Europe. Major changes in the business climate and a large untapped market have made the former Soviet Union, Poland, Hungary, and other central and eastern European countries intriguing options for joint ventures and new plants.

Site Layout. Just as it dictates the kind and location of facility, the type of business will determine the layout of the site selected. For each kind of business, production and operations managers must meet different needs. Different kinds of production require varying space for assembly lines, workstations, or other specific arrangements for work layouts.

The manager must plan the layout in detail before the site is chosen. The plan must account for the needed square footage, work areas, office and conference areas, storage, and shipping needs. To draw up specific plans, managers use templates, models, drawings, and the latest computer techniques.

Managing Materials, Purchasing, and Inventory.   Materials management, purchasing, and inventory control cover the planning, ordering, and internal storage and distribution of supplies and materials needed for production. Other names used for these areas include *material handling, procurement, supply room management,* and *inventory management.*

Some variations occur in the way authority and responsibility are organized. In some companies the purchasing department purchases every good or service bought from outside sources. In others the purchasing function covers only those materials and supplies used in the actual production process.

In large companies the materials manager may oversee the functions of purchasing and inventory control, or inventory control may be part of production control, depending on its scope. Inventory control may handle only inventory of components and subassemblies, or it may cover all inventories—of supplies, raw materials, components, and subassemblies, and even finished products.

In recent years two important systems have been created to handle materials management and inventory control. Just-in-time (JIT) inventory control and materials requirements planning (MRP) have greatly refined the degree to which materials and inventory control can be managed and scheduled.

Just-in-time (JIT) manufacturing requires that the exact quantity of defect-free raw materials, parts, and subassemblies are produced just in time for the next stage of the manufacturing process. This concept extends backward to suppliers and forward to the final customer. The goal of JIT manufacturing is to match the output of manufacturing with market demand, thus eliminating waste.

An efficient JIT system can result in low inventories of purchased parts and raw materials, work in process, and finished goods. It saves warehouse and work area space while lowering the costs of carrying large inventories. Reducing inventory can also expose other production problems. A sometimes tardy supplier can be covered if the firm carries a large inventory. Smaller inventories spotlight the efficiency of all sources. A delinquent supplier will be replaced.

Since JIT systems have little finished goods inventory, machine breakdowns are costly. Thus careful attention to maintaining efficient equipment becomes a high priority. Machines must be in top working order to fulfill the JIT demands. A top-quality repair team that can move into immediate action must be available if JIT is to work effectively.

Materials requirements planning (MRP) is a computer-driven system for analyzing and projecting materials needs and then scheduling their arrival at the right work site, at the right time, in the right quantities. MRP works closely with the master production schedule (which we'll discuss shortly) and takes into account such variables as lead time in ordering.

MRP focuses on "getting the right materials to the right place at the right time." In most cases, making "right" decisions requires a computer to handle all the materials and components involved. The MRP program analyzes data from inventory, the master production schedule, and the bill of materials. The output includes inventory status, planned order timing, and changes in due dates because of rescheduling.

MRP is used in companies involved in assembly operations. Firms that produce large volumes of tools, generators, turbines, appliances, and motors are particularly attracted to MRP. It is also useful in companies that order a high number of units.

Together, JIT and MRP provide a system that saves time and dollars. They have helped managers control the amount of inventory required to keep production moving smoothly.

With JIT and MRP, suppliers of parts and subassemblies can plan in much closer time tolerances. In very large operations, such as the Detroit auto assemblies, nearby suppliers are actually hooked up by computer to follow the progress of assembly-line work. From this vantage point, their trucks can arrive nearly at the moment the materials are needed. Lead times on orders are greatly reduced, and costs of storing inventory drop sharply.

Scheduling.   The production, or manufacturing, manager is responsible for the company's main goal: producing goods in the amounts and sequence planned and on schedule. This function is critical to the firm's success. Three elements of management—planning, organizing, and controlling—can be clearly seen in the production manager's tasks. Planning the use of labor, facilities, and materials for fulfilling the production schedule is a complex, ongoing task. The manager will usually have more than one product to plan for, with the resultant needs for changes in materials, production processes, energy, and labor.

A *master production schedule* must be created. It will show when the manager plans to produce each product and in what quantities. The production manager is responsible for meeting the dates, quantities, and cost commitments on the schedule. The master schedule will affect the efforts and success of every department in the company. Therefore it should also reflect the needs of the finance, marketing, shipping, and all other departments.

Production managers must plan for flexibility, to enable the production area to change from one process to another on short notice. They may use a number of tactics to meet emergencies or make changes in the plan. Requesting overtime, hiring temporary workers, cross-training workers so they can do more than one job, and many other methods are available.

Flexibility as well as adherence to schedule can be achieved with the use of the **program evaluation and review technique (PERT) chart**. PERT was developed in the 1950s from the joint efforts of Lockheed Aircraft, the U.S. Navy Special Projects Office, and the consulting firm of Booz Allen & Hamilton. They were working on the Polaris missile project and wanted to provide the United States with an advantage over what was then the Soviet Union in time of completion.

An important part of PERT is the construction of a chart, a graphical system for tracking events that must take place to accomplish a task. A PERT chart is one of the most effective tools of modern management. Five steps are followed in creating a PERT chart:

1. Break the project to be accomplished into events or completed actions; label each with the amount of time needed to do it.

2. List the first event of the task.

3. List the event that follows the first one; draw a line with an arrow from the first event to the next one, showing the sequence. (If two events follow, draw arrows to both events to show that one event leads to two, or even more, events.)

4. Chart all the events needed to complete the project in the same way, to completion.

5. Label the arrows with the amount of time it takes to complete each activity.

Exhibit B.1 presents a PERT chart for the replacement of a machine in a manufacturing plant. The letters represent the activities necessary to replace the machine. The numbers in the circles represent completed activities, called events; number 1 is the origin of the project. For instance, B represents securing bids and awarding contracts; 3 represents that bids have been secured and contracts awarded. Each activity is also assigned an expected time for completion; removing existing equipment is expected to take two weeks.

EXHIBIT B . I
Example of a PERT Chart

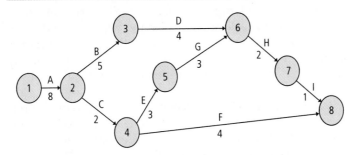

Activity	Description	Completion Time (Days)	Prerequisites
A	Prepare specifications	8	None
B	Secure bids and award contracts	5	A
C	Remove existing equipment	2	A
D	Train operators for new machine	4	A, B
E	Electrical modifications	3	A, C
F	Paint	4	A, C
G	Install machine	3	A, C, E
H	Test machine	2	A, B, D
I	Reschedule production	1	A, B, D, H

As Exhibit B.1 shows, some activities must be completed before others, while some can be completed simultaneously. The prerequisites are shown in the figure. For example, specifications must be prepared and old equipment must be removed before painting. All activities must be accomplished before the final event, rescheduling production. The longest path from start to completion of the project in terms of time needed to complete the activities is called the **critical path.** In this case, the critical path is 1-2-3-6-7-8, which takes 20 days. Thus the project cannot be completed in less than 20 days.

The PERT chart can be used to track exactly where a product or project is in its development and what needs to be done next to keep it on schedule. Bottlenecks can be identified and corrected. For example, if the third event in a sequence always involves a delay, the production manager can identify the problem and make changes as needed.

The PERT chart has its limitations. It is only as good in planning as its user's ability to identify all the steps in a chain of events. Because it helps break down the production tasks into clearly separate segments, PERT also helps to identify needs and uses for computerized manufacturing programs, temporary workers, and overtime techniques. This breakdown is helpful in the current climate of rapid change in production techniques, numbers of products, and kinds of new products. The public presents an ever-ready market for newer, more appealing products; getting the products to the consumer is up to the production staff. Until recently, companies could expect to bring out a new product line or new models in the line no more frequently than every year. Today, in many industries, new products are inserted into the master schedule—and from there into the marketplace—as fast as they can be designed.

Managing Quality Control. The production or quality control manager may be responsible for defining standards with exact specifications or for issuing guidelines regarding exact specifications set by an outside agency. Standards are set by hundreds of regulating agencies, such as the federal Food and Drug Administration (FDA) and Bureau of Standards. These standards affect color, size, shape, taste, texture, durability, and many other properties of goods produced in the United States. From toothpaste to rocket fuel, American products are tested and standardized to a greater degree than any others in the world. Government contracts can be lost and consumer purchasing can fall rapidly if standards are not met.

The quality control manager must select or devise procedures to test the quality of products, establish troubleshooting procedures, pinpoint causes of any defects in products, and correct any problems rapidly to minimize losses. Customer complaints or returns of defective products must also be analyzed so that necessary corrections can be made.

Complaints and returns from customers can build up and result in lost customers and sales. Therefore a quality control expert must develop a system that reduces the chances that low-quality products or services get to the customers. A four-step program can help keep the perception of poor quality from being associated with the company.

Step 1 Define Quality Characteristics

The first step involves defining the quality characteristics desired by the customer or client; this means finding out what customers want. Examining customer preferences, technical specifications, marketing suggestions, and competitive products provides necessary information. Customer preferences are extremely significant, since repeat sales likely depend on a reasonable degree of customer satisfaction. A Rolex watch customer wants accuracy, a long service life, and style. But a Timex watch customer has other quality standards and preferences. The Timex keeps reasonably accurate time and sells at a much lower price than the Rolex. The quality characteristics of Rolex watches meet and depend on different customer preferences than the quality characteristics of Timex watches.

Step 2 Establish Quality Standards

Once the quality characteristics have been defined, the next step is to establish the desired quality levels. Quality standards serve as the reference point for comparing the ideal to what actually exists. Standards for factors such as size, color, weight, texture, accuracy, reliability, time of delivery, and support are set by management.

The cost of achieving and sustaining a specific level of quality must be estimated and compared to the cost of potential rejections. The **quality funnel principle** suggests that the closer to the start of the production process, the lower the cost of rejection. As the product or service progresses through the process, more resources are invested; the greater the amount of resources invested, the higher the cost of rejection. The greater cost is incurred when the customer or client is the source of rejection. In that case the cost of processing the complaint and the cost of lost goodwill are added to the cost of resources. For example, complaints about Ford's Explorer were costly in the form of lost repeat sales, customer lawsuits, and recalls to repair defective parts.

Step 3 Develop Quality Review Program

The methods for quality review, where and by whom reviews will be reported and analyzed, and other review procedures must be formalized. One important decision involves how many products will be checked for quality. Will all products be inspected, or only a representative sampling? The greater the number of products inspected, the greater the costs associated with quality review. Representative sampling is less costly but creates

(1) the risk that more low-quality products will get into customers' hands, (2) a greater likelihood that customer goodwill can be tarnished, and (3) the need to decide on what number of defects or poor-quality products will be acceptable.

Sampling procedures can take many forms. Some organizations use a random spot check. A random selection of the product is inspected for quality. When a formal random spot check is used, the results can be meaningful and can provide adequate control. Decisions about which plan to use involve making inferences about the entire procedure, based on samples. Representative sampling presupposes that defective products will occasionally slip through the quality check network.

Step 4 Build Quality Commitment

A commitment to quality among an organization's work force has three ingredients:

- *Quality focus*. From top management to operating employees, all employees must sincerely believe that quality of all outputs is the accepted practice. Satisfying customer or client quality needs must be the goal of all employees.

- *Quality intelligence*. Employees must be aware of the acceptable quality standards and how those standards can be met.

- *Quality skills*. Employees must have the skills and abilities to achieve the quality standards set by management.

The employees' commitment to producing high-quality output is imperative. The numerous approaches include job enrichment, goal setting, positive reinforcement, and team development. Participative management (an approach with many adherents) involves employees in important management decisions.

Index